Windows NT™ Networking Guide

Microsoft®

WINDOWS NT RESOURCE KIT

Microsoft PRESS®

For Windows NT Workstation and Windows NT Server Version 3.5

PUBLISHED BY
Microsoft Press
A Division of Microsoft Corporation
One Microsoft Way
Redmond, Washington 98052-6399

Library of Congress Cataloging-in-Publication Data
Windows NT networking guide : for Windows NT workstation and
  Windows NT server version 3.5 / by Microsoft Corporation.
       p.   cm.
    Includes index.
    ISBN 1-55615-656-1
    1. Computer networks.   2. Microsoft Windows NT.   I. Microsoft
Corporation.
TK5105.5.M548   1995
005.7'13--dc20   94-45565
                                                                                  CIP

Printed and bound in the United States of America.

    1 2 3 4 5 6 7 8 9   QMQM   0 9 8 7 6 5

Distributed to the book trade in Canada by Macmillan of Canada, a division of Canada Publishing
Corporation.

A CIP catalogue record for this book is available from the British Library.

Microsoft Press books are available through booksellers and distributors worldwide. For further
information about international editions, contact your local Microsoft Corporation office. Or
contact Microsoft Press International directly at fax number (206) 936-7329.

3+Open and 3Com are registered trademarks of 3Com Corporation. PostScript is a registered trademark of
Adobe Systems, Inc. AT&T is a registered trademark of American Telephone and Telegraph Company.
Apple, AppleTalk, and Macintosh are registered trademarks of Apple Computer, Inc. Banyan and VINES are
registered trademarks of Banyan Systems, Inc. CompuServe is a registered trademark of CompuServe, Inc.
ArcNet is a registered trademark of Datapoint Corporation. Open VMS is a registered trademark and DEC,
DECnet, Pathworks, and VMS are trademarks of Digital Equipment Corporation. pcANYWHERE is a
registered trademark of Dynamic Microprocessor Associates, Inc. Hewlett Packard and HP are registered
trademarks of Hewlett-Packard Company. AIX, IBM, and OS/2 are registered trademarks and AFP is a
trademark of International Business Machines Corporation. Lotus and Lotus Notes are registered trademarks
of Lotus Development Corporation. Microsoft, MS, MS-DOS, MSX, and Win32 are registered trademarks
and Windows and Windows NT are trademarks of Microsoft Corporation in the U.S.A. and other countries.
NT is a trademark of Northern Telecom Limited in the U.S.A. and other countries. Novell and NetWare are
registered trademarks of Novell, Inc. UNIX is a registered trademark of Novell, Inc., in the U.S.A. and other
countries, licensed exclusively through X/Open Company, Ltd. Sun and Sun Microsystems are registered
trademarks of Sun Microsystems, Inc. SYBASE is a registered trademark of Sybase, Inc.

This book is dedicated to the system administrators who keep us all connected. We hope this book makes your job easier.

Contributors to this book include the following:

Technical Writers:
Chris Dragich, Jeff Howard, Sharon Kay,
Doralee Moynihan, Annie Pearson, and Jim Purcell

Technical Consultants:
J. Allard, Pradeep Bahl, Sudheer Dhulipalla, James Gilroy, Tom Hazel, Steve Heaney,
Jan Keller, Leslie Link, James McDaniel, Kerry Schwartz, and Cliff Van Dyke

Technical Editor:
Sonia Marie Moore

Project Lead:
Peggy Etchevers

Indexer:
Jane Dow

Production Team:
Karye Cattrell, Yong Ok Chung, and Cathy Pfarr

Graphic Designer:
Sue Wyble

Graphic Artists:
Gwen Grey, Elizabeth Read, and Stephen Winard

Contents

PART II   Using Windows NT Networking

PART III   TCP/IP

PART IV   Windows NT and the Internet

Figures and Tables

Tables

Introduction

Welcome to the *Microsoft Windows NT Resource Kit Volume 2: Windows NT Networking Guide.*

The *Windows NT Resource Kit* also includes the following volumes:

- *Volume 1: Windows NT Resource Guide,* which provides information to help administrators better understand how to install, manage, and integrate Windows NT™ in a network or multiuser environment.
- *Volume 3: Windows NT Messages,* which provides information on local and remote debugging and on interpreting error messages.
- *Volume 4: Optimizing Windows NT,* which provides a step-by-step approach to understanding all the basic performance management techniques.

The *Windows NT Networking Guide* is designed for people who are, or who want to become, expert users of Microsoft® Windows NT Workstation and Microsoft Windows NT Server networking features. The *Windows NT Networking Guide* presents detailed, easy-to-read technical information to help you better manage how Windows NT is used at your site. It contains specific networking information for system administrators who are responsible for installing, managing, and integrating Windows NT in both small and large networks.

The *Windows NT Networking Guide* is a technical supplement to the documentation included as part of the Windows NT product and does not replace that information as the source for learning how to use Windows NT networking features and utilities.

You should also use it in conjunction with the *Windows NT Resource Guide* since there are multiple cross-references between the two books. In addition, the tools for both books are contained on a single compact disc (CD) and in a single set of 3.5-inch floppy disks. (The CD is bound into the back cover of the *Windows NT Resource Guide,* and the floppy disks are available upon request from MS-Press.) See the "Introduction" section of the *Windows NT Resource Guide* for a partial list of the available tools. A complete list is available on the CD in the README.WRI file with instructions on how to use them in the RKTOOLS.HLP file.

This introduction includes two kinds of information you can use to get started:

- The first section outlines the contents of this book, so that you can quickly find technical details about specific elements of Windows NT networking.
- The second section describes the conventions used to present information in this book.

About the Networking Guide

This guide includes the following chapters. Additional tables of contents are included in each part to help you quickly find the information you want.

Part I, About Windows NT Networking

Chapter 1, "Windows NT Networking Architecture," contains information for the support professional who may not have a local area network background. This chapter provides a technical discussion of networking concepts and discusses the networking components included with Windows NT.

Chapter 2, "Network Interoperability," describes how Windows NT works together with your existing Novell® networks, IBM® mainframe systems, and UNIX® systems.

Chapter 3, "Windows NT User Environments," explains the use of home directories and logon scripts in customizing the environment of individual users or related groups of users.

Chapter 4, "Network Security and Administration," describes how security is implemented for workgroups and domains under Windows NT, including local logon and pass-through validation for trusted domains and network browsing.

Chapter 5, "Windows NT Browser," explains how members of a Windows NT network can browse the resources of the network.

Part II, Using Windows NT Networking

Chapter 6, "Using NBF with Windows NT," describes NetBEUI Frame, the implementation of the NetBIOS Extended User Interface protocol under Windows NT, including how network traffic and sessions are managed.

Chapter 7, "Using DLC with Windows NT," presents details about the Data Link Control (DLC) protocol device driver in Windows NT that provides connectivity to IBM mainframes and to local area network printers attached directly to the network.

Chapter 8, "Client-Server Connectivity on Windows NT," discusses how MS-DOS®, Windows®, Windows NT, and OS/2® client workstations communicate with Windows NT databases, focusing on Microsoft SQL Server as an example of a distributed application.

Chapter 9, "Using Remote Access Service," explains the technical details of Windows NT RAS including security, interoperability, and scripting capabilities.

Part III, TCP/IP

Chapter 10, "Overview of Microsoft TCP/IP for Windows NT," describes the elements that make up Microsoft TCP/IP and provides an overview of how you can use Microsoft TCP/IP to support various networking solutions.

Chapter 11, "Installing and Configuring Microsoft TCP/IP and SNMP," describes the process for installing and configuring Microsoft TCP/IP, SNMP, and Remote Access Service (RAS) with TCP/IP on a computer running Windows NT.

Chapter 12, "Networking Concepts for TCP/IP," presents key TCP/IP networking concepts for networking administrators interested in a technical discussion of the elements that make up TCP/IP.

Chapter 13, "Installing and Configuring DHCP Servers," presents the procedures and strategies for setting up servers to support the Dynamic Host Configuration Protocol for Windows networks.

Chapter 14, "Installing and Configuring WINS Servers," presents the procedures and strategies for setting up Windows Internet Name Service servers.

Chapter 15, "Setting Up LMHOSTS," provides guidelines and tips for using LMHOSTS files for name resolution on networks.

Chapter 16, "Using the Microsoft FTP Server Service," describes how to install, configure, and administer the Microsoft FTP Server service.

Chapter 17, "Using Performance Monitor with TCP/IP Services," describes how to use the performance counters for TCP/IP, FTP Server service, DHCP servers, and WINS servers.

Chapter 18, "Internetwork Printing and TCP/IP," describes how to install TCP/IP printing and create TCP/IP printers on Windows NT computers with Microsoft TCP/IP.

Chapter 19, "Troubleshooting TCP/IP," describes how to troubleshoot IP connections and use the diagnostic utilities to get information that will help solve networking problems.

xxii Windows NT Networking Guide

Part IV, Windows NT and the Internet

Chapter 20, "Using Windows NT on the Internet," describes typical scenarios for connecting a Window NT computer or network to the Internet and the logistical details involved in doing that.

Chapter 21, "Setting Up Internet Servers and Clients on Windows NT Computers," describes how to set up Internet servers and clients on a Windows NT computer.

Chapter 22, "Remote Access Service and the Internet," provides technical details about using RAS for Internet connections, including as an Internet Gateway Server and as a router to the Internet for small networks.

Part V, Appendixes

Appendix A, "TCP/IP Utilities Reference," describes the TCP/IP utilities and provides syntax and notes.

Appendix B, "MIB Object Types for Windows NT," describes the LAN Manager MIB II objects provided when you install SNMP with Windows NT.

Appendix C, "Windows Sockets Application," lists third-party vendors who have created software based on the Windows Sockets standard to provide utilities and applications that run in heterogeneous networks using TCP/IP. This appendix also lists Internet sources for public-domain software based on Windows Sockets.

Conventions in This Manual

This document assumes that you have read the Windows NT documentation set and that you are familiar with using menus, dialog boxes, and other features of the Windows operating system family of products. It also assumes that you have installed Windows NT on your system and that you are using a mouse. For keyboard equivalents to menu and mouse actions, see the Microsoft Windows NT online Help.

This document uses several conventions to help you identify information. The following table describes the typographical conventions used in the *Windows NT Networking Guide.*

Convention	Used for
bold	MS-DOS–style command and utility names such as **copy** or **ping** and switches such as **/?** or **-h**. Also used for Registry value names, such as **IniFileMapping** and OS/2 application programming interfaces (APIs).
italic	Parameters for which you can supply specific values. For example, the Windows NT root directory appears in a path name as *systemroot*\SYSTEM32, where *systemroot* can be C:\WINNT35 or some other value.
ALL CAPITALS	Directory names, filenames, and acronyms. For example, DLC stands for Data Link Control; C:\PAGEFILE.SYS is a file in the boot sector.
Monospace	Sample text from batch and .INI files, Registry paths, and screen text in non-Windows–based applications.

Other conventions in this document include the following:

- "MS-DOS" refers to Microsoft MS-DOS version 3.3 or later.
- "Windows-based application" is used as a shorthand term to refer to an application that is designed to run with 16-bit Windows and does not run without Windows. All 16-bit and 32-bit Windows applications follow similar conventions for the arrangement of menus, dialog box styles, and keyboard and mouse use.

- "MS-DOS–based application" is used as a shorthand term to refer to an application that is designed to run with MS-DOS but not specifically with Windows or Windows NT and is not able to take full advantage of their graphical or memory management features.

- "Command prompt" refers to the command line where you type MS-DOS–style commands. Typically, you see characters such as C:\> to show the location of the command prompt on your screen. In Windows NT, you can double-click the MS-DOS Prompt icon in Program Manager to use the command prompt.

- An instruction to "type" any information means to press a key or a sequence of keys, and then press the ENTER key.

- Mouse instructions in this document, such as "Click the OK button" or "Drag an icon in File Manager," use the same meanings as the descriptions of mouse actions in the *Windows NT System Guide* and the Windows online tutorial.

PART I

About Windows NT Networking

C H A P T E R   1

Windows NT Networking Architecture

Windows NT is a complete operating system with fully integrated networking capabilities. These capabilities differentiate Windows NT from other operating systems such as MS-DOS, OS/2, and UNIX for which network capabilities are installed separately from the core operating system.

Integrated networking support means that Windows NT offers these features:

- Support for both peer-to-peer and client-server networking. All Windows NT computers can act as both network clients and servers, sharing files and printers with other computers and exchanging messages over the network. Windows NT Server also includes features needed for full-scale servers, such as domain management tools.

- The ability to easily add networking software and hardware. The networking software integrated into Windows NT lets you easily add protocol drivers, network card drivers, and other network software. Windows NT includes four transport protocols—IPX/SPX (NWLink), TCP/IP, NBF (Windows NT NetBEUI), and DLC.

- Interoperability with existing networks. Windows NT systems can communicate using a variety of transport protocols and network adapters. It can also communicate over a variety of different vendors' networks.

- Support for distributed applications. Windows NT provides a transparent Remote Procedure Call (RPC) facility. It also supports NetBIOS, Sockets, and the Windows Network (WNet) APIs and named pipes and mailslots, for backward compatibility with LAN Manager installations and applications.

- Remote access to networks. Windows NT Remote Access Service (RAS) clients can dial into any PPP or SLIP server. Windows NT RAS servers support any remote clients using IPX, TCP/IP, or NetBEUI using PPP. For additional information about RAS, see Chapter 9, "Using Remote Access Service."

- Print and File sharing, and AppleTalk® routing for Macintosh® clients.

This chapter describes the Windows NT networking architecture and how
it achieves each of these goals. For perspective, the next section provides a
brief explanation of two industry-standard models for networking—the Open
System Interconnection (OSI) reference model and the Institute of Electrical and
Electronic Engineers (IEEE) 802 project model. The remainder of the chapter
describes the Windows NT networking components as they relate to the OSI
and IEEE models and as they relate to the overall Windows NT architecture.

Overview of Networking

In the early years of networking, several large companies, including IBM,
Honeywell, and Digital Equipment Corporation (DEC™), each had its own standard
for how computers could be connected together. These standards described the
mechanisms necessary to move data from one computer to another. These early
standards, however, were not entirely compatible. Networks adhering to IBM
Systems Network Architecture (SNA) could not communicate directly with
networks using DEC Digital Network Architecture (DNA), for example.

In later years, standards organizations, including the International Standards
Organization (ISO) and the Institute of Electrical and Electronic Engineers (IEEE),
developed models that became globally recognized and accepted as the standards
for designing any computer network. Both models describe networking in terms of
functional layers.

OSI Reference Model

ISO developed a model called the Open Systems Interconnection (OSI) reference model. It is used to describe the flow of data between the physical connection to the network and the end-user application. This model is the best known and most widely used model to describe networking environments.

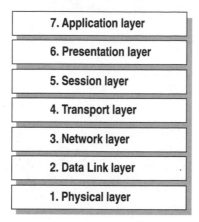

Figure 1.1   Open Systems Interconnection (OSI) Reference Model

As shown in Figure 1.1, the OSI layers are numbered from bottom to top. The most basic functions, such as putting data bits onto the network cable, are on the bottom, while functions attending to the details of applications are at the top.

In the OSI model, the purpose of each layer is to provide services to the next higher layer, shielding the higher layer from the details of how the services are actually implemented. The layers are abstracted in such a way that each layer believes it is communicating with the same layer on the other computer. In reality, each layer communicates only with adjacent layers on one computer. That is, for information to pass from Layer 5 on Computer A to Layer 5 on Computer B, it actually follows the route illustrated by Figure 1.2.

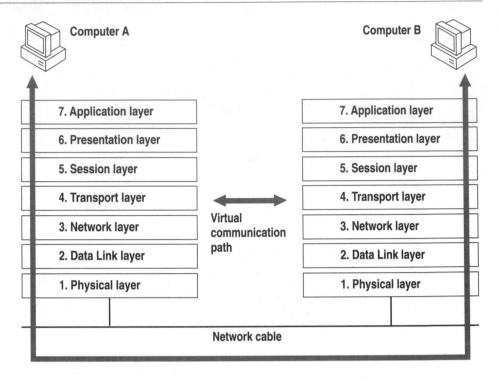

Figure 1.2   Communication Between OSI Layers

The following list describes the purpose of each of the seven layers of the OSI model and identifies services that they provide to adjacent layers.

1. The Physical Layer addresses the transmission of the unstructured raw bit stream over a physical medium (that is, the networking cable). The Physical Layer relates the electrical/optical, mechanical, and functional interfaces to the cable. The Physical Layer also carries the signals that transmit data generated by all the higher layers.

    This layer defines how the cable is attached to the network adapter card. For example, it defines how many pins the connector has and what each pin is used for. It describes the topology used to connect computers together (Token Ring, Ethernet, or some other). It also defines which transmission technique will be used to send data over the network cable.

2. The Data Link Layer packages raw bits from the Physical Layer into *data frames*, which are logical, structured packets in which data can be placed. The exact format of the frame used by the network depends on the topology. That is, a Token Ring network data frame is laid out differently than an Ethernet frame. The Data Link Layer is responsible for providing the error-free transfer of these frames from one computer to another through the Physical Layer. This allows the Network Layer to assume virtually error-free transmission over the network connection. Frames contain source and destination addresses so that the sending and receiving computers can recognize and retrieve their own frames on the network.

3. The Network Layer is responsible for addressing messages and translating logical addresses and names into physical addresses. This layer also determines the route from the source to the destination computer. It determines which path the data should take based on network conditions, priority of service, and other factors. It also manages traffic problems on the network, such as switching, routing, and controlling the congestion of data packets.

   The Network Layer bundles small data frames together for transmission across the network. It also restructures large frames into smaller packets. On the receiving end, the Network Layer reassembles the data packets into their original frame structure.

4. The Transport Layer takes care of error recognition and recovery. It also ensures reliable delivery of host messages originating at the Application Layer. Similar to how the Network Layer handles data frames, this layer repackages messages —dividing long messages into several packets and collecting small messages together in one packet—to provide for their efficient transmission over the network. At the receiving end, the Transport Layer unpacks the messages, reassembles the original messages, and sends an acknowledgment of receipt.

5. The Session Layer allows two applications on different computers to establish, use, and end a connection called a *session*. This layer performs name recognition and the functions needed to allow two applications to communicate over the network, such as security functions.

   The Session Layer provides synchronization between user tasks by placing checkpoints in the data stream. This way, if the network fails, only the data after the last checkpoint has to be retransmitted. This layer also implements dialog control between communicating processes, regulating which side transmits, when, for how long, and so on.

6. The Presentation Layer determines the form used to exchange data between networked computers. It can be called the network's translator. At the sending computer, this layer translates data from a format received from the Application Layer into a commonly recognized, intermediary format. At the receiving end, this layer translates the intermediary format into a format useful to that computer's Application Layer.

   The Presentation Layer also manages network security issues by providing services such as data encryption. It also provides rules for data transfer and provides data compression to reduce the number of bits that need to be transmitted.

7. The Application Layer serves as the window for application processes to access network services. This layer represents the services that directly support the user applications such as software for file transfers, database access, and electronic mail.

IEEE 802 Model

Another networking model developed by the IEEE further defines sublayers of the Data Link Layer. The IEEE 802 project (named for the year and month it began—February 1980) defines the *Media Access Control* (MAC) and the *Logical Link Control* (LLC) sublayers.

As Figure 1.3 shows, the Media Access Control sublayer is the lower of the two sublayers, providing shared access for the computers' network adapter cards to the Physical Layer. The MAC Layer communicates directly with the network adapter card and is responsible for delivering error-free data between two computers on the network.

The Logical Link Control sublayer, the upper sublayer, manages data link communication and defines the use of logical interface points [called Service Access Points (SAPs)] that other computers can reference and use to transfer information from the LLC sublayer to the upper OSI layers. Two protocols running on the same computer would use separate SAPs.

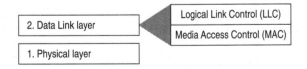

Figure 1.3   Logical Link Control and Media Access Control Sublayers

Project 802 resulted in a number of documents, including three key standards for network topologies:

- 802.3 defines standards for bus networks, such as Ethernet, that use a mechanism called Carrier Sense Multiple Access with Collision Detection (CSMA/CD).
- 802.4 defines standards for token-passing bus networks. (The ArcNet® architecture is similar to this standard in many ways.)
- 802.5 defines standards for Token-Ring networks.

IEEE defined functionality for the LLC Layer in standard 802.2 and defined functionality for the MAC and Physical Layers in standards 802.3, 802.4, and 802.5.

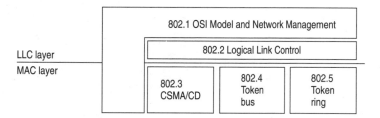

Figure 1.4   Project 802 Standards as Related to LLC and MAC Layers

This chapter describes the layered components of the Windows NT networking architecture, beginning with an overall description of that architecture.

Windows NT Networking Model

As with other architecture components of Windows NT, the networking architecture is built of layers. This helps provide expandability by allowing other functions and services to be added. Figure 1.5 shows all of the components that make up the Windows NT networking model.

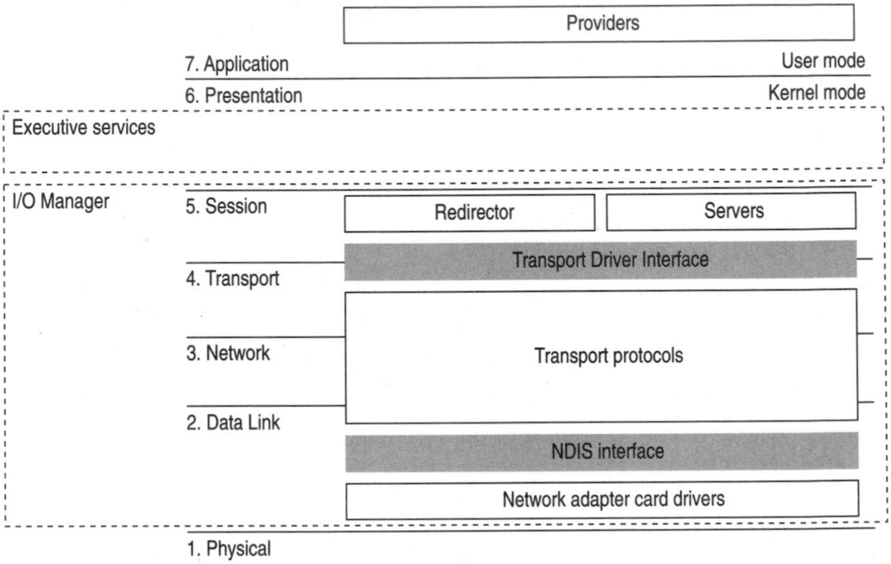

Figure 1.5   Windows NT Networking Model

Each of the Windows NT networking layers performs these functions.

The Windows NT networking model begins at the MAC sublayer where *network adapter card drivers* reside. These drivers link Windows NT to the network via corresponding network adapter cards. Windows NT includes RAS to allow network access to computers for people who work at home or on the road. For more information, see "Remote Access for Windows NT Clients," later in this chapter.

The network model includes two important interfaces—the *NDIS 3.0 Interface* and the *Transport Driver Interface* (TDI). These interfaces isolate one layer from the next by allowing an adjacent component to be written to a single standard rather than many. For example, a network adapter card driver (below the NDIS interface) does not need to include blocks of code specifically written for each transport protocol it uses. Instead, the driver is written to the NDIS interface, which solicits services from the appropriate NDIS-conformant transport protocol(s). These interfaces are included in the Windows NT networking model to allow for portable, interchangeable modules.

Between the two interfaces are *transport protocols*, which act as data organizers for the network. A transport protocol defines how data should be presented to the next receiving layer and packages the data accordingly. It passes data to the network adapter card driver through the NDIS Interface and to the redirector through the TDI.

Above the TDI are *redirectors,* which "redirect" local requests for network resources to the network.

For interconnectivity with other vendors' networks, Windows NT allows multiple redirectors. For each redirector, the Windows NT computer must also have a corresponding *provider* DLL (supplied by the network vendor). A Multiple Provider Router determines the appropriate provider and then routes the application request via the provider to the corresponding redirector.

The rest of this chapter describes these Windows NT networking components in detail.

NDIS-Compatible Network Adapter Card Drivers

Until the late 1980s, many of the implementations of transport protocols were tied to a proprietary implementation of a MAC-Layer interface defining how the protocol would converse with the network adapter card. This made it difficult for network adapter card vendors to support the different network operating systems available on the market. Each network adapter card vendor had to create proprietary interface drivers to support a variety of protocol implementations for use with several network operating system environments.

In 1989, Microsoft and 3Com jointly developed a standard defining an interface for communication between the MAC Layer and protocol drivers higher in the OSI model. This standard is known as the Network Device Interface Specification (NDIS). NDIS allows for a flexible environment of data exchange. It defines the software interface—called the NDIS interface—used by transport protocols to communicate with the network adapter card driver.

The flexibility of NDIS comes from the standardized implementation used by the network industry. Any NDIS-conformant protocol can pass data to any NDIS-conformant network adapter card driver, and vice versa. A process called *binding* is used to establish the initial communication channel between the protocol driver and the network adapter card driver.

Windows NT currently supports device drivers and transport protocols written to NDIS version 3.0.

NDIS allows multiple network adapter cards on a single computer. Each network adapter card can support multiple transport protocols. The advantage of supporting multiple protocol drivers on a single network card is that Windows NT computers can have simultaneous access to different types of network servers, each using a different transport protocol. For example, a computer can have access to both a Windows NT Server using NBF (the Windows NT implementation of NetBEUI) and a UNIX server via TCP/IP simultaneously.

Unlike previous NDIS implementations, Windows NT does not need a protocol manager module to link the various components at each layer together. Instead, Windows NT uses the information in the Registry (described in Chapter 10, "Overview of the Windows NT Registry" of the *Windows NT Resource Guide*) and a small piece of code called the *NDIS wrapper* that surrounds the network adapter card driver.

Transport Protocols

Sandwiched between the NDIS interface and the TDI are transport protocol device drivers. These drivers communicate with a network adapter card via a NDIS-compliant device driver.

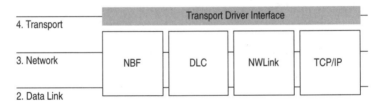

Figure 1.6   Transport Protocols

Windows NT includes these transports:

- NBF is a transport protocol derived from NetBEUI and provides compatibility with existing LAN Manager, LAN Server, and MS-Net installations. (For more information, see Chapter 6, "Using NBF with Windows NT.")

- TCP/IP is a popular routable protocol for wide-area networks.

- NWLink is an NDIS-compliant version of Internetwork Packet Exchange (IPX/SPX) compatible protocol. It can be used to establish connections between Windows NT computers and either MS-DOS, OS/2, Windows, or other Windows NT computers via RPC, Sockets, or Novell NetBIOS.

- Microsoft Data Link Control (DLC) provides an interface for access to mainframes and network attached printers. (For more information, see Chapter 7, "Using DLC with Windows NT.")

- AppleTalk supports Services for Macintosh in Windows NT Server. Developers using Windows NT Workstation can also install the AppleTalk protocol, as needed, when developing AppleTalk-compliant programs.

Transport Protocols and Streams

Windows NT supports Streams-compliant protocols provided by third parties. These protocols use Streams as an intermediary between the protocol and next interface layer (NDIS on the bottom and TDI on top). Calls to the transport protocol driver must first go through the upper layer of the Streams device driver to the protocol, then back through the lower layer of Streams to the NDIS device driver.

Using Streams makes it easier for developers to port other protocol stacks to Windows NT. It also encourages protocol stacks to be organized in a modular, stackable style, which is in keeping with the original OSI model.

Transport Driver Interface

The Windows NT networking model was designed to provide a platform on which other vendors can develop distributed applications. The NDIS boundary helps to do this by providing a unified interface at a significant break point in the model. At another significant breakpoint, namely the Session Layer of the OSI model, Windows NT includes another boundary layer. The TDI provides a common interface for networking components that communicate at the Session Layer. These boundaries allow software components above and below a level to be mixed and matched without reprogramming.

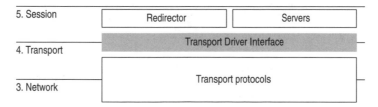

Figure 1.7   The Transport Driver Interface

The TDI is not a single program but a protocol specification to which the upper bounds of transport protocol device drivers are written. (Windows NT also includes a TDI driver that handles IRQ packet traffic from multiple TDI providers.) At this layer, networking software provides a virtual connection between the local redirector and each local or remote destination with which the redirector communicates. Similar connections are made between the server and the sources of the requests it receives.

Windows NT Workstations and Servers

Above all, the goal of a network is to share resources in one location on the network and to use them from another location on the network. On a network, computers can be organized in one of two ways:

- On networks using a classic *client-server model,* dedicated servers share resources and client workstations can access those resources.
- On networks using the *peer-to-peer networking model* (also called workgroup computing), each computer can act as both client workstation and server. Computers running

Windows NT allows you to configure your network using either or both of these models. Windows NT Workstation can use the peer-to-peer model with as many as ten users simultaneously connected to each workstation.

In the Windows NT architecture, two software components—called the server and the redirector—provide server and workstation functionality. Both of these components reside above the TDI and are implemented as file system drivers.

Being implemented as file system drivers has several benefits. Applications can call a single API (namely, Windows NT I/O functions) to access files on local and remote computers. From the I/O Manager's perspective, there is no difference between accessing files stored on a remote networked computer and accessing those stored locally on a hard disk. The redirector and server can directly call other drivers and other kernel-mode components such as the Cache Manager, thus optimizing performance. Each can be loaded and unloaded dynamically. In addition, the Windows NT redirector can coexist with other redirectors (discussed more fully in the section called "Interoperating with Other Networks," later in this chapter).

Windows NT Redirector

The redirector is the component through which one computer gains access to another computer. The Windows NT redirector allows connection to other Windows NT computers as well as to LAN Manager, LAN Server, and MS-Net servers. This redirector communicates to the protocol stacks to which it is bound via the TDI. Because network connections are not entirely reliable, it is up to the redirector to reestablish connections when they go down.

As illustrated by Figure 1.8, when a process on a Windows NT workstation tries to open a file on a remote computer, these steps occur:

1. The process calls the I/O Manager, asking for the file to be opened.

2. The I/O Manager recognizes that the request is for a file on a remote computer, so it passes it to the redirector file system driver.

3. The redirector passes the request to lower-level network drivers, which transmit it to the remote server for processing.

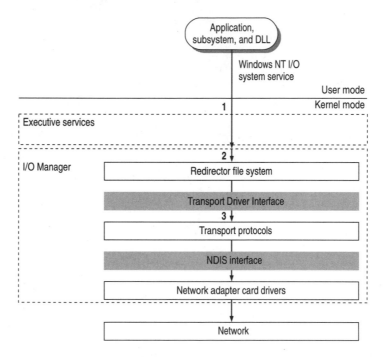

Figure 1.8   Client-Side Processing Using the Redirector

Windows NT Server

The server component entertains the connections requested by client-side redirectors and provides them with access to the resources they request. When a Windows NT server receives a request from a remote workstation to read a file on the server, these steps occur (as shown in Figure 1.9):

1. The low-level network drivers receive the request and pass it to the server driver.

2. The server passes a file-read request to the appropriate local file system driver.

3. The local file system driver calls a lower-level disk driver to access the file.

4. The data is passed back to the local file system driver.

5. The local file system driver passes the data back to the server.

6. The server passes the data to the lower-level network drivers for transmission back to the client computer.

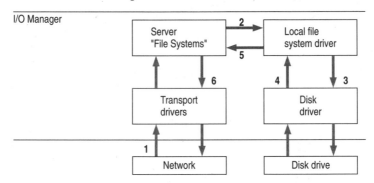

Figure 1.9   Server-Side Processing Using the Server

Interoperating with Other Networks

As mentioned before, the Windows NT redirector allows connections to LAN Manager, LAN Server, and MS-Net servers. It can also coexist with redirectors for other networks, such as Novell NetWare® and Banyan® VINES®.

While Windows NT includes integrated networking, its open design provides for transparent access to other networks. For example, a Windows NT user can concurrently access files stored on Windows NT and NetWare servers.

For details about interoperating with other networks, see Chapter 2, "Network Interoperability."

Providers and the Provider Interface Layer

For each additional type of network (NetWare, VINES, or some other), you must install a component called a *provider*. The provider is the component that allows a Windows NT computer to communicate with the network. Windows NT includes a provider for the Windows NT network. It also includes the Client Service for NetWare with Windows NT Workstation and the Gateway Service for NetWare with Windows NT Server, with which a Windows NT computer can connect as a client to a NetWare network. Other provider DLLs are supplied by the appropriate network vendors.

From the application viewpoint, there are two sets of commands that can cause network traffic—uniform naming convention (UNC) commands and WNet commands.

UNC is a method of identifying a shared resource on a network. UNC names start with two backslashes followed by the server name. All other fields in the name are separated by a single backslash. Although it's enough to simply specify the servername to list a server's shared resources, a full UNC name is in this form:

```
\\server\share\subdirectory\filename
```

WNet is part of the Win32® API and is specifically designed to allow applications on Windows NT workstations to connect to multiple networks, browse the resources of computers on those networks, and transfer data between computers of various networks. File Manager, for example, uses the WNet interface to provide its network browsing and connection facilities.

As shown in Figure 1.10, the provider layer spans the line between kernel and user modes to manage commands that may cause network traffic. The provider layer also includes two components to route UNC and WNet requests to the appropriate provider:

- The Multiple UNC Provider (MUP) receives UNC commands and locates the redirector that can make a connection to the UNC name.

- The Multiple Provider Router (MPR) receives WNet commands and passes the request to each redirector in turn until one is found that can satisfy the request.

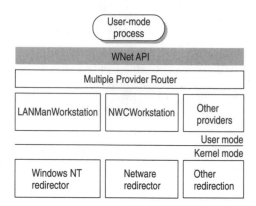

Figure 1.10   Provider Interface Components

Note I/O calls, such as Open, can contain both an UNC name and WNet calls.

Multiple UNC Provider

The MUP is a kernel-mode component whose job is to locate UNC names. When an application sends a command containing UNC names, MUP routes each UNC name to one of the registered UNC providers, including LanmanWorkstation and any others that may be installed. When a provider indicates that it can communicate with the server, MUP sends the remainder of the command to the provider.

When applications make I/O calls that contain UNC names, the MUP directs them to the appropriate redirector file system driver. The call is routed to its redirector based on the handle on the I/O call.

Multiple Provider Router

Through the MPR, Windows NT provides an open interface that enables consistent access to third-party network file systems. The key to the MPR is that all file systems, regardless of type and physical location, are accessible through the same set of file system APIs.

Applications, including File Manager, make file system requests through the Windows NT Win32 API. The MPR ensures that requests are directed to the proper file system. Local file requests are sent to the local disk, remote requests to Windows-based servers are sent to the proper server by the Windows redirector, requests to NetWare-based servers are handled by the NetWare Client for Windows NT and sent to the NetWare server, and so on.

Because applications access all types of files through a single set of APIs, any application can access any kind of server without affecting the user.

Distributed Applications and Windows NT

Any application you run on Windows NT can take advantage of networking resources because networking components are built into Windows NT. In addition, Windows NT includes several mechanisms that support and benefit distributed applications.

A *distributed application* is one that has two parts—a front-end to run on the client computer and a back-end to run on the server. In distributed computing, the goal is to divide the computing task into two sections. The front-end requires minimal resources and runs on the client's workstation. The back-end requires large amounts of data, number crunching, or specialized hardware and runs on the server. A connection between the client and the server at a process-to-process level allows data to flow in both directions between the client and server.

Microsoft Mail, Microsoft Schedule+, SQL Server, and SNA Server are examples of distributed applications.

As described in the next section, Windows NT includes NetBIOS and Windows Sockets interfaces for building distributed applications. In addition, Windows NT supports peer-to-peer named pipes, mailslots, and remote procedure calls (RPC). On Windows NT, for example, an electronic mail product could include a messaging service using named pipes and asynchronous communication that runs with any transport protocol or network card.

Of named pipes, mailslots, and RPC, RPC is the most portable mechanism. RPCs use other interprocess communication (IPC) mechanisms—including named pipes and the NetBIOS and Windows Sockets interfaces—to transfer functions and data between client and server computers.

Named pipes and mailslots are implemented to provide backward compatibility with existing LAN Manager installations and applications.

For more information about using distributed applications with Windows NT, see Chapter 8, "Client-Server Connectivity on Windows NT."

NetBIOS and Windows Sockets

Besides redirectors, Windows NT includes two other components that provide links to remote computers—NetBIOS and Windows Sockets. Windows NT includes NetBIOS and Windows Sockets interfaces for building distributed applications. (Windows NT also includes three other interprocess communication mechanisms—named pipes, mailslots, and remote procedure calls—for use by distributed applications. These are described later in this chapter.)

The NetBIOS and Windows Sockets APIs are supplied by separate DLLs. These DLLs communicate with corresponding drivers in the Windows NT Executive. As shown by Figure 1.11, the NetBIOS and Windows Sockets drivers then bypass the Windows NT redirector and communicate with protocol drivers directly using the TDI.

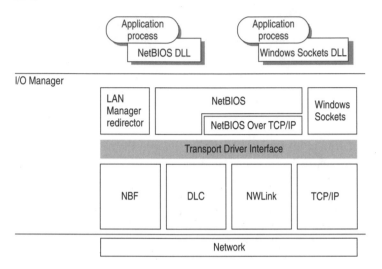

Figure 1.11   NetBIOS and Windows Sockets Support

NetBIOS

NetBIOS is the Network Basic Input/Output System—a session-level interface used by applications to communicate with NetBIOS-compliant transports such as NetBEUI Frame (NBF). The network redirector is an example of a NetBIOS application. The NetBIOS interface is responsible for establishing logical names on the network, establishing sessions between two logical names on the network, and supporting reliable data transfer between computers that have established a session.

This Session-Layer interface was originally developed by Sytek, Inc., for IBM's broadband computer network. At that time, NetBIOS was included on a ROM chip on the network adapter card. Sytek also developed a NetBIOS for IBM's Token-Ring network, this time implemented as a device driver. Several other vendors have since produced versions of this interface.

In order to support the emerging network industry standard, Microsoft developed the NetBIOS interface for MS-Net and LAN Manager products, and also included this interface with the Windows for Workgroups product.

NetBIOS uses a unique logical name to identify a workstation for handling communications between nodes. A NetBIOS name is a unique alphanumeric name consisting of one to 15 characters. To carry on two-way communication between computers, NetBIOS establishes a logical connection, or *session*, between them. Once a logical connection is established, computers can then exchange data in the form of NetBIOS requests or in the form of a Server Message Block (SMB).

Server Message Blocks

The SMB protocol (developed jointly by Microsoft, Intel, and IBM) defines a series of commands used to pass information between networked computers and can be broken into four message types—session control, file, printer, and message. Session control consists of commands that start and end a redirector connection to a shared resource at the server. The file SMB messages are used by the redirector to gain access to files at the server. The printer SMB messages are used by the redirector to send data to a print queue at a server and to get status information about the print queue. The message SMB type allows an application to send messages to or receive messages from another workstation.

The redirector packages network control block (NCB) requests meant for remote computers in a structure known as a system message block (SMB). SMBs can be sent over the network to a remote device. The redirector also uses SMBs to make requests to the protocol stack of the local computer, such as "Create a session with the file server."

The provider DLL listens for SMB messages destined for it and removes the data portion of the SMB request so that it can be processed by a local device.

SMBs provide interoperability between different versions of the Microsoft family of networking products and other networks that use SMBs, including these:

MS OS/2 LAN Manager	DEC PATHWORKS™
Microsoft Windows for Workgroups	Microsoft LAN Manager for UNIX
IBM LAN Server	3Com® 3+Open®
MS-DOS LAN Manager	MS-Net

Windows Sockets

Windows Sockets is a Windows implementation of the widely used UC Berkeley Sockets API. Microsoft TCP/IP, NWLink, and AppleTalk protocols use this interface.

A *socket* provides an endpoint to a connection; two sockets form a complete path. A socket works as a bidirectional pipe for incoming and outgoing data between networked computers. The Windows Sockets API is a networking API tailored for use by programmers using the Microsoft Windows family of products. Windows Sockets is a public specification based on Berkeley UNIX Sockets and aims to do the following:

- Provide a familiar networking API to programmers using Windows or UNIX

- Offer binary compatibility between heterogeneous Windows-based TCP/IP stack and utilities vendors

- Support both connection-oriented and connectionless protocols

Most users will use programs that comply with Windows Sockets, such as FTP or Telnet. (However, developers who are interested in developing a Windows Sockets application can find specifications for Windows Sockets on the Internet.)

Named Pipes and Mailslots

Named pipes and mailslots are actually written as file systems, unlike other IPC mechanisms. Thus, the Registry lists entries for the Named Pipes File System (NPFS) and the Mailslot File System (MSFS). As file systems they share common functionality, such as caching, with the other file systems. Additionally, processes on the local computer can use named pipes and mailslots to communicate with one another without going through networking components. Remote access to named pipes and mailslots, as with all of the file systems, is provided through the redirector.

Named pipes are based on OS/2 API calls, but in Windows NT they include additional asynchronous support and increased security.

Another new feature added to named pipes is impersonation, which allows a server to change its security identifier so that it matches the client's. For example, suppose a database server system uses named pipes to receive read and write requests from clients. When a request comes in, the database server program can impersonate the client before attempting to perform the request. So even if the server program does have authority to perform the function, the client may not, and the request would be denied. (For more information on impersonation, see Chapter 2, "Windows NT Security Model" of the *Windows NT Resource Guide*.)

Mailslot APIs in Windows NT are a subset of those in Microsoft OS/2 LAN Manager. Windows NT implements only second-class mailslots, not first-class mailslots. Second-class mailslots provide *connectionless* messaging for broadcast messages and so on. Delivery of the message is not guaranteed, although the delivery rate on most networks is very high. Second-class mailslots are most useful for identifying other computers or services on a network and for wide-scale notification of a service.

Remote Procedure Calls

Much of the original design work for an RPC facility was started by Sun Microsystems®. This work was continued by the Open Software Foundation (OSF) as part of their overall Data Communications Exchange (DCE) standard. The Microsoft RPC facility is compatible with the OSF/DCE-standard RPC. It is important to note that it is compatible and not compliant. Compliance in this case means starting with the OSF source code and building on it. The Microsoft RPC facility is completely interoperable with other DCE-based RPC systems such as the ones for HP® and IBM AIX® systems.

The RPC mechanism is unique because it uses the other IPC mechanisms to establish communications between the client and the server. RPC can use named pipes, NetBIOS, or Windows Sockets to communicate with remote systems. If the client and server are on the same computer, it can use the Local Procedure Call (LPC) facility to transfer information between processes and subsystems. This makes RPC the most flexible and portable of the Windows NT IPC mechanisms.

RPC is based on the concepts used for creating structured programs, which can be viewed as having a "backbone" to which a series of "ribs" can be attached. The backbone is the mainstream logic of the program, which should rarely change. The ribs are the procedures the backbone calls on to do work or perform functions.

In traditional programs, these ribs are statically linked. By using DLLs, structured programs can dynamically link the ribs. With DLLs, the procedure code and the backbone code are in different modules. The DLL can thus be modified or updated without changes to the backbone. RPC means that the backbone and the ribs can exist on different computers, as shown in Figure 1.12.

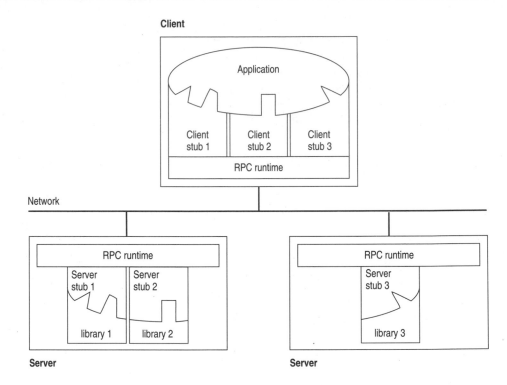

Figure 1.12   Remote Procedure Call Facility

In this figure, the client application was developed with a specially compiled *stub* library. The client application thinks it is calling its own subroutines. In reality, these stubs transfer the data and the function down to a module called the RPC Runtime. This module is responsible for finding the server that can satisfy the RPC command. Once found, the function and data are sent to the server, where it is picked up by the RPC Runtime module on the server. The server piece then loads the needed library for the function, builds the appropriate data structure, and calls the function. The function thinks it is being called by the client application. When the function is completed, any return values are collected, formatted, and sent back to the client via the RPC Runtime modules. When the function returns to the client application it has the appropriate returned data, or it has an indication that the function failed in stream.

Remote Access Service

Windows NT 3.5 Remote Access Service (RAS) connects remote or mobile workers to corporate networks. Optimized for client-server computing, RAS is implemented primarily as a software solution, and is available on all of Microsoft's operating systems.

To understand the RAS architecture, it is important to make the distinction between RAS and remote control solutions, such as Cubix and pcANYWHERE®. RAS is a software-based multi-protocol router; remote control solutions work by sharing screen, keyboard and mouse control over a WAN connection. In a remote control solution, users share a CPU or multiple CPU's on the server. In contrast, a Windows NT RAS server's CPU is dedicated to communications, not to running applications.

Point-to-Point Protocol (PPP)

Windows NT supports the Point-to-Point Protocol (PPP) in RAS. PPP is a set of industry standard framing and authentication protocols. PPP negotiates configuration parameters for multiple layers of the OSI model.

PPP support in Windows NT 3.5 (and Windows 95) means that computers running Windows can dial into remote networks through any server that complies with the PPP standard. PPP compliance also enables a Windows NT Server to receive calls from, and provide network access to, other vendors' remote access software.

The PPP architecture also enables clients to load any combination of IPX, TCP/IP, and NetBEUI. Applications written to the Windows Sockets, NetBIOS, or IPX interface can now be run on a remote Windows NT Workstation. The following illustrates the PPP architecture of RAS.

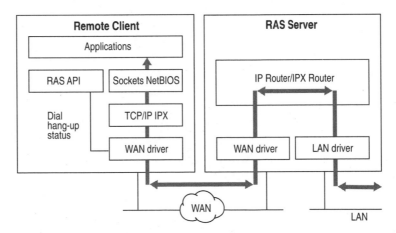

Figure 1.13   PPP Architecture of RAS

RAS Connection Sequence

Understanding the RAS connection sequence will help you understand the PPP protocol.

Upon connecting to a remote computer, PPP negotiation begins.

First, framing rules are established between the remote computer and server. This allows continued communication (frame transfer) to occur.

Next the RAS server authenticates the remote user using the PPP authentication protocols (PAP, CHAP, SPAP). The protocols invoked depend on the security configurations of the remote client and server.

Once authenticated, the Network Control Protocols (NCPs) are used to enable and configure the server for the LAN protocol that will be used on the remote client.

When the PPP connection sequence has completed successfully, the remote client and RAS server can begin to transfer data using any supported protocol, such as Windows Sockets, RPC, or NetBIOS. The following illustrates where the PPP protocol are on the OSI model.

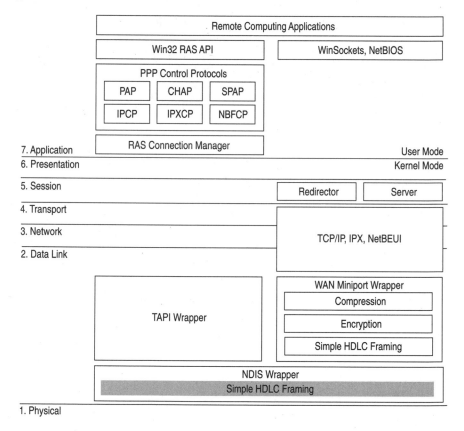

Figure 1.14   Location of the PPP Protocol on the OSI Model

If your remote client is configured to use the NetBIOS gateway or SLIP, this sequence is invalid.

NetBIOS Gateway

Windows NT continues to support NetBIOS gateways, the architecture used in previous version of Windows NT and LAN Manager. Remote users connect using NetBEUI, and the RAS server translates packets, if necessary, to IPX or TCP/IP. This enables users to share network resources in a multi-protocol LAN, but prevents them from running applications which rely on IPX or TCP/IP on the client. The NetBIOS gateway is used by default when remote clients are using NetBEUI. The following illustrates the NetBIOS gateway architecture of RAS.

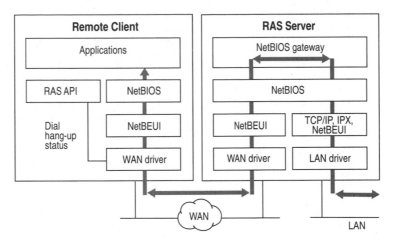

Figure 1.15   NetBIOS Gateway Architecture of RAS

An example of the NetBIOS gateway capability is remote network access for Lotus® Notes® users. While Lotus Notes does offer dial up connectivity, dial up is limited to the Notes application only. RAS complements this connectivity by providing a low-cost, high-performance remote network connection for Notes® users which not only connects Notes, but offers file and print services, and access to other network resources.

Serial Line Internet Protocol (SLIP)

Serial Line Internet Protocol (SLIP), is an older communications standard found in UNIX environments. SLIP does not provide the automatic negotiation of network configuration and encrypted authentication that PPP can provide. SLIP requires user intervention. Windows NT 3.5 RAS can be configured as a SLIP client, enabling Windows NT users to dial into an existing SLIP server. RAS does not provide a SLIP server in Windows NT Server.

See the RASPHONE.HLP online Help file on the Windows NT distribution disks (or, if RAS has been installed, *systemroot***SYSTEM32**) for more information about RAS.

Services for Macintosh

Through Windows NT Services for Macintosh, Macintosh users can connect to a Windows NT server the same way they would connect to an AppleShare server. Windows NT Services for Macintosh will support an unlimited number of simultaneous AFP™ connections to a Windows NT server, and Macintosh sessions will be integrated with Windows NT sessions. The per-session memory overhead is approximately 15K.

Existing versions of LAN Manager Services for the Macintosh can be easily upgraded to Windows NT Services for Macintosh. OS/2-based volumes that already exist are converted with permissions intact. In addition, graphical installation, administration, and configuration utilities are integrated with existing Windows NT administration tools. Windows NT Services for Macintosh requires System 6.0.7 or higher and is AFP 2.1-compliant; however, AFP 2.0 clients are supported. AFP 2.1 compliance provides support for logon messages and server messages.

Support for Macintosh networking is built into the core operating system for Windows NT Server. Windows NT Services for Macintosh includes a full AFP 2.0 file server. All Macintosh file system attributes, such as resource data forks, 32-bit directory IDs, and so on, are supported. As a file server, all filenames, icons, and access permissions are intelligently managed for different networks. For example, a Word for Windows file will appear on the Macintosh with the correct Word for Macintosh icons. These applications can also be launched from the File Server as Macintosh applications. When files are deleted, there will be no orphaned resource forks left to be cleaned up.

Windows NT Services for Macintosh fully supports and complies with Windows NT security. It presents the AFP security model to Macintosh users and allows them to access files on volumes that reside on CD-ROM or other read-only media. The AFP server also supports both cleartext and encrypted passwords at logon time. The administrator has the option to configure the server not to accept cleartext passwords.

Services for Macintosh can be administered from Control Panel and can be started transparently if the administrator has configured the server to use this facility.

Macintosh-accessible volumes can be created from File Manager. Services for Macintosh automatically creates a Public Files volume at installation time. Windows NT file and directory permissions are automatically translated into corresponding Macintosh permissions.

Windows NT Services for Macintosh has the same functionality as the LAN Manager Services for Macintosh 1.0 MacPrint. In addition, administration and configuration are easier. There is a user interface for publishing a print queue on AppleTalk and a user interface for choosing an AppleTalk printer as a destination device. The Windows NT print subsystem handles AppleTalk despooling errors gracefully, and uses the built-in printer support in Windows NT. (The PPD file scheme of Macintosh Services 1.0 is not used.) Services for Macintosh also has a PostScript-compatible engine that allows Macintoshes to print to any Windows NT printer as if they were printing to a LaserWriter.

Additional Reading

For additional information on topics related to networking and the Windows NT networking model, see the following resources:

ANSI/IEEE standard 802.2 - 1985 (ISO/DIS 8802/2): *IEEE Standards for Local Area Networks—Logical Link Control Standard.*

ANSI/IEEE standard 802.3 - 1985 (ISO/DIS 8802/3): *IEEE Standards for Local Area Networks—Carrier Sense Multiple Access with Collision Detection (CSMA/CD) Access Method and Physical Layer Specifications*; American National Standards Institute; January 12, 1989.

ANSI/IEEE standard 802.4 - 1985 (ISO/DIS 8802/4): *IEEE Standards for Local Area Networks—Token-Passing Bus Access Method and Physical Layer Specifications*; American National Standards Institute; December 17, 1984.

ANSI/IEEE standard 802.5 - 1985 (ISO/DIS 8802/5): *IEEE Standards for Local Area Networks—Token-Ring Access Method and Physical Layer Specifications*; American National Standards Institute; June 2, 1989.

Beatty, Dana. "Programming to the OS/2 IEEE 802.2 API." *OS/2 Notebook*. Ed. Dick Conklin. Redmond, WA: Microsoft Press, 1990.

Haugdahl, J. Scott. *Inside NetBIOS*. Minneapolis: Architecture Technology Corporation, 1990.

Haugdahl, J. Scott. *Inside NetBIOS (2nd Edition)*. Minneapolis, Minn: Architecture Technology Corporation, 1988.

Haugdahl, J. Scott. *Inside Token-Ring (3rd Edition)*. Minneapolis, Minn: Architecture Technology Corporation, 1990.

IBM Token-Ring Network Architecture Reference (6165877), November 1985.

IBM Token-Ring Network PC Adapter Technical Reference (69X7830).

International Business Machines. *Local Area Network: Technical Reference (SC30-3383-2)*. New York: 1988.

International Standard 7498: *Information processing systems—Open Systems Interconnection—Basic Reference Model (First edition)*; American National Standards Institute, November 15, 1984. The OSI model.

Martin, James. *Local Areas Networks: Architecture and Implementations*. Englewood Cliffs, NJ: Prentice Hall: 1989.

Microsoft Corporation, 3Com Corporation. *SMB Specification*. This may be obtained from the files library in the Microsoft Client Server Computing forum on CompuServe (GO MSNETWORK).

Microsoft Corporation. *Microsoft LAN Manager Resource Kit*. Microsoft Corporation, 1992.

Microsoft. *Computer Dictionary*. Redmond, WA: Microsoft Press, 1991.

Microsoft. *Microsoft LAN Manager MS-DLC Protocol Driver*. Redmond, WA: Microsoft Press, 1991.

Microsoft. *Microsoft/3Com LAN Manager Network Driver Interface Specification*. Redmond, WA: Microsoft Press, 1990.

Miller, Mark. *LAN Protocol Handbook*. Redwood City, CA: M & T Books, 1990.

Miller, Mark. *LAN Troubleshooting Handbook*. Redwood City, CA: M & T Books, 1990.

Tanenbaum, Andrew. *Computer Networks (2nd Edition)*. Englewood Cliffs, NJ: Prentice Hall, 1988

The Ethernet. A Local Area Network. (Data Link Layer and Physical Layer Specifications); version 2.0, November 1982. Also known as the "Ethernet Blue Book."

C H A P T E R   2

Network Interoperability

In addition to Windows-based networking, Windows NT supports network interoperability with computers running a wide range of operating systems and network protocols. This support makes it easy to incorporate computers running Windows NT into existing networks so you can take advantage of the advanced features of Windows NT without disrupting your enterprise.

The networking architecture of Windows NT is protocol-independent, providing standard interfaces for applications—such as Windows Sockets, remote procedure calls (RPC), and NetBIOS—and device drivers. Besides making it easier to implement a particular protocol stack for Windows NT, this architecture also enables a Windows NT computer to run multiple protocols on a single network adapter card. As a result, a Windows NT computer can simultaneously communicate with a number of different network systems.

Of particular interest to most network administrators is how to provide access by and to computers running Windows NT Workstation and Windows NT Server in the following environments:

- Novell NetWare networks
- UNIX networks
- SNA networks for IBM mainframe and midrange computers

This chapter provides an overview of some of the issues and benefits involved in using Windows NT computers in these environments.

Using Windows NT with NetWare

Windows NT computers can easily be integrated into a predominantly NetWare environment, making the benefits of an advanced operating system available to an existing network.

A network administrator contemplating a mixed network environment is naturally concerned about how the various components will be able to communicate with each other. In the case of a mixed Windows-based networking and NetWare environment, the network administrator wants to ensure that Windows NT Workstation computers added to the network are able to use file and print resources on existing NetWare servers, and that existing NetWare clients can access client-server applications running on Windows NT Servers. The following figure shows how the various components of the network relate to each other.

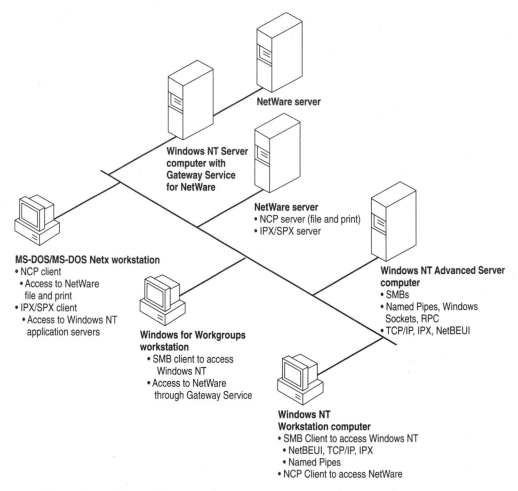

Figure 2.1   Mixed Windows-based and NetWare Environment

The following sections discuss how Windows NT computers can effectively function either as a client of NetWare servers or as an application server for NetWare clients.

Windows NT Servers on a NetWare Network

Many organizations that use NetWare are seeking solutions for downsizing or reengineering existing applications that run on minicomputers or mainframes. NetWare servers are designed to function primarily as file and print servers, so they do not support such business-critical applications well. NetWare servers do not feature preemptive multitasking or protected virtual memory, essential features for client-server applications. On the other hand, Windows NT Server makes an ideal platform for such demanding applications because of its scalability, fault tolerance, 32-bit architecture, and threaded, preemptive multitasking with full memory protection.

NetWare administrators can take advantage of the advanced features of Windows NT Servers on an existing NetWare network without interfering with client systems' access to file and printer resources on NetWare servers. For example, a NetWare administrator can add Windows NT Server computers running SQL Server to the network so client workstations can take advantage of a distributed high-performance relational database system while still being able to use files and printers shared by their usual NetWare servers. Such a solution requires no additional hardware or software to provide the necessary connectivity.

To function as an application server for NetWare clients, a computer running Windows NT Server must be running the built-in NWLink IPX/SPX-compatible protocol stack (NWLink). Connections over NWLink can be made via Remote Procedure Calls (RPC), Windows Sockets, Novell NetBIOS, or the NWLink NetBIOS installed with NWLink. Because NWLink is NDIS-compliant, the Windows NT computer can simultaneously run other protocol stacks, such as NetBEUI Frame (NBF) or TCP/IP, through which it can communicate with non-NetWare computers.

Windows NT Clients on a NetWare Network

Windows NT was designed from the start with integrated network support in mind. Because the network support built into Windows NT is independent of the underlying network system, the same user interface and tools work with all networks that run on Windows NT. For example, with File Manager the user can browse and connect to any NetWare or Windows-networking server on the network.

With the Client Service for NetWare, a Windows NT Workstation computer can access file and print resources on NetWare servers as easily as it accesses resources on Windows-based networking servers. With the Gateway Service for NetWare, a Windows NT Server computer can not only access NetWare file and print resources, but also share these resources with Windows-based networking clients that have no NetWare connectivity software. To the Microsoft networking clients, the NetWare resource looks like any other shared resource on the Windows NT Server computer.

The Windows NT architecture includes an open interface called the multiple provider router (MPR) that enables consistent access to third-party network file systems. The MPR makes all file systems, regardless of type and physical location, accessible through the same set of file-system application programming interfaces (APIs). Applications (and components of the Windows NT shell) make file-system requests through the Windows NT Win32 API. The MPR ensures that requests are directed to the proper file system: local file requests are sent to the local disk, remote requests to Windows-based servers are sent to the proper server by the Windows NT redirector, and requests to NetWare servers are sent to the appropriate server by the Client or Gateway Service for NetWare.

For more information about NWLink and the Client and Gateway Services for NetWare, see the *Windows NT Installation Guide* or *Windows NT Server Services for NetWare Networks.*

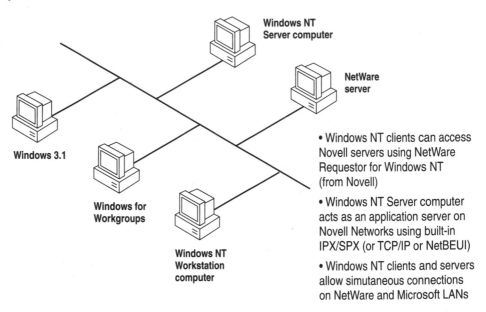

Figure 2.2   Windows NT Computers as NetWare Clients or Application Servers

Additional Considerations Regarding Mixed Networking Environments

Before adding computers running Windows NT (or other non-NetWare operating systems) to a NetWare network, a NetWare administrator should anticipate some of the potential problems that might arise.

One source of possible difficulty for NetWare administrators is that Windows NT NetWare clients do not run NetWare logon scripts. However, Windows NT can run its own logon scripts, and the ability of Windows NT to maintain persistent connections through logon scripts and user profiles provides much the same functionality as NetWare logon scripts in many instances.

Another area of difficulty is backing up Windows NT NetWare clients. Novell servers do not provide tape backup services for their Windows NT clients without third-party software. A Windows NT computer equipped with a supported tape drive can back up other Windows NT computers, as well as NetWare servers and computers running Windows networking software.

Finally, Windows NT can act as a client only for a NetWare server running NetWare version 3.*x* and earlier. Windows NT can access servers running NetWare 4.*x* through the server's Bindery Emulation Mode that emulates version 3.*x*.

Integrating Windows NT and UNIX Systems

With its advanced configuration management tools, Windows NT is especially suited for integrating with most of the UNIX variants that are likely to be found on many networks. Among the Windows NT features that make it easy to interoperate with UNIX systems are:

- Built-in TCP/IP protocol and utilities.
- Support for character and graphics terminal emulation.
- Advanced file transfer and data sharing capabilities.
- Distributed processing support.
- Application portability.

The following sections provide further information about these features. With DHCP and WINS, combined with the DNS server and other TCP/IP tools provided in this resource kit, integrating Windows NT and UNIX systems is easier than ever. For full details on TCP/IP in the Windows NT environment, see Part III, "TCP/IP," and Part IV, "Windows NT and the Internet."

TCP/IP Protocol

At the protocol level, Windows NT includes a fast, robust implementation of the Transport Control Protocol/Internet Protocol (TCP/IP) protocol stack, the most commonly used protocol among UNIX systems. Using TCP/IP, Windows NT computers can communicate with UNIX systems without additional networking software. (TCP/IP also provides efficient communication on wide-area networks, even when no UNIX systems are involved.) The TCP/IP protocol stack for Windows NT is NDIS-compliant and so can be used in conjunction with NetBEUI Frame (NBF) and other NDIS-compliant protocols. It includes an internet protocol (IP) router, serial line internet protocol (SLIP), and point-to-point protocol (PPP) support.

In addition to the TCP/IP protocol itself, Windows NT also includes more than a dozen TCP/IP utilities that make it easier for experienced UNIX users to access UNIX systems from Windows NT and to administer the TCP/IP networking on their own computer. Additional tools are included on the CD-ROM accompanying this resource kit.

Windows NT also provides facilities for integrating computers running Windows NT into networks managed through Simple Network Management Protocol (SNMP), which is commonly used to manage TCP/IP networks. Through its SNMP service, a Windows NT computer can report its current status to an SNMP management system on a TCP/IP network, either in response to a request from a management system or automatically when a significant event occurs on the Windows NT computer.

For more information, see Part III, "TCP/IP."

Character and Graphics Terminal Support

The TCP/IP Telnet utility is built into the Windows Terminal accessory to make it easy for a Windows NT computer to have character-oriented terminal access to UNIX systems via TCP/IP. Telnet provides basic terminal emulation of TTY (scrolling), as well as emulation of DEC VT-100 (ANSI) and VT-52 terminals.

Even in the traditionally character-oriented UNIX environment, many applications are moving to graphical user interfaces. X Windows is a commonly used standard for graphical interfaces in networked UNIX environments. A number of third-party companies are also developing X Servers to enable Windows NT users to access and run X-based applications on UNIX systems. (In X Windows terminology, an X Server runs on a client workstation to provide graphics output on behalf of an X Client program running on an applications server.) Several third-party vendors are also developing X Client libraries for Windows NT as well; this eventually will enable UNIX (or other systems with X Server capabilities) to access client-server applications running on a Windows NT computer. Companies developing X Servers and X Client libraries for Windows NT include Hummingbird, Congruent, and Digital Equipment Corporation.

File Transfer and Data Sharing

One of the fundamental reasons for connecting computers on a network is to enable them to exchange files and data. Windows NT supports standard facilities for transferring files and sharing data between Windows NT and UNIX systems.

Included with Windows NT itself are both client and server versions of File Transfer Protocol (FTP). FTP makes it possible for Windows NT computers to exchange files with diverse systems, particularly UNIX systems.

Where more advanced data sharing capabilities are required, computers running Windows NT can access data on UNIX systems (including data on remotely mountable file systems, such as NFS, RFS, and AFS) through Microsoft LAN Manager for UNIX (LMU), an implementation of Microsoft Windows networking for servers running UNIX variants. LMU is based on server message blocks (SMBs), a set of protocols developed by Microsoft that are now part of the X/Open standard.

Finally, a number of third-party companies (including NetManage, Beame and Whiteside, Intergraph, and Process Software) have developed versions of Sun's Network File System (NFS) for Windows NT. NFS is a widely used tool for sharing files among various UNIX systems.

Distributed Processing Support

As more and more enterprises adopt the client-server paradigm for their networks, standards-based distributed processing becomes a key factor in the success of that effort. Windows NT provides direct support for several types of industry-standard distributed processing.

The Remote Procedure Call (RPC) facility of Windows NT is wire-compatible with the Open Software Foundation's Distributed Computing Environment (DCE) RPC. Using this RPC, developers can create applications that include not only Windows NT computers, but all systems that support DCE-compatible RPCs, such as systems from Hewlett Packard® and Digital Equipment Corporation.

In addition to RPCs, Windows NT supports Windows Sockets. Windows Sockets provides an API that is compatible with Berkeley-style sockets, a mechanism that is widely used by different UNIX versions for distributed computing.

For more information about RPC and Windows Sockets, see Chapter 1, "Windows NT Networking Architecture."

Perhaps most importantly, Windows Open Services Architecture (WOSA), whose development is being led by Microsoft, specifies an open set of APIs for integrating Windows-based computers with back-end services on a broad range of vendors' systems. WOSA consists of an extensible set of APIs that enable Windows-based desktop applications to access available information without having to know anything about the type of network in use, the types of computers in the enterprise, or the types of back-end services available. As a result, should the network, computers, or services change, desktop applications built using WOSA won't require rewriting. The first two WOSA components address database and electronic messaging: Open Database Connectivity (ODBC) and Messaging API (MAPI). Work is underway for additional standards, including directory, security, and software licensing services.

Common Application Support

For most users, the key measure of interoperability is the ability to run the same applications on multiple platforms. Three key factors are furthering this type of interoperability between UNIX and Windows NT computers.

One factor is the relative ease with which many UNIX independent software vendors (ISVs) are able to port their high-end business and technical applications to the Win32 API of Windows NT. Aiding this process is the fact that most UNIX applications are written in standard C and so are readily adapted to other operating systems (such as Windows NT) for which standard C libraries have been developed. A wide variety of third-party porting aids (including items as diverse asXlibs, GNU tools, and X Client libraries) are available through commercial sources and from Internet. Because application developers are finding it so easy to port their traditionally UNIX-based applications to Windows NT, increasing numbers of such applications will be available for both UNIX platforms and for computers running Windows NT.

Another factor is that Windows NT fully supports programs that conform to the IEEE 1003.1-1990 standard commonly known as POSIX.1 (derived from Portable Operating System Interface). This standard defines a basic set of operating-system services available to character-based applications. Programs that adhere to the POSIX standard can be easily ported from one operating system to another. See Chapter 17, "POSIX Compatibility," of the *Windows NT Resource Guide* for more information.

Another factor is that third-party products from vendors such as Bristol Technologies are available that enable UNIX to run Windows-based applications. Additionally, there are third-party products, such as Consensys Portage, that enable Windows NT to run UNIX-based applications.

Connecting Windows NT and IBM SNA Hosts

A growing trend in many types of enterprises is downsizing mainframe-based applications to run on personal computer client-server networks. Many of these downsized applications will still require access to data and applications residing on IBM System Network Architecture (SNA) hosts, mainframes and midrange computers. Companies have invested large amounts of money, time, and effort in their host systems and so want to be able to make the best use of that investment even as they move toward distributed client-server computing. This section discusses how Windows NT computers can be connected to IBM SNA hosts to leverage the high capacity of SNA hosts in a distributed environment.

Basic Connectivity Using the Built-in DLC Protocol

A computer running Windows NT can communicate with IBM SNA hosts (as well as other network devices) across an Ethernet or token ring LAN through the Data Link Control (DLC) protocol that is built into Windows NT. The DLC protocol device driver enables a basic level of connectivity with other computers running the DLC protocol stack. For example, a Windows NT computer can connect to and communicate with an IBM mainframe through its 37x5 Front-end processor (FEP) using a 3270 terminal emulator and the DLC protocol. See Chapter 7, "Using DLC with Windows NT," for more information.

SNA Server for Windows NT

Although such simple one-to-one connections can suffice for many basic operations, most enterprises require more flexible connectivity between IBM host computers and local area networks (LANs). To meet this need, Microsoft SNA Server exploits client-server architecture to link desktop personal computers to IBM mainframe and midrange computers that are accessible using the Systems Network Architecture (SNA) protocols. The client personal computers can run Windows NT, Windows, MS-DOS, OS/2, or the Macintosh operating system and can use standard LAN protocols to connect to the server; only the computer running SNA Server must run the SNA protocol. Each personal computer user can have multiple 3270 and 5250 sessions for concurrent terminal and printer emulation, including file-transfer and Emulator High-Level Language API (EHLLAPI) applications. SNA Server for Windows NT also provides support for the following APIs for distributed SNA applications:

- Advanced Program-to-Program Communications (APPC) for applications that communicate peer-to-peer with other APPC applications using the LU 6.2 protocol

- Common Programming Interface for Communications (CPI-C) for applications that communicate peer-to-peer with IBM Systems Application Architecture (SAA) applications using the LU 6.2 protocol

- Common Service Verbs (CSV) for applications that communicate with NetView and enable tracing of API calls

- Logical Unit APIs (LUA) for applications (using LUA/Request Unit Interface or LUA/Session Level Interface APIs) that need direct access to LU 0, 1, 2, and 3 data streams

The client-server architecture of SNA Server makes it possible to off-load communications processing from client systems, permitting them to use their system resources more efficiently. Client personal computers do not have to run one protocol to access the LAN and another to access the SNA host. Instead, each personal computer can run Microsoft-based networking (named pipes), TCP/IP, IPX/SPX, AppleTalk®, or Banyan® VINES®, within a single-protocol or mixed network, to access the SNA server. The SNA server routes the connection to the appropriate host computer via the SNA protocol. The SNA server automatically balances the user load across multiple host connections and servers to provide optimal throughput.

The client-server architecture also provides Windows NT-based applications with the ability to access information on IBM mainframes and midrange computers. For example, using SNA Server, mail servers can access PROFS, and Microsoft SQL Server can access DB2 information.

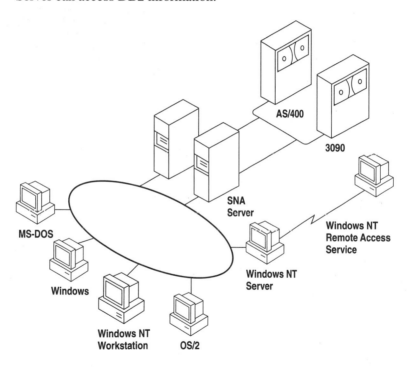

Figure 2.3   SNA Server Connecting LANs to IBM Host Computers

DSPU Support

In addition to standard personal computer connections, SNA Server supports Downstream Physical Units (DSPUs), any SNA device or personal computer running a full PU 2.0 (SNA cluster controller) protocol stack. These systems use the SNA server as a concentrator gateway for connecting to IBM hosts. Examples of some of the DSPU clients that SNA Server supports are IBM OS/2 Communications Manager/2 clients and IBM 3174 cluster controllers. The DSPU protocols that SNA Server supports are DLC over token ring or Ethernet, Synchronous Data Link Control (SDLC), and OSI-standard X.25/QLLC (Qualified Logical Link Control).

NetView Support

SNA Server provides API support for bidirectional communications with NetView, IBM's mainframe-centered network management system. SNA Server can send application- or system-defined Windows NT event-log messages to NetView and can enable Windows NT commands to be executed from the NetView console. For example, if an SNA Server database is stopped on the LAN, an alert can be sent to the NetView console. A data center operator can then send a command from the NetView console to the Windows NT computer to restart the server.

SNA Server also supports Response-Time Monitor (RTM) and user-defined alerts for third-party 3270 emulators.

Centralized Management

Network administrators can administer all SNA servers from a centralized location, such as from a LAN workstation or a NetView console. For example, a company with offices in several cities could have one or more SNA Servers at each site. The MIS department at corporate headquarters can manage all of these SNA servers, performing all administrative functions remotely.

Integration with Windows NT

SNA Server is supported on all the hardware platforms supported by Windows NT. SNA Server relies on the built-in security of Windows NT, so administrators need to manage only a single set of user accounts. SNA Server also is fully integrated with Windows NT system monitoring and management services, and provides automatic server and connection fault tolerance. SNA Server for Windows NT is completely 32-bit and multithreaded for maximum performance, scalability, and reliability.

SNA Server is fully compliant with Microsoft's Windows Open Services Architecture (WOSA), providing a consistent interface to enterprise computing environments and hiding the complexities of connectivity from applications.

Server Capabilities

SNA Server provides for as many as 250 simultaneous host connections by each server and up to 2,000 users and 10,000 sessions per server.

C H A P T E R   3

Windows NT User Environments

Each user on a Windows NT network works in a unique environment. The user environment is composed of such things as the file and print resources that are available, the configuration of Program Manager icons, screen wallpaper or background, automatic network connections, and applications that run on startup. One important element of the user environment is a directory assigned to a user or to a defined user group on either a workstation or a server where the user can store files. This directory is called a *home directory*.

A user's environment is determined primarily by a *user profile*, which you can create and maintain on a Windows NT Server computer using the User Profile Editor administrative tool. For information on the User Profile Editor, see the *Windows NT Server System Guide.* Some elements of the user environment are more easily controlled by creating a script that is executed whenever the user logs on to a Windows NT Workstation computer or a Windows NT Server computer. Such a script is called a *logon script*.

This chapter explains how to create home directories and logon scripts. It also describes special parameters you can use in logon scripts so the same script runs in different user environments with the expected result for each individual user.

Home Directories

A home directory is a private storage space assigned to a user or group of users. Users typically store their private data in their home directory, and they can normally restrict or grant access to other users. When a user opens a Command Prompt window, the default directory is the user's home directory. The home directory can also be specified as the default working directory for applications.

If hard disk space on your network's client workstations is limited, you might want to assign each user a home directory on a Windows NT Server computer. Or, if you want to limit a user's access to the files and directories on a workstation, you can create a home directory on the workstation and give the user only List permission on all other directories.

Assigning a Home Directory

On a Windows NT Workstation computer, home directories are assigned in User Manager. On a Windows NT Server computer, home directories are assigned in User Manager for Domains. The home directory that is used depends on whether the user logs on to the workstation account or the domain account.

The home directory can be specified by a local path name, such as C:\USERS\BILL, or by a universal naming convention (UNC) name, such as \\MYSERVER\USERS\BILL. The UNC name is the better option for large networks, because the system administrator can more easily see where users' home directories are located.

By default, the home directory is the \USERS\DEFAULT directory that is created during installation of Windows NT. The most common way to assign a home directory is to specify it using the following syntax:

\USERS*accountname*

   –Or–

\USERS*groupname*

where *accountname* is the username given to the account or where *groupname* is the name of a local or global group whose members all share the same home directory.

▶ **To assign a home directory**

1. From the Administrative Tools group in Program Manager, double-click the User Manager or User Manager for Domains icon, depending on whether you are using a Windows NT Workstation computer or Windows NT Server computer.

2. Double-click the name of the user or group whose home directory you want to assign.

   The User Properties dialog box appears.

3. Choose the Profile button to display the User Environment Profile dialog box.

4. Enter the full path specification of the home directory in the Local Path box of the Home Directory group box.

   If you are specifying a remote home directory, specify a disk drive letter and provide the full path (not just the sharename) to the directory. For instance, if the home directory is \JEFFHO on share \\SERVER1\USERS, enter the path \\SERVER1\USERS\JEFFHO.

Note If you want the user to control access to the home directory, give the user Full Control permission for the directory. You will probably also give members of the Administrator or Domain Admins group Full Control permission and give all other users No Access or List permission only. For information on setting directory permissions, see Chapter 4, "File Manager," of the *Windows NT System Guide.*

If you specify a nonexistent directory when you define or modify a user account, Windows NT automatically creates the directory.

When a user logs on to a domain, Windows NT automatically tries to connect to the home directory defined in the user's domain account using the following rules.

- If the computer where the home directory resides is not available, the user's home directory on the local computer is used (if there is one).

- If the home directory specified does not exist or the user does not have a home directory, then the user is connected to the \USERS\DEFAULT directory of the computer that processes the logon.

- If the \USERS\DEFAULT directory does not exist, then the user is connected to the \USERS directory.

Note Windows NT Server connects the user to the home directory specified in the domain user account only when the logon is from a Windows NT or Windows for Workgroups 3.11 client. LAN Manager 2.*x* clients can connect to the home directory by typing the following command at the command prompt:

net use <*drive*>: **/home**

Specifying the Home Directory in a Logon Script or Batch File

Windows NT provides three environment parameters you can use in a logon script or other batch file to specify the location of the home directory, or in Program Manager to specify the working directory of an application. Logon scripts are described later in this chapter. If a home directory has not been defined for the user, the default values are used as shown in the following table.

Table 3.1   Environment Parameters for Logon Scripts and Batch Files

Parameter name	Definition	Default value
%homedrive%	Drive where the home directory is located	Drive where the Windows NT system files are installed
%homepath%	Path name of the home directory	\USERS\DEFAULT
%homeshare%	UNC name of the shared directory containing the home directory, or a local or redirected drive letter	No default value

If the \USERS\DEFAULT directory does not exist on the drive specified by the **%homedrive%** parameter, the value of the **%homepath%** parameter is set by default to the \USERS directory on that drive. If the \USERS directory does not exist, the **%homepath%** parameter is set to the root directory specified by the **%homedrive%** parameter.

When the user opens a Command Prompt window, the default directory is the equivalent of **%homedrive%%homepath%**. If a user's home directory is specified on a remote computer and that computer is not available, the default directory of the Command Prompt on a Windows NT Workstation computer is the user's home directory on the local workstation.

You might also want to specify the working directory of each application as **%homedrive%%homepath%**. That way, all File Open and Save As dialog boxes default to the user's home directory.

Logon Scripts

A logon script is a .BAT, .CMD, or .EXE file that is run automatically when a user logs on at a Windows NT network client running either Windows NT Workstation or MS-DOS. A logon script can automatically configure the user's environment to perform such tasks as making network connections, running applications, and setting environment variables upon startup.

User profiles can do everything that logon scripts can do, and more. However, there are several reasons to use logon scripts instead of, or in addition to, user profiles:

- You have users that use MS-DOS workstations. User profiles work only on Windows NT workstations.

- You want to manage part of the user's environment, such as network connections, without managing or dictating the entire environment.

- You use only personal profiles, and you want to create common network connections for multiple users.

- You already have LAN Manager 2.*x* running on your network, and you want to continue to use the logon scripts you created for that system.

- Logon scripts are easier to create and maintain than user profiles.

You can assign a different logon script to each user or create logon scripts for use by multiple users. Whenever that user logs on, the logon script is downloaded and run. To assign a user a logon script, you designate the name of the logon script file in the user environment profile defined in User Manager on a Windows NT Workstation computer, or User Manager for Domains on a Windows NT Server computer. Specify only the filename, not the full pathname.

The default file extension for logon scripts is .CMD for client workstations running OS/2 2.1 and .BAT for all other client computers. You can define a different file type as the logon script by specifying the file extension. If the same logon script must run at both Intel-based and RISC-based workstations, it must be a .BAT file that runs the appropriate .EXE file or files on the workstation. Use the **%processor%** parameter in the logon script to run the appropriate .EXE file no matter which processor is being used.

You specify the path to the logon script using the Server option of Control Panel. For detailed information, see online Help. By default, Windows NT looks for logon scripts on the primary domain controller in the directory *systemroot*\SYSTEM32\REPL\IMPORT\SCRIPTS, where *systemroot* is the disk drive and directory in which Windows NT Server was installed.

If you use logon scripts in a domain with more than one domain controller, you should replicate the logon scripts to all the backup domain controllers. All servers in a domain can authorize logon requests, and the logon script for a user must be located on the server that approves the user's logon request. By replicating logon scripts, you ensure that logon scripts are always available to users, yet you still need to maintain only one copy of each script.

The filename for each user's logon script is defined with other user account information in User Manager for Domains. If you change the path to the logon scripts, this change is not replicated to the client workstations. The path must be updated manually in the Server option of Control Panel for each client computer.

To simplify the replication of logon scripts, Windows NT Server creates a \SCRIPTS subdirectory under both the default import and export directories used for replication. If you replicate logon scripts, you must be sure to use the Server option of Control panel or Server Manager to change the logon script path to *systemroot*\SYSTEM32\REPL\IMPORT\SCRIPTS or *systemroot*\SYSTEM32\REPL\EXPORT\ SCRIPTS, as appropriate. For more information, see the Server Manager chapter of the *Windows NT Server System Guide*.

When you use replicated logon scripts, you identify one of the domain controllers as the export server and all the others as import servers. The export server for the logon scripts is normally, but does not have to be, the primary domain controller (PDC).

Logon Scripts and LAN Manager 2.x

When a user at a workstation running LAN Manager 2.*x* logs on to a Windows NT Server computer, LAN Manager tries to run the user's logon script. LAN Manager 2.*x* does not, however, recognize the logon script parameters described earlier in this chapter. Logon scripts for LAN Manager 2.*x* workstations should instead use the **NetWkstaGetInfo** or **NetUserGetInfo** parameter to obtain the necessary values.

Logon Scripts and Windows for Workgroups

By default, Windows for Workgroups does not run a logon script when a user logs on to a Windows NT Server computer. To run a logon script from Windows for Workgroups, you must configure Windows for Workgroups to log on to the Windows NT domain on startup.

▶ **To log on to the Windows NT domain on startup from a Windows for Workgroups computer**

1. From Control Panel, double-click the Network option.

2. In the Microsoft Windows Network dialog box, choose the Startup button to display the Startup Settings dialog box.

3. In the Options for Enterprise Networking box, select the Log On To Windows NT or LAN Manager Domain checkbox.

4. In the Domain box, type the name of the Windows NT domain you want to log on to.

5. In the Startup Settings dialog box, choose the OK button.

6. In the Microsoft Windows Network dialog box, choose the OK button.

Windows for Workgroups does not recognize logon script parameters, and application programming interface (API) calls made from a logon script return an error.

Troubleshooting Logon Scripts

Use this list to troubleshoot the most common problems with logon scripts:

- Make sure the logon script is in the directory specified in the Server option of Control Panel. When Windows NT is installed, the logon script directory is as follows:

```
systemroot\system32\repl\import\scripts
```

The only valid path option is a subdirectory of the default logon script directory. If the path is any other directory or it uses the environment variable **%homepath%**, the logon script fails.

- If the logon script is on an NTFS partition, make sure the user has Read permission for the logon script directory. If no permissions have been explicitly assigned, the logon script might fail without providing an error message.

- Make sure the logon script has a filename extension of either .CMD or .BAT. The .EXE extension is also supported, but only for genuine executable programs. If you use a nondefault file extension for your processor, be sure to specify it with the filename of the logon script.

  Attempting to use the .EXE extension for a script file results in the following error message:

  NTVDM CPU has encountered an illegal instruction.

  If this error message appears, close the window in which the logon script is running.

- If the logon script is to run on a Windows for Workgroups computer, make sure the Windows NT domain name is specified as a startup option in the Network option of Control Panel.

- Make sure any new or modified logon scripts have been replicated to all domain controllers. Replication of logon scripts happens periodically, not immediately. To manually force replication, use Server Manager. See the Server Manager chapter of the *Windows NT Server System Guide* for detailed information.

Environment Parameters for Logon Scripts

If you want to use the same logon script for various users, you can use the environment parameters shown in the following table to reduce development and maintenance time.

Table 3.2   Environment Parameters for Logon Scripts

Parameter	Description
%homedir%	Redirected drive letter on user's computer that refers to the share point for the user's home directory
%homedrive%	Local or redirected drive where the home directory is located
%homepath%	Path name of the home directory
%homeshare%	UNC name of the shared directory containing the home directory, or a local or redirected drive letter
%os%	The operating system of the user's workstation
%processor_architecture%	The processor architecture (such as Intel) of the user's workstation
%processor_level%	The type of processor (such as 486) of the user's workstation
%userdomain%	The domain containing the user's account
%username%	The user name of the user

Environment Variables for Logon Scripts

The environment variables shown in the following table can be set by the logon script.

Table 3.3   Environment Variables for Logon Scripts

Variable	Description
ComSpec	Directory for CMD.EXE
LibPath	Directories to search for dynamic link libraries (DLLs)
OS2LibPath	Directories to search for dynamic link libraries (DLLs) under OS/2 subsystem
Path	Directories to search for executable program files
WinDir	Directory in which Windows NT is installed

C H A P T E R 4

Network Security and Administration

Each domain and computer in a workgroup maintains its own user accounts information. Even on a multidomain network, if account information for an individual user is coordinated across all parts of the network, the user can access any server or domain with a single logon. If the user's accounts are allowed to become unsynchronized, the following problems can occur:

- The user can't browse a domain or server for which he or she has permissions.
- The user can't access a shared resource.
- The user must type a password each time he or she browses or tries to access a resource.

This chapter provides tips for helping you avoid problems related to network logon. It describes how user accounts and other security information are maintained within workgroups and domains and how security information can be shared by trusted domains.

Before reading this chapter, be sure to read the *Windows NT Server Concepts and Planning Guide* for a thorough discussion of domain organization strategies and user environment management techniques.

Windows NT User Accounts

Windows NT needs only a single logon, even for a heterogeneous networking environment, in part because security in Windows NT is assigned by user rather than by resource. Resource-based security models require a separate password for each resource a user wants to access.

In Windows NT, the network administrator creates an account for each user wanting to use network resources. As described in Chapter 2, "Windows NT Security Model," of the *Windows NT Resource Guide,* Windows NT maintains a user account containing a unique security ID within the user accounts database. Windows NT also keeps track of permissions and user rights for the user. When a person logs on, the *Security Accounts Manager* (SAM) checks the user's logon information against data in its user accounts database to authenticate the logon. Then, when access is granted, the *Local Security Authority* (LSA) creates a security access token for that user.

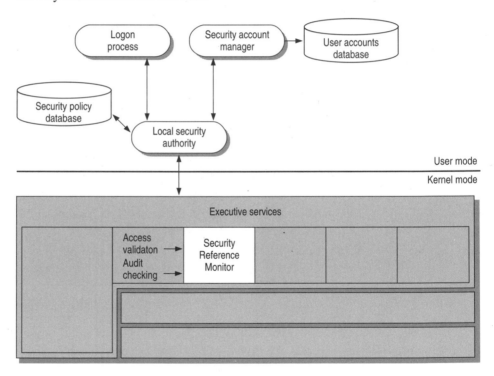

Figure 4.1　Windows NT Security Model

Note A user who forgets his or her password might assume that he or she can gain access to a resource via the Guest account; this is not the case. Because Windows NT recognizes the username, it compares the user's logon information only with the account information for that username. If the password does not match, no access is granted.

By default, the Guest account on Windows NT Server is disabled so that only those users with recognized accounts can access the system. As described in the *Windows NT Server Concepts and Planning Guide*, Windows NT uses the Guest account for people with an unrecognized user account, including users logging on from untrusted domains. Domains and trust relations are explained later in this chapter.

Depending on the way your corporation's network is organized, a given user might, in fact, have more than one account, perhaps one granting access to the local computer or workgroup and another for domains on the network. The user account database used to authenticate a logon doesn't necessarily reside on the user's local computer. Its location depends on whether the computer is part of a workgroup or a domain and whether the user is logging on to the local computer, to the home domain, or to another domain.

In the Windows NT security model, there are two types of user accounts:

- A *global user account* is a normal user account that fits into the Windows NT model described in this chapter. User accounts on Windows NT Workstation computers and on Windows NT Server computers that are not domain controllers are global accounts. Global users are authenticated by the primary domain controller (PDC) or backup domain controller (BDC) on a domain, or through trust relationships.

- A *local user account* is a user account that fully participates in a domain but is available only by remote logon and is authenticated only by user information available locally on the machine that is processing the logon. For example, a local user might be a member of a Windows for Workgroups, LAN Manager 2.*x,* or Novell network. Local user accounts are available only within their domain; they cannot be authenticated through trust relationships.

Workgroups and Domains

A *workgroup* is simply an organizational unit, a way to group computers that don't belong to a domain. In a workgroup, each computer keeps track of its own user and group account information and does not share this information with other computers. Each Windows NT computer that participates in a workgroup maintains its own security policy and security account databases.

Users on a workgroup are considered global users, as explained in the previous section. Logons to another computer are authenticated on the remote computer only by valid username and password.

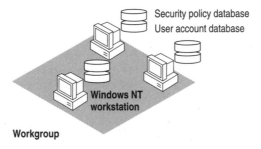

Figure 4.2   Computers Participating in a Workgroup

A workgroup is a good network configuration for a small group of computers with not many user accounts, where network administration is not an issue, or in an environment with a mix of Microsoft networks that does not include Windows NT Server computers.

A *domain* is a group of servers that share common security policy and user account databases. One Windows NT Server computer acts as the primary domain controller (PDC), which maintains the centralized security databases for the domain. Other Windows NT Server computers in the domain function as backup domain controllers and can authenticate logon requests. Domains can also contain Windows NT Server computers that do not act as domain controllers, Windows NT Workstation computers, LAN Manager 2.*x* servers, and other workstations such as those running Windows for Workgroups and MS-DOS. Users of a Windows NT Server domain are authenticated by the primary domain controller or by a backup domain controller. Logon credentials include the username, password, and domain name.

With Windows NT, administrators have full centralized control over security. To eliminate any single point of failure on a Windows NT Server domain, the user account database, including the logon scripts (which are discussed in Chapter 3, "Windows NT User Environments") is automatically replicated to the backup domain controllers.

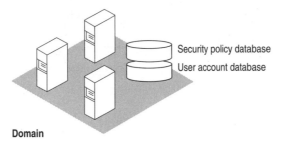

Security policy database
User account database

Domain

Figure 4.3   Computers Participating in a Domain

Domains and workgroups can interoperate and are identical in terms of browsing. If a Windows NT computer is not participating in a domain, it is by default part of a workgroup (even if the workgroup is only one computer) and can be browsed as part of that workgroup. For more information, see Chapter 5, "Windows NT Browser."

LAN Manager 2.x Domains

A Windows NT computer can connect to standalone LAN Manager 2.x servers and LAN Manager 2.x servers participating in a LAN Manager 2.x domain. LAN Manager 2.x and Windows NT computers interoperate because they both use *server message blocks* (SMBs) to communicate between the redirector and server software. The NetBEUI Frame (NBF) and TCP/IP protocols used by Windows NT are also interoperable with NetBEUI and TCP/IP protocols written for LAN Manager 2.x.

Note LAN Manager 2.x servers can act as backup domain controllers in a Windows NT Server domain. Both local and global user accounts are replicated to LAN Manager 2.x servers acting as BDCs. Because LAN Manager 2.x does not support trust relationships or local groups, a LAN Manager 2.x server can never be a primary domain controller.

Avoiding Multiple PDCs

A common configuration problem is having multiple PDCs on a domain. This type of configuration problem is described in the following scenario.

A system administrator installs a Windows NT Server computer called \\MAIN_UNIT, which is designated during installation as the PDC of a domain called MyDomain. Later, the system administrator shuts down and turns off the PDC, \\MAIN_UNIT. Then the system administrator installs another server, called \\SECOND_UNIT, which is also installed as the PDC. Because \\MAIN_UNIT is not currently on the network, MyDomain has no PDC, and the installation of \\SECOND_UNIT proceeds without error.

Now the system administrator turns \\MAIN_UNIT back on. When the Netlogon service (described later in this chapter) discovers another PDC on the network, it fails, and \\MAIN_UNIT can no longer participate in the domain.

The system administrator now has a serious problem. It is not possible to simply demote \\MAIN_UNIT from a PDC to a BDC and continue. The *Security ID* (SID) for \\MAIN_UNIT will not be recognized by the current PDC, \\SECOND_UNIT. In fact, \\MAIN_UNIT cannot join MyDomain in any capacity. This happens because when a PDC is created, a unique domain SID is also created. All BDCs and user accounts within the domain share this domain SID as a prefix to their own SIDs. When \\SECOND_UNIT is installed as a PDC, its SID prefix is different from that of \\MAIN_UNIT, and the two computers can never participate in the same domain.

In addition, the system administrator cannot change the name of \\MAIN_UNIT and rejoin MyDomain, because the SID is fixed once the Windows NT Server is installed. If \\MAIN_UNIT is to be the PDC of MyDomain, the system administrator must shut down both \\MAIN_UNIT and \\SECOND_UNIT, start up \\MAIN_UNIT, and then reinstall Windows NT Server on \\SECOND_UNIT, designating it a BDC during setup.

To avoid this problem, \\SECOND_UNIT should be installed as a backup domain controller while \\MAIN_UNIT is running. If \\MAIN_UNIT is taken offline at this point, \\SECOND_UNIT can be promoted to PDC. (In general, it should not be necessary to designate a new PDC unless the original PDC is going to be down for a long time.) When \\MAIN_UNIT is ready to go online again, \\SECOND_UNIT can be demoted to a BDC. The SID for \\MAIN_UNIT is recognized by \\SECOND_UNIT, and when \\MAIN_UNIT is restarted, it becomes the PDC again.

Interdomain Trust Relationships

With Windows NT Server, the user accounts and global groups from one domain can be used in another domain. When a domain is configured to allow accounts from another domain to have access to its resources, it effectively *trusts* the other domain. The *trusted* domain has made its accounts available to be used in the *trusting* domain. These trusted accounts are available on Windows NT Server computers and Windows NT Workstation computers participating in the trusting domain.

Hint By using trust relationships in your multidomain network, you reduce the need for duplicate user account information and reduce the risk of problems caused by unsynchronized account information.

The *trust relationship* is the link between two domains that enables a user with an account in one domain to have access to resources on another domain. The trusting domain is allowing the trusted domain to return to the trusting domain a list of global groups and other information about users who are authenticated in the trusted domain. There is an implicit trust relationship between a Windows NT Workstation participating in a domain and its PDC.

The following figure illustrates a trust relationship between two domains, where the London domain trusts the Topeka domain.

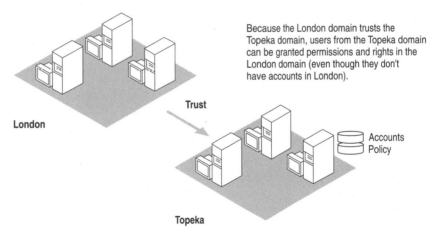

Because the London domain trusts the Topeka domain, users from the Topeka domain can be granted permissions and rights in the London domain (even though they don't have accounts in London).

Trust

London

Accounts
Policy

Topeka

Figure 4.4   Trusted Domain

In this example, the following statements are true because the London domain trusts the Topeka domain:

- Users defined in the Topeka domain can access resources in the London domain without creating an account within that domain.

- Topeka appears in the From box at the initial logon screen of Windows NT computers in the London domain. Thus, a user from the Topeka domain can log on at a computer in the London domain.

When trust relationships are defined, user accounts and global groups can be given rights and permissions in domains other than the domain where these accounts are located. Administration is then much easier, because you need to create each user account only once on your entire network, and then the user account can be given access to any computer on your network (provided you set up domains and trust relationships to allow it).

Note   Trust relationships can be configured only between two Windows NT Server domains. Workgroups and LAN Manager 2.*x* domains cannot be configured to use trust relationships.

Changes to Computers in the Trusting and Trusted Domains

When one domain is permitted to trust another, User Manager for Domains creates an interdomain trust account in the Security Accounts Manager (SAM) of the trusted domain. This account is like any other global user account, except that the USER_INTERDOMAIN_TRUST_ACCOUNT bit in the control field for the account is set. The interdomain trust account is used only by the primary domain controller and is invisible in User Manager for Domains. The password is randomly generated and is maintained by User Manager for Domains.

When this trust relationship is established, the Netlogon service on the trusting domain attempts discovery on the trusted domain, as described later in this chapter, and the interdomain trust account is authenticated by a domain controller on the trusted domain.

When one domain trusts another, a trusted domain object is created in the LSA of the trusting domain, and a Secret object is created in the LSA of the trusting domain.

Access to Files in a Trusting Domain

Users from the trusted domain can be given rights and permissions to objects in the trusting domain using File Manager, just as if they were members of the trusting domain. Subject to account privilege, users in the trusted domain can browse resources in the trusting domain.

For example, suppose the London domain trusts the Topeka domain. User EmilyP, who is a member of the Topeka domain, wants to access MYFILE.TXT, which is a file located on a Windows NT Server computer in the London domain. When EmilyP attempts to log on to the server in London, her user account information is not transferred to the London domain's user database. Because London trusts Topeka, the London domain has access to user information in the Topeka domain's user account database. Authenticating a user logon in this manner is called *pass-through authentication,* a concept that is discussed in greater detail later in this chapter.

One-way Trust Relationships

Trust relationships are defined in only one direction. In the previous example, just because the London domain trusts the Topeka domain does not mean that the Topeka domain trusts the London domain. For a two-way trust relationship, each domain must be configured to trust the other.

Trust relationships are not transitive. For example, if the London domain trusts the Topeka domain and the Topeka domain trusts the Melbourne domain, that does not mean that the London domain trusts the Melbourne domain. For the London domain to trust the Melbourne domain, a trust relationship must be explicitly established.

Users and computers from the trusting domain have no special status on the trusted domain. The names of trusting domains do not appear in the From box of the Logon dialog box, nor do users from the trusting domain appear in the File Manager of computers in the trusted domain.

Setting Up Domains

The way you configure your network into domains depends on your administrative resources and the size of your network. This section describes the most common domain models:

- Single domain
- Master domain
- Multiple master domain
- Multiple trust

Single Domain

In the single domain model, there is only one domain. Because there are no other domains, there are no trust relationships to administer. This model is the best implementation for organizations with fewer than 10,000 users in which trust among departments is not an issue. This model offers centralized management of all user accounts, and local groups have to be defined only once. In an organization with multiple domains where there is no need to share information among domains, the best configuration is often multiple single domains.

If, however, you anticipate significant growth in your organization, you might want to consider a more flexible model, such as the multiple master domain model described later in this section. If your organization grows beyond 10,000 users, the single domain model can no longer support all your users, and there might be a great deal of administrative work involved in reconfiguring your user database.

Master Domain

In an organization with fewer than 10,000 users in which trust among departments is an issue, the master domain model is a suitable option. In this model, one domain, the master domain, is trusted by all other domains, but does not trust any of them. Trust relationships among the other domains can be defined and administered as necessary.

The master domain model offers the benefits of both central administration and multiple domains. In an organization with a number of departments, each department can administer its own resources, but user accounts and global groups still need to be defined only once, in the master domain.

As with the single domain model, however, the user population is limited to 10,000, because all user accounts are maintained in one place, the master domain. Further, local groups must be defined for each domain, which can require significantly more administration if you use local groups extensively.

Multiple Master Domain

For large organizations, or those which anticipate substantial growth, the multiple master domain model might be the best solution. In this model, there is more than one master domain, each of which trusts all the other master domains, and all of which are trusted by all the other domains. None of the master domains trusts any of the subdomains.

This model works best when computer resources are grouped in some logical fashion, such as by department or by location. Because a multiple master domain model can support as many as 10,000 users per master domain, it works well for large organizations. And because all the master domains trust each other, only one copy of each user account is needed.

The administrative requirements for a multiple master domain model can be considerably greater than for a single domain or master domain model. Local and global groups might have to be defined several times, there are more trust relationships to manage, and not all user accounts reside in the same domain.

Multiple Trust

In the multiple trust model, all domains trust all other domains. This model is the simplest to understand, but if many domains are involved it is the most complex to administer.

Like the multiple master domain model, the multiple trust model is scalable as the organization grows: it can support as many as 10,000 users for each domain (not for each master domain, as in the multiple master domain model). Because each domain has full control over its own user accounts, the multiple trust model can work well for a company without a centralized management information services (MIS) department. If, however, the organization has many domains, there can be a very large number of trust relationships to manage. And because domain administration is decentralized, it is harder to assure the integrity of global groups that other domains might use.

Local and Global Groups

You can place a set of users with the same administrative requirements into user groups. User groups make system administration much simpler, because you can assign all members of a group the same logon script, file rights and permissions, and user profile. If some aspect of the group's administrative requirements changes, you can make the change in just one place for all the users in the group.

User groups can be local or global. The terms *local group* and *global group* refer not to the contents of the group, but to the scope of the group's availability. A local group is available only on the domain controllers within the domain in which it is created, while a global group is available within its own domain and in any trusting domain. A trusting domain can, therefore, use a global group to control rights and permissions given members of a trusted domain.

Global Groups

A global group contains only individual user accounts (no groups) from the domain in which it is created. Once created, a global group can be assigned permissions and rights, either in its own domain or in any trusting domain. A global group is a good way to export a group of users as a single unit to another domain. For example, in a trusting domain you can grant identical permissions to a particular file to a global group, which then pertain to all individual members of that group.

Global groups are available only on Windows NT Server domains. When Windows NT Server is installed on a computer, it is configured with two predefined global groups:

- Domain Admins
- Domain Users

Local Groups

A local group is a good way to import a group of users and global groups from other domains into a single unit for use in the local domain. A local group can contain user accounts or global groups from one or more domains. The group can be assigned privileges and rights only within its own domain. Local groups created on a Windows NT Workstation computer or a Windows NT Server computer in a workgroup are available only on that computer.

The following predefined local groups are available on Windows NT Workstation and Windows NT Server computers:

- Administrators
- Users
- Guests
- Backup operators
- Replicator

The following additional predefined local groups are available only on Windows NT Server computers acting as primary or backup domain controllers:

- Account operators
- Print operators
- Server operators

Another predefined local group, Power Users, is available only on Windows NT Workstation computers or on Windows NT Server computers that are not acting as domain controllers.

Logons and Authentication

When you log on to a workgroup computer, your logon information is compared with the local user accounts database. When you log on to a computer that participates in a domain, you choose whether to log on locally, or to the domain. (If your domain trusts another domain, you can alternately choose to log on there.)

Note Windows NT Server computers store only domain accounts. To log on to a Windows NT Server computer, you must use a domain account.

For example, suppose AnnM has an account on a domain (MyDomain), as well as an account on a Windows NT workstation (MyWksta) belonging to that domain. When AnnM logs onto her workstation account, the local authentication software uses the information stored in the workstation user accounts database to authenticate the logon. If AnnM logs onto the domain from that workstation, the local authentication software sends the logon request to the domain for authentication. Although they share the same username, each account has a unique security ID.

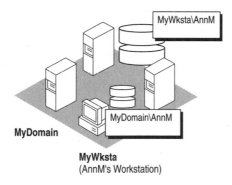

Figure 4.5   Logging On Locally Versus Logging On to the Domain

As described in Chapter 2, "Windows NT Security Model," of the *Windows NT Resource Guide,* the Local Security Authority (LSA) creates a security access token for each user accessing the system. This happens when the user logs on and is authenticated (that is, during interactive logon). The LSA also creates a security access token when a user establishes a connection from a remote computer. This procedure is called a *remote logon.*

For example, suppose AnnM logs on and is authenticated by her local computer and then wants to access a printer controlled by a Windows NT Server computer in domain MyDomain. When she tries to connect to the printer (assuming she hasn't already connected to some other resource in the domain), she is actually performing a remote logon. One of the servers in MyDomain checks the domain's central user accounts database for information to authenticate her account for the domain and then creates a security access token for AnnM, and allows AnnM access.

Note This type of scenario becomes complex when AnnM uses different passwords for different accounts. For example, if her local password doesn't match the password for her domain account, when she tries to browse the domain or connect to a resource in the domain, a message like the following is displayed on the screen:

```
System error 5 has occurred
Access is denied
```

While tools such as File Manager prompt for a valid password, the command-line interface and some applications simply deny access. It is always a better idea to have one set of credentials that apply everywhere in a trusted enterprise.

From an administrative viewpoint, it is important to understand where the user account information is stored. A user's account is either in a private local user accounts database or in a domain user accounts database shared by all the Windows NT Server computers in the domain.

The Netlogon Service

The Netlogon service provides users logging on with a single access point to a domain's primary domain controller and all backup domain controllers. The Netlogon service replicates any changes to the security database to all domain controllers in the domain, including the SAM, BuiltIn, and LSA databases described in Chapter 2, "Windows NT Security Model," of the *Windows NT Resource Guide.* The SAM database is limited only by the number of Registry entries permitted and by the performance limits of the computer hardware. The maximum number of accounts of all types the SAM database supports is 10,000.

The Netlogon service on a Windows NT Server computer fully synchronizes its user database when the domain controller is first installed, or when the domain controller is brought back online after being offline, and the PDC's change log is full when the server returns online.

The Netlogon service accepts logon requests from any client and provides complete authentication information from the SAM database. It can authenticate logon requests as a member of a trusting or trusted domain.

The Netlogon service runs on any Windows NT computer that is a member of a domain. It requires the Workstation service and the "Access This Computer from Network" right, which is set in User Manager on Windows NT Workstation computers or servers, or User Manager for Domains on domain controllers. A domain controller also requires that the Server service be running.

User Authentication

On a Windows NT Workstation computer or a Windows NT Server computer that is not a domain controller, the Netlogon service processes logon requests for the local computer and passes through logon requests to a domain server.

The Netlogon service processes authenticates a logon request in three steps:

1. Discovery
2. Secure channel setup
3. Pass-through authentication (where necessary)

Discovery

When a user logs on to a domain from a Windows NT Workstation computer or a Windows NT Server computer that is not a domain controller, the computer must determine the location of a domain controller in its domain. If the computer is part of a workgroup, not a domain, the Netlogon service terminates. (If the workstation is not connected to a network, Windows NT treats it like a member of a workgroup consisting of one member.)

When a Windows NT Workstation computer or a Windows NT Server computer that is not a domain controller starts up, it attempts to locate a Windows NT Server computer in each trusted domain. (There is an implicit trust between the client and domain controllers in its own domain.) In either case, the server located can be either a primary domain controller (PDC) or a backup domain controller (BDC). The act of locating a domain controller to connect to is called *discovery*. Once a domain controller has been discovered, it is used for subsequent user authentication.

When a domain controller is started up, the Netlogon service attempts discovery with all trusted domains. (Discovery is not necessary on the domain controller's own domain, because it has access to its own SAM database.) Each domain is called three times in intervals of five seconds before discovery fails. If a trusted domain does not respond to a discovery attempt, the domain controller attempts another discovery every 15 minutes until it locates a domain controller on the trusted domain. If the domain controller receives an authorization request for the trusted domain for which discovery has not yet been successful, it attempts another discovery immediately, no matter when the last discovery was attempted.

Secure Communication Channel

Before a connection between two Windows NT computers is allowed, each computer's Netlogon service must be satisfied that the computer at the other end of the connection is identifying itself correctly. To do this, each computer's Netlogon service issues and verifies challenge and challenge response information. When this information is successfully completed, a secure channel is established and a communication session set up between the two computers' Netlogon services. The session can be ended without terminating the secure channel. The secure channel is used to pass subsequent network API calls between the two computers. The secure communication channel is used to pass the username and encrypted password during pass-through authentication. Pass-through authentication is discussed in detail later in this chapter.

The Netlogon service maintains security on these communication channels by using user-level security to create the channel. The following special internal user accounts are created:

- *Workstation trust* accounts, which allow a domain workstation to perform pass-through authentication for a Windows NT Server computer in the domain, as described later in this chapter

- *Server trust* accounts, which allow Windows NT Server computers to get copies of the master domain database from the domain controller

- *Interdomain trust* accounts, which allow a Windows NT Server computer to perform pass-through authentication to another domain

The Netlogon service attempts to set up a secure channel when it is started, as soon as discovery is completed. Failing that, Netlogon retries every 15 minutes or whenever an action requiring pass-through authentication occurs. To reduce network overhead among trusted domains, the Netlogon service on a domain controller creates a secure channel only when it is needed.

Note If the secure channel cannot be created at logon (for example, because the domain controllers are offline), the Netlogon service starts anyway. If the user's interactive logon uses the same domain name and username, the user's interactive logon is successfully completed using cached credentials.

A Windows NT computer stores the information used to authenticate the last several (ten, by default) users who logged on interactively. That way, if all the domain controllers are down at the same time, the last several users who connected to the computer can still log on. Additionally, the credentials of all users who have logged on from the local computer are stored in the local SAM database.

Pass-through Authentication

Pass-through authentication occurs when a user account must be authenticated, but the local computer can't authenticate the account itself. In this case, the username and password are forwarded to a Windows NT Server computer that can authenticate the user, and the user's information is returned to the requesting computer.

Pass-through authentication occurs in the following instances:

- At interactive logon when a user at a Windows NT Workstation computer or a Windows NT Server computer that is not a domain controller is logging onto a domain or trusted domain

- At remote logon when the domain specified is a trusted domain

Figure 4.6 illustrates pass-through authentication. In this example, AnnM wants to access a computer in the London domain. Because the London domain trusts AnnM's home domain (Topeka), it asks the Topeka domain to authenticate AnnM's account information.

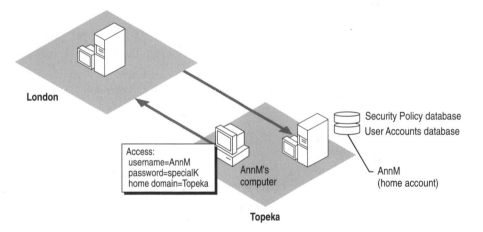

Figure 4.6   Pass-Through Authentication

The Netlogon service provides this pass-through authentication. Each Windows NT computer participating in the domain must be running the Netlogon and Workstation services. (Netlogon is dependent on the Workstation service.) The Netlogon service communicates with the Netlogon service on the remote computer, as illustrated in Figure 4.7.

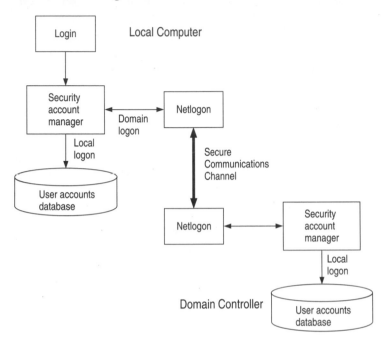

Figure 4.7   Netlogon Requirements for Domain Logons

If the user account is in a trusted domain, the request must first be passed from the computer in the trusting domain to a domain controller in its domain. The domain controller then passes the request to a domain controller in the trusted domain, which authenticates the user account information and then returns the user information by the reverse route.

Interactive Logon

The interactive logon can occur in any user accounts database where a user has an account. Depending on the type of Windows NT computer and how it has been configured, the From box (in the Logon dialog box) lists the local computer and/or domains where user accounts can be authenticated.

Summary of Interactive Logon Authentication

The following table shows the logon options for someone using a Windows NT computer in a workgroup, a domain, and a domain with a trust relationship. The unique identifier used by Windows NT after logon depends on the location of the database used to log on the user. The third column in this table describes the unique identifier used in each case. Any network connection requests sent elsewhere on the network include this unique identifier.

Table 4.1   Summary of Interactive Logon Authentication

Computer is in	User can logon at	Unique identifier
Workgroup	Local database	Computername and username
Domain	Local database Domain database	Computername and username Domain name and username
Domain with a trust relationship	Local database Home domain database Trusted domain database	Computername and username Domain name and username Trusted domain name and username
Domain without a trust relationship	Local database	Computername and username Untrusting domain name and username

Remote Logon

A security access token created at interactive logon is assigned to the initial process created for the user. When the user tries to access a resource on another computer, the security access token is placed in a table in the remote server process. The server process creates a security ID for the user and maps it to the user's security access token. This security ID is sent back to the client redirector and is used in all further server message block (SMB) communication between the server and client. Whenever a resource request comes in from the client, the security ID identifies the user to the server process. The security access token that maps to the user ID identifies the user to the remote security subsystem.

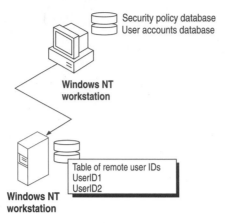

Figure 4.8   Remote Logon

The following list shows the steps in a successful remote logon at a Windows NT Workstation computer or Windows NT Server computer.

1. The username, password, and domain name (the data entered in the Welcome dialog box) of the logged on user are sent from the user's computer to the remote Windows NT server.

2. The authenticating computer's SAM compares the logon username and password with information in the user accounts database.

3. If the access is authorized, the authenticating computer's LSA constructs a security access token and passes it to the server process, which creates a user ID referencing the security access token.

4. The user ID is then returned to the client computer for use in all subsequent requests to the server.

   After the session has been created, the client computer sends requests marked with the user ID it received during session setup. The server matches the user ID with the proper access token kept in an internal table. This security access token at the remote computer is used for access authentication at the remote computer by that user.

Remote Logon at a LAN Manager 2.x Server

Remote logon at a LAN Manager 2.x server is basically the same as remote logon to a Windows NT computer. However, instead of comparing the user's logon information against a centralized user accounts database, the LAN Manager 2.x server compares the information with its local user accounts database. This database may be the server's own standalone database or a domain database shared by a group of servers. LAN Manager 2.x servers cannot use pass-through authentication.

Accessing resources on a LAN Manager 2.*x* server is similar to accessing resources on a Windows NT computer, except that the LAN Manager 2.*x* server does not use a security access token to identify resource requests. Instead, the security ID maps to the username, which is used to process resource requests.

If the LAN Manager 2.*x* server is in the same domain as a Windows NT Server computer, the server logon is identical to that used when accessing another Windows NT Server computer (except that the LAN Manager 2.*x* server does not generate or use security access tokens).

If the LAN Manager 2.*x* server is in another domain, the server logon is identical to logon for a Windows NT Workstation computer that is a member of a workgroup. This is true even for a trusted domain, since LAN Manager 2.*x* servers don't support trust relationships. An account must exist either in the LAN Manager 2.*x* server's domain or at the stand-alone server itself.

Summary of Remote Logon Authentication

This section summarizes the various remote logon scenarios.

▶ **Workgroup computer connecting to a Windows NT computer in a domain**

Interactive logon for the user at the workgroup computer (the client) is performed by the local user accounts database.

The client's username and a function of the password are passed to the specific server in the domain to which the client is trying to connect. This server checks the username and password with information in its local user accounts database. If there is a match, access to this server is allowed.

▶ **Domain computer connecting to a Windows NT computer in the same domain**

Interactive logon for the user at the client computer was performed by the domain's user accounts database.

The client's domain name, username, and a function of the password are passed to the computer being accessed, which passes them to a Windows NT Server computer in the domain.

The Windows NT Server computer verifies that the domain name for the client matches this domain.

Next the Windows NT Server computer check the username and password against the domain's user accounts database. If there is a match, access is allowed.

   ▸ **Domain client in a trusted domain connecting to a Windows NT computer**

   Interactive logon for the user at the client computer is performed by the domain's user accounts database.

   The client's domain name, username, and a function of the password are passed to the computer being accessed. That computer passes the logon information to a Windows NT Server in the domain.

   The Windows NT Server computer verifies that the client's domain is a trusted domain and then passes the client's identification information to a Windows NT Server computer in that trusted domain.

   A Windows NT Server computer in the trusted domain (that is, the same domain as the client computer) checks the username and password against the domain's user accounts database. If there is a match, access is allowed.

Common Logon Scenarios

The following examples describe various logon scenarios in a Windows NT environment.

Example 1: Logging On to a Member of a Workgroup

For a computer running Windows NT and participating in a workgroup, the logon information is compared with the local user accounts database. When a user logs on, the From box lists only the name of the local computer. The user cannot specify another workgroup or domain for logon. There is no discovery, because the Netlogon service is not running. If the user attempts access to another Windows NT computer, authentication proceeds as discussed in "Example 4: Logging On to an Untrusted Domain," later in this chapter.

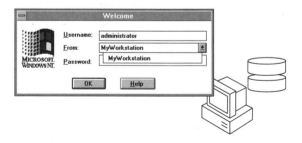

Figure 4.9   Initial Logon and Local Databases for a Windows NT Workstation

After successful authentication, the username and password are cached by the computer's redirector for use when connecting to remote resources.

Example 2: Logging On to the Home Domain

From a Windows NT computer participating in a domain, a user can choose to have his or her logon information authenticated by the local computer or by a domain controller in its domain. If the user account is a domain account, a domain controller's SAM for the home domain or a trusted domain authenticates the logon. The workstation itself connects to a domain with a workstation trust account.

The From box lists the name of the local computer, the name of the home domain in which the computer participates, and the names of any trusted domains.

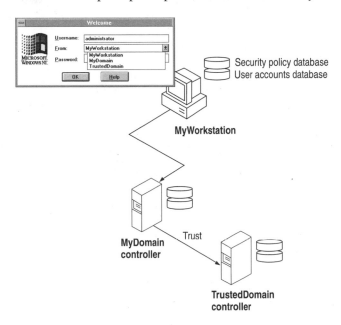

Figure 4.10   Logging On from a Domain Workstation

The security access token generated in an interactive logon is maintained on the computer where the user is logged on.

Example 3: Logging On to a Trusted Domain

When a user at a Windows NT Workstation computer in a domain, or a Windows NT Server computer that is participating in a domain but not as a domain controller, attempts to log on to a trusted domain, the user's credentials are not authenticated on the local computer. The logon request is passed to a domain controller on the trusted domain and is authenticated there.

If the username is not valid and the Guest account of the computer on the computer the user is logging on to is enabled, the user is logged on to the trusted domain as a guest. If the Guest account is disabled, or if the username is valid but the password is not, the logon attempt fails with access denied. The Guest account is used only for remote logons.

The **net use** command prompts for a password if there is no corresponding user account in the trusted domain, or if there is a corresponding user account but the password does match the one supplied by the trusting domain. In situations where the **net use** command would require a password, the **net view** command simply fails with access denied.

The From box lists the domain and trusted domains for this computer.

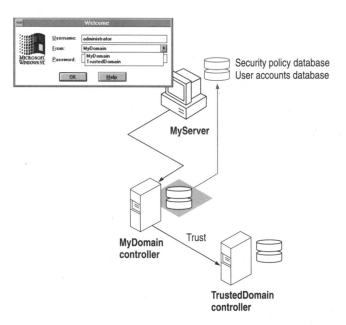

Figure 4.11   Authentication by a Trusted Domain Controller

Example 4: Logging On to an Untrusted Domain

If a client workstation or server connects by remote logon to a Windows NT computer and the domain name specified is not trusted by the domain the client workstation or server that the user is logged on to, the client computer checks its own user account for the username and password supplied. If the credentials are valid, the client logs the user on. If the username is not valid and the client's Guest account is enabled, the computer logs the user on as a guest and passes the credentials to the untrusted domain.

Example 5: Logging on Without Specifying a Domain Name

For workstations running Windows for Workgroups 3.1 or LAN Manager 2.0, the domain of the Windows NT computer being connected to might not be specified. For a user connecting to an individual or workgroup workstation, user credentials are authenticated only on the local computer. If the username is not valid and a Guest account is enabled, the user is logged on as a guest.

If the client is connecting to a domain of which the workstation is a member, user credentials are authenticated first by the workstation itself, and then by a domain controller. If the username is not valid for the domain and the domain controller's Guest account is enabled, the user is logged to the Guest account of the machine being connected to. If the username is valid but the password is not, or if the Guest account is disabled, the user is again prompted for a password, and then the logon attempt fails with access denied.

For a user logging onto a trusted domain from a domain workstation, it is not obvious where the user's domain account is defined. User credentials are authenticated in the following order until the user is successfully logged on: first by the workstation itself, then by the local domain server, and finally by the trusted domain. If all these logon attempts fail, the user is connected, if possible, to the local workstation's Guest account.

Troubleshooting Logon Problems

This section discusses the two categories of typical problems users might face that relate to logons:

- Problems when trying to view a server's shared resources
- Problems when trying to access one of those resources

Viewing a Server's Shared Resources

Suppose AnnM logs on to a Windows NT domain with the password Yippee. She wants to view the shared resources on a server named \\PRODUCTS, but her password there is Yahoo. Because of this situation, Ann sees the following message displayed on the screen:

```
Error 5: Access has been denied.
```

AnnM asks the administrator of \\PRODUCTS to change her password, but the administrator leaves the User Must Change Password At Next Logon checkbox checked. When AnnM tries to view the server's shared resources this time, she sees the following message displayed on the screen:

```
Error 2242: The password of this user has expired.
```

When the administrator of \\PRODUCTS clears the User Must Change Password At Next Logon checkbox, AnnM is finally able to see the server's shared resources.

Accessing a Server's Shared Resources

Suppose AnnM is logged on to a Windows NT domain with the password Yippee but wants to connect to a shared directory on \\PRODUCTS, where her password is Yahoo. Even though \\PRODUCTS has a Guest account because there is an account for AnnM, she is not allowed to gain access via the Guest account. Instead, Windows NT prompts AnnM for the valid password on \\PRODUCTS.

On the other hand, JeffH wants to access the same shared directory and has no account on \\PRODUCTS. He is allowed access to this resource via the Guest account for \\PRODUCTS and is assigned the permissions associated with that account.

WAN Environments

In a WAN environment, timeout parameters are automatically tuned by both Windows NT Workstation and Windows NT Server. Session setup times out after 45 seconds.

Using the LMHOSTS file, a directed mailslot can be sent directly to a computer's internet protocol (IP) address to establish a trust relationship. For information on the LMHOSTS file, see Chapter 15, "Setting Up LMHOSTS."

C H A P T E R 5

Windows NT Browser

Users on a Windows NT network often need to know what domains and computers are accessible from their local computer. Viewing all the network resources available is known as *browsing*. The Windows NT Browser system maintains a list, called the *browse list,* of all the domains and servers available. For instance, when a user attempts to connect to a network drive using File Manager, the list of servers that is displayed in the Shared Directories box of the Connect Network Drive dialog box is the browse list, and it is provided by a browser in the local computer's domain.

Note For the purposes of this discussion, the term *server* refers to any computer that can provide resources to the rest of the network. A Windows NT Workstation computer, for instance, is a server in the context of the Browser system if it can share file or print resources with other computers on the network. The computer does not have to be actually sharing resources to be considered a server. In this chapter, specific references to Windows NT Server computers are always made explicitly.

The Windows NT browser system consists of a *master browser*, *backup browsers*, and client systems. The master browser maintains the browse list and periodically sends copies to the backup browsers. When a browser client needs information, it obtains the current browse list by remotely sending a **NetServerEnum2** application programming interface (API) call to either the master browser or a backup browser. (A **NetServerEnum** API call is also supported for compatibility with Microsoft LAN Manager networks.)

The centralized browser architecture reduces the number of *broadcast datagrams.* A datagram is a network packet that is sent to a mailslot on a specified computer (a *directed datagram)* or to a mailslot on any number of computers (a *broadcast datagram).* The centralized browser architecture also reduces the demands on the client's CPU and memory.

Specifying a Browser Computer

Whether a computer running Windows NT Workstation computer or a Windows NT Server computer can become a browser is determined in the Registry by the MaintainServerList entry under the HKEY_LOCAL_MACHINE \SYSTEM\CurrentControlSet\Services\Browser\Parameters key. The possible values for the MaintainServerList entry are shown in the following table:

Table 5.1   Values for the MaintainServerList Entry

Value	Meaning
No	This computer will never be a browser.
Yes	This computer will become a browser. At startup, the server tries to contact the master browser to get a current browse list. If the master browser cannot be found, this computer forces a browser election, and can become the master browser. For more information on browser elections, see "Determining Browser Roles," later in this chapter.
	This is the default value for Windows NT Server computers.
Auto	This computer is a *potential browser*. Whether it becomes a browser depends on the number of existing browsers. This computer is notified by the master browser if it should become a backup browser.
	This is the default value for Windows NT Workstation computers.

On any computer with a value of Yes or Auto for the MaintainServerList, Windows NT Setup configures the Browser service to start automatically when the computer starts.

Another setting in the HKEY_LOCAL_MACHINE\SYSTEM\CurrentControlSet\Services\Browser\Para meters key in the registry has a bearing on which servers become master browsers and backup browsers. Setting the IsDomainMasterBrowser entry to True or Yes on a computer makes that computer a *preferred master browser*. A preferred master browser computer has an advantage over other computers in master browser elections. Also, whenever a preferred master browser computer is started, it forces a browser election. For more information on browser elections, see "Determining Browser Roles," later in this chapter.

Number of Browsers in Domains and Workgroups

In a Windows NT Server domain, every Windows NT Server computer is a browser. One Windows NT Server computer in the domain, the primary domain controller if there is one, is the master browser, and the other Windows NT Server computers are backup browsers. If there is more than one Windows NT Server computer in the domain, no Windows NT Workstation computer will ever be a master browser in the domain.

In a workgroup containing Windows NT Workstation computers, there is always one master browser. If there are at least two Windows NT Workstation computers in the workgroup, there is also one backup browser. For every 32 Windows NT Workstation computers in the workgroup, there is another backup browser.

Determining Browser Roles

At certain times in each domain or workgroup, it is necessary to force an election of the master browser. This section explains how the election works.

When a Windows NT computer needs to force a master browser election, it notifies the other browsers on the system by broadcasting an *election datagram*. The election datagram contains the sending browser's election version and election criteria, as explained later in this section. The election version is a constant value that identifies the version of the browser election protocol.

When a browser receives an election datagram, the receiving browser examines the datagram and first compares the election version with its own. If the receiving browser has a higher election version than any other browser, it wins the election regardless of the election criteria. If the election versions are identical for both computers, the election criteria are compared.

The election criteria is a 4-byte hexadecimal value. If there is a tie on the basis of election version, the tie is broken by the value of the election criteria.

- If the browser has a higher election criteria than the issuer of the election datagram, the browser issues its own election datagram and enters the "election in progress" state.

- If the browser does not have a higher election criteria than the issuer of the election datagram, the browser attempts to determine which system is the new master browser.

Specific groups of bytes are masked and their values set according to the following list:

```
Operating System Type:              0xFF000000
    Windows NT Server:              0x20000000
    Windows NT Workstation:         0x10000000
    Windows for Workgroups:         0x01000000

Election Version:                   0x00FFFF00
Per Version Criteria:               0x000000FF
    Primary Domain Controller:      0x00000080
    WINS client:            0x00000020
    Preferred Master browser            0x00000008
    Running Master browser:         0x00000004
    MaintainServerList=yes          0x00000002
    Running Backup Browser          0x00000001
```

If there is still a tie, the browser that has been running longest is the winner. If there is still a tie, the browser that has a lexically lower name is the winner. For example, a server with a name of A becomes master browser instead of a server with a name of B.

When a browser receives an election datagram indicating that it wins the election, the browser enters the *running election* state. In the running election state, the browser sends an election request after a delay based on the browser's current browser role:

- Master browsers delay for 200ms.
- Backup browsers delay for 400ms.
- All other browsers delay for 800ms.

The browser broadcasts up to four election datagrams. If, after four election datagrams, no other browser has responded with an election criteria that would win the election, the browser becomes the master browser. If the browser receives an election datagram indicating that another system would win the election, the browser demotes itself to backup browser. To avoid unnecessary network traffic, a browser that has lost an election does not broadcast any unsent election datagrams.

Browsers

The master browser and backup browsers in each domain have certain duties to maintain the browse list.

Role of Master Browsers

The master browser maintains the browse list, the list of all servers in the master browser's domain or workgroup, and the list of all domains on the network. For a domain that spans more than one subnetwork, the master browser maintains the browse list for the portion of the domain on its subnetwork.

Individual servers announce their presence to the master browser by sending a directed datagram called a *server announcement* to the domain or workgroup's master browser. Computers running Windows NT Server, Windows NT Workstation, Windows for Workgroups, and LAN Manager servers send server announcements. When the master browser receives a server announcement from a computer, it adds that computer to the browse list.

The master browser also returns lists of backup browsers (in the local subnetwork of a TCP/IP-based network, if the domain spans more than one subnetwork) to computers running Windows NT Server, Windows NT Workstation, and Windows for Workgroups. If a TCP/IP subnetwork comprises more than one domain, each domain has its own master browser and backup browsers. On networks using the NetBEUI Frame (NBF) or NWLink IPX/SPX-compatible network protocol, name queries are sent across routers, so there is always only one master browser for each domain.

When a computer starts and the computer's MaintainServerList registry entry is set to Auto, the master browser must tell that computer whether or not to become a backup browser.

When a computer first becomes a master browser, it can force all servers to register with it if its browse list is empty. The master browse computer does this by broadcasting a *RequestAnnouncement* datagram. All computers that receive a RequestAnnouncement datagram must respond by sending a server announcement at a random time within the next 30 seconds. The randomized delay ensures that the network and the master browser itself are not overwhelmed with responses.

When a master browser receives a server announcement from another computer that claims to be the master browser, the receiving master browser demotes itself and forces an election. This action ensures that there is always only one master browser in each domain or workgroup.

Note   The list of servers that the master browser maintains is limited to 64K of data. This limits the number of computers that can be in a browse list in a single workgroup or domain to 2000-3000 computers.

Role of Domain Master Browsers

The primary domain controller (PDC) of a domain is given a bias in browser elections to ensure that it becomes the master browser. The browser service running on a domain's primary domain controller has the special additional role of being the *domain master browser*.

For a domain that uses TCP/IP and spans more than one subnetwork, each subnetwork functions as an independent browsing entity, with its own master browser and backup browsers. To browse across the WAN to other subnetworks, at least one browser running Windows NT Server is required on the domain for each subnetwork. On the subnetwork with the PDC, this Windows NT Server computer is typically the PDC, which functions as the domain master browser.

When a domain spans multiple subnetworks, the master browsers for each subnetwork announces itself as the master browsers to the domain master browser using a directed MasterBrowserAnnouncement datagram. The domain master browser then sends a remote **NetServerEnum** API call to each master browser to collect each subnetwork's list of servers. The domain master browser merges the server list from each subnetwork master browser with its own server list to form the browse list for the domain. This process is repeated every 15 minutes to ensure that the domain master browser has a complete browse list of all the servers in the domain.

The master browser on each subnetwork also sends a remote **NetServerEnum** API call to the domain master browser to obtain the complete browse list for the domain. This browse list is thus available to browser clients on the subnetwork.

Note Windows NT workgroups cannot span multiple subnetworks. Any Windows NT workgroup that spans subnetworks actually functions as two separate workgroups, with identical names.

Role of Backup Browsers

Backup browsers call the master browser every 15 minutes to get the latest copy of the browse list, as well as a list of domains. Each backup browser caches these lists and returns the list of servers to any clients that send a remote **NetServerEnum** API call to the backup browser. If the backup browser cannot find the master browser, it forces an election.

How Computers Announce Themselves

When a computer is started, it announces itself by sending a server announcement to the domain or workgroup's master browser every minute. As the computer continues running, the time between server announcements is increased until it eventually becomes once every 12 minutes.

If the master browser has not received a server announcement from a computer for three announcement periods, the computer is removed from the browse list.

Note   There might be up to a 36-minute delay between the time a server goes down and the time it is removed from the browse list.

Domain Announcements

Client computers sometimes need to retrieve lists of domains, as well as lists of servers in those domains. The Windows NT **NetServerEnum** API has a level of information to allow this.

When a browser becomes a master browser, it broadcasts a DomainAnnouncement datagram every minute for the first five minutes, and then broadcasts once every 15 minutes after that. Master browsers on other domains receive these DomainAnnouncement datagrams and add the specified domain to the browse list.

DomainAnnouncement datagrams contain the name of the domain, the name of the domain master browser, and whether the master browser is running Windows NT Server or Windows NT Workstation. If the master browser if running Windows NT Server, the datagram also specifies whether that browser is the domain's PDC.

If a domain has not announced itself for three consecutive announcement periods, the domain is removed from the browse list.

Note   A domain might be down for as long as 45 minutes before it is removed from the browse list.

The domain master browser augments this list of domains with the list of domains that have registered a domain NetBIOS address with the Windows Internet Name Service (WINS). Checking against WINS ensures that the browser maintains a complete list of domain names in an environment with subnetworks. For information on special NetBIOS names, see "Managing Special Names" in Chapter 14, "Installing and Configuring WINS Servers."

How Clients Receive Browser Information

When an application running on a client issues a **NetServerEnum** API call, the client sends the API call to a browser.

If this is the first time a **NetServerEnum** API call has been issued by an application running on the client, the client must first determine which computers are the browsers in its workgroup or domain. The client does this by sending a QueryBrowserServers directed datagram. This request is processed by the master browser for the domain and subnetwork on which the client is located. The master browser then returns a list of browsers active in the workgroup or domain being queried. The client selects the names of three browsers from the list, and then stores these names for future use. For future **NetServerEnum** API calls, a browser is chosen randomly from the three browser names that were saved by the client.

If the client cannot find the master browser after three attempts, the client issues a *ForceElection* broadcast to the domain being queried. A ForceElection broadcast forces the election of a new master browser in the domain. To indicate that the master browser could not be found, the client then returns an error (ERROR_BAD_NETPATH) to the application. For more information on browser elections, see "Determining Browser Roles," earlier in this chapter.

Browser Failures

When a server fails, it stops announcing itself. When the master browser does not receive a server announcement for three of the server's current announcement periods, the master browser removes the non-browser from the browse list. It might take up to an additional 15 minutes for the backup browsers to retrieve the updated browse list from the master browser, so it could take as long as 51 minutes from the time a server fails to when it is removed from all browse lists.

Because a backup browser announces itself in the same way as a server, the procedure when a backup browser fails is the same as that for a server. If the name of this backup browser has been given to any clients, attempts made by those clients to contact this backup browser fail. The client then retries the **NetServerEnum** API call on another backup browser on the client's list of browsers. If all the backup browsers that a client knows have failed, the client attempts to get a new list of backup browsers from the master browser. If the client is unable to contact the master browser, it forces a browser election.

When a master browser fails, the backup browsers detect the failure within 15 minutes. After a master browser failure is detected, the first backup browser to detect the failure forces an election to select a new master browser. In addition, it is possible that between the time the master browser fails and the election of a new master browser happens, the domain will disappear from the list of domains in the browse list. If a client performs its first **NetServerEnum** API call after the old master browser has failed but before a backup browser detects the failure, the client forces an election. If a master browser fails and there are no backup browsers, browsing in the workgroup or domain will not function correctly.

When a domain master browser fails, other master browsers see only servers on the same local subnetwork. Eventually, all servers that are not on the local subnetwork are removed from the browse list.

Browser Components

The Browser system consists of two components:

- Browser service
- Datagram Receiver

The Browser service is the user-mode portion that is responsible for maintaining the browse list, remotely making API calls, and managing the various roles a browser can have. It resides within the LanmanServer service (*systemroot*\SYSTEM32\SERVICES.EXE) and is supported by *systemroot*\SYSTEM32\BROWSER.DLL. The browser's registry entries are under the HKEY_LOCAL_MACHINE\SYSTEM\CurrentControlSet \Services\Browser key.

The datagram receiver is the kernel-mode portion of the browser, and is simply a datagram and mailslot receiver. It receives directed and broadcast datagrams of interest to the workstation and server services. It provides kernel-level support for the **NetServerEnum** API, as well as support for remote mailslot reception (second-class datagram-based mailslot messages) and the request announcement services.

The datagram receiver file is *systemroot*\SYSTEM32\BROWSER.SYS. The datagram receiver's registry entries are in the HKEY_LOCAL_MACHINE \SYSTEM\CurrentControlSet\Services\DGRcvr key.

Mailslot Names

All browser datagrams destined for LAN Manager, Windows for Workgroups, Windows NT Workstation, or Windows NT Server computers are sent to the mailslot name \MAILSLOT\LANMAN.

Browser datagrams that are destined only for Windows NT Workstation or Windows NT Server computers are sent to the mailslot name \MAILSLOT\MSBROWSE.

LAN Manager Interoperability

In order for Windows NT browsers and LAN Manager browsers to work together, you might have to perform some configuration tasks.

Making Windows NT Servers Visible to LAN Manager Clients

To make a Windows NT server visible to LAN Manager clients, you must configure the Windows NT server to announce itself to LAN Manager 2.*x* servers. You can do this by using the Networks option in Control Panel or by changing the LMannounce entry in the Registry.

▶ **To make a Windows NT server visible to LAN Manager clients using the Control Panel**

1. On the Windows NT computer, double-click the Network option in Control Panel to display the Network Settings dialog box.

2. Select Sever from the Installed Network Software box, and then choose the Configure button to display the Server dialog box.

3. Select Make Browser Broadcasts to LAN Manager 2.*x* Clients check box, and then choose the OK button.

▶ **To make a Windows NT browser visible to LAN Manager clients using the Windows NT Registry**

1. Run the REGEDT32.EXE file from File Manager or Program Manager to start the Registry Editor.

2. Locate the following key:

   HKEY_LOCAL_MACHINE\SYSTEM\CurrentControlSet\Services\LanmanServer\Parameters

3. Change the value of the LMannounce entry to **1**.

For more information about the Windows NT Registry, see Chapters 10 through 14 in the *Windows NT Resource Guide*.

Making LAN Manager Domains Visible to Windows NT Browsers

You can make up to four LAN Manager-only domains visible to a Windows NT Browser. You can do this by using the Control Panel or configuring the Registry of the Windows NT browser. The LAN Manager domains you add to the Windows NT browse list this way will be visible to all members of the Windows NT browser's domain.

▶ **To make LAN Manager domains visible to a Windows NT browser using the Control Panel**

1. On the Windows NT computer, double-click the Networks option in Control Panel to display the Network Settings dialog box.

2. Select Computer Browser from the Installed Network Software box, and then choose the Configure button to display the Browser Configuration dialog box.

3. For each LAN Manager domain you want to add, type the LAN Manager domain name in the box on the left, and then choose the Add button.

4. When finished adding up to four domains, choose the OK button.

▶ **To make LAN Manager domains visible to a Windows NT browser using the Windows NT Registry**

1. Run the REGEDT32.EXE file from File Manager or Program Manager of the Windows NT browser to start the Registry Editor.

2. Locate the following key:

   HKEY_LOCAL_MACHINE\SYSTEM\CurrentControlSet\Services\LanmanServer\Parameters

3. In the OtherDomains entry, add the names of the LAN Manager domains that you want to be made visible to the Windows NT browser.

For more information about the Windows NT Registry, see chapters 10 through 14 in the *Windows NT Resource Guide*.

P A R T   I I

Using Windows NT Networking

C H A P T E R 6

Using NBF with Windows NT

NetBEUI Frame (NBF) is the implementation of the NetBIOS Extended User Interface (NetBEUI) protocol driver used in Windows NT. This protocol provides compatibility with existing LANs that use the NetBEUI protocol.

This chapter describes how NBF handles connection-oriented and connectionless network traffic, and it also describes NBF's unique method for handling resources to create a virtually infinite number of connections. The topics include the following:

- Overview of NetBEUI and NBF
- NBF and network traffic
- NBF and sessions
- Session limits

Overview of NetBEUI and NBF

The NetBEUI protocol, first introduced by IBM in 1985, was written to the NetBIOS interface and designed as a small, efficient protocol for use on department-sized LANs of 20 to 200 workstations. This original design assumed that broader connectivity services could be added by including gateways as the network grew. (As described later in this chapter, NBF breaks the session limit that restricted NetBEUI's reach.)

The NetBEUI protocol provides powerful flow control and tuning parameters plus robust error detection. Microsoft has supported the NetBEUI protocol in all of its networking products since Microsoft's first networking product, MS-Net, was introduced in the mid-1980s.

NetBEUI is the precursor to the NetBEUI Frame (NBF) protocol included with Windows NT. NBF provides compatibility with existing LAN Manager and MS-Net installations, and with IBM LAN Server installations. On Windows NT, the NetBIOS interface is supported under MS-DOS, 16-bit Windows, and Win32 subsystem environments.

NBF and Network Traffic

The NBF protocol, like NetBEUI, provides for both connectionless or connection-oriented traffic. Connectionless communications can be either unreliable or reliable. NBF and NetBEUI provide only *unreliable connectionless*, not reliable connectionless communications.

Unreliable communication is similar to sending a letter in the mail. No response is generated by the receiver of the letter to ensure the sender that the letter made it to its destination. In comparison, reliable connectionless communications is like a registered letter whose sender is notified that the letter arrived.

Connection-oriented communications provide reliable communications between two computers in a way that is analogous to a phone call, where two callers connect, a conversation occurs, and then the connection is dropped when the conversation ends. A reliable connection requires more overhead than connectionless communications do.

NBF communicates via the NDIS interface at the Logical Link Control (LLC) sublayer. A connection at the LLC sublayer is called a *link*, which is uniquely defined by the adapter's address and the destination service access point (DSAP). A service access point (SAP) can be thought of as the address of a port to a layer as defined by the OSI model. Because NBF is a NetBIOS implementation, it uses the NetBIOS SAP (0xF0). While the 802.2 protocol governs the overall flow of data, the primitives are responsible for passing the data from one layer to the next. The primitives are passed through the SAPs between layers.

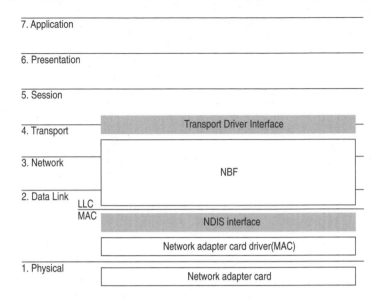

Figure 6.1   NBF Communicates via the NDIS Interface at the LLC Sublayer

Connectionless Traffic

For connectionless traffic that requires a response from a remote computer, NBF sends out a certain number of frames, depending on the command. The total number is based on *retry* Registry value entries, such as **NameQueryRetries**. The time between sending each frame is determined by *timeout* Registry entries, such as **NameQueryTimeout**.

Three types of NetBIOS commands generate connectionless traffic: name claim and resolution, datagrams, and miscellaneous commands. These commands are sent as UI (Unnumbered Information) frames at the LLC sublayer.

To see how Windows NT uses retry and timeout values from the Registry, consider what happens when Windows NT registers computernames via NBF using the NetBIOS **Add.Name** command. When NBF receives the **Add.Name** command, it broadcasts ADD_NAME_QUERY frames a total of **AddNameQueryRetries** times and sends these broadcasts at a time interval of **AddNameQueryTimeout**. This allows computers on the network enough time to inform the sending computer whether the name is already registered as a unique name on another computer or a group name on the network.

Note   All Registry values discussed in this chapter are found under the following Registry path:

```
HKEY_LOCAL_MACHINE\SYSTEM\CurrentControlSet\Services\Nbf
```

Connection-Oriented Traffic

The **net use** command is an example of a connection-oriented communication, as illustrated in Figure 6.2.

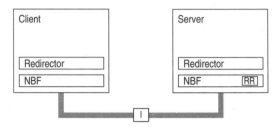

Figure 6.2   Connection-oriented Network Traffic

When a user types **net use** at the command line to connect to a shared resource, NBF must first locate the server by sending UI-frames, and then initialize the link. This is handled by the redirector when it makes a connection to the NBF drivers via the Transport Driver Interface (TDI) boundary. NBF begins the sequence by generating a NetBIOS Find Name frame. Once the server is found, a session is set up with UC Class-II frames following the standard 802.2 protocol (802.2 governs the overall flow of data).

The client computer sends an SABME (Set Asynchronous Balance Mode Extended) frame, and the server returns a UA (Unnumbered Acknowledgment) frame. Then the client sends an RR (Receive Ready) frame, notifying the server that it is ready to receive I-frames whose sequence number is currently 0. The server acknowledges this frame.

Once the LLC-level session is established, additional NetBEUI-level information is exchanged. The client sends a Session Initialize frame, and then the server responds with a Session Confirm frame. At this point, the NetBEUI-level session is ready to handle application-level frames (Server Message Blocks, or SMBs).

Reliable transfer is achieved with link-oriented frames by numbering the I-frames. This allows the receiving computer to determine whether the frames were lost and in what order they were received.

NBF uses two techniques to improve performance for connection-oriented traffic: use of adaptive sliding windows and use of link timers. These techniques are described in the next two sections.

Adaptive Sliding Window Protocol

NBF uses an adaptive sliding window algorithm to improve performance while reducing network congestion and providing flow control. A sliding window algorithm allows a sender to dynamically tune the number of LLC frames sent before an acknowledgment is requested. Figure 6.3 shows frames traveling through a two-way pipe.

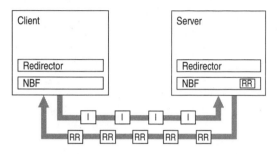

Figure 6.3   Adaptive Sliding Window

If the sender could feed only one frame into the pipe and then had to wait for an acknowledgment (ACK), the sender's pipe would be underused. If the sender can send multiple frames before an ACK is returned, the sender can keep the pipe full, thereby using the full bandwidth of the pipe. The frames would travel forward, and then ACKs for the received frames would travel back. The number of frames that the sender is allowed to send before it must wait for an ACK is referred to as the *send window*. In general, NBF has no receive window, unless it detects that the remote is a version of IBM LAN Server, which never polls; in this case, NBF uses a receive window based on the value of **MaximumIncomingFrames** in the Registry.

The adaptive sliding window protocol tries to determine the best sizes for the send window for the current network conditions. Ideally, the windows should be big enough so that maximum throughput can be realized. However, if the window gets too big, the receiver could get overloaded and drop frames. For big windows, dropped frames cause significant network traffic because more frames have to be retransmitted. Lost frames might be a problem on slow links or when frames have to pass over multiple hops to find the receiving station. Lost frames coupled with large send windows generate multiple retransmissions. This traffic overhead might make an already congested network worse. By limiting the send window size, traffic is throttled, and congestion control is exercised.

Link Timers

NBF uses three timers: the response timer (T1), the acknowledgment timer (T2), and the inactivity timer (Ti). These timers help regulate network traffic and are controlled by the values of the **DefaultT1Timeout**, **DefaultT2Timeout**, and **DefaultTiTimeout** Registry entries, respectively.

The response timer is used to determine how long the sender should wait before it assumes the I-frame is lost. After T1 milliseconds, NBF sends an RR frame that has not been acknowledged and doubles the value for T1. If the RR frame is not acknowledged after the number of retries defined by the value of **LLCRetries**, the link is dropped.

Where the return traffic does not allow the receiver to send an I-frame within a legitimate time period, the acknowledgment timer begins, and then the ACK is sent. The value for this timer is set by the T2 variable, with a default value of 150 milliseconds. If the sender has to wait until the T2 timer starts in order to receive a response, the link might be underused while the sender waits for the ACK. This rare situation can occur over slow links. On the other hand, if the timer value is too low, the timer starts and sends unnecessary ACKs, generating excess traffic. NBF is optimized so that the last frame the sender wants to send is sent with the POLL bit turned on. This forces the receiver to send an ACK immediately.

The inactivity timer, Ti, is used to detect whether the link has gone down. The default value for Ti is 30 seconds. If Ti milliseconds pass without activity on the link, NBF sends an I-frame for polling. This is then ACKed, and the link is maintained.

Note   Remember that T2 <= T1 <= Ti.

NBF and Sessions

Each process within Windows NT that uses NetBIOS can communicate with up to 254 different computers. The implementation of NetBIOS under Windows NT requires the application to do a few more things than have traditionally been done on other platforms, but the capacity for doing up to 254 sessions from within each process is well worth the price. Prior implementations of NetBIOS had the 254-session limit for the entire computer, including the workstation and server components.

Note that the 254-session limit does not apply to the default workstation or server components. The workstation and server services avoid the problem by writing directly to the TDI rather than calling NetBIOS directly. This is a handle-based (32-bit) interface.

NBF also has a unique method of handling resources to create a virtually infinite (memory permitting) number of connections, as described in the next section.

Session Limits

The 254-session limit is based on a key variable in the NetBIOS architecture called the *Local Session Number* (LSN). This is a one-byte number (0 to 255) with several numbers reserved for system use. When two computers establish a session via NBF, there is an exchange of LSNs.

The LSNs on the two computers might be different. They do not have to match, but a computer always uses the same LSN for a given session. This number is assigned when a program issues a CALL NCB (Network Control Block). The number is actually shared between the two computers in the initial frame sent from the calling computer to the listening computer. Figure 6.4 shows this session-creation frame exchange.

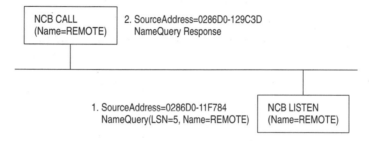

Figure 6.4   Broadcast of NameQuery

The initial frame is a NameQuery frame. In previous implementations of NBF, this frame was broadcast onto the network. All computers read the frame and check to see if they have the name in their name space and if there is a LISTEN NCB pending on the name. If there is a LISTEN NCB pending, the computer assigns a new LSN for itself, and then adds it to the response frame and satisfies the LISTEN NCB, which now contains just the LSN used on that computer. Even though both computers know the LSN of the other, the information is not used. The more important information for the two communicating partners is the network addresses that are part of the frames. As the frames are exchanged, each partner picks up the address of the other in the source address component of the frame received. The NBF protocol keeps the network address of the remote partner so that subsequent frames can be addressed directly.

Note   This process applies for NBF connections. NetBIOS connections established via TCP/IP and RFC1001/1002 or NBP are handled differently.

Windows NT has to use the same NameQuery frame to establish connections with remote computers via NBF; otherwise, it would not be able to talk to existing workstations and servers. The NameQuery frame transmitted must contain the 1-byte-wide LSN to be used.

Breaking the 254-Session Limit

NBF breaks the 254-session barrier by using a combination of two matrices, one maintained by NBF, and one maintained by NetBIOS.

The NBF system maintains a two-dimensional matrix, as shown in Figure 6.5. Along the side of this matrix are the LSN numbers 1 to 254. Across the top are the network addresses for the different computers that it has sessions with. In the cell defined by the LSN and network address is the TDI handle, which relates back to the process that established the connection (either the CALL or LISTEN).

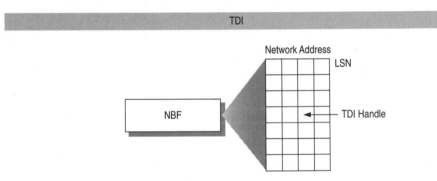

Figure 6.5   NBF and Its LSN Matrix

Note   The matrix concept and its contents are for illustration purposes only. The physical storage algorithm and exact contents are beyond the scope of this chapter.

The NameQuery frame from Windows NT contains the LSN number associated with the TDI handle that satisfies either the NCB CALL or the LISTEN. In the case of a CALL, it is not broadcast but is addressed directly to the recipient.

The remaining mystery is how NBF gets the network address of the recipient to add to its matrix when doing the CALL. (It's easy on the LISTEN side because the address is in the NameQuery frame received.)

As shown in Figure 6.6, NBF uses two NameQuery frames.

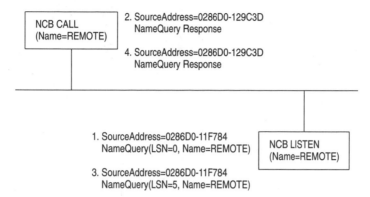

Figure 6.6   Two NameQuery Frames in Windows NT NBF

For the numbered items in Figure 6.6:

1. The first frame is the FindName format of the NameQuery.
   However, an LSN of 0 is special; it indicates that it is a FindName. The
   FindName is broadcast; when the remote computer responds to the
   frame, NBF has the network address it needs to add an entry to the table.

2. The second NameQuery is then sent directly to the remote station, with the LSN
   filled in as a CALL command. The FindName will be successfully returned by
   the remote computer, even if no LISTEN NCB is posted against the name.

3. If no LISTEN NCB is posted against the name, frame (3) is sent.

4. The same frame is responded to by frame (4).

NBF must also address another problem—the LSN from the NBF table cannot be
the one returned to the process issuing the CALL or LISTEN commands. NBF may
have established connections with multiple remote computers with LSN=5, for
example. Windows NT must return each process an LSN number that uniquely
defines its session.

As stated earlier, NBF uses the TDI handle to know which LSN and network
address to send frames to, and each process has its own set of LSNs available to it.
Therefore, there must be a component between the originating process and the TDI
interface of NBF that translates a process ID and an LSN into a TDI handle. The
component in the middle is called NETBIOS.SYS.

This concept is illustrated in Figure 6.7, although the table maintained by
NETBIOS.SYS is actually 254 LSNs per LANA number per process. (In
Windows NT, each binding path is represented by a LANA number). In reality,
each process can have up to 254 sessions per LANA number, not just a total of 254
sessions.

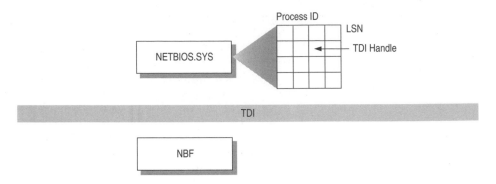

Figure 6.7   NETBIOS.SYS Matrix

NETBIOS.SYS builds a second matrix that has LSNs down the side, process IDs along the top, and TDI handles in the cells. It is the LSN from this table that is passed back to the originating process.

Figure 6.8 presents a top-down view of the architecture.

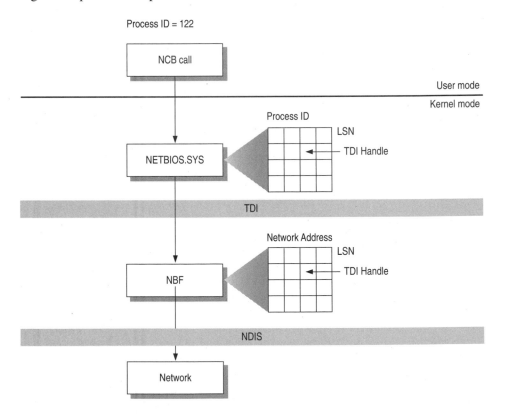

Figure 6.8   Another View of the NetBIOS Architecture

For example, suppose a process needs to establish a session with a remote computer. Before the process can issue the CALL NCB, it must issue a RESET NCB. This command signals NETBIOS.SYS to allocate space in its TDI handle table, among other things. Once the RESET is satisfied, the process issues a CALL NCB to make a connection with a specific remote computer. This NCB is directed down to the NETBIOS.SYS device driver. The driver opens a new TDI handle to NBF and sends the command to NBF.

NBF issues the first NAME_QUERY with LSN=0 to find the remote computer. When the remote computer responds, the network address is extracted from the frame, and a column in the NBF table is created. The second NAME_QUERY with an LSN is sent directly to the remote computer. When that frame is returned successfully, NBF returns from the TDI call to the NETBIOS.SYS driver with a successful status code.

NETBIOS.SYS then fills in the LSN from its table into the NCB and satisfies it back to the calling process.

CHAPTER 7

Using DLC with Windows NT

A Data Link Control (DLC) protocol interface device driver is included in Windows NT Workstation and Windows NT Server. The DLC protocol is traditionally used to provide connectivity to IBM mainframes. It is also used to provide connectivity to local area network printers that are directly attached to the network, instead of to a specific computer.

This chapter provides details about the DLC protocol device driver for Windows NT.

Overview

The Data Link Control (DLC) protocol driver provided with Windows NT allows the computer to communicate with other computers running the DLC protocol stack (for example, an IBM mainframe) and other network peripherals (for example, printers such as a Hewlett-Packard HP 4Si that use a network adapter card to connect directly to the network).

Windows NT DLC contains an 802.2 Logical Link Control (LLC) Finite State Machine, which is used when transmitting and receiving type 2 connection-oriented frames. DLC can also transmit and receive type 1 connectionless frames, such as Unnumbered Information (UI) frames. Type 1 and 2 frames can be transmitted and received simultaneously.

Windows NT DLC works with either token ring or Ethernet MAC drivers and can transmit and receive Digital.Intel.Xerox (DIX) format frames when bound to an Ethernet MAC.

The DLC interface can be accessed from 32-bit Windows NT-based programs and from 16-bit MS-DOS–based and 16-bit Windows-based programs. The 32-bit interface conforms largely to the CCB2 interface, the segmented 16-bit pointers being replaced with flat 32-bit pointers. The 16-bit interface conforms to the CCB1 interface.

Note For definitions of the CCB interfaces, see the *IBM Local Area Network Technical Reference*.

Loading the DLC Driver on Windows NT

The DLC driver can be loaded when the system is first installed, or any time thereafter, using the Network option in Control Panel.

The order of the bindings section is significant to DLC because an adapter is specified at the DLC interface as a number—typically 0 or 1 (although Windows NT DLC can support up to 16 physical adapters). The number corresponds to the index of the adapter in the DLC bindings section. If you have only one network adapter card installed, DLC applications use a value of 0 to refer to this adapter, and you need not make any changes to the bindings.

If you have more than one adapter card, you might want to modify the bindings.

▶ **To change the order of the bindings**

1. From the Network Control Panel, choose Bindings.

2. From the Show Bindings For box, choose DLC Protocol.

   You will see a list of bindings, such as the following:

   ```
   DLC Protocol -> ARC Built-in Ethernet Adapter Driver ->
      [01] ARC Built-in Ethernet Adapter
   DLC Protocol -> IBM Token Ring Adapter Driver ->
      [02] IBM Token Ring Adapter
   ```

   The numbers in brackets refer to the order in which the adapters were installed. In this example, DLC currently refers to the Ethernet adapter as adapter #0 and the Token Ring adapter as adapter #1.

   If you have software (such as a 3270 emulator program) that allows you to specify an adapter number at run time, you might decide to keep the current setup and change the adapter number when you run the software. Typically, however, the software uses adapter #0, expecting an IBM Token Ring card to be the primary adapter. In this case, you will need to change the order of the bindings list.

3. To change the order of an item in the list, highlight the item, and then use the up- and down-arrow buttons to reposition it in the list.

   For example, suppose you wanted to change the above bindings so that the IBM Token Ring adapter corresponds to adapter #0 and the ARC Ethernet adapter corresponds to adapter #1. Highlight the line containing IBM Token Ring Adapter Driver, and click once on the up-arrow button. The bindings are now correctly ordered for your application software, and you do not need to modify the program configuration.

4. Choose OK to keep the modified bindings list.

DLC Driver Parameters in the Registry

Unlike other Windows NT protocol drivers, DLC does not bind to a MAC driver until an adapter open command is issued. When an adapter is opened for the first time, the DLC protocol driver writes some default values into the Registry for that adapter. These values control the various timers that DLC uses, whether DIX frames should be used over an Ethernet link, and whether bits in a destination address should be swapped (used when going over a bridge that swaps destination addresses).

The timer entries in the Registry are supplied because program-supplied timer values might not be sufficient. There are three timers used by DLC link communication:

- T1 is the response timer.
- T2 is the acknowledgment delay timer.
- Ti is the inactivity timer.

Each timer is split into two groups—**TxTickOne** and **TxTickTwo**, where x is 1, 2, or i.

Typically, these timer values are set when a program opens an adapter and/or creates a Service Access Point (SAP).

The Registry contains entries used to modify timer values. Registry entries for DLC are found in the following location:

```
HKEY_LOCAL_MACHINE\SYSTEM\CurrentControlSet\Services\DLC\Parameters
   \<Adapter Name>
```

When you edit a timer entry value, the change takes effect the next time the adapter is opened (for example, by rerunning the application). For more information, including the ranges and default values for the timers, see "DLC System Driver Entries" in Chapter 14, "Registry Value Entries."

Communicating with SNA Hosts Using DLC and SNA

One of the major uses of the DLC protocol today is connecting personal computers to SNA hosts, that is, IBM mainframe or midrange computers such as the AS/400. With the increased popularity of local area networks in the mid-1980s, IBM introduced two new connectivity options for its hosts. With the Token Ring Interface Connection (TIC), any SNA host can communicate with a token ring network. With the LAN Interface Connection (LIC), an AS/400 computer can communicate with an Ethernet network.

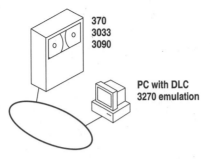

Figure 7.1   Mainframe Connectivity Path Using Token Ring

The SNA hosts already possessed a rich protocol stack in Systems Network Architecture (SNA). SNA provides equivalent functionality to the OSI Network, Transport, Session, and Presentation levels (although functionality might differ at each level). Because the DLC layer and the OSI Data Link layer are almost identical in functionality, a programming interface was developed for the DLC layer and exposed to programmers wanting to use this level of interface. The interface is described in the IEEE 802.2 standard.

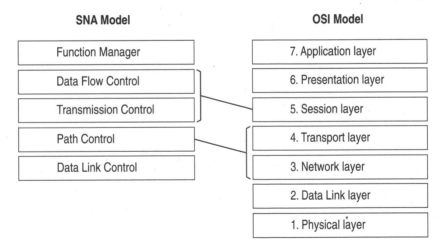

Figure 7.2   Comparison of SNA and OSI Models

SNA Server uses the DLC protocol device driver when communicating to mainframes via the token ring interface. Detailed configuration and installation information is provided in the *Microsoft SNA Server Installation Guide* and the *Microsoft SNA Server Administration Guide.*

Using DLC to Connect to HP Printers

DLC is used to provide connectivity to local area network printers that are directly attached to the network, not to a specific computer.

Printing via the DLC protocol device driver starts by creating a printer that uses the HPMON.DLL printer driver. All commands are performed in the Print Manager utility.

▷ **To connect to a printer that is directly attached to the network**

1. From the Printer menu in Print Manager, choose Create Printer.

2. In the Print To box, select Other.

3. In the Print Destinations dialog box, select Hewlett-Packard Network Port.

4. In the Add Hewlett-Packard Network Peripheral Port dialog box, select the network adapter card that will communicate with the printer.

From the Add Hewlett-Packard Network Peripheral Port dialog box, you can cause Windows NT to automatically search for printers connected to your network. You can also adjust the DLC Timers for this application. DLC timers are described in "DLC Driver Parameters in the Registry," earlier in this chapter.

For more specific information, see the online Help associated with the Add Hewlett-Packard Network Peripheral Port dialog box.

Changing the Locally Administered Address

There might be times when you want to change or override the network address of the network adapter card when running the DLC protocol. You might want to do this, for example, when communicating directly to a mainframe. Certain configurations of mainframe software require the network address of the devices connecting to it to follow a set format, so it might be necessary to change the card's network address. You can do this through the Registry Editor.

Note The following example is for an IBM Token Ring adapter. This parameter is supported on other network adapters as well, but not necessarily all.

The following instructions do not apply when connecting to a mainframe via SNA Server. The modifications needed to the network address are handled during the installation process.

▶ **To change the address of an adapter card**

1. From the File menu of Program Manager, choose the Run command.

2. In the Command Line box of the Run dialog box, type REGEDT32.EXE, and then choose the OK button.

3. When the Registry Editor starts, select the following key:

   `HKEY_LOCAL_MACHINE\SYSTEM\CurrentControlSet\Services\ibmTOKMC01`

4. From the Edit menu, choose Add Value. For Value, type **NetworkAddress,** and select REG_SZ for data. Choose OK.

5. Type the 12-digit Locally Administered Address (LAA) that you need to communicate to the mainframe. If you don't know this address, see your network administrator or operations group.

6. Exit the Registry Editor and restart your computer.

   (You must restart the computer for the modification to take effect.)

7. From the command prompt, run the following command to report the active MAC address:

   `net config rdr`

   If the MAC address is the one you entered in the Registry Editor, the LAA has taken effect.

For more information about using Registry Editor, see Chapter 11, "Registry Editor and Registry Administration," of the *Windows NT Resource Guide.* For information about specific DLC-related Registry Entries, see Chapter 14, "Registry Value Entries," of the *Windows NT Resource Guide.*

C H A P T E R   8

Client-Server Connectivity on Windows NT

Client-server computing systems must be able to access data that resides on different hardware platforms, different operating systems, different network operating systems, and different database management systems (DBMSs). This chapter discusses specifically how client workstations communicate with databases stored on Windows NT computers. Primarily, this chapter covers details about MS-DOS, Windows, Windows NT Workstation, and OS/2 client workstations.

This chapter explains client-server connectivity on Windows NT using Microsoft SQL Server as an example. For information on other client-server databases developed for Windows NT, see the appropriate vendor documentation.

SQL Server

Microsoft SQL Server 4.21 has been completely reengineered for Windows NT. SQL Server includes the following enhancements and performance improvements that were not part of previous versions of SQL Server:

- A new Symmetric Server architecture allows SQL Server to scale from notebook computers to symmetric multiprocessor servers, with support for Intel-based and RISC-based computers. This architecture dynamically balances the processor load across multiple CPUs and provides a preemptive multithreaded design for improved performance and reliability.

- Windows NT provides preemptive scheduling, virtual paged memory management, symmetric multiprocessing, and asynchronous I/O, the foundation of a mission-critical database server platform. Integration with the Windows NT operating system improves operational control and ease of use. Administrators can manage multiple SQL Servers across distributed networks using graphical tools for configuration, security, database administration, performance monitoring, event notification, and unattended backup.

- Unified logon security with Windows NT security means that authorized users do not have to maintain separate SQL Server logon passwords and can bypass a separate logon process for SQL Server. Additionally, SQL Server applications can take advantage of Windows NT security features, which include encrypted passwords, password aging, domain-wide user accounts, and Windows-based user administration.

- Windows NT provides an ideal platform for building powerful 32-bit client-server applications for Microsoft SQL Server. The *Microsoft SQL Server Programmer's Toolkit* contains a 32-bit Win32-based version of the Microsoft DB-Library™ application programming interface.

- Microsoft SQL Server is fully interoperable with Microsoft SQL Server for OS/2, as well as with SYBASE SQL Server for the UNIX and VMS operating systems. Existing applications will work unchanged. Microsoft SQL Server operates across all corporate network environments, including Novell NetWare and TCP/IP-based LANs.

The key to enterprise interoperability is network independence. Microsoft SQL Server can support clients communicating over multiple heterogeneous networks simultaneously, with no need for additional integration products. SQL Server communicates on named pipes (over either NetBEUI or TCP/IP network protocols) with Windows, Windows NT, MS-DOS, and OS/2 clients. In addition, SQL Server can simultaneously support TCP/IP Sockets for communication with Macintosh, UNIX, or VMS clients and SPX Sockets for communications in a Novell NetWare environment. It also supports DECnet™ Sockets, AppleTalk, and Banyan VINES. Microsoft SQL Server leverages the power, ease of use, and scalability offered by the Windows NT operating system to manage large databases for mission-critical applications.

Data Access Mechanisms

Figure 8.1 illustrates the key interfaces used to access data in a Microsoft SQL Server client-server environment. These include application programming interfaces (APIs), data stream protocols, interprocess communication (IPC) mechanisms, network protocols, and the Tabular Data System (TDS) protocol.

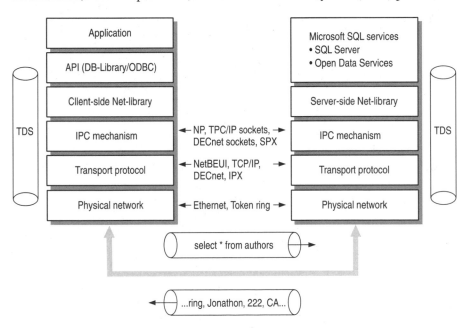

Figure 8.1   Levels and Interfaces Within the Microsoft SQL Server Architecture

The following sections describe each of these interfaces to SQL Server.

Application Programming Interfaces

Each back-end database typically has its own application programming interface (API) through which it communicates with clients. A client application needing to access multiple back-end databases must be able to transform requests and data transfers into each of the corresponding APIs. Client-server applications communicate with Microsoft SQL Server through two APIs—Open Database Connectivity (ODBC) and DB-Library.

ODBC is an API for generic database connectivity for Windows and Windows NT platforms. It is designed to be a general-purpose call-level interface (CLI) for any database, including nonrelational DBMSs. The ODBC interface provides the needed functionality for applications that must access multiple DBMSs from different vendors. Application developers can develop, compile, and ship an application without targeting a specific DBMS, provided that DBMS-specific features are not used. ODBC ensures interoperability by forcing all clients to adhere to a standard interface. The ODBC driver automatically interprets a command for a specific data source.

DB-Library is a set of API calls designed specifically so multiplatform client applications can interact with Microsoft SQL Server. DB-Library provides the needed functionality for applications requiring client support for MS-DOS and OS/2, as well as for Microsoft Windows and Windows NT. It is also equivalent to the SYBASE Open Client interface on UNIX, VMS, and Macintosh systems.

Data Stream Protocols

Every DBMS uses a logical data stream protocol that enables the transfer of requests, data, status, error messages, and so on, between the DBMS and its clients. The API uses interprocess communication (IPC) mechanisms supported by the operating system and network to package and transport this logical protocol.

The data stream protocol for Microsoft SQL Server is called Tabular Data Stream (TDS). TDS is also used by Open Data Services and SYBASE® software to transfer requests and responses between the client and the server. Because TDS is a logical data stream protocol, it requires physical network IPC mechanisms to transmit the data. The Net-Library architecture described later in this chapter provides a method of sending TDS across a physical network connection.

Data stream protocols are typically proprietary, developed and optimized to work exclusively with a particular DBMS. An application accessing multiple databases must, therefore, be able to use multiple data stream protocols. Using ODBC helps resolve this problem for application developers.

With ODBC implementations, the data stream protocol differences are resolved at the driver level. Each driver emits the data stream using the protocol established by the server. The SQL Server ODBC driver emits TDS directly; it does not translate or otherwise encapsulate DB-Library function calls.

Interprocess Communication Mechanisms

The choice of IPC mechanism is constrained by the operating system and network being used. For example, Microsoft SQL Server for OS/2 uses named pipes as its IPC mechanism, SYBASE SQL Server on UNIX uses TCP/IP sockets, and SYBASE on VMS uses DECnet Sockets. In a heterogeneous environment, multiple IPC mechanisms might be used on a single computer.

SQL Server for Windows NT can communicate over multiple IPC mechanisms. SQL Server communicates on named pipes (over either NetBEUI or TCP/IP network protocols) with Windows, Windows NT, MS-DOS, and OS/2 clients. It can also simultaneously support TCP/IP Sockets for communication with Macintosh, UNIX, or VMS clients and SPX sockets for communications in a Novell NetWare environment. SQL Server also supports Banyan VINES, DECnet Sockets, and AppleTalk.

Network Protocols

A network protocol is used to transport the data stream protocol over a network. It can be considered as the plumbing that supports the IPC mechanisms used by the data stream protocol, as well as supporting basic network operations such as file transfers and print sharing.

Back-end databases can reside on a local area network (LAN) that connects it with the client application, or it can reside at a remote site, connected via a wide area network (WAN) and/or gateway. In both cases, it is possible that the network protocols or physical network supported by the various back-end databases are different from those supported by the client or each other. In these cases, a client application must use different network protocols to communicate with various back-end databases.

The network transport protocols supported within SQL Server include NetBEUI, TCP/IP, SPX/IPX using NWLink, DECnet, AppleTalk, and VINES IP.

Net-Library Architecture

Microsoft SQL Server Net-Library architecture for client-server applications is based on the Net-Library concept that abstracts the client and server applications from the underlying network protocols being used. Figure 8.2 shows how SQL Server and related products can be accessed from practically any network environment.

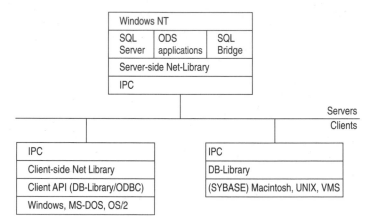

Figure 8.2   Net-Library Architecture

The Net-Library architecture provides a method of sending TDS (used by Microsoft SQL Server, Open Data Services, and SYBASE) via an IPC across a physical network connection. The Net-Library architecture also provides a transparent interface to the DB-Library APIs and the SQL Server driver for ODBC.

Net-Libraries are linked dynamically at run time. With the Microsoft Windows NT, Windows, and OS/2 operating systems, Net-Libraries are implemented as DLLs, and multiple Net-Libraries can be loaded simultaneously. With MS-DOS, Net-Libraries are implemented as terminate-and-stay-resident (TSR) programs, and only one can be loaded at a time.

The Net-Library architecture can be divided into two components—server-side Net-Libraries and client-side Net-Libraries.

Server-Side Net-Library Architecture

Microsoft SQL Server uses the server-side Net-Library architecture that was first introduced with Microsoft SQL Bridge. It can accept client requests across multiple network protocols at the same time.

Figure 8.3 illustrates the integration of server-side Net-Libraries with the various SQL Server–based products on the Windows NT platform.

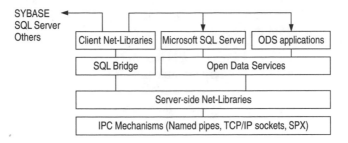

Figure 8.3   Server-Side Net-Library Architecture on the Windows NT Platform

The default Net-Library is named pipes.

When a server-side Net-Library is loaded by an application such as SQL Server, the Net-Library implements a network-specific way of establishing communication with clients and, in some cases, registers its presence on the network. SQL Server looks at the Windows NT Registry to determine which Net-Library to load on startup and which parameters to pass to it. The SQL Server Monitor process also uses a server-side Net-Library to communicate with clients and to search the following Registry key for network-specific parameters:

```
HKEY_LOCAL_MACHINE\SOFTWARE\Microsoft\SQLServer\Server
```

At startup, SQL Server specifies a value for the *server_name* parameter in the SRV_CONFIG structure of Open Data Services. This value identifies which Registry key SQL Server will search for values of the **ListenOn** and *connection_string* Registry entries. (By default, SQL Server looks in HKEY_LOCAL_MACHINE\SOFTWARE\Microsoft\SQLServer\Server.)

Each *connection_string* Registry value is read and passed on to the associated Net-Library (for example, named pipes) that is listed in the **ListenOn** field in the Server subkey. Each Net-Library acts upon the *connection_string* differently.

If there is no *connection_string* associated with the Net-Library, SQL Server does one of the following:

- If the Registry entry is under the SQL#Server\Server subkey, no connection string is passed as the default.
- If the Registry entry is not under SQL#Server\Server, *server_name* is passed as the default.

If the *server_name* subkey and the SQL#Server\Server subtree do not exist, or the Registry cannot be accessed, SQL Server assumes that the named pipes DLL (for the default Net-Library) is loaded, and no parameter is passed. (Named pipes access can be turned off by using the Registry Editor to explicitly delete the named pipes entry from the SQL#Server\Server subkey.)

Remote stored procedure calls and the Microsoft SQL Administrator tool also use the DB-Library/Net-Library architecture under Windows NT.

Client-Side Net-Library Architecture

When a call is made to open a connection to SQL Server, the API involved (DB-Library or the SQL Server driver for ODBC) determines which client-side Net-Library should be loaded to communicate with SQL Server or Open Data Services. (This process is described in more detail later in this chapter.)

Figure 8.4 shows client-side Net-Libraries used to communicate with SQL Server on the server side.

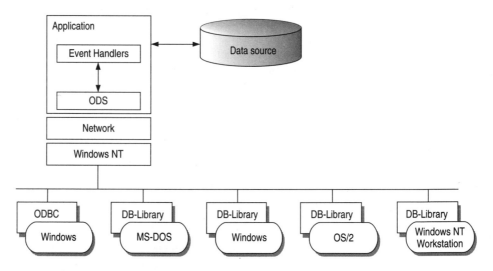

Figure 8.4   Client-Side Net-Library Architecture

Win32 DB-Library Architecture

Internally, a separate operating system thread is spawned for each connection that DB-Library makes with SQL Server. Each instance of the DB-Library DLL that is loaded by a calling process gets a private data area, while sharing code.

The Win32 DB-Library architecture differs from the implementation with Windows 3.x. In Windows 3.x, the DB-Library DLL has a single data segment that is shared among all calling processes. W3DBLIB.DLL maintains DB-Library connections as a linked list of connections in a single data segment. This architecture is required, because in Windows 3.x DLLs have a single data segment that is shared among all calling processes. This necessitates the initialization and clean up of the DB-Library DLL data structures through calls to the **dbinit** and **dbwinexit** functions.

The DB-Library functions for Win32 are located in NTWDBLIB.DLL, and the named pipe Net-Library is located in DBNMPNTW.DLL. (Be sure to set the PATH environment variable to include the directory where the DLLs reside.)

Another file, NTWDBLIB.LIB, contains import definitions that your applications for the Win32 API use. Set the LIB environment variable to include the directory where NTWDBLIB.LIB resides.

DB-Library resolves server names differently depending on the client platform.

Resolving Server Names for Clients Based on Windows, MS-DOS, OS/2, and Windows NT

When **dbopen** (the DB-Library function that initiates a client conversation with SQL Server) is called with the name of a SQL Server to connect to, DB-Library uses configuration information to determine which client-side Net-Library to load.

The client-side Net-Library configuration is stored in the following locations:

Client	Net-Library configuration is stored in
Windows 3.x	WIN.INI
MS-DOS	Environment variable
OS/2	OS2.INI
Windows NT	Windows NT Registry

DB-Library scans the **[SQLSERVER]** section of WIN.INI, OS2.INI, or the \SQLServer\Client\ConnectTo subtree of the Windows NT Registry looking for a logical name that matches the *servername* parameter specified in the call to **dbopen**. All items in the **[SQLSERVER]** section of the .INI file or in the Registry subtree have this format:

```
logical-name=Net-Lib-DLL-name[,network-specific-parameters]
```

Note Although some Net-Libraries need values for *network-specific-parameters*, this is optional for others that instead use defaults or determine the network-specific information required themselves.

DB-Library uses the following logic to determine which Net-Library to load:

- If a matching logical name is found in the .INI file or in the Windows NT Registry, DB-Library loads the specified Net-Library DLL. If network-specific parameters are present in the .INI entry or the Windows NT Registry, these are passed unmodified by DB-Library to the Net-Library DLL.

- If no matching logical name is found in the .INI file or in the Windows NT Registry, the DLL name (and optionally, the network-specific parameters) of the entry named DSQUERY will be used to load the required Net-Library. So, if you don't have a specific server name but do have a DSQUERY entry, that entry will be used as the default.

- If there is neither a specific logical name nor a DSQUERY entry in the .INI file or in the Windows NT Registry, DB-Library loads the named pipes Net-Library (for example, DBNMPP3.DLL for the Windows operating system) and passes it the *servername* parameter from **dbopen**. With Microsoft SQL Server using named pipes, you typically never need to make a .INI entry. If you use any other Net-Library, you must make at least one entry.

The following examples illustrate this logic:

- **forecast=dbnmp3**

  The Windows named pipe Net-Library is used, and it connects to SQL Server \\Forecast using the standard named pipe, \pipe\sql\query.

- **sales=dbnmp3,\\server1\pipe\sql2\query**

  The Windows named pipe Net-Library is used, and it connects to \\server1, where SQL Server has been started using an alternate named pipe, \pipe\sql2\query.

Note SQL Server can be directed to use an alternate pipe by adding an entry to the ListenOn field in the Registry under the following tree:

`HKEY_LOCAL_MACHINE\SOFTWARE\Microsoft\SQLServer\Server`

- **dsquery=dbmsspx3**

  The SPX Net-Library is used, and the *servername* parameter from **dbopen** is used. This Net-Library requires no specific network connection information because it queries the NetWare Bindery to determine the location of the server running the Network Manager service specified in the *servername* parameter.

- **unixsrv=sybtcpw,131,107.005.21,3180**

  The SYBASE TCP/IP Net-Library is used, and DB-Library passes the IP address and port number contained in the initialization string to the Net-Library.

Note The SQL Server ODBC driver uses the same Net-Libraries as DB-Library to communicate with SQL Server, Open Data Services, and SQL Bridge.

Resolving Server Names for MS-DOS–Based Clients

With MS-DOS, only one Net-Library TSR can be loaded, so there is no .INI configuration. Instead, MS-DOS environment variables are used to specify any network-specific connection information. Environment variables have the following format:

`logical-name=network-specific-parameters`

The Net-Library used is the currently loaded TSR. If the *servername* parameter passed to **dbopen** corresponds to a currently set environment variable, DB-Library passes the information contained in the environment string to the currently loaded Net-Library. In turn, Net-Library uses this information to determine server location and network-specific information parameters, if present. If no environment variable matches the *servername* passed to **dbopen**, DB-Library passes the *servername* parameter from **dbopen** to the currently loaded Net-Library.

New DB-Library Function Identifies SQL Servers

DB-Library version 4.20.20 and later includes a new function (**dbserverenum**) that enables applications to identify SQL Servers available on the network, regardless of which network operating system is being used. For details on the **dbserverenum** function, see the *Microsoft SQL Server Programmer's Reference for C*.

Configuration of the Net-Library

The Net-Library files and IPCs for each network protocol supported by Microsoft SQL Server are listed in the following table. These files are installed automatically using the SQL Server Setup utility on the server side and the SQL Client Configuration Utility on the Windows, Windows NT, MS-DOS, and OS/2 client side. The AUTOEXEC.BAT file is used to load the MS-DOS client Net-Library.

The server-side Net-Library is used by SQL Server and ODS applications. If SQL Server and ODS are on the same computer, ODS uses an alternate pipe.

Table 8.1 shows which files you need when installing SQL Server on various network operating systems with various network protocols. Use the following table to determine exactly which files need to be in place for servers and clients.

You can also use this table for troubleshooting, should there be difficulty in connecting a client workstation to Microsoft SQL Server.

Table 8.1   Server-Side and Client-Side Net-Library Files

Network interface	Network protocol	Network clients supported	Client-side Net-Library	Server-side Net-Library	Comments
Named Pipes	NetBEUI or TCP/IP	LAN Manager, Windows for Workgroups, and Windows NT clients	DBNMPIPE.EXE (MS-DOS), DBNMP3.DLL (Windows), DBNMPP.DLL (OS/2), DBNMPNTW.DLL (Windows NT)	SSNMPNTW.DLL	This network setup provides SQL Server Integrated Security with the Windows NT User Account Database.
	NWLink	Windows NT clients	DBNMPNTW.DLL (Windows NT)	SSNMPNTW.DLL	
Windows Sockets	TCP/IP	UNIX and MAC clients	Part of SYBASE Open Client	SSMSSOCN.DLL	This configuration provides multiple vendor integration.

Table 8.1   Server-Side and Client-Side Net-Library Files *(continued)*

Network interface	Network protocol	Network clients supported	Client-side Net-Library	Server-side Net-Library	Comments
		PC clients: FTP PC/TCP, HP ARPA Services, Wollongong PathWay, Novell LAN WorkPlace, AT&T® StarGroup, Sun PC-NFS, DEC PATHWORKS (DECnet), Microsoft TCP/IP for LAN Manager, and so on	DBMSSOCN.DLL (Windows NT), DBMSSOC3.DLL (Windows), DBMSSOC.EXE (MS-DOS)	SSMSSOCN.DLL	The corresponding Net-Libraries are available from SYBASE.
Windows Sockets	NWLink (IPX/SPX)	Novell NetWare 3.10+ (MS-DOS and Windows) and OS/2 Requestor, NSD004 (OS/2) clients	DBMSSPX.EXE (DOS), DBMSSPX3.DLL (Windows), DBMSSPXP.DLL (OS/2)	Novell: SSMSSPXN.DLL	The servername is registered with the Novell bindery service.
	NWLink		DBMSSPXN.DLL (Windows NT)		
VINES Sockets	VINES IP	Banyan VINES, 4.11 (rev.5)+ and Windows NT clients	DBMSVINE.EXE (DOS), DBMSVIN3.DLL (Windows), DBMSVINP.DLL (OS/2), DBMSVINN.DLL (Windows NT)	Banyan VINES: SSMSVINN.DLL	Registers to StreetTalk as the given service. Banyan VINES will automatically handle lookups of partial names or nicknames.

Notes   NWLink is a Microsoft implementation of the IPX/SPX protocol. Alternative software available through Novell is fully expected sometime in the near future.

Using NetBEUI as the network protocol, the client workstation always uses a broadcast to locate the SQL Server(s) on the network. Also, with TCP/IP the client workstation always uses a broadcast to locate the SQL Server(s), provided that the servername and IP address are not located in the LMHOST file on the workstations.

Novell Connectivity

As shown by Table 8.1, in a Novell NetWare environment, SQL Server requires NWLink (installed through Network Control Panel) and the SSMSSPXN.DLL. This DLL is automatically installed on the server side, with the appropriate Registry entries, when you use SQL Server Setup and choose Change Network Support, then NWLink IPX/SPX.

The following is a sample of what is added to the Registry for Microsoft SQL Server on a Novell Network:

```
HKEY LOCAL_MACHINE\SOFTWARE\Microsoft\SQLServer\Server
ListenOn: REG_MULTI_SZ: SSNMPNTW, \\.\pipe\sql\query
    SSMSSPXN, CORAL (computername)
```

Windows and OS/2 client workstations require the Novell NetWare 3.10 or higher level of IPX. The SQL Client Configuration Utility that ships with SQL Server is used to specify the default network that the Windows and OS/2 clients will use. By choosing Novell IPX/SPX, the required DBMSSPX3.DLL is automatically installed on the Windows client side, and DBMSSPXP.DLL is installed on the OS/2 client side. This adds the appropriate entries in the WIN.INI file or the OS/2.INI file, respectively.

The following is a sample of what is added to the WIN.INI for Windows clients communicating with Microsoft SQL Server on a Novell Network:

```
[SQLSERVER]
DSQUERY=DBMSSPX3
```

MS-DOS clients require the same level of IPX that the Windows workstations do. DBMSSPX.EXE must be installed on the MS-DOS computer. This TSR can be loaded either manually or from AUOTEXEC.BAT.

Windows NT client workstations use NWLink, which is installed through Network Control Panel. After installation, use the Client Configuration Utility to specify that the default network is Novell IPX/SPX. This, in turn, installs the required DBMSSPXN.DLL on the Windows NT client side.

The following is a sample Registry entry for Windows NT clients communicating with Microsoft SQL Server on a Novell Network:

```
HKEY_LOCAL_MACHINE\SOFTWARE\Microsoft\SQLServer\Client\ConnectTo
DSQUERY: REG_SZ: DBMSSPXN
```

C H A P T E R   9

Using Remote Access Service

Windows NT 3.5 Remote Access Service (RAS) connects remote or mobile workers to corporate networks. Optimized for client-server computing, Remote Access Service (RAS) is implemented primarily as a software solution, and is included in all of Microsoft's operating systems.

The goals in designing RAS were to make it:

- Secure
- Interoperable
- Economical
- Scalable
- High performance
- Easy to use
- Extensible

RAS Capabilities and Functionality

RAS provides transparent network access for computer running Windows NT, Windows for Workgroups, MS-DOS version 3.1 or later (RAS version 1.1a), and MS OS/2 version 3.1 (RAS version 1.1).

Users run the RAS graphical phone book on a remote computer, and then initiate a connection to the RAS server using a local modem, X.25, or ISDN card. The RAS server, running on a Windows NT Server-based computer connected to the corporate network, authenticates the users and services the sessions until terminated by the user or network administrator. All services that are typically available to a LAN-connected user (including file- and print-sharing, database access and messaging) are enabled via the RAS connection. The following figure depicts the RAS architecture:

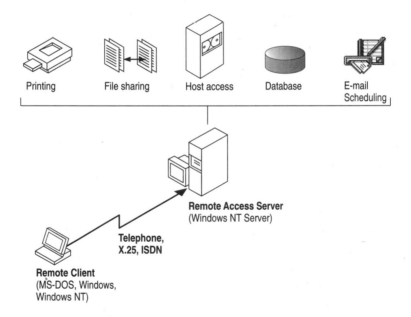

Figure 9.1   RAS Architecture

Note that the remote clients use standard tools to access resources. For example, the Windows File Manager is used to make drive connections, and Print Manager is used to connect printers. Connections made while LAN-connected via these tools are persistent, so users don't need to re-connect to network resources during their remote sessions. Since drive letters and UNC (Universal Naming Convention) names are fully supported via RAS, most commercial and custom applications work without any modification.

Connectivity is achieved in one of three ways: via a standard modem, ISDN card, or X.25. The asynchronous modem is the most popular means of connecting, with ISDN emerging as a high-speed alternative. X.25 is a standard for many companies doing business internationally.

Remote Access Versus Remote Control

In understanding the RAS architecture, it is important to make the distinction between RAS and remote control solutions, such as Cubix and pcANYWHERE. RAS is a software-based multi-protocol router; remote control solutions work by sharing screen, keyboard and mouse over the wire. In a remote control solution, users share a CPU or multiple CPU's on the server. The RAS server's CPU is dedicated to communications, not to running applications.

This architectural difference has significant implications in two areas: scalability and software applications architecture.

In the area of scalability, consider the differing approach to increasing the capacity or performance of a remote-control server. For best performance, an additional or upgraded CPU or computer would need to be purchased for every port to be added or upgraded. With RAS, additional ports can be added without upgrading the server computer. When it does require an upgrade, the RAS Server would generally get additional RAM, a less costly approach than with remote-control. With Windows NT, a single server can scale to support hundreds of remote users, using far fewer hardware resources than a remote control solution.

In software applications architecture, the RAS client normally executes applications from the remote workstation. Contrast this with the remote control client, which runs applications from the host-side CPU. The RAS arrangement is better suited to graphical, client-server—based applications, and because network traffic is reduced, the user achieves higher performance. Remote control, however, can be useful in non-client-server environments.

RAS Features in Windows NT 3.5

Microsoft's Remote Access Server first shipped with LAN Manager 2.1 in 1991. It was included with the Windows NT 3.1 operating system, and has now been significantly enhanced for Windows NT 3.5. RAS features the following capabilities:

- Multiprotocol routing via PPP support
- Internet support
- Improved integration with NetWare® networks
- Increased number of simultaneous connections
- Software data compression
- Data encryption
- Availability of the RAS APIs

Multi-protocol Routing via PPP Support

The underlying RAS architecture allows clients to run any combination of the network protocols NetBEUI, TCP/IP, or IPX during a RAS session. This means that Windows Sockets and NetWare-aware, as well as NetBIOS applications, can be run remotely. The Point-to-Point Protocol (PPP) is used as the framing mechanism on the wire. Using PPP enables a high degree of interoperability with existing remote access services.

Internet Support

RAS enables Windows NT and the next version of Windows, Windows95, to provide complete services to the Internet. A Windows NT Server 3.5-based computer can be configured as an Internet service provider, offering dial-up Internet connections to a client workstation running Windows NT 3.5 or Windows95. A computer running Windows NT Workstation 3.5 can dial into an Internet-connected computer running Windows NT Server 3.5, or to any one of a variety of industry-standard PPP or SLIP-based Internet servers.

Improved Integration with NetWare Networks

Windows NT 3.5 and RAS fully integrate into a NetWare network. The RAS clients are running IPX and/or NetBIOS, so all applications that typically work when directly connected to the network, continue to work when remotely connected. The RAS server now supports IPX routing, enabling remote clients to gain access to all NetWare resources via the RAS server.

Increased Number of Simultaneous Connections

Windows NT Server 3.5 supports up to 256 simultaneous connections. The Windows NT Workstation provides a single RAS connection, primarily for personal use or for very small networks.

Software Data Compression

Software data compression in RAS allows users to boost their effective throughput. Data is compressed by the RAS client, sent over the wire in a compressed format, and then decompressed by the server. In typical use, RAS software compression doubles effective throughput.

Data Encryption

Remote Access Service provides data encryption, in addition to password encryption, to provide privacy for sensitive data. While most RAS users do not need encryption, government agencies, law enforcement organizations, financial institutions, and others benefit from it. Microsoft RAS uses the RC4 encryption algorithm of RSA Data Security Inc.

RAS APIs

In April 1994, Microsoft published the 16-bit and 32-bit RAS APIs, which allow corporate developers and solution providers to create custom, remote-enabled applications that can establish a remote connection, use network resources, and re-connect in the event of a communications link failure. Applications developed using these tools will be compatible with Windows95, Windows NT Workstation and Server 3.5, and Windows for Workgroups 3.11.

Security

Microsoft's RAS provides security at the operating system, file system, and network layers, as well as data encryption and event auditing. Some of the security features are inherited from the Windows NT operating system, while others are specific to RAS itself. Every stage of the process—such as user authentication, data transmission, resource access, logoff and auditing—can be secured. The next section describes RAS security in detail.

Windows NT Security

Windows NT, the host for RAS, is a secure operating environment. Windows NT was designed to meet the requirements for C-2 level (U.S. Department of Defense) security, meaning that access to system resources can be discretely controlled, and all access to the system can be recorded and audited. A Windows NT Server-based computer, provided it is secured physically, can be locked-down using software. Any access to the system requires a password and leaves an audit trail.

Windows NT Server provides for enterprise-wide security using a *trusted domain, single-network logon* model. A domain is simply a collection of servers that are administered together. Trusted domains establish relationships whereby the users and groups of one domain can be granted access to resources in a trusting domain. This eliminates the need for duplicate entry of user accounts across a multi-server network. Finally, under the single-network-logon model, once a user is authenticated, the user carries access credentials. Anytime the user attempts to gain access to a resource anywhere on the network, Windows NT automatically presents the user's credentials. If trusted domains are used, the user may never have to present a password after initial logon, even though his account exists on one server in one domain only.

The single-network logon model extends to RAS users. RAS access is granted from the pool of all Windows NT user accounts. An administrator grants a single user, group of users, or all users the right to dial into the network. Then, users use their domain login to connect via RAS. Once the user has been authenticated by RAS, they can use resources throughout the domain and in any trusted domains.

Finally, Windows NT provides the Event Viewer for auditing. All system, application, and security events are recorded to a central secure database which, with proper privileges, can be viewed from anywhere on the network. Any attempts to violate system security, start or stop services without authorization, or gain access to protected resources, is recorded in the Event Log and can be viewed by the administrator.

Authentication

Authentication is an important concern for many corporations. This section answers some of the most frequently-asked questions, such as:

- How can our system insure the privacy of passwords?
- Can our system include a security mechanism in addition to that provided by RAS and Windows NT?
- Is the call-back feature supported?

Authentication Protocols

The Challenge Handshake Authentication Protocol (CHAP) is used by the Remote Access Server to negotiate the most secure form of encrypted authentication supported by both server and client. CHAP uses a challenge-response mechanism with one-way encryption on the response. CHAP allows the RAS server to negotiate downward from the most-secure to the least-secure encryption mechanism, and protects passwords transmitted in the process.

Table 9.1   Security Levels and RAS Encryption Protocols

Level of security	Type of encryption	RAS encryption protocol
High	One-way	CHAP, MD5
Medium	Two-way	SPAP
Low	Clear-text	PAP

CHAP allows different types of encryption algorithms to be used. Specifically, RAS uses DES and RSA Security Inc.'s MD5. Microsoft RAS uses DES encryption when both the client and the server are using RAS. DES encryption, the U.S. government standard, was designed to protect against password discovery and playback. Windows NT 3.5, Windows for Workgroups, and Windows95 will *always* negotiate DES-encrypted authentication when communicating with each other. When connecting to third-party remote access servers or client software, RAS can negotiate SPAP or clear-text authentication if the third party product does not support encrypted authentication.

MD5, an encryption scheme used by various PPP vendors for encrypted authentication, can be negotiated by the Microsoft RAS client when connecting to other vendors' remote access servers. MD5 is not available in the RAS server.

SPAP, the Shiva Password Authentication Protocol, is a two-way (reversible) encryption mechanism employed by Shiva. Windows NT Workstation 3.5, when connecting to a Shiva LAN Rover, uses SPAP; as does a Shiva client connecting to a Windows NT Server 3.5. This form of authentication is more secure than clear text, but less secure than CHAP.

PAP uses clear-text passwords and is the least sophisticated authentication protocol. It is typically negotiated if the remote workstation and server cannot negotiate a more secure form of validation.

The Microsoft RAS server has an option that prevents clear-text passwords from being negotiated. This option enables system administrators to enforce a high level of security.

Third-party Security Hosts

RAS supports third-party security hosts. The security host sits between the remote user and the RAS Server.

The security host generally provides an extra layer of security by requiring a hardware key of some sort in order to provide authentication. Verification that the remote user is in physical possession of the key takes place before they are given access to the RAS Server. This open architecture allows customers to choose from a variety of security hosts to augment the security in RAS.

As an additional measure of security, RAS offers call-back. Call-back security enables administrators to require remote users to dial from a specific predetermined location (e.g. telephone number at home) or to call back a user from any location, in order to use low-cost communications lines. In the case of secured call back, the user initiates a call, and connects with the RAS Server. The RAS Server then drops the call, and calls back a moment later to the pre-assigned call-back number. This security method will generally thwart most impersonators.

Network Access Restrictions

Remote access to the network under RAS is controlled by the system administrator. In addition to the tools provided with Windows NT Server (authentication, trusted domains, event auditing, C2 security design, etc.), the RAS Admin tool gives an administrator the ability to grant or revoke remote access privileges on a user-by-user basis. This means that even though RAS is running on a Windows NT Server-based computer, access to the network must be explicitly granted for each user who is to be authorized to enter the network via RAS.

This process ensures that remote access must be explicitly granted, and provides a convenient means for setting call back restrictions.

Microsoft's RAS provides an additional measure of security. The RAS Administrator provides a switch that allows access to be granted to all resources that the RAS host computer can see, or just resources local to the computer. This allows a customer to tightly control what information is available to remote users, and to limit their exposure in the event of a security breach.

Data Encryption

Data encryption protects data and ensures secure dial-up communications. This is especially important for financial institutions, law-enforcement and government agencies, and corporations that require secure data transfer. For installations where total security is required, the RAS administrator can set the RAS server to force encrypted communications. Users connecting to that server automatically encrypt all data sent.

Interoperability

Because LAN's are evolving quickly from islands of information to fully-connected networks of diverse operating systems, protocols, and file systems, Microsoft has defined interoperability as a key feature in Windows NT and RAS and has concentrated on the following areas to ensure smooth integration into the heterogeneous networks of today and tomorrow:

- Flexible hardware options
- PPP, an underlying protocol for interoperability
- A ramp to the Internet
- Seamless integration with NetWare networks
- Interoperability with other third-party remote access vendors

Flexible Hardware Options

Microsoft's Remote Access Service offers the broadest hardware support of any remote access vendor. Currently, over 1,700 computers, 300 modems, and 11 multi-port serial adapters are supported. By selecting a remote access solution with very broad hardware support, customers can gain flexibility in their system design. A complete listing of the hardware devices supported by RAS can be found in the Windows NT Hardware Compatibility List (HCL). The HCL ships with Windows NT, and can also be found on the Microsoft Download Service (206-936-MSDL) or on CompuServe (GO WINNT).

Point-to-Point Protocol: The Enabling Technology

Previous versions of RAS functioned as NetBIOS gateways. Users would make their connections using NetBEUI/ NetBIOS, and then inherit other protocols from the server. This method enabled users to share network resources in a multi-vendor LAN environment, but limited them from running applications which relied on the presence of a protocol other than NetBEUI on the client-side. The enhanced architecture is as follows:

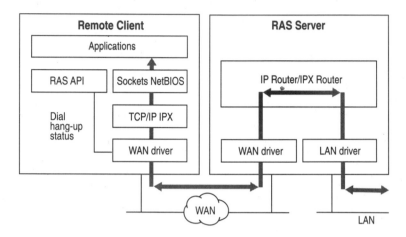

Figure 9.2   PPP Architecture

While this architecture continues to support the NetBIOS gateway, it also offers some exciting new possibilities. This architecture enables clients to load any combination of NetBEUI, IPX, and TCP/IP. Applications written to the Windows Sockets, NetBIOS, or IPX interface can now be run on a Windows NT Workstation. This architecture will be the basis for the RAS client in Windows95 as well.

Multi-protocol routing is just one of the benefits of Microsoft's move to the Point-to-Point Protocol (PPP) in RAS. The Point-to-Point Protocol is a set of industry standard protocols that enable remote access solutions to interoperate in a multi-vendor network. PPP support in Windows NT 3.5 and Windows95 means that workstations running Windows can dial into remote networks through any industry-standard PPP server. It also enables a Windows NT Server to receive calls from, and provide network access to, other vendors' remote access workstation software.

And while multi-protocol support is an important new feature of Microsoft's RAS, NetBIOS gateway support continues to be an important part of its feature set.

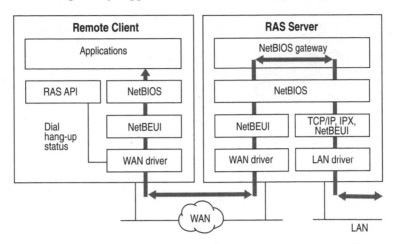

Figure 9.3   NetBIOS Gateway Architecture

An example of the NetBIOS gateway capability is remote network access for Lotus Notes users. While Lotus Notes does offer dial-up connectivity, dial up is limited to the Notes application only. RAS complements this connectivity by providing a low-cost, high-performance remote network connection for Notes® users, which not only connects Notes, but offers file and print services, and access to other network resources.

Many customers who are interested in PPP interoperability, are also concerned with SLIP. SLIP, the Serial Line Internet Protocol, is an older communications standard found in UNIX environments. SLIP does not provide automatic negotiation of network configuration; it requires user intervention. It also does not support encrypted authentication. Microsoft supports SLIP on the client side, so that the clients running Windows NT 3.5 may dial into an existing SLIP server. RAS does not provide a SLIP server in Windows NT version 3.5.

Using Terminal and Script Settings for Remote Logons

When you use RAS to connect to a remote computer, the remote computer will probably require a specific series of commands and responses to successfully log you on to the remote system. The sequence is identical each time you log on to the remote system.

If both the remote server and client are Windows NT 3.5 computers, connection and logon can be completely automated using Windows NT built-in security. If you log on to the Windows NT RAS client using a username and password that is valid on the remote network, and select the Authenticate Using Current User Name and Password check box in the Edit Phone Book Entry dialog box, Windows NT RAS will automatically connect to the remote Windows NT 3.5 RAS server.

If the remote computer you are logging on to is not a Windows NT 3.5 computer, you must configure the Security settings for each RAS entry to handle the log on requirements for the remote device you are connecting to. The remote logon will be either manual using a Terminal screen that allows you to interact with the remote computer, or you can automate the remote log on using scripts that are stored in SWITCH.INF or PAD.INF (for X.25 networks).

This section explains how to use the RAS Terminal screen and also describes how to create and use automatic scripts for logon to remote computers.

Using RAS Terminal for Remote Logons

If a remote computer you dial in to requires a log on procedure, you must configure the Security settings for that RAS entry to use a RAS Terminal log on as described in the procedure below. After RAS connects to the remote system, a character-based window will appear and display the log on sequence from the remote computer. You use this screen to interact with the remote computer for logging on. Alternatively, you can automate the manual log on through RAS Terminal as described in the next section, "Automating Remote Log Ons Using SWITCH.INF Scripts."

▶ **To configure a Windows NT 3.5 RAS entry to use Terminal after dialing**

1. In Remote Access, select the entry you want to connect to.
2. Choose the Edit button.
3. If the Security button is not visible, choose the Advanced button.
4. Choose the Security button. (In Windows NT 3.1 and Windows for Workgroups 3.11, this button is labeled Switch).
5. In the After Dialing box, select Terminal. (In Windows NT 3.1 and Windows for Workgroups 3.11, this box is labeled Post-Connect).
6. Choose the OK button until you return to the main Remote Access Screen.

After you dial and connect to this entry, the After Dial Terminal screen will appear and you will see prompts from the remote computer. You then log on to the remote computer using the After Dial Terminal dialog box. After you have completed all interaction with the remote computer, choose the Done button to close the After Dial Terminal dialog box.

Automating Remote Log Ons Using SWITCH.INF Scripts

You can use the SWITCH.INF file (or PAD.INF on X.25 networks) to automate the log on process instead of using the manual RAS Terminal describe in the previous section, "Using RAS Terminal for Remote Log Ons."

Creating Scripts for RAS

SWITCH.INF is like a set of small batch files (scripts) contained in one file. A SWITCH.INF script has four elements: a section header, commands, responses, and comments.

Section headers divide SWITCH.INF into individual scripts. A section header starts a script.

Each line in a script is a command or a response. A command comes from the local RAS client. The commands you can issue from a Windows NT computer are listed below.

A response is from the remote device or computer. To write an automatic script, you must know the required responses for a specific device. The commands and responses must be in the exact order the remote device expects them. Branching statements, such as GOTO or IF, are not supported. The required sequence of commands and responses for a specific intermediary device should be in the documentation for the device, or if you are connecting to a commercial service, from the support staff of that service.

The SWITCH.INF file can contain scripts for each intermediary devices or online service that the RAS user will call. The scripts are activated by configuring Remote Access phonebook entries as described below in the section "Activating SWITCH.INF Scripts."

Note RAS permits you to embed your username and password only in clear text in the SWITCH.INF file. The ability to use macros that obtain your username and password from your own RAS phone book file (*username*.PBK) will be included in an upcoming, interim release of Windows NT. This functionality may be available by the time you are reading this. Check the RASPHONE.HLP file on your current system for the availability of these macros and for more information about creating scripts with SWITCH.INF.

Section Headers

A section header marks the beginning of a script for a certain intermediary device and must not exceed 31 characters. The section header is enclosed in square brackets. For example:

```
[Route 66 Login]
```

Comment Lines

Comment lines must have a semicolon (;) in column one and can appear anywhere in the file. Comment lines can contain information for those who maintain the SWITCH.INF file. For example:

```
; This script was created by MariaG on September 29, 1995
```

Commands

A command comes from the local computer. A response comes from the remote device or computer.

You use the **COMMAND=** statement to send commands to the intermediary device. The **COMMAND=** statement can be used three ways, as described below:

COMMAND=
> **COMMAND=** by itself causes a 2-second delay, depending on CPU speed and whether or not caching software like SMARTDRV.DRV is running. Using **COMMAND=** as a delay is important because the intermediary device may not be able to process all commands if they are send at once.

COMMAND=*custom string*
> This sends *custom string* but will also cause a slight delay of several hundred milliseconds (depending on CPU speed and caching software installed) to give the intermediary device time to process *custom string* and prepare for the next command.

COMMAND=*custom string <cr>*
> This causes *custom string* to be sent instantaneously because of the carriage return (*<cr>*) at the end of the line.

You must consult the documentation from the remote device to determine the required strings to be send with the **COMMAND=** command.

Response Related Keywords

Each command line is followed by one or more response lines. You must consult the documentation from the remote device to determine the possible response strings.

In addition to the response strings you obtain for the remote device (or online service), response lines can contain one of the following keywords:

OK=*custom response string <macro>*
   The script continues to the next line.

CONNECT=*custom response string <macro>*
   Used at the end of a successful script.

ERROR=*custom response string <macro>*
   Causes RAS to display a generic error message.

ERROR_DIAGNOSTICS=*custom response string* **<diagnostics>**
   Causes RAS to display the specific cause for an error returned by the device. Not all devices report specific errors. Use **ERROR=** if you device does not return specific errors.

NoResponse
   Used when no response will come from the remote device.

These commands are usually combined. **CONNECT=** is usually the last line executed unless an **ERROR** line follows it and the intermediary device reports an error.

RAS on the local computer always expects a response from the remote device and will wait until a response is received unless a **NoResponse** statement follows the **COMMAND=** line. If there is no statement for a response following a **COMMAND=** line, the **COMMAND=** line will execute and stop.

Reserved Macro Words

Reserved macro keyword are enclosed in angle brackets

<cr>
   Inserts a carriage return.

<lf>
   Inserts a line feed.

<match>

Reports a match if the string enclosed in quotation marks is found in the device response. For example, <match> "Smith" matches Jane Smith and John Smith III.

<?>

Inserts a wildcard character, for example, CO<?><?>2 matches COOL2 or COAT2, but not COOL3.

<hXX> (XX are hexadecimal digits)

Allows any hexadecimal character to appear in a string including the zero byte, <h00>.

<ignore>

Ignores the rest of a response from the macro on. For example, <cr><lf>CONNECTV-<ignore> reads the following responses as the same: "crlfCONNECTV-1.1" and "crlfCONNECTV-2.3."

<diagnostics>

Passes specific error information from a device to RAS. This enables RAS to display the specific error to RAS users. Otherwise, a nonspecific error message will appear.

Activating SWITCH.INF Scripts

You can configure a RAS entry to execute a SWITCH.INF script before dialing, after dialing, or both. For example, to automate a remote log on to a remote host, you would first create the script in SWITCH.INF, and then configure the RAS entry to use the created script after dialing.

▶   **To activate a script in Windows NT 3.5**

1. In Remote Access, select the entry you want to connect to.

2. Choose the Edit button.

3. If the Security button is not visible, choose the Advanced button.

   Choose the Security button. (In Windows NT 3.1 and Windows for Workgroups 3.11, this button is labeled Switch).

   In the After Dialing box, select the name of the script. The section header in SWITCH.INF is what will appear as the name of the script. (In Windows NT 3.1 and Windows for Workgroups 3.11, this box is labeled Post-Connect).

4. Choose the OK button until you return to the main Remote Access Screen.

When you dial this entry, the selected script will execute after RAS dials and connects to the remote host.

Troubleshooting Scripts Using DEVICE.LOG

Windows NT 3.1 and 3.5 (and Windows for Workgroups 3.11) allow you to log all information passed between RAS, the modem, and the intermediate device, including errors reported by the intermediate device. This can allow you to find errors that prevent your scripts from working.

The DEVICE.LOG file is created by turning logging on in the registry. The DEVICE.LOG file is in the SYSTEM32\RAS subdirectory of your Windows NT directory.

▶ **To create DEVICE.LOG**

1. Hang up any connections, and then exit from Remote Access.

2. Start the Registry Editor by running the REGEDT32.EXE program.

3. Go to HKEY_LOCAL_MACHINE, and then access the following key:
   \SYSTEM\CurrentControlSet\Services\RasMan\Parameters

   Change the value of the Logging parameter to 1. When changed, the parameter should look like this:

   Logging:REG_DWORD:0x1

Logging begins when you restart Remote Access or start the Remote Access Server service (if your computer is receiving calls). You do not need to shutdown and restart Windows NT.

If an error is encountered during script execution, execution halts. You must determine the problem by looking in DEVICE.LOG, make the necessary corrections to the script, and then restart RAS.

To turn logging on in Windows for Workgroups 3.11, edit the SYSTEM.INI file and in the [Remote Access] section add the line LOGGING=1. The text file DEVICE.LOG will be created automatically in the Windows directory when RAS is started.

Using Scripts with Other Microsoft RAS Clients

Microsoft RAS version 1.0 does not have the capability to invoke RAS Terminal or use scripts in .INF files.

Microsoft RAS version 1.1 supports PAD.INF only. Note that the syntax used in the PAD.INF file differs slightly different from subsequent versions of Microsoft RAS.

Microsoft RAS for Windows for Workgroups version 3.11, Windows NT version 3.1 and version 3.5 support RAS Terminal and scripts in SWITCH.INF and PAD.INF.

Resource Directory

This resource directory provides contact information on many of the vendors that provide RAS-related equipment and support. It is not intended as an all-inclusive list of RAS-related products.

Digiboard
6400 Flying Cloud Drive
Eden Prairie, MN 55344
(612) 943-9020
Multi-port Serial Adapters,
ISDN Adapters

Eicon Technology Corp.
2196 - 32nd Avenue (Lachine)
Montreal, Quebec H8T 3H7
Canada
(514) 631-2592
X.25 Adapters

NetManage, Inc.
20823 Stevens Creek Blvd.
Cupertino, CA 95014
Phone: (408) 973-7171
Fax: (408) 257-6405
Terminal Emulation, File Transfer,
X Windows, E-mail, NFS, TN3270,
BIND, SNMP

Security Dynamics
One Alewife Center
Cambridge, MA 02140 USA
Phone (617) 547-7820
Fax (617) 354 8836

Advanced network security
and authorization products

Digital Pathways Inc
201 Ravendale Drive
Mountain View, CA 94043-5216
Phone (415) 964 0707
Fax (415) 961 7487
Advanced network security
and authorization products

Racal
480 Spring Park Place
Suite 900
Herndon, Virginia 22070
Phone (703) 437 9333
Fax (703) 471 0892
Advanced network security
and authorization products

SpartaCom, Inc.
10, avenue du Québec
Bât. F4
B.P. 537
F-91946 Courtaboeuf Cedex
France
Phone (33-1) 69.07.17.80
Fax (33-1) 69.29.09.19

PART III

TCP/IP

C H A P T E R   1 0

Overview of Microsoft TCP/IP for Windows NT

Transmission Control Protocol/Internet Protocol (TCP/IP) is a networking protocol that provides communication across interconnected networks made up of computers with diverse hardware architectures and various operating systems. TCP/IP can be used to communicate with Windows NT systems, with devices that use other Microsoft networking products, and with non-Microsoft systems, such as UNIX systems.

This chapter introduces Microsoft TCP/IP for Windows NT. The topics in this chapter include the following:

- Advantages of adding TCP/IP to a Windows NT configuration
- Microsoft TCP/IP core technology and third-party add-ons
- Windows NT solutions in TCP/IP internetworks

For more detailed information on TCP/IP and its integration with Microsoft Windows NT and other networking products, see Chapter 12, "Networking Concepts for TCP/IP."

Advantages of Adding TCP/IP to a Windows NT Configuration

The TCP/IP protocol family is a standard set of networking protocols, or rules, that govern how data is passed between computers on a network. TCP/IP is used to connect the Internet, the worldwide internetwork connecting over two million universities, research labs, U.S. defense installations, and corporations. These same protocols can be used in private internetworks that connect several local area networks.

Microsoft TCP/IP for Windows NT enables enterprise networking and connectivity on Windows NT computers. Adding TCP/IP to a Windows NT configuration offers the following advantages:

- A standard, routable enterprise networking protocol that is the most complete and accepted protocol available. All modern operating systems offer TCP/IP support, and most large networks rely on TCP/IP for much of their network traffic.

- A technology for connecting dissimilar systems. Many standard connectivity utilities are available to access and transfer data between dissimilar systems, including File Transfer Protocol (FTP) and Terminal Emulation Protocol (Telnet). Several of these standard utilities are included with Windows NT.

- A robust, scalable, cross-platform client-server framework. Microsoft TCP/IP supports the Windows Sockets 1.1 interface, which is ideal for developing client-server applications that can run with Windows Sockets-compliant stacks from other vendors. Many public-domain Internet tools are also written to the Windows Sockets standard. Windows Sockets applications can also take advantage of other networking protocols such as Microsoft NWLink, the Microsoft implementation of the IPX/SPX protocols used in Novell® NetWare® networks.

- The enabling technology necessary to connect Windows NT to the global Internet. TCP/IP, Point to Point Protocol (PPP), and Windows Sockets 1.1 provide the foundation needed to connect and use Internet services.

Microsoft TCP/IP Core Technology and Third-Party Add-Ons

Microsoft TCP/IP provides all the elements necessary to implement these protocols for networking. Microsoft TCP/IP includes the following:

- Core TCP/IP protocols, including the Transmission Control Protocol (TCP), Internet Protocol (IP), User Datagram Protocol (UDP), Address Resolution Protocol (ARP), and Internet Control Message Protocol (ICMP). This suite of Internet protocols provides a set of standards for how computers communicate and how networks are interconnected. Support is also provided for PPP and Serial-Line IP (SLIP), which are protocols used for dial-up access to TCP/IP networks, including the Internet.

- Support for application interfaces, including Windows Sockets 1.1 for network programming, remote procedure call (RPC) for communicating between systems, NetBIOS for establishing logical names and sessions on the network, and network dynamic data exchange (Network DDE) for sharing information embedded in documents across the network.

- Basic TCP/IP connectivity utilities, including **finger**, **ftp**, **lpr**, **rcp**, **rexec**, **rsh**, **telnet**, and **tftp**. These utilities allow Windows NT users to interact with and use resources on non-Microsoft hosts, such as UNIX workstations.

- TCP/IP diagnostic tools, including **arp**, **hostname**, **ipconfig**, **lpq**, **nbtstat**, **netstat**, **ping**, **route**, and **tracert**. These utilities can be used to detect and resolve TCP/IP networking problems.

- Services and related administrative tools, including the FTP Server service for transferring files between remote computers, Windows Internet Name Service (WINS) for dynamically registering and querying computer names on an internetwork, Dynamic Host Configuration Protocol (DHCP) service for automatically configuring TCP/IP on Windows NT computers, and TCP/IP printing for accessing printers connected to a UNIX computer or connected directly to the network via TCP/IP.

- Simple Network Management Protocol (SNMP) agent. This component allows a Windows NT computer to be administered remotely using management tools such as SunNet Manager or HP Open View. SNMP can also be used to monitor DHCP servers and to monitor and configure WINS servers.

- The client software for simple network protocols, including Character Generator, Daytime, Discard, Echo, and Quote of the Day. These protocols allow a Windows NT computer to respond to requests from other systems that support these protocols. When these protocols are installed, a sample QUOTES files is also installed in the *\systemroot*\SYSTEM32\DRIVERS\ETC directory.

- Path MTU Discovery, which provides the ability to determine the datagram size for all routers between Windows NT computers and any other systems on the WAN. Microsoft TCP/IP also supports the Internet Gateway Multicast Protocol (IGMP), which is used by new workgroup software products.

The following figure shows the elements of Microsoft TCP/IP alongside the variety of additional applications and connectivity utilities provided by Microsoft and other third-party vendors.

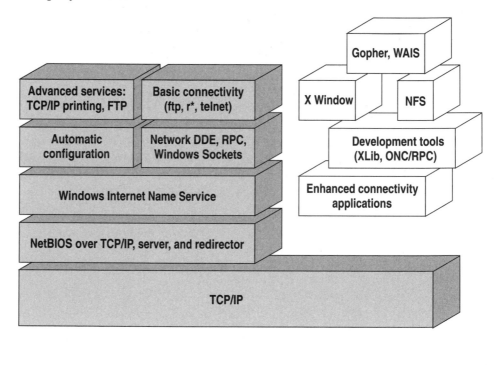

Figure 10.1   Microsoft TCP/IP Core Technology and Third-party Add-ons

TCP/IP standards are defined in *Requests for Comments* (RFCs), which are published by the Internet Engineering Task Force (IETF) and other working groups. The relevant RFCs supported in this version of Microsoft TCP/IP (and for Microsoft Remote Access Service) are described in the following table.

Table 10.1   Requests for Comments (RFCs) Supported by Microsoft TCP/IP

RFC	Title
768	User Datagram Protocol (UDP)
783	Trivial File Transfer Protocol (TFTP)
791	Internet Protocol (IP)
792	Internet Control Message Protocol (ICMP)
793	Transmission Control Protocol (TCP)
826	Address Resolution Protocol (ARP)
854	Telnet Protocol (TELNET)
862	Echo Protocol (ECHO)
863	Discard Protocol (DISCARD)
864	Character Generator Protocol (CHARGEN)
865	Quote of the Day Protocol (QUOTE)
867	Daytime Protocol (DAYTIME)
894	IP over Ethernet
919, 922	IP Broadcast Datagrams (broadcasting with subnets)
959	File Transfer Protocol (FTP)
1001, 1002	NetBIOS Service Protocols
1034, 1035	Domain Name System (DOMAIN)
1042	IP over Token Ring
1055	Transmission of IP over Serial Lines (IP-SLIP)
1112	Internet Gateway Multicast Protocol (IGMP)
1122, 1123	Host Requirements (communications and applications)
1134	Point to Point Protocol (PPP)
1144	Compressing TCP/IP Headers for Low-Speed Serial Links
1157	Simple Network Management Protocol (SNMP)

Table 10.1   Key Requests for Comments (RFCs) Supported by Microsoft TCP/IP
(continued)

RFC	Title
1179	Line Printer Daemon Protocol
1188	IP over FDDI
1191	Path MTU Discovery
1201	IP over ARCNET
1231	IEEE 802.5 Token Ring MIB (MIB-II)
1332	PPP Internet Protocol Control Protocol (IPCP)
1334	PPP Authentication Protocols
1533	DHCP Options and BOOTP Vendor Extensions
1534	Interoperation Between DHCP and BOOTP
1541	Dynamic Host Configuration Protocol (DHCP)
1542	Clarifications and Extensions for the Bootstrap Protocol
1547	Requirements for Point to Point Protocol (PPP)
1548	Point to Point Protocol (PPP)
1549	PPP in High-level Data Link Control (HDLC) Framing
1552	PPP Internetwork Packet Exchange Control Protocol (IPXCP)
1553	IPX Header Compression
1570	Link Control Protocol (LCP) Extensions
Draft RFCs	NetBIOS Frame Control Protocol (NBFCP); PPP over ISDN; PPP over X.25; Compression Control Protocol

All RFCs can be found on the Internet via ds.internic.net.

In this version of Windows NT, Microsoft TCP/IP does not include a complete suite of TCP/IP connectivity utilities, Network File System (NFS) support, or some TCP/IP server services (daemons) such as **routed** and **telnetd**. Many such applications and utilities that are available in the public domain or from third-party vendors are compatible with Microsoft TCP/IP.

Tip For Windows for Workgroups computers and MS-DOS–based computers on a Microsoft network, you can install the new version of Microsoft TCP/IP—32 for Windows for Workgroups and the Microsoft Network Client version 2.0 for MS-DOS from the Windows NT Server 3.5 compact disc. This software includes the DHCP and WINS clients and other elements of the new Microsoft TCP/IP software. For information about installing these clients, see Chapter 9, "Network Client Administrator," in the *Windows NT Server Installation Guide*.

Windows NT Solutions in TCP/IP Internetworks

When TCP/IP is used as a transport protocol with Windows NT, Windows NT computers can communicate with other kinds of systems without additional networking software. Microsoft TCP/IP in combination with other parts of Windows NT provides a scalable solution for enterprise networks that include a mix of system types and software on many platforms.

This section summarizes how TCP/IP works with Windows NT to provide enterprise networking solutions. For information about how the elements discussed in this section fit within the networking architecture, see "TCP/IP and Windows NT Networking" in Chapter 12, "Networking Concepts for TCP/IP."

Using TCP/IP for Scalability in Windows Networks

TCP/IP delivers a scalable internetworking technology widely supported by hardware and software vendors.

When TCP/IP is used as the enterprise-networking protocol, the Windows-based networking solutions from Microsoft can be used on an existing internetwork to provide client and server support for TCP/IP and connectivity utilities. These solutions include:

- Microsoft Windows NT Workstation 3.5, with enhancements to support wide area networks (WAN), TCP/IP printing, extended LMHOSTS file, Windows Sockets 1.1, FTP Server service software, and DHCP and WINS client software.

- Microsoft Windows NT Server 3.5, with the same enhancements as Windows NT, plus DHCP server and WINS server software to support the implementation of these new protocols.

- Microsoft TCP/IP-32 for Windows for Workgroups 3.11, with Windows Sockets support, can be used to provide access for Windows for Workgroups computers to Windows NT, LAN Manager, and other TCP/IP systems. Microsoft TCP/IP-32 includes DHCP and WINS client software.

- Microsoft LAN Manager, including both client and server support for Windows Sockets, and MS-DOS–based connectivity utilities. The Microsoft Network Client 2.0 software on the Windows NT Server compact disc includes new Microsoft TCP/IP support with DHCP and WINS clients.

The current version of TCP/IP for Windows NT also supports IP routing in systems with multiple network adapters attached to separate physical networks (multihomed systems).

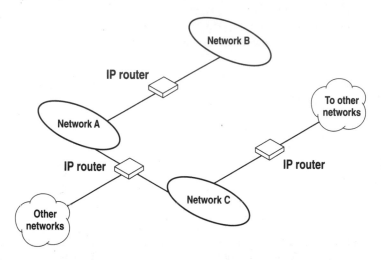

Figure 10.2   TCP/IP for Windows NT Supports IP Routing for Multihomed Systems

Using TCP/IP for Connectivity to the Internet

Microsoft TCP/IP provides Windows-based networking with a set of internetworking protocols based on open standards.

Microsoft TCP/IP for Windows NT includes many common connectivity applications such as **ftp**, **rsh**, and **telnet** that support file transfer, remote process execution, and terminal emulation for communication on the Internet and between non-Microsoft network systems.

TCP/IP applications created by researchers and other users, such as Gopher and NCSA Mosaic, are in the public domain or are available through other vendors as both 16-bit and 32-bit Windows-based applications. Any of these applications that follow the Windows Sockets 1.1 standard are compatible with Windows NT. Such applications allow a Windows NT computer to act as a powerful Internet client using the extensive internetworking components with public-domain viewers and applications to access Internet resources.

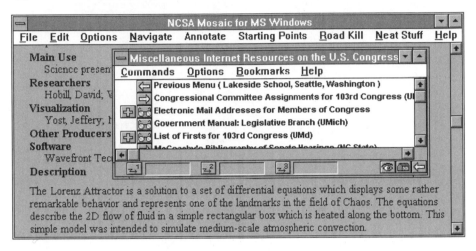

Tip   Public-domain Windows-based utilities such as LPR and Gopher can be obtained on the Internet via ftp.cica.indiana.edu in the /pub/win3/nt or /pub/win3/winsock directory, or via the same directories on ftp.cdrom.com.

TCP/IP for Heterogeneous Networking

Because most modern operating systems (in addition to Windows NT) support TCP/IP protocols, an internetwork with mixed system types can share information using simple networking applications and utilities. With TCP/IP as a connectivity protocol, Windows NT can communicate with many non-Microsoft systems, including:

- Internet hosts
- Apple® Macintosh® systems
- IBM mainframes
- UNIX systems
- Open VMS™ systems
- Printers with network adapters connected directly to the network

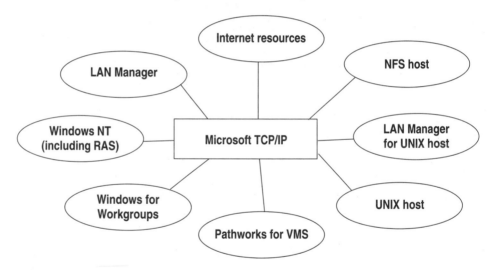

Figure 10.3   Microsoft TCP/IP Connectivity

Microsoft TCP/IP provides a framework for interoperable heterogeneous networking. The modular architecture of Windows NT networking with its transport-independent services contributes to the strength of this framework. For example, Windows NT supports these transport protocols, among many others:

- IPX/SPX for use in NetWare environments, using the Microsoft NWLink transport. Besides providing interoperability with NetWare networks, IPX/SPX is a fast LAN transport for Windows-based networking as well.
- TCP/IP for internetworks based on IP technologies. TCP/IP is the preferred transport for internetworks and provides interoperability with UNIX and other TCP/IP-based networks.

- NetBEUI as the protocol for local area networking on smaller networks and compatibility with existing LAN Manager and IBM LAN Server networks.

- AppleTalk for connecting to and sharing resources with Macintosh systems.

Other transport protocols provided by third-party vendors, such as DECnet and OSI, can also be used by Windows NT networking services.

Windows NT provides standard network programming interfaces through the Windows Sockets, RPC, and NetBIOS interfaces. Developers can take advantage of this heterogeneous client-server platform to create custom applications that will run on any system in the enterprise. An example of such a service is Microsoft SQL Server, which uses Windows Sockets 1.1 to provide access to NetWare, MS-DOS–based, Windows NT, and UNIX clients.

Using TCP/IP with Third-Party Software

TCP/IP is a common denominator for heterogeneous networking, and Windows Sockets is a standard used by application developers. Together they provide a framework for cross-platform client-server development. TCP/IP-aware applications from vendors that comply with the Windows Sockets standards can run over virtually any TCP/IP implementation.

The Windows Sockets standard ensures compatibility with Windows-based TCP/IP utilities developed by more than 30 vendors. This includes third-party applications for the X Window System, sophisticated terminal emulation software, NFS, electronic mail packages, and more. Because Windows NT offers compatibility with 16-bit Windows Sockets, applications created for Windows 3.x Windows Sockets run over Windows NT without modification or recompilation.

For example, third-party applications for X Window provide strong connectivity solutions by means of X Window servers, database servers, and terminal emulation. With such applications, a Windows NT computer can work as an X Window server platform while retaining compatibility with applications created for Windows NT, Windows 3.1, and MS-DOS on the same system. Other third-party software includes X Window client libraries for Windows NT, which allow developers to write X Window client applications on Windows NT that can be run and displayed remotely on X Window server systems.

The Windows Sockets API is a networking API used by programmers creating applications for both the Microsoft Windows NT and Windows operating systems. Windows Sockets is an open standard that is part of the Microsoft Windows Open System Architecture (WOSA) initiative. It is a public specification based on Berkeley UNIX sockets, which means that UNIX applications can be quickly ported to Microsoft Windows and Windows NT. Windows Sockets provides a single standard programming interface supported by all the major vendors implementing TCP/IP for Windows systems.

The Windows NT TCP/IP utilities use Windows Sockets, as do 32-bit TCP/IP applications developed by third parties. Windows NT also uses the Windows Sockets interface to support Services for Macintosh and IPX/SPX in NWLink. Under Windows NT, 16-bit Windows-based applications created under the Windows Sockets standard will run without modification or recompilation. Most TCP/IP users will use programs that comply with the Windows Sockets standard, such as **ftp** or **telnet** or third-party applications.

The Windows Sockets standard allows a developer to create an application with a single common interface and a single executable that can run over many of the TCP/IP implementations provided by vendors. The goals for Windows Sockets are the following:

- Provide a familiar networking API to programmers using Windows NT, Windows for Workgroups, or UNIX

- Offer binary compatibility between vendors for heterogeneous Windows-based TCP/IP stacks and utilities

- Support both connection-oriented and connectionless protocols

Typical Windows Sockets applications include graphic connectivity utilities, terminal emulation software, Simple Mail Transfer Protocol (SMTP) and electronic mail clients, network printing utilities, SQL client applications, and corporate client-server applications.

If you are interested in developing a Windows Sockets application, specifications for Windows Sockets are available on the Internet from ftp.microsoft.com, on CompuServe® in the MSL library, and in the Microsoft Win32 Software Developers Kit.

▶ **To get a copy of the Windows Sockets specification via anonymous FTP**

1. Make sure you have write permission in your current working directory.

2. At the command prompt, start **ftp**, and then connect to **ftp.microsoft.com** (or **198.105.232.1**).

3. Log on as **anonymous**.

4. Type your electronic mail address for the *password*.

5. Type **cd \advsys\winsock\spec11**, and then press ENTER.

6. Use the **dir** command to see the list of available file types. If you want binary data such as in the Microsoft Word version, type **bin**, and then press ENTER.

7. Determine the file with the format you want [for example, ASCII (.TXT), PostScript® (.PS), or Microsoft Word (.DOC)], and then type **get winsock.***ext* where *ext* is the format that you want, such as **winsock.doc** for the Microsoft Word version.

▶ **To get a copy of the Windows Sockets specification from CompuServe**

1. At the command prompt, type **go msl**, and then press ENTER.

2. Browse using the keywords **windows sockets**.

3. Choose the file with the format you want [ASCII (.TXT), PostScript (.PS), or Microsoft Word for Windows (.DOC)], and then type **get winsock**.*ext.*

There is also an electronic mailing list designed for discussion of Windows Sockets programming.

▶ **To subscribe to the Windows Sockets mailing list**

• Send electronic mail to listserv@sunsite.unc.edu with a message body that contains **subscribe winsock** *user's-email-address.*

   You can use the same procedure to subscribe to two mailing lists called **winsock-hackers** and **winsock-users**.

C H A P T E R   1 1

Installing and Configuring Microsoft TCP/IP and SNMP

This chapter explains how to install Microsoft TCP/IP and the SNMP service for Windows NT and how to configure the protocols on your computer.

The TCP/IP protocol family can be installed as part of Custom Setup when you install Windows NT, following the steps described in this chapter. Also, if you upgrade to a new version of Windows NT, Setup automatically installs the new TCP/IP protocol and preserves your previous TCP/IP settings. This chapter assumes that Windows NT has been successfully installed on your computer but TCP/IP has not been installed.

The following topics appear in this chapter:

- Before installing Microsoft TCP/IP
- Installing TCP/IP
- Configuring TCP/IP
- Configuring TCP/IP to use DNS
- Configuring advanced TCP/IP options
- Configuring SNMP
- Removing TCP/IP components
- Configuring Remote Access Service (RAS) for use with TCP/IP

You must be logged on as a member of the Administrators group to install and configure all elements of TCP/IP.

Before Installing Microsoft TCP/IP

Important The values that you use for manually configuring TCP/IP and SNMP must be supplied by the network administrator.

Check with your network administrator to find out the following information before you install Microsoft TCP/IP on a Windows NT computer:

- Whether you can use Dynamic Host Configuration Protocol (DHCP) to configure TCP/IP. You can choose this option if a DHCP server is installed on your internetwork. You cannot choose this option if this computer will be a DHCP server. For information, see "Using Dynamic Host Configuration Protocol" later in this chapter.

- Whether this computer will be a DHCP server. This option is available only for Windows NT Server. For information, see Chapter 13, "Installing and Configuring DHCP Servers."

- Whether this computer will be a Windows Internet Name Service (WINS) server. This option is available only for Windows NT Server. For information, see Chapter 14, "Installing and Configuring WINS Servers."

- Whether this computer will be a WINS proxy agent. For information, see "Windows Internet Name Service and Broadcast Name Resolution" in Chapter 12, "Networking Concepts for TCP/IP."

If you cannot use DHCP for automatic configuration, you need to obtain the following values from the network administrator so you can configure TCP/IP manually:

- The IP address and subnet mask for each network adapter card installed on the computer. For information, see "IP Addressing" in Chapter 12, "Networking Concepts for TCP/IP."

- The IP address for the default local gateways (IP routers).

- Whether your computer will use Domain Name System (DNS) and, if so, the IP addresses and DNS domain name of the DNS servers on the internetwork. For information, see "Domain Name System Addressing" in Chapter 12 "Networking Concepts for TCP/IP."

- The IP addresses for WINS servers, if WINS servers are available on your network.

You need to know the following information before you install the Simple Network Management Protocol (SNMP) service on your computer, as described in "Configuring SNMP" later in this chapter:

- Community names in your network
- Trap destination for each community
- IP addresses or computer names for SNMP management hosts

Although the Windows NT SNMP management agent supports management consoles over both IPX and UDP protocols, SNMP must be installed in conjunction with the other TCP/IP services. Once SNMP is installed, no additional configuration is needed to manage over IPX. If IPX is installed, SNMP automatically runs with it.

Installing TCP/IP

You must be logged on as a member of the Administrators group for the local computer to install and configure TCP/IP.

▶ **To install Microsoft TCP/IP on a Windows NT computer**

1. Double-click the Network icon in Control Panel to display the Network Settings dialog box.

2. Choose the Add Software button to display the Add Network Software dialog box.

3. Select TCP/IP Protocol And Related Components from the Network Software box, and then choose the Continue button.

4. In the Windows NT TCP/IP Installation Options dialog box, select the options for the TCP/IP components you want to install, as described in the table that follows this procedure. If any TCP/IP elements have been installed previously, they are dimmed and not available. When you have selected the options you want, choose the Continue button.

   While you are installing or configuring TCP/IP, you can read the hint bar at the bottom of each TCP/IP dialog box for information about a selected item, or choose the Help button to get detailed online information.

   Windows NT Setup displays a message prompting for the full path to the Windows NT distribution files.

5. In the Windows NT Setup dialog box, enter the full path to the Windows NT distribution files, and then choose the Continue button.

    You can specify a drive letter for floppy disks, a CD-ROM drive, or a shared network directory, or you can specify the Universal Naming Convention (UNC) path name for a network resource, such as \\NTSETUP\MASTER.

    All necessary files are copied to your hard disk.

    Note If you are installing from floppy disks, Windows NT Setup might request disks more than once. This behavior is normal and not an error condition.

    ---

6. If you selected the options for installing the SNMP and FTP Server services, you are automatically requested to configure these services.

    Follow the directions provided in the online Help for these dialog boxes. For additional details, see "Configuring SNMP" later in this chapter, and see also Chapter 16, "Using the Microsoft FTP Server Service."

7. In the Network Settings dialog box, choose the OK button.

    If you selected the Enable Automatic DHCP Configuration option and a DHCP server is available on your network, all configuration settings for TCP/IP are completed automatically, as described in "Using Dynamic Host Configuration Protocol" later in this chapter.

    If you did not check the Enable Automatic DHCP Configuration option, continue with the configuration procedures described in "Configuring TCP/IP Manually" later in this chapter. TCP/IP must be configured in order to operate.

    If you checked the DHCP Server Service or WINS Server Service options, you must complete the configuration steps described in Chapter 13, "Installing and Configuring DHCP Servers," and Chapter 14, "Installing and Configuring WINS Servers."

Table 11.1   Windows NT TCP/IP Installation Options

Option	Usage
TCP/IP Internetworking	Includes the TCP/IP protocol, NetBIOS over TCP/IP and Windows Sockets interfaces, and the TCP/IP diagnostic utilities. These elements are installed automatically.
Connectivity Utilities	Installs the TCP/IP utilities. Select this option to install the connectivity utilities described in Appendix A, "TCP/IP Utilities Reference."
SNMP Service	Installs the SNMP service. Select this option to allow this computer to be administered remotely using management tools such as Sun Net Manager or HP Open View. This option also allows you to monitor statistics for the TCP/IP services and WINS servers using Performance Monitor, as described in Chapter 17, "Using Performance Monitor with TCP/IP Services."
TCP/IP Network Printing Support	Enables this computer to print directly over the network using TCP/IP. Select this option if you want to print to UNIX print queues or TCP/IP printers that are connected directly to the network, as described in Chapter 18, "Internetwork Printing with TCP/IP."
	This option must be installed if you want to use the **Lpdsvr** service so that UNIX computers can print to Windows NT printers.
FTP Server Service	Enables files on this computer to be shared over the network with remote computers that support FTP and TCP/IP (especially non-Microsoft network computers). Select this option if you want to use TCP/IP to share files with other computers, as described in Chapter 16, "Using the Microsoft FTP Server Service."
Simple TCP/IP Services	Provides the client software for the Character Generator, Daytime, Discard, Echo, and Quote of the Day services. Select this option to allow this computer to respond to requests from other systems that support these protocols.

Table 11.1   Windows NT TCP/IP Installation Options *(continued)*

Option	Usage
DHCP Server Service	Installs the server software to support automatic configuration and addressing for computers using TCP/IP on your internetwork. This option is available only for Windows NT Server. Select this option if this computer is to be a DHCP Server, as described in Chapter 13, "Installing and Configuring DHCP Servers."
	If you select this option, you must manually configure the IP address, subnet mask, and default gateway for this computer.
WINS Server Service	Installs the server software to support WINS, a dynamic name resolution service for computers on a Windows internetwork. This option is available only for Windows NT Server. Select this option if this computer is to be installed as a primary or secondary WINS server, as described in Chapter 14, "Installing and Configuring WINS Servers."
	Do not select this option if this computer will be a WINS proxy agent.
Enable Automatic DHCP Configuration	Turns on automatic configuration of TCP/IP parameters for this computer. Select this option if there is a DHCP server on your internetwork to support dynamic host configuration. This option is the preferred method for configuring TCP/IP on most Windows NT computers.
	This option is not available if the DHCP Server Service or WINS Server Service option is selected.

If you have trouble installing Microsoft TCP/IP on your computer, follow the suggestions in the error messages displayed on the screen. You can also use diagnostic utilities such as **ping** to isolate network hardware problems and incompatible configurations. For information, see Chapter 19, "Troubleshooting TCP/IP."

After TCP/IP is installed, the *systemroot*\SYSTEM32\DRIVERS\ETC directory contains several files, including default HOSTS, NETWORKS, PROTOCOLS, QUOTES, and SERVICES files plus a sample LMHOSTS.SAM file that describes the format for this file.

Configuring TCP/IP

For TCP/IP to work on your computer, it must be configured with the IP addresses, subnet mask, and default gateway for each network adapter on the computer. Microsoft TCP/IP can be configured using two different methods:

- If there is a DHCP server on your internetwork, it can automatically configure TCP/IP for your computer using DHCP.

- If there is no DHCP server, or if you are configuring a Windows NT Server computer to be a DHCP server, you must manually configure all TCP/IP settings.

These configuration methods are described in the following sections.

Using DHCP

The best method for ensuring easy and accurate installation of TCP/IP is to use automatic DHCP configuration, which uses DHCP to configure your local computer with the correct IP address, subnet mask, and default gateway.

You can take advantage of this method for configuring TCP/IP if there is a DHCP server installed on your network. The network administrator can tell you if this option is available. You cannot use DHCP configuration for a server that you are installing as a DHCP server or a WINS server. You must configure TCP/IP settings manually for DHCP servers, as described in "Configuring TCP/IP Manually" later in this chapter.

▶ **To configure TCP/IP using DHCP**

1. Make sure the Enable Automatic DHCP Configuration option is checked in either the Windows NT TCP/IP Installation Options dialog box or the TCP/IP Configuration dialog box.

2. When you restart the computer after completing TCP/IP installation, the DHCP server automatically provides the correct configuration information for your computer.

If you subsequently attempt to configure TCP/IP in the Network Settings dialog box, the system warns you that any manual settings will override the automatic settings provided by DHCP. As a general rule, you should not change the automatic settings unless you specifically want to override a setting provided by DHCP. For detailed information about DHCP, see "Dynamic Host Configuration Protocol" in Chapter 12, "Networking Concepts for TCP/IP."

Configuring TCP/IP Manually

After the Microsoft TCP/IP protocol software is installed on your computer, you must manually provide valid addressing information if you are installing TCP/IP on a DHCP server or a WINS Server, or if you cannot use automatic DHCP configuration.

For a WINS server computer that has more than one network adapter card, WINS always binds to the first adapter in the list of adapters bound by TCP/IP. Make sure that this adapter address is not set to 0, and that the binding order of IP addresses is not disturbed.

You must be logged on as a member of the Administrators group for the local computer to configure TCP/IP.

Caution Be sure to use the values for IP addresses and subnet masks that are supplied by your network administrator to avoid duplicate addresses. If duplicate addresses do occur, this can cause some computers on the network to function unpredictably. For more information, see "IP Addressing" in Chapter 12, "Networking Concepts for TCP/IP."

▶ **To manually configure the TCP/IP protocol**

1. Complete one of the following tasks:

   If you are installing TCP/IP, perform the following steps.

   - Complete all options in the Windows NT TCP/IP Installation Options dialog box, and then choose OK to display the Network Settings dialog box.

   - Choose the OK button to display the Microsoft TCP/IP Configuration dialog box.

   –Or–

   If you are reconfiguring TCP/IP, perform the following steps.

   - Double-click the Network option in Control Panel to display the Network Settings dialog box.

- In the Installed Network Software box, select TCP/IP Protocol, and then choose the Configure button to display the TCP/IP Configuration dialog box.

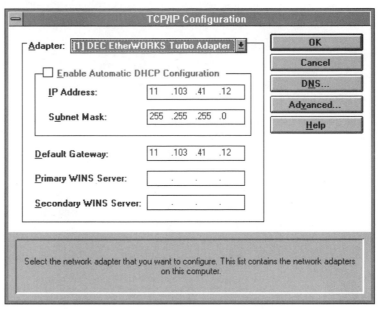

2. In the Adapter box, select the network adapter for which you want to set IP addresses.

   The Adapter list contains all network adapters to which IP is bound on this computer. This list includes all adapters installed on this computer.

   You must set specific IP addressing information for each bound adapter with correct values provided by the network administrator. The bindings for a network adapter determine how network protocols and other layers of network software work together.

3. For each bound network adapter, type values in the IP Address and Subnet Mask boxes.

   - The value in the IP Address box identifies the IP address for your local computer or, if more than one network card is installed in the computer, for the network adapter card selected in the Adapter box.

- The value in the Subnet Mask box identifies the network membership for the selected network adapter and its host ID. This allows the computer to separate the IP address into host and network IDs. The subnet mask defaults to an appropriate value, as shown in the following table:

Table 11.2   Subnet Mask Defaults

Address class	Range of first octet in IP address	Subnet mask
Class A	1–126	255.0.0.0
Class B	128–191	255.255.0.0
Class C	192–223	255.255.255.0

4. For each network adapter on the computer, type the correct IP address value in the Default Gateway box, as provided by the network administrator.

   This value specifies the IP address of the default gateway (or IP router) used to forward packets to other networks or subnets. This value should be the IP address of your local gateway.

   This parameter is required only for systems on internetworks. If this parameter is not provided, IP functionality is limited to the local subnet unless a route is specified with the TCP/IP **route** utility, as described in Appendix A, "TCP/IP Utilities Reference."

   If your computer has multiple network cards, additional default gateways can be added using the Advanced Microsoft TCP/IP Configuration dialog box, as described later in this chapter.

5. If there are WINS servers installed on your network and you want to use WINS in combination with broadcast name queries to resolve computer names, type IP addresses in the boxes for the primary and, optionally, the secondary WINS servers.

   The network administrator should provide the correct values for these parameters. These are global values for the computer, not just individual adapters.

   If an address for a WINS server is not specified, this computer uses name query broadcasts (the b-node mode for NetBIOS over TCP/IP) plus the local LMHOSTS file to resolve computer names to IP addresses. Broadcast resolution is limited to the local network.

Note   WINS name resolution is enabled and configured automatically for a computer that is configured with DHCP.

On a WINS server, NetBIOS over TCP/IP (NETBT.SYS) uses WINS on the local computer as the primary name server, regardless of how name resolution might be configured. Also, NetBIOS over TCP/IP binds to the first IP address on a network adapter and ignores any additional addresses.

For overview information about name resolution options, see "Name Resolution for Windows Networking" in Chapter 12 "Networking Concepts for TCP/IP." For detailed information about installing and configuring WINS servers, see Chapter 14, "Installing and Configuring WINS Servers."

6. If you want to configure the advanced TCP/IP options for multiple gateways and other items, choose the Advanced button, and then continue with the configuration procedure, as described in "Configuring Advanced TCP/IP Options" later in this chapter.

7. If you want to use DNS for host name resolution, choose the DNS button, and then continue with the configuration procedure, as described in the next section.

8. If you do not want to configure DNS or advanced options, or if you have completed the other configuration procedures, choose the OK button. When the Network Settings dialog box is displayed again, choose the OK button.

   Microsoft TCP/IP has been configured. If you are installing TCP/IP for the first time, you must restart the computer for the configuration to take effect. If you are changing your existing configuration, you do not have to restart your computer.

After TCP/IP is installed, the *systemroot*\SYSTEM32\DRIVERS\ETC directory contains a default HOSTS file and a sample LMHOSTS.SAM file. The network administrator might require that replacement HOSTS and LMHOSTS files be used instead of these default files.

Configuring TCP/IP to Use DNS

Although TCP/IP uses IP addresses to identify and reach computers, users typically prefer to use computer names. DNS is a naming service generally used in the UNIX networking community to provide standard naming conventions for IP workstations. Windows Sockets applications and TCP/IP utilities, such as **ftp** and **telnet**, can also use DNS in addition to the HOSTS file to find systems when connecting to foreign hosts or systems on your network.

Contact the network administrator to find out whether you should configure your computer to use DNS. Usually, you can use DNS if you are using TCP/IP to communicate over the Internet or if your private internetwork uses DNS to distribute host information. For information, see "Domain Name System Addressing" in Chapter 12, "Networking Concepts for TCP/IP."

Microsoft TCP/IP includes DNS client software for resolving Internet or UNIX system names. Microsoft Windows networking provides dynamic name resolution for NetBIOS computer names via WINS servers and NetBIOS over TCP/IP.

DNS configuration is global for all network adapters installed on a computer.

▶ **To configure TCP/IP DNS connectivity**

1. Double-click the Network option in Control Panel to display the Network Settings dialog box.

2. In the Installed Network Software box, select TCP/IP Protocol, and then choose the Configure button to display the TCP/IP Configuration dialog box.

3. Choose the DNS button to display the DNS Configuration dialog box.

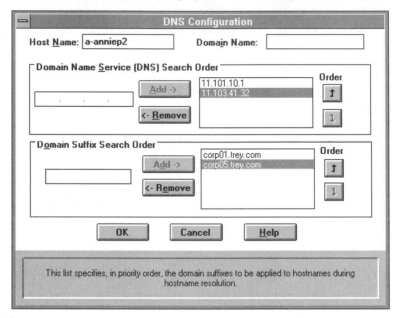

Names are displayed in the Host Name box and Domain Name box.

4. Complete one or both of the following optional tasks:

- Type a new name in the Host Name box (usually your computer name).

  The host name can be any combination of A–Z letters, 0–9 numerals, and the hyphen (-) character.

  Note Some characters that can be used in Windows NT computer names, particularly the underscore, cannot be used in host names.

  By default, this value is the Windows NT computer name, but the network administrator can assign another host name without affecting the computer name. The host name is used to identify the local computer by name for authentication by some utilities. Other TCP/IP-based utilities, such as **rexec**, can use this value to learn the name of the local computer. Host names are stored on DNS servers in a table that maps names to IP addresses for use by DNS.

- Type a new name in the Domain Name box.

The DNS Domain Name can be any combination of A–Z letters, 0–9 numerals, and the hyphen (-) plus the period (.) character used as a separator.

The DNS Domain Name is usually an organization name followed by a period and an extension that indicates the type of organization, such as microsoft.com. The DNS Domain Name is used with the host name to create a fully qualified domain name (FQDN) for the computer. The FQDN is the host name followed by a period (.) followed by the domain name. For example, this could be **corp01.research.trey.com**, where **corp01** is the host name and **research.trey.com** is the domain name. During DNS queries, the local domain name is appended to short names.

Note A DNS domain is not the same as a Windows NT or LAN Manager domain.

---

5. In the Domain Name System (DNS) Search Order box, type the IP address of the DNS server that will provide name resolution, and then choose the Add button to move the IP address to the list on the right.

The network administrator should provide the correct values for this parameter.

You can add up to three IP addresses for DNS servers. The servers running DNS will be queried in the order listed. To change the order of the IP addresses, select an IP address to move, and then use the up- and down-arrow buttons. To remove an IP address, select the IP address, and then choose the Remove button.

6. In the Domain Suffix Search Order box, type the domain suffixes to add to your domain suffix search list, and then choose the Add button.

This list specifies the DNS domain suffixes to be appended to host names during name resolution. You can add up to six domain suffixes. To change the search order of the domain suffixes, select a domain name to move, and then use the up- and down-arrow buttons. To remove a domain name, select the domain name, and then choose the Remove button.

7. When you are done setting DNS options, choose the OK button.

8. When the TCP/IP Configuration dialog box reappears, choose the OK button. When the Network Settings dialog box reappears, choose the OK button.

The settings take effect after you restart the computer.

Configuring Advanced TCP/IP Options

If your computer has multiple network adapters connected to different networks using TCP/IP, you can choose the Advanced button in the TCP/IP Configuration dialog box to configure options for the adapters or to configure alternate default gateways.

▶ **To configure or reconfigure advanced TCP/IP options**

1. Double-click the Network option in Control Panel to display the Network Settings dialog box.

2. In the Installed Network Software box, select TCP/IP Protocol, and then choose the Configure button to display the TCP/IP Configuration dialog box.

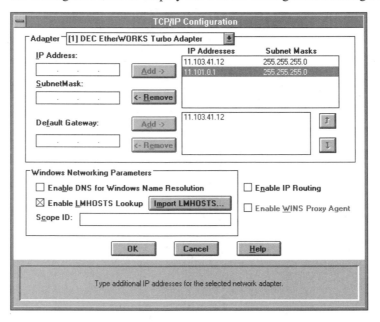

3. Choose the Advanced button to display the Advanced Microsoft TCP/IP Configuration dialog box.

4. In the Adapter box, select the network adapter for which you want to specify advanced configuration values.

   The IP address and default gateway settings in this dialog box are defined only for the selected network adapter.

5. In the IP Address and SubnetMask boxes, type an additional IP address and subnet mask for the selected adapter, and then choose the Add button to move the IP address to the list on the right.

   The network administrator should provide the correct values for this parameter.

   Optionally, if your network card uses multiple IP addresses, repeat this process for each additional IP address. You can specify up to five additional IP addresses and subnet masks for identifying the selected network adapter. This can be useful for a computer connected to one physical network that contains multiple logical IP networks.

6. In the Default Gateway box, type the IP address for an additional gateway that the selected adapter can use, and then choose the Add button to move the IP address to the list on the right.

   Repeat this process for each additional gateway. The network administrator should provide the correct values for this parameter.

   This list specifies up to five additional default gateways for the selected network adapter.

   To change the priority order for the gateways, select an address to move and use the up- or down-arrow buttons. To remove a gateway, select it, and then choose the Remove button.

7. If you want to use DNS for DNS name resolution on Windows networks, select the Enable DNS For Windows Name Resolution option.

   If this option is selected, the system finds the DNS server by using the IP address specified in the DNS Configuration dialog box, as described earlier in this chapter. Selecting this option enables DNS name resolution for use by Windows networking applications.

8. If you want to use the LMHOSTS file for NetBIOS name resolution on Windows networks, select the Enable LMHOSTS Lookup option.

   If you already have a configured LMHOSTS file, choose the Import LMHOSTS button and specify the directory path for the LMHOSTS file you want to use. By default, Windows NT uses the LMHOSTS file found in *systemroot*\SYSTEM32\DRIVERS\ETC.

   For any method of name resolution used in a Windows NT network, the LMHOSTS file is consulted last after querying WINS or using broadcasts, but before DNS is consulted.

9. In the Scope ID box, type the computer's scope identifier, if required on an internetwork that uses NetBIOS over TCP/IP.

   To communicate with each other, all computers on a TCP/IP internetwork must have the same scope ID. Usually, this value is left blank. A scope ID might be assigned to a group of computers that will communicate only with each other and no other systems. Such computers can find each other if their scope IDs are identical. Scope IDs are used only for communication based on NetBIOS over TCP/IP.

   A computer can have only one scope ID, even if it has more than one adapter card with access to more than one network. If such a multihomed computer is a DHCP client, with DHCP servers on each network, the scope ID of the two networks should be identical. If they are not identical, the last adapter card to be configured will write its scope ID to the Registry, which could result in unexpected behavior and a loss of connectivity to one of the networks. It is best in this case to set the scope ID manually. Any manually configured value overrides values provided by the DHCP server.

   The network administrator should provide the correct value, if required.

10. To turn on static IP routing, check the Enable IP Routing option.

    This option allows this computer to participate with other static routers on a network. You should check this option if you have two or more network cards and your network uses static routing, which also requires the addition of static routing tables. For information about creating static routing tables, see the **route** utility in Appendix A, "TCP/IP Utilities Reference."

    This option is not available if your computer has only one network adapter and one IP address. Also, this option does not support routers running the Routing Information Protocol (RIP).

11. If you want this computer to be used to resolve names based on the WINS database, select the Enable WINS Proxy Agent option.

    This option allows the computer to answer name queries for remote computers, so other computers configured for broadcast name resolution can benefit from the name resolution services provided by a WINS server.

    This option is available only if you entered a value for a primary WINS server in the TCP/IP Configuration dialog box, as described in "Configuring TCP/IP" earlier in this chapter. However, the proxy agent cannot be run on a computer that is also a WINS server.

    Consult with the network administrator to determine whether your computer should be configured as a WINS proxy agent, as only a few computers on each subnetwork should be configured for this feature.

12. When you are done setting advanced options, choose the OK button. When the TCP/IP Configuration dialog box reappears, choose the OK button. When the Network Settings dialog box reappears, choose the OK button to complete advanced TCP/IP configuration.

You must restart the computer for the changes to take effect.

Configuring SNMP

The SNMP service is installed when you select the SNMP Service option in the Windows NT TCP/IP Installation Options dialog box. After the SNMP service software is installed on your computer, you must configure it with valid information for SNMP to operate.

You must be logged on as a member of the Administrators group for the local computer to configure SNMP.

The SNMP configuration information identifies communities and trap destinations.

- A *community* is a group of hosts to which a Windows NT computer running the SNMP service belongs. You can specify one or more communities to which the Windows NT computer using SNMP will send traps. The community name is placed in the SNMP packet when the trap is sent.

    When the SNMP service receives a request for information that does not contain the correct community name and does not match an accepted host name for the service, the SNMP service can send a trap to the trap destination(s), indicating that the request failed authentication.

- *Trap destinations* are the names or IP addresses of hosts to which you want the SNMP service to send traps with the selected community name.

You might want to use SNMP for statistics, but might not care about identifying communities or traps. In this case, you can specify the "public" community name when you configure the SNMP service.

▶ **To configure the SNMP service**

1. Double-click the Network option in Control Panel to display the Network Settings dialog box.

2. In the Installed Network Software box, select SNMP Service, and then choose the Configure button to display the SNMP Service Configuration dialog box.

3. To identify each community to which you want this computer to send traps, type the name in the Community Names box. After typing each name, choose the Add button to move the name to the Send Traps With Community Names list on the left.

   Typically, all hosts belong to public, which is the standard name for the common community of all hosts. To delete an entry in the list, select it, and then choose the Remove button.

   Note Community names are case sensitive.

   ---

4. To specify hosts for each community you send traps to, after you have added the community and while it is still highlighted, type the hosts in the IP Host/Address Or IPX Address box. Then choose the Add button to move the host name or IP address to the Trap Destination for the *selected community* list on the left.

   You can enter a host name, its IP address, or its IPX address.

   To delete an entry in the list, select it, and then choose the Remove button.

5. To enable additional security for the SNMP service, choose the Security button. Continue with the configuration procedure, as described in the next section, "Configuring SNMP Security."

6. To specify Agent information (comments about the user, location, and services), choose the Agent button, and then continue with the configuration procedure, as described in "Configuring SNMP Agent Information" later in this chapter.

7. When you have completed all procedures, choose the OK button. When the Network Settings dialog box reappears, choose the OK button.

   The Microsoft SNMP service has been configured and is ready to start. It is not necessary to reboot the computer.

Configuring SNMP Security

SNMP security allows you to specify the communities and hosts a computer will accept requests from, and to specify whether to send an authentication trap when an unauthorized community or host requests information.

▶ **To configure SNMP security**

1. Double-click the Network option in Control Panel to display the Network Settings dialog box.

2. In the Installed Network Software list box, select SNMP Service, and then choose the Configure button.

3. In the SNMP Service Configuration dialog box, choose the Security button.

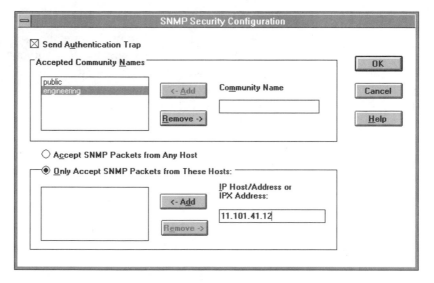

4. If you want to send a trap for failed authentications, select the Send Authentication Trap check box in the SNMP Security Configuration dialog box.

5. In the Community Name box, type the community names in which you will accept requests. Choose the Add button after typing each name to move the name to the Accepted Community Names list on the left.

   A host must belong to a community that appears on this list for the SNMP service to accept requests from that host. Typically, all hosts belong to public, which is the standard name for the common community of all hosts. To delete an entry in the list, select it, and then choose the Remove button.

6. Select an option to specify whether to accept SNMP packets from any host or from only specified hosts.

   - If the Accept SNMP Packets From Any Host option is selected, no SNMP packets are rejected on the basis of source host ID. The list of hosts under Only Accept SNMP Packets From These Hosts has no effect.

   - If the Only Accept SNMP Packets From These Hosts option is selected, SNMP packets will be accepted only from the hosts listed. In the IP Host/Address Or IPX Address box, type the host names, IP addresses, or IPX addresses of the hosts from which you will accept requests. Then choose the Add button to move the host name or IP address to the list box on the left. To delete an entry in the list, select it, and then choose the Remove button.

7. Choose the OK button.

   The SNMP Service Configuration dialog box reappears.

   To specify Agent information (comments about the user, location, and services), choose the Agent button. Continue with the configuration procedure, as described in the next section.

8. After you complete all procedures, choose the OK button. When the Network Settings dialog box reappears, choose the OK button.

   The Microsoft SNMP service and SNMP security have been configured and are ready to start. You do not need to reboot the computer.

Configuring SNMP Agent Information

SNMP agent information allows you to specify comments about the user and the physical location of the computer and to indicate the types of service to report. The types of service that can be reported are based on the computer's configuration.

▶ **To configure SNMP agent information**

1. Double-click the Network option in Control Panel to display the Network Settings dialog box.

2. In the Installed Network Software list box, select SNMP Service, and then choose the Configure button to display the SNMP Service Configuration dialog box.

3. Choose the Agent button to display the SNMP Agent dialog box.

```
┌─────────────────────────────────────────────────────────────┐
│ ─                       SNMP Agent                           │
├─────────────────────────────────────────────────────────────┤
│                                                              │
│   Contact:      │ Ernest Aydelotte          │      ┌────OK────┐│
│                                                    └──────────┘│
│   Location:     │ Bldg. 7, room 823         │      ┌──Cancel──┐│
│                                                    └──────────┘│
│  ┌─ Service ──────────────────────────────────┐   ┌───Help───┐│
│  │   ☐ Physical        ☐ Datalink / Subnetwork │   └──────────┘│
│  │                                             │              │
│  │   ☐ Internet        ☒ End-to-End            │              │
│  │                                             │              │
│  │   ☒ Applications                            │              │
│  └─────────────────────────────────────────────┘              │
│                                                              │
└─────────────────────────────────────────────────────────────┘
```

4. In the Contact box and Location box, type the computer user's name and the computer's physical location.

   These comments are used as text only. They cannot include embedded control characters.

5. In the Service group box, select all options that indicate network capabilities provided by your Windows NT computer.

   SNMP must have this information to manage the enabled services.

If you have installed additional TCP/IP services, such as a bridge or router, you should consult RFC 1213 for additional information.

Table 11.3   SNMP Service Options

Option	Description
Physical	Select this option if this Windows NT computer manages any physical TCP/IP device, such as a repeater.
Datalink/Subnetwork	Select this option if this Windows NT computer manages a TCP/IP subnetwork or datalink, such as a bridge.
Internet	Select this option if this Windows NT computer acts as an IP gateway.
End-to-End	Select this option if this Windows NT computer acts as an IP host. This option should be selected for all Windows NT installations.
Applications	Select this option if this Windows NT computer includes any applications that use TCP/IP, such as electronic mail. This option should be selected for all Windows NT installations.

6. Choose the OK button.

7. When the SNMP Service Configuration dialog box reappears, choose the OK button. When the Network Settings dialog box reappears, choose the OK button.

SNMP is now ready to operate. You do not need to restart the computer.

Removing TCP/IP Components

If you want to remove the TCP/IP protocol or any of the services installed on a computer, use the Network option in Control Panel to remove it.

When you remove network software, Windows NT warns you that the action permanently removes that component. You cannot reinstall a component that has been removed until after you restart the computer.

▶ **To remove any TCP/IP component**

1. Double-click the Network option in Control Panel to display the Network Settings dialog box.

2. In the Installed Network Software list, select the component that you want to remove.

3. Choose the Remove button to permanently remove the component.

Configuring RAS for Use with TCP/IP

Windows NT users who install Remote Access Service (RAS) for remote networking maintain all the benefits of TCP/IP networking, including access to the WINS and DNS capabilities of Microsoft TCP/IP. RAS clients can be configured to use Point to Point Protocol (PPP) or Serial Line Internet Protocol (SLIP) to allow TCP/IP dial-up support for existing TCP/IP internetworks and the Internet. When PPP is configured on a Windows NT Remote Access server, it can function as a router for RAS clients. SLIP client software is provided to support older implementations; it does not support multiple protocols.

As with all network services, you install RAS by using the Network option in Control Panel. During RAS installation and configuration, you can specify the network protocol settings to use for RAS connections, which also enables you to specify TCP/IP configuration settings. When the network administrator installs a Microsoft RAS server, IP addresses are reserved for use by RAS clients.

Users with RAS client computers can use the Remote Access program to enter and maintain names and telephone numbers of remote networks. RAS clients can connect to and disconnect from these networks through the Remote Access program. You can also use the Remote Access Phone Book application to select the network protocols to use for a specific Phone Book entry. If TCP/IP is installed, the Phone Book automatically selects TCP/IP over PPP as the protocol.

If a RAS client computer has a serial COM port, you can use the Remote Access Phone Book application to configure SLIP for use with a selected Phone Book entry. If you configure a RAS client computer to use the SLIP option, when you dial in for a connection to the selected Phone Book entry, the Terminal screen appears, and you can begin an interactive session with a SLIP server. When you use SLIP, Remote Access Phone Book bypasses user authentication. You will not be asked for a username and password.

For complete information about setting up RAS servers and clients and using RAS with Windows NT, see *Windows NT Server Remote Access Service*.

C H A P T E R   1 2

Networking Concepts for TCP/IP

This chapter describes how TCP/IP fits in the Windows NT network architecture and explains the various components of the Internet Protocol suite and IP addressing. As part of the discussion on name resolution in Windows-based networking, this chapter also describes NetBIOS over TCP/IP (NBT) and Domain Name System (DNS). For additional information about these topics, see the books listed in the "Welcome" section of this manual.

This chapter also provides conceptual information about two key features for Microsoft TCP/IP: Dynamic Host Configuration Protocol (DHCP) and Windows Internet Name Service (WINS).

The following topics appear in this chapter:

- TCP/IP and Windows NT networking
- Internet protocol suite
- IP addressing
- Name resolution for Windows-based networking
- SNMP

TCP/IP and Windows NT Networking

The architecture of the Microsoft Windows NT operating system with integrated networking is protocol-independent. This architecture, illustrated in the following figure, provides Windows NT file, print, and other services over any network protocol that uses exports from the TDI interface. The protocols package network requests for applications in their respective formats, and then send the requests to the appropriate network adapter via the *network device interface specification* (NDIS) interface. The NDIS specification allows multiple network protocols to reside over a wide variety of network adapters and media types.

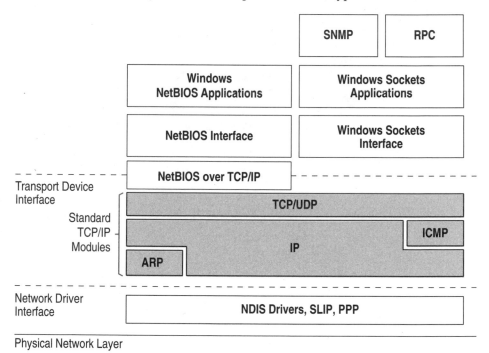

Figure 12.1   Architectural Model of Windows NT with TCP/IP

Under the Windows NT transport-independent architecture, TCP/IP is a protocol family that can be used to offer Windows-based networking capabilities. The TCP/IP protocol gives Windows NT, Windows for Workgroups, and LAN Manager computers transparent access to each other and allows communication with non-Microsoft systems in the enterprise network.

Internet Protocol Suite

TCP/IP refers to the Internet suite of protocols. It includes a set of standards that specify how computers communicate and gives conventions for connecting networks and routing traffic through the connections.

The Internet protocols are a result of a Defense Advanced Research Projects Agency (DARPA) research project on network interconnection in the late 1970s. It was mandated on all United States defense long-haul networks in 1983 but was not widely accepted until it was integrated with 4.2 Berkeley Software Distribution (BSD) UNIX. The popularity of TCP/IP is based on the following features:

- *Robust client-server framework.* TCP/IP is an excellent client-server application platform, especially in wide area network (WAN) environments.
- *Information sharing.* Thousands of academic, military, scientific, and commercial organizations share data, electronic mail, and services on the Internet using TCP/IP.
- *General availability.* Implementations of TCP/IP are available on nearly every popular computer operating system. Source code is widely available for many implementations. Vendors for bridges, routers, and network analyzers all offer support for the TCP/IP protocol suite within their products.

The following discussion introduces the components of the IP protocol suite. Some knowledge of the architecture and interaction between TCP/IP components is useful for both administrators and users, but most of the details discussed here are transparent when you are actually using TCP/IP.

Transmission Control Protocol and Internet Protocol

Transmission Control Protocol (TCP) and Internet Protocol (IP) are only two members of the IP protocol suite. IP is a protocol that provides packet delivery for all other protocols within the TCP/IP family. IP provides a best-effort, connectionless delivery system for computer data. That is, IP packets are not guaranteed to arrive at their destination, nor are they guaranteed to be received in the sequence in which they were sent. The protocol's checksum feature confirms only the IP header's integrity. Thus, responsibility for the data contained within the IP packet (and the sequencing) is assured only by using higher-level protocols.

Perhaps the most common higher-level IP protocol is TCP. TCP supplies a reliable, connection-based protocol over (or encapsulated within) IP. TCP guarantees the delivery of packets, ensures proper sequencing of the data, and provides a checksum feature that validates both the packet header and its data for accuracy. In the event that the network either corrupts or loses a TCP/IP packet during transmission, TCP is responsible for retransmitting the faulty packet. This reliability makes TCP/IP the protocol of choice for session-based data transmission, client-server applications, and critical services, such as electronic mail.

This reliability has a price. TCP headers require the use of additional bits to provide proper sequencing of information, as well as a mandatory checksum to ensure reliability of both the TCP header and the packet data. To guarantee successful data delivery, the protocol also requires the recipient to acknowledge successful receipt of data.

Such acknowledgments (or ACKs) generate additional network traffic, diminishing the level of data throughput in favor of reliability. To reduce the impact on performance, most hosts send an acknowledgment for every other segment or when an ACK timeout expires.

User Datagram Protocol

If reliability is not essential, User Datagram Protocol (UDP), a TCP complement, offers a connectionless datagram service that guarantees neither delivery nor correct sequencing of delivered packets (much like IP). Higher-level protocols or applications might provide reliability mechanisms in addition to UDP/IP. UDP data checksums are optional, providing a way to exchange data over highly reliable networks without unnecessarily consuming network resources or processing time. When UDP checksums are used, they validate the integrity of both the header and data. ACKs are also not enforced by the UDP protocol; this is left to higher-level protocols.

UDP also offers one-to-many service capabilities, because it can be either broadcast or multicast.

Address Resolution Protocol and Internet Control Message Protocol

Two other protocols in the IP suite perform important functions, although these are not directly related to the transport of data: Address Resolution Protocol (ARP) and Internet Control Message Protocol (ICMP). ARP and ICMP are maintenance protocols that support the IP framework and are usually invisible to users and applications.

IP packets contain both source and destination IP addresses, but the hardware address of the destination computer system must also be known. IP acquires a system's hardware address by broadcasting a special inquiry packet (an ARP *request packet*) containing the IP address of the system with which it is attempting to communicate. All of the ARP-enabled nodes on the local IP network detect these broadcasts, and the system that owns the IP address in question replies by sending its hardware address to the requesting computer system in an ARP reply packet. The hardware/IP address mapping is then stored in the requesting system's ARP cache for subsequent use. Because the ARP reply can also be broadcast to the network, it is likely that other nodes on the network can use this information to update their own ARP caches. (You can use the **arp** utility to view the ARP tables.)

ICMP allows two nodes on an IP network to share IP status and error information. This information can be used by higher-level protocols to recover from transmission problems or by network administrators to detect network trouble. Although ICMP packets are encapsulated within IP packets, they are not considered to be a higher-level protocol (ICMP is required in every TCP/IP implementation). The **ping** utility makes use of the ICMP *echo request* and *echo reply* packets to determine whether a particular IP node (computer system) on a network is functional. For this reason, the **ping** utility is useful for diagnosing IP network or gateway failures.

IP Addressing

A *host* is any device attached to the network that uses TCP/IP. To receive and deliver packets successfully between hosts, TCP/IP relies on three values, that the user provides: IP address, subnet mask, and default gateway.

The network administrator provides each of these values for configuring TCP/IP on a computer. Windows NT users on networks with DHCP servers can take advantage of automatic system configuration and do not need to manually configure TCP/IP parameters. This section provides details about IP addresses, subnet masks, and IP gateways.

IP Addresses

Every host interface, or node, on a TCP/IP network is identified by a unique IP address. This address is used to identify a host on a network; it also specifies routing information in an internetwork. The *IP address* identifies a computer as a 32-bit address that is unique across a TCP/IP network. An address is usually represented in dotted-decimal notation, which depicts each octet (eight bits, or one byte) of an IP address as its decimal value and separates each octet with a period. An IP address looks like this:

```
102.54.94.97
```

Important   Because IP addresses identify nodes on an interconnected network, each host on the internetwork must be assigned a unique IP address, valid for its particular network.

Network ID and Host ID

Although an IP address is a single value, it contains two pieces of information: the network ID and the host (or system) ID for your computer.

- The *network ID* identifies a group of computers and other devices that are all located on the same logical network, which are separated or interconnected by routers. In internetworks (networks formed by a collection of local area networks), there is a unique network ID for each network.

- The *host ID* identifies your computer within a particular network ID. (A host is any device that is attached to the network and uses TCP/IP.)

Networks that connect to the public Internet must obtain an official network ID from the InterNIC to guarantee IP network ID uniqueness. The InterNIC can be contacted via electronic mail at info@internic.net (for the United States, 1–800–444–4345 or, for Canada and overseas, 619–455–4600). Internet registration requests can be sent to hostmaster@internic.net. You can also use FTP to connect to is.internic.net, then log in as **anonymous**, and then change to the /INFOSOURCE/FAQ directory.

After receiving a network ID, the local network administrator must assign unique host IDs for computers within the local network. Although private networks not connected to the Internet can choose to use their own network identifier, obtaining a valid network ID from InterNIC allows a private network to connect to the Internet in the future without reassigning addresses.

The Internet community has defined address *classes* to accommodate networks of varying sizes. Each network class can be discerned from the first octet of its IP address. The following table summarizes the relationship between the first octet of a given address and its network ID and host ID fields. It also identifies the total number of network IDs and host IDs for each address class that participates in the Internet addressing scheme. This sample uses w.x.y.z to designate the bytes of the IP address.

Table 12.1   IP Address Classes

Class	w values[1,2]	Network ID	Host ID	Available networks	Available hosts per net
A	1–126	w	x.y.z	126	16,777,214
B	128–191	w.x	y.z	16,384	65,534
C	192–223	w.x.y	z	2,097,151	254

1 Inclusive range for the first octet in the IP address.

2 The address 127 is reserved for loopback testing and interprocess communication on the local computer; it is not a valid network address. Addresses 224 and above are reserved for special protocols (IGMP multicast and others), and cannot be used as host addresses.

A network host uses the network ID and host ID to determine which packets it should receive or ignore and to determine the scope of its transmissions (only nodes with the same network ID accept each other's IP-level broadcasts).

Because the sender's IP address is included in every outgoing IP packet, it is useful for the receiving computer system to derive the originating network ID and host ID from the IP address field. This task is done by using subnet masks, as described in the following section.

Subnet Masks

Subnet masks are 32-bit values that allow the recipient of IP packets to distinguish the network ID portion of the IP address from the host ID. Like an IP address, the value of a subnet mask is frequently represented in dotted-decimal notation. Subnet masks are determined by assigning 1's to bits that belong to the network ID and 0's to the bits that belong to the host ID. Once the bits are in place, the 32-bit value is converted to dotted-decimal notation, as shown in the following table.

Table 12.2   Default Subnet Masks for Standard IP Address Classes

Address class	Bits for subnet mask	Subnet mask
Class A	11111111 00000000 00000000 00000000	255.0.0.0
Class B	11111111 11111111 00000000 00000000	255.255.0.0
Class C	11111111 11111111 11111111 00000000	255.255.255.0

The result enables TCP/IP to determine the host and network IDs of the local computer. For example, when the IP address is 102.54.94.97 and the subnet mask is 255.255.0.0, the network ID is 102.54 and the host ID is 94.97.

Although configuring a host with a subnet mask might seem redundant after examining the previous tables (since the class of a host is easily determined), subnet masks are also used to further segment an assigned network ID among several local networks.

For example, suppose a network is assigned the Class-B network address 144.100. This is one of over 16,000 Class-B addresses capable of serving more than 65,000 nodes. However, the worldwide corporate network to which this ID is assigned is composed of 12 international LANs with 75 to 100 nodes each. Instead of applying for 11 more network IDs, it is better to use subnetting to make more effective use of the assigned ID 144.100. The third octet of the IP address can be used as a subnet ID, to define the subnet mask 255.255.255.0. This arrangement splits the Class-B address into 254 subnets: 144.100.1 through 144.100.254, each of which can have 254 nodes. (Host IDs 0 and 255 should not be assigned to a computer; they are used as broadcast addresses, which are typically recognized by all computers.) Any 12 of these network addresses could be assigned to the international LANs in this example. Within each LAN, each computer is assigned a unique host ID, and they all have the subnet mask 255.255.255.0.

The preceding example demonstrates a simple (and common) subnet scheme for Class-B addresses. Sometimes it is necessary to segment only portions of an octet, using only a few bits to specify subnet IDs (such as when subnets exceed 256 nodes). Each user should check with the local network administrator to determine the network's subnet policy and the correct subnet mask. For all systems on the local network, the subnet mask must be the same for that network ID.

Important All computers on a logical network must use the same subnet mask and network ID; otherwise, addressing and routing problems can occur.

Routing and IP Gateways

TCP/IP networks are connected by *gateways* (or routers), which have knowledge of the networks connected in the internetwork. Although each IP host can maintain static routes for specific destinations, usually the default gateway is used to find remote destinations. (The *default gateway* is needed only for computers that are part of an internetwork.)

When IP prepares to send a packet, it inserts the local (source) IP address and the destination address of the packet in the IP header and checks whether the network ID of the destination matches the network ID of the source. If they match, the packet is sent directly to the destination computer on the local network. If the network IDs do not match, the routing table is examined for static routes. If none are found, the packet is forwarded to the default gateway for delivery.

The default gateway is a computer connected to the local subnet and other networks that has knowledge of the network IDs for other networks in the internetwork and how to reach them. Because the default gateway knows the network IDs of the other networks in the internetwork, it can forward the packet to other gateways until the packet is eventually delivered to a gateway connected to the specified destination. This process is known as *routing*.

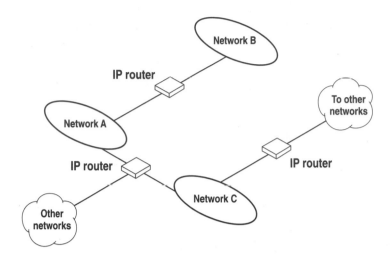

Figure 12.2   Internetwork Routing Through Gateways

On networks that are not part of an internetwork, IP gateways are not required. If a network is part of an internetwork and a system does not specify a default gateway (or if the gateway computer is not operating properly), only communication beyond the local subnet is impaired. Users can add static routes by using the **route** utility to specify a route for a particular system. Static routes always override the use of default gateways.

If the default gateway becomes unavailable, the computer cannot communicate outside its own subnet. Multiple default gateways can be assigned to prevent such a problem. When a computer is configured with multiple default gateways, retransmission problems result in the system trying the other routers in the configuration to ensure internetworking communications capabilities. To configure multiple default gateways in Windows NT, you must provide an IP address for each gateway in the Advanced Microsoft TCP/IP Configuration dialog box, as described in Chapter 11, "Installing and Configuring Microsoft TCP/IP and SNMP."

Dynamic Host Configuration Protocol

Assigning and maintaining IP address information can be an administrative burden for network administrators responsible for internetwork connections. Contributing to this burden is the problem that many users do not have the knowledge necessary to configure their own computers for internetworking and must therefore rely on their administrators.

The Dynamic Host Configuration Protocol (DHCP) was established to relieve this administrative burden. DHCP provides safe, reliable, and simple TCP/IP network configuration, ensures that address conflicts do not occur, and helps conserve the use of IP addresses through centralized management of address allocation. DHCP offers dynamic configuration of IP addresses for computers. The system administrator controls how IP addresses are assigned by specifying *lease* durations, which specify how long a computer can use an assigned IP address before having to renew the lease with the DHCP server.

As an example of how maintenance tasks are made easy with DHCP, the IP address is released automatically for a DHCP client computer that is removed from a subnet, and a new address for the new subnet is automatically assigned when that computer reconnects on another subnet. Neither the user nor the network administrator needs to intervene to supply new configuration information. This is a most significant feature for mobile computer users with portables that are docked at different computers, or for computers that are moved to different offices frequently.

The DHCP client and server services for Windows NT are implemented under Requests for Comments (RFCs) 1533, 1534, 1541, and 1542.

The following illustration shows an example of a DHCP server providing configuration information on two subnets. If, for example, ClientC is moved to Subnet 1, the DHCP server automatically supplies new TCP/IP configuration information the next time that ClientC is started.

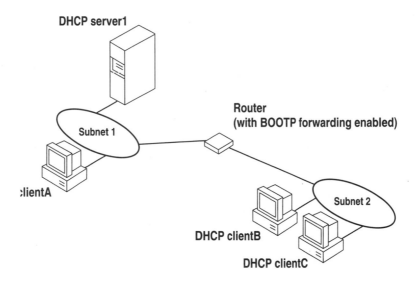

Figure 12.3   DHCP Clients and Servers on a Routed Network

DHCP uses a client-server model and is based on leases for IP addresses. During system startup (the *initializing* state), a DHCP client computer sends a *discover message* that is broadcast to the local network and might be relayed to all DHCP servers on the private internetwork. Each DHCP server that receives the discover message responds with an *offer message* containing an IP address and valid configuration information for the client that sent the request.

The DHCP client collects the configuration offerings from the servers and enters a *selecting* state. When the client enters the *requesting* state, it chooses one of the configurations and sends a *request message* that identifies the DHCP server for the selected configuration.

The selected DHCP server sends a *DHCP acknowledgment message* that contains the address first sent during the discovery stage, plus a valid lease for the address and the TCP/IP network configuration parameters for the client. After the client receives the acknowledgment, it enters a *bound* state and can now participate on the TCP/IP network and complete its system startup. Client computers that have local storage save the received address for use during subsequent system startup. As the lease approaches its expiration date, it attempts to renew its lease with the DHCP server, and is assigned a new address if the current IP address lease cannot be renewed.

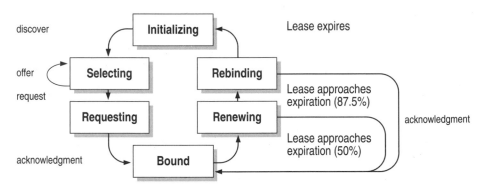

Figure 12.4   DHCP Client State Transition During System Startup

In Windows NT Server, the network administrator uses DHCP Manager to define local policies for address allocation, leases, and other options. For information about using this tool, see Chapter 13, "Installing and Configuring DHCP Servers." For information about the steps for setting up TCP/IP using DHCP, see "Configuring TCP/IP" in Chapter 11, "Installing and Configuring Microsoft TCP/IP and SNMP." For information about setting up DHCP relaying, see the documentation for your router.

Name Resolution for Windows-Based Networking

Configuring Windows NT with TCP/IP requires the IP address and computer name, which are unique identifiers for the computer on the network. The IP address, as described earlier in this chapter, is the unique address by which all other TCP/IP devices on the internetwork recognize that computer. For TCP/IP and the Internet, the computer name is the globally known system name plus a DNS domain name. (On the local network, the computer name is the NetBIOS name that was defined during Windows NT Setup.)

Computers use IP addresses to identify each other, but users usually find it easier to work with computer names. A mechanism must be available on a TCP/IP network to resolve computer names to IP addresses. To ensure that both computer name and address are unique, the Windows NT computer using TCP/IP registers its name and IP address on the network during system startup. A Windows NT computer can use one or more of the following methods to ensure accurate name resolution in TCP/IP internetworks:

- Windows Internet Name Service

  Windows NT computers can use WINS if one or more WINS servers are available that contain a dynamic database mapping computer names to IP addresses. WINS can be used in conjunction with broadcast name resolution for an internetwork where other name resolution methods are inadequate. As described in the following section, WINS is a NetBIOS over TCP/IP (NBT) mode of operation defined in RFC 1001/1002 as p-node.

- Broadcast name resolution

  Windows NT computers can also use broadcast name resolution, which is a NetBIOS over TCP/IP mode of operation defined in RFC 1001/1002 as b-node. This method relies on a computer making IP-level broadcasts to register its name by announcing it on the network. Each computer in the broadcast area is responsible for challenging attempts to register a duplicate name and for responding to name queries for its registered name.

- DNS name resolution

  The Domain Name System (DNS) provides a way to look up name mappings when connecting a computer to foreign hosts using NetBIOS over TCP/IP or Windows Sockets applications, such as FTP. DNS is a distributed database designed to relieve the traffic problems that arose with the exploding growth of the Internet in the early 1980s.

- An LMHOSTS file to specify the NetBIOS computer name and IP address mappings, or a HOSTS file to specify the DNS name and IP address

On a local computer, the HOSTS file (used by Windows Sockets applications to find TCP/IP host names) and LMHOSTS file (used by NetBIOS over TCP/IP to find Microsoft networking computer names) can be used to list known IP addresses mapped with corresponding computer names. The LMHOSTS file is still used for name resolution in Windows NT for small-scale networks or remote subnets where WINS is not available.

This section provides details about name resolution in Windows NT after first presenting some background information about the modes of NetBIOS over TCP/IP that can be used in Microsoft networks.

NetBIOS over TCP/IP and Name Resolution

NetBIOS over TCP/IP (NBT) is the session-layer network service that performs name-to-IP address mapping for name resolution. This section describes the modes of NBT, as defined in RFCs 1001 and 1002 to specify how NetBIOS should be implemented over TCP/IP.

The modes of NBT define how network resources are identified and accessed. The two most important aspects of the related naming activities are registration and resolution. *Registration* is the process used to acquire a unique name for each node (computer system) on the network. A computer typically registers itself when it starts. *Resolution* is the process used to determine the specific address for a computer name.

The NBT modes include the following:

- *b-node*, which uses broadcasts to resolve names
- *p-node*, which uses point-to-point communications with a name server to resolve names
- *m-node*, which uses b-node first (broadcasts), and then p-node (name queries) if the broadcast fails to resolve a name
- *h-node*, which uses p-node first for name queries, and then b-node if the name service is unavailable or if the name is not registered in the WINS database

If WINS servers are specified by either a DHCP server or the TCP/IP configuration specified in the Network option of Control Panel, Windows NT 3.5 defaults to h-node. Otherwise, the default node type is b-node, unless another node type has been set as an option by the DHCP server.

For DHCP users on a Windows NT network, the node type is assigned by the DHCP server. A DHCP client computer can have only one NetBIOS node type, no matter how many adapter cards it has. On a multihomed computer with access to more than one network, the node type must be the same on both networks. When WINS servers are in place on the network, NBT resolves names on a client computer by communicating with the WINS server. If you want to configure a multihomed computer with some network adapter cards using b-node and some using h-node, configure WINS server addresses for the adapter cards that are to run in h-mode. The presence of a WINS address on an adapter card effectively overrides the b-node setting.

When WINS servers are not in place, NBT uses b-node broadcasts to resolve names. NBT in Windows NT can also use LMHOSTS files and DNS for name resolution, depending on how TCP/IP is configured on a particular computer. In Windows NT 3.5, the NETBT.SYS module provides the NBT functionality that supports name registration and resolution modes.

Windows NT version 3.5 supports all of the NBT modes described in the following sections. NBT is also used with the LAN Manager 2.x Server message protocol.

B-Node

The b-node mode uses broadcasts for name registration and resolution. That is, if NT_PC1 wants to communicate with NT_PC2, it broadcasts to all machines that it is looking for NT_PC2, and then it waits a specified time for NT_PC2 to respond. B-node has two major problems:

- In a large environment, it loads the network with broadcasts.

- Routers do not forward broadcasts, so computers that are on opposite sides of a router never hear the requests.

P-Node

The p-node mode addresses the issues that b-node does not solve. In a p-node environment, computers neither create nor respond to broadcasts. All computers register themselves with the WINS server, which is a NetBIOS Name Server (NBNS) with enhancements. The WINS server is responsible for knowing computer names and addresses and for ensuring no duplicate names exist on the network. All computers must be configured to know the address of the WINS server.

In this environment, when NT_PC1 wants to communicate with NT_PC2, it queries the WINS server for the address of NT_PC2. When NT_PC1 gets the appropriate address from the WINS server, it goes directly to NT_PC2 without broadcasting. Because the name queries go directly to the WINS server, p-node avoids loading the network with broadcasts. Because broadcasts are not used and because the address is received directly, computers can span routers.

The most significant problems with p-node are the following:

- All computers must be configured to know the address of the WINS server (although this is typically configured via DHCP)
- If for any reason the WINS server is down, computers that rely on the WINS server to resolve addresses cannot get to any other systems on the network, even if they are on the local network

M-Node

The m-node mode was created primarily to solve the problems associated with b-node and p-node. This mode uses a combination of b-node and p-node. In an m-node environment, a computer first attempts registration and resolution using b-node. If that is successful, it then switches to the p-node. Because this uses b-node first, it does not solve the problem of generating broadcast traffic on the network. However, m-node can cross routers. Also, because b-node is always tried first, computers on the same side of a router continue to operate as usual if the WINS server is down.

M-node uses broadcasts for performance optimization, because in most environments local resources are used more frequently than remote resources. Also, in a Windows NT network, m-node can cause problems with NetLogon in routed environments.

H-Node

The h-node mode, which is currently in RFC draft form, is also a combination of b-node and p-node that uses broadcasts as a last effort. Because p-node is used first, no broadcasts are generated if the WINS server is running, and computers can span routers. If the WINS server is down, b-node is used, so computers on the same side of a router continue to operate as usual.

The h-node mode does more than change the order for using b-node and p-node. If the WINS server is down so that local broadcasts (b-node) must be used, the computer continues to poll the WINS server. As soon as the WINS server can be reached again, the system switches back to p-node. Also, optionally on a Windows network, h-node can be configured to use the LMHOSTS file after broadcast name resolution fails.

The h-node mode solves the most significant problems associated with broadcasts and operating in a routed environment. For Microsoft TCP/IP users who configure TCP/IP manually, h-node is used by default, unless the user does not specify addresses for WINS servers when configuring TCP/IP.

B-Node with LMHOSTS and Combinations

Another variation is also used in Microsoft networks to span routers without a
WINS server and p-node mode. In this mode, b-node uses a list of computers and
addresses stored in an LMHOSTS file. If a b-node attempt fails, the system looks in
LMHOSTS to find a name and then uses the associated address to cross the router.
However, each computer must have this list, which creates an administrative burden
in maintaining and distributing the list. Both Windows for Workgroups 3.11 and
LAN Manager 2.*x* used such a modified b-node system. Windows NT uses this
method if WINS servers are not used on the network. In Windows NT, some
extensions have been added to this file to make it easier to manage (as described in
Chapter 15, "Setting Up LMHOSTS"), but modified b-node is not an ideal solution.

Some sites might need to use both b-node and p-node modes at the same site.
Although this configuration can work, administrators must exercise extreme
caution in doing so, using it only for transition situations. Because p-node hosts
disregard broadcasts and b-node hosts rely on broadcasts for name resolution, the
two hosts can potentially be configured with the same NetBIOS name, leading to
unpredictable results. Notice that if a computer configured to use b-node has a static
mapping in the WINS database, a computer configured to use p-node cannot use the
same computer name.

Windows NT computers can also be configured as WINS proxy agents to help the
transition to using WINS. For more details, see the next section.

Windows Internet Name Service and Broadcast Name Resolution

WINS provides a distributed database for registering and querying dynamic
computer name-to-IP address mappings in a routed network environment. If you are
administering a routed network, WINS is your best first choice for name resolution,
because it is designed to solve the problems that occur with name resolution in
complex internetworks.

WINS reduces the use of local broadcasts for name resolution and allows users to
easily locate systems on remote networks. Furthermore, when dynamic addressing
through DHCP results in new IP addresses for computers that move between
subnets, the changes are automatically updated in the WINS database. Neither the
user nor the network administrator needs to make manual accommodations for name
resolution in such a case.

The WINS protocol is based on and is compatible with the protocols defined for NBNS in RFCs 1001/1002, so it is interoperable with any other implementations of these RFCs.

This section provides an overview of how WINS and name query broadcasts provide name resolution on Windows networks. For information about setting up WINS servers, see Chapter 14, "Installing and Configuring WINS Servers."

WINS in a Routed Environment

WINS consists of two components: the WINS server, which handles name queries and registrations, and the client software, which queries for computer name resolution.

Windows-based networking clients (WINS-enabled Windows NT or Windows for Workgroups 3.11 computers) can use WINS directly. Non-WINS computers on the internetwork that are b-node compatible as described in RFCs 1001 and 1002 can access WINS through proxies, which are WINS-enabled computers that listen to name query broadcasts and then respond for names that are not on the local subnet or are p-node computers.

On a Windows NT network, users can browse transparently across routers. To allow browsing without WINS, the network administrator must ensure that the users' primary domain has Windows NT Server or Windows NT Workstation computers on both sides of the router to act as master browsers. These computers need correctly configured LMHOSTS files with entries for the domain controllers across the subnet.

With WINS, such strategies are not necessary because the WINS servers and proxies transparently provide the support necessary for browsing across routers where domains span the routers.

The following figure shows a small internetwork, with three local area networks connected by a router. Two of the subnets include WINS name servers, which can be used by clients on both subnets. WINS-enabled computers, including proxies, access the WINS server directly, and the computers using broadcasts access the WINS server through proxies. Proxies only pass name query packets and verify that registrations do not duplicate existing systems in the WINS database. Proxies, however, do not register b-node systems in the WINS database.

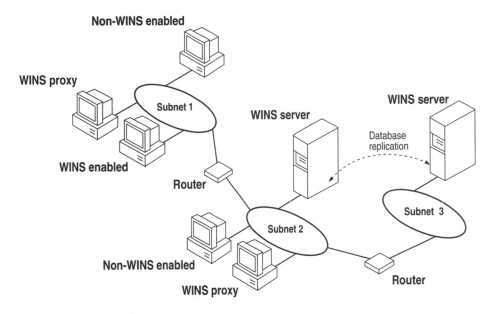

Figure 12.5   Example of an Internetwork with WINS Servers

The proxy communicates with the WINS server to resolve names (rather than maintaining its own database) and then caches the names for a certain time. The proxy serves as an intermediary, by either communicating with the WINS server or supplying a name-to-IP address mapping from its cache. The following illustration shows the relationships among WINS servers and clients, including proxies for non-WINS computers and the replication between WINS servers.

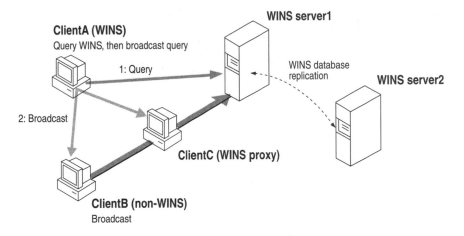

Figure 12.6   Example of Clients and Servers Using WINS

In the above figure, ClientA can resolve names by first querying the WINS server and, if that fails, then using broadcast name queries. ClientB, which is not WINS-enabled, can only resolve names using broadcast name queries, but when ClientC receives the broadcast, it forwards the request to the WINS server and returns the address to ClientB.

However, a complex environment presents additional problems. For example, an internetwork might consist of two subnets, with all the computers belonging to DomainA attached to Subnet1, all the computers in DomainB attached to Subnet2, and computers from DomainC attached to either of the subnets. In this case, without WINS, DomainA computers can browse Subnet1, DomainB computers can browse Subnet2, and DomainC computers can browse both subnets as long as the primary domain controller for DomainC is available. With WINS, computers from all domains can browse all subnets if their WINS servers share databases.

If the Windows NT client computer is also DHCP-enabled and the administrator specifies WINS server information as part of the DHCP options, the computer usually will be automatically configured with WINS server information. You can manually configure WINS settings, as described in Chapter 11, "Installing and Configuring Microsoft TCP/IP and SNMP":

- To enable WINS name resolution for a computer that does not use DHCP, specify WINS server addresses in the TCP/IP Configuration dialog box.

- To designate a proxy, check the Enable WINS Proxy Agent option in the Advanced Microsoft TCP/IP Configuration dialog box.

With WINS servers in place on the internetwork, names are resolved using two basic methods, depending on whether WINS resolution is available and enabled on the particular computer. Whatever name resolution method is used, the process is transparent to the user after the system is configured.

If WINS is not enabled   The computer registers its name by broadcasting *name registration request* packets to the local subnet via UDP datagrams. To find a particular computer, the non-WINS computer broadcasts *name query request* packets on the local subnet, although this broadcast cannot be passed on through IP routers. If local name resolution fails, the local LMHOSTS file is consulted. These processes are followed whether the computer is a network server, a workstation, or other device.

If WINS is enabled   The computer first queries the WINS server, and if that does not succeed, it broadcasts its name registration and query requests via UDP datagrams (h-node), in the following series of steps:

1. During TCP/IP configuration, the computer's name is registered with the WINS server, and then the IP address of the WINS server is stored locally so the WINS server can be found on the internetwork. The WINS database is replicated among all WINS servers on the internetwork.

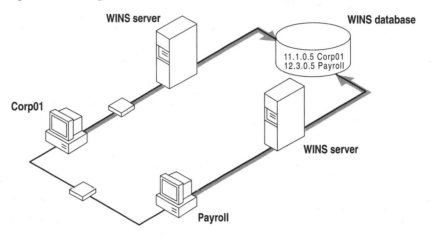

Figure 12.7   Name Registration in the WINS Database

2. A *name query request* is sent first to the WINS server, including requests from remote clients that are routed through an IP router. This request is a UDP datagram. If the name is found in the WINS database, the client can establish a session based on the address mapping received from WINS.

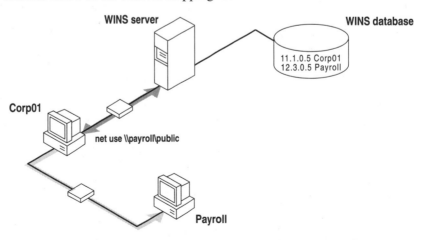

Figure 12.8   Processing a Name Query Request

3. If querying the WINS server does not succeed and if the client computer is configured as an h-node, the computer broadcasts *name query request* packets in the same manner as a non-WINS-enabled computer.

4. Finally, if other methods fail, the local LMHOSTS file is checked. This also includes a search of any centralized LMHOSTS files referred to in #INCLUDE statements, as described in Chapter 15, "Setting Up LMHOSTS."

WINS servers accept and respond to UDP name queries. Any name-to-IP address mapping registered with a WINS server can be provided reliably as a response to a name query. However, a mapping in the database does not ensure that the related device is currently running, only that a computer claimed the particular IP address and it is a currently valid mapping.

WINS Name Registration

Name registration ensures that the computer's name and IP address are unique for each device.

If WINS is enabled   The name registration request is sent directly to the WINS server to be added to the database. A WINS server accepts or rejects a computer name registration depending on the current contents of its database. If the database contains a different address for that name, WINS challenges the current entry to determine whether that device still claims the name. If another device is using that name, WINS rejects the new name registration request. Otherwise, WINS accepts the entry and adds it to its local database together with a timestamp, an incremental unique version number, and other information.

If WINS is not enabled   For a non-WINS computer to register its name, a *name registration request* packet is broadcast to the local network, stating its computer name and IP address. Any device on the network that previously claimed that name challenges the name registration with a *negative name registration response*, resulting in an error. If the registration request is not contested within a specific time period, the computer adopts that name and address.

Once a non-WINS computer has claimed a name, it must challenge duplicate name registration attempts and respond positively to name queries issued on its registered name by sending a *positive name query response*. This response contains the IP address of the computer so that the two systems can establish a session.

WINS Name Release

When a computer finishes with a particular name (such as when the Workstation service or Server service is stopped), it no longer challenges other registration requests for the name. This is referred to as *releasing a name*.

If WINS is enabled   Whenever a computer is shut down properly, it releases its name to the WINS server, which marks the related database entry as *released*. If the entry remains released for a certain period of time, the WINS server marks it as *extinct*, and the version number is updated so that the database changes will be propagated among the WINS servers. *Extinct* entries remain in the database for a designated period of time to enable the change to be propagated to all WINS servers.

If a name is marked released at a WINS server and a new registration arrives using that name but a different address, the WINS server can immediately give that name to the requesting client because it knows that the old client is no longer using that name. (This might happen, for example, when a DHCP-enabled laptop changes subnets.) If that computer released its name during an orderly shutdown, the WINS server does not challenge the name. If the computer restarts because of a system reset, the name registration with a new address causes the WINS server to challenge the registration, but the challenge fails and the registration will succeed, because the computer no longer has the old address.

If WINS is not enabled   When a non-WINS computer releases a name, a broadcast is made to allow any systems on the network that might have cached the name to remove it. Upon receiving name query packets specifying the deleted name, the computer simply ignores the request, allowing other computers on the network to acquire the name that it has released.

For non-WINS computers to be accessible from other subnets, their names must be added as static entries to the WINS database or in the LMHOSTS file(s) on the remote system(s), because they will only respond to name queries that originate on their local subnet.

WINS Name Renewal

A *renewal* is a timed reregistration of a computer's name with the WINS server. The timestamp for an entry indicates the entry's expiration date and time. If the entry is owned by the local WINS server, the name is released at the time specified unless the client has reregistered. An entry defined as static never expires. If the entry is owned by another WINS server, the entry is revalidated at the time specified. If it does not exist in the database of the WINS server that owns the entry, it is removed from the local WINS database. A request for name renewal is treated the same as a new name registration.

Renewal provides registration reliability through periodic reregistering of names with the WINS servers. The default renewal interval for entries in the WINS database is four days. WINS clients register and refresh every two days. Because this setting reduces network traffic and allows WINS to serve many more nodes than before, you should not lower it. The primary and backup WINS servers should have the same renewal interval.

IP Addressing for RAS

Remote Access Service (RAS) provides remote networking for telecommuters, mobile workers, and system administrators who monitor and manage servers at multiple branch offices. Users with RAS on a Windows NT computer can dial in to remotely access their networks for services such as file and printer sharing, electronic mail, scheduling, and SQL database access.

Windows NT RAS works with IP routing for RAS servers so that RAS clients can use TCP/IP networks. (RAS can also work with IPX routing for clients that use NetWare networks.) Windows NT also uses the industry-standard Point to Point Protocol (PPP) and Serial Line IP (SLIP) standards. These standards ensure that Windows NT is interoperable with third-party remote-access server and client software. RAS clients can use DNS and WINS for name resolution services, and it can create TCP sessions with systems on the local network.

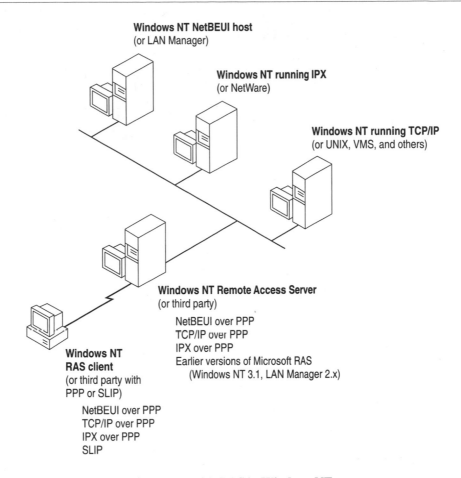

Figure 12.9   Network Access with RAS in Windows NT

The RAS server provides a pool of IP addresses that are reserved for static configuration during RAS installation. The IP addresses are automatically assigned to RAS clients using PPP when they dial in. If the administrator sets up the RAS server to use a static pool of addresses, all clients dialing into a particular RAS server are assigned the same network ID as the RAS server plus unique host IDs. (Of course, the network administrator must also reserve that range of static addresses on the DHCP server, if present, to make sure that those addresses are not assigned.)

RAS clients can connect to multiple TCP/IP networks that are logically joined (but physically separate) networks sharing the same address space. When using multiple connections, the RAS client can still use DNS and WINS for name resolution.

For complete details about RAS, see the *Windows NT Server Remote Access Service* manual.

Name Resolution with Host Files

For computers located on remote subnets where WINS is not used, the HOSTS and LMHOSTS files provide mappings for names to IP addresses. This is the name resolution method used on internetworks before DNS and WINS were developed. The HOSTS file can be used as a local DNS equivalent. The LMHOSTS file can be used as a local WINS equivalent. Each of these files is also known as a *host table*. Sample versions of LMHOSTS and HOSTS files are added to the *\systemroot*\SYSTEM32\DRIVERS\ETC directory when you install Microsoft TCP/IP. These files can be edited using any ASCII editor, such as Notepad or Edit, which are part of Windows NT.

Microsoft TCP/IP can be configured to search HOSTS, the local host table file, for mappings of remote host names to IP addresses. The HOSTS file format is the same as the format for host tables in the 4.3 Berkeley Software Distribution (BSD) UNIX */etc/hosts* file. For example, the entry for a computer with an address of 192.102.73.6 and a host name of trey-research.com looks like this:

```
192.102.73.6         trey-research.com
```

If you want a Windows NT Server to join a domain and perform domain operations, such as browsing or acting as a backup domain controller, when the primary domain controller (PDC) is on the other side of a router, you must add the Windows NT computer and domain names to the DNS server or the local HOSTS file, with the IP address of the PDC as the domain address. Here is a sample HOSTS file entry:

```
11.11.11.45     controller  controller.domain      controller.domain.company
11.11.11.45     domain
```

Where *controller* is the Windows NT computer name of the PDC and *domain* is the name of the Windows NT domain (not the DNS domain).

Edit the sample HOSTS file that is created when you install TCP/IP to include remote host names and their IP addresses for each computer with which you will communicate. This sample file also explains the syntax of the HOSTS file.

The LMHOSTS file is a local text file that maps IP addresses to NetBIOS computer names for Windows-networking computers that you will communicate with outside of the local subnet. For example, the LMHOSTS table file entry for a computer with an address of 192.45.36.5 and a computer name of Finance1 looks like this:

```
192.45.36.5     finance1
```

The LMHOSTS file is read when WINS or broadcast name resolution fails, and resolved entries are stored in a system cache for later access.

When the computer uses the replicator service and does not use WINS, LMHOSTS entries are required on import and export servers for any computers on different subnets participating in the replication. The LMHOSTS file is also used for small-scale networks that do not have servers. For more information about the LMHOSTS file, see Chapter 15, "Setting Up LMHOSTS."

Domain Name System Addressing

The Domain Name System (DNS) is a distributed database providing a hierarchical naming system for identifying hosts on the Internet. DNS was developed to solve the problems that arose when the number of hosts on the Internet grew dramatically in the early 1980s. The specifications for DNS are defined in RFCs 1034 and 1035. Although DNS might seem similar to WINS, there is a major difference: DNS requires static configuration for computer name-to-IP address mapping, while WINS is fully dynamic and requires far less administration.

The DNS database is a tree structure called the domain name space, where each domain (node in the tree structure) is named and can contain subdomains. The domain name identifies the domain's position in the database in relation to its parent domain, with a period (.) separating each part of the names for the network nodes of the DNS domain.

The root of the DNS database is managed by the Internet Network Information Center. The top-level domains were assigned organizationally and by country. These domain names follow the international standard ISO 3166. Two-letter and three-letter abbreviations are used for countries, and various abbreviations are reserved for use by organizations, as shown in the following example.

Table 12.3   Abbreviations Used in DNS Domain Names

DNS domain name abbreviation	Type of organization
com	Commercial (for example, microsoft.com)
edu	Educational (for example, mit.edu for Massachusetts Institute of Technology)
gov	Government (for example, nsf.gov for the National Science Foundation)
org	Noncommercial organizations (for example, fidonet.org for FidoNet)
net	Networking organizations (for example nsf.net for NSFNET)

Each DNS domain is administered by different organizations, which usually break their domains into subdomains and assign administration of the subdomains to other organizations. Each domain has a unique name, and each of the subdomains have unique names within their domains. The label for each network domain is a name of up to 63 characters. The *fully qualified domain name* (FQDN), which includes the names of all network domains leading back to the root, is unique for each host on the Internet. A particular DNS name could be similar to the following, for a commercial host:

```
accounting.trey.com
```

DNS uses a client-server model, where the DNS servers contain information about a portion of the DNS database and make this information available to clients, called *resolvers*, that query the name server across the network. DNS *name servers* are programs that store information about parts of the domain name space called *zones*. The administrator for a domain sets up name servers that contain the database files with all the resource records describing all hosts in their zones. DNS resolvers are clients that are trying to use name servers to gain information about the domain name space.

Windows NT includes the DNS resolver functionality used by NetBIOS over TCP/IP and by Windows Sockets connectivity applications such as **ftp** and **telnet** to query the name server and interpret the responses.

The key task for DNS is to present friendly names for users and then resolve those names to IP addresses, as required by the internetwork. Name resolution is provided through DNS by the name servers, which interpret the information in a FQDN to find its specific address. If a local name server doesn't contain the data requested in a query, it sends back names and addresses of other name servers that could contain the information. The resolver then queries the other name servers until it finds the specific name and address it needs. This process is made faster because name servers continuously cache the information learned about the domain name space as the result of queries.

All the resolver software necessary for using DNS on the Internet is installed with Microsoft TCP/IP. To use DNS for TCP/IP name resolution, you specify options in the DNS Configuration dialog box. For more information, see Chapter 11, "Installing and Configuring Microsoft TCP/IP and SNMP."

On computers with Windows NT Server 3.5, Windows NT Workstation 3.5, or Windows for Workgroups 3.11 with Microsoft TCP/IP-32 installed, Windows Socket applications can use either DNS or NetBIOS over TCP/IP for name resolution.

The following table compares DNS versus WINS name resolution.

Table 12.4   WINS Versus DNS Name Resolution

Name provider capabilities	WINS	DNS
Provides scalable naming authority for large internetworks	Yes	Yes
Provides a dynamic, distributed naming authority for TCP/IP network names	Yes	Not dynamic
Supports MX records for electronic mail	No	Yes
Supports recursion and referral for name resolution	No	Yes
Provides hierarchical naming and resolution scheme	No	Yes
Includes DNS name server	No	Yes
Includes DNS name resolution client	Yes	Yes
Provides static name resolution	Yes (optional)	Yes (only)
Queries DNS servers	Yes[1]	Yes
Provides name server in operating system	Yes	No
Resolves NetBIOS-compatible names	Yes	No
Provides a name resolution solution for large peer-based TCP/IP networks (50,000+ systems)	Yes	No
Supports automatic name registration	For WINS clients only	No
Supports dynamic NetBIOS name registration and resolution	Yes	No
Supports managing hosts configured via DHCP	Yes	No
Supports easy administration, including browsing and managing dynamic and static registrations	Yes	No
Centralizes management of the name database	Yes	No
Defines server replication partners and policies	Yes	No
Alleviates LMHOSTS management requirements	Yes	No
Reduces IP broadcast traffic in Windows-based internetworks	Yes	No

[1] Queries DNS servers via Windows Sockets applications or, for Windows-based networking applications, via NetBIOS over TCP/IP (after using WINS first)

SNMP

Simple Network Management Protocol (SNMP) is used by administrators to monitor and control remote hosts and gateways on an internetwork. The Windows NT SNMP service allows a Windows NT computer to be monitored remotely but does not include an application to monitor other SNMP systems on the network.

Note You must install the SNMP service to use the TCP/IP performance counters in Performance Monitor, as described in Chapter 17, "Using Performance Monitor with TCP/IP Services."

SNMP is a network management protocol widely used in TCP/IP networks. These kinds of protocols are used to communicate between a management program run by an administrator and the network management agent running on a host or gateway. These protocols define the form and meaning of the messages exchanged, the representation of names and values in the messages, and administrative relationships among hosts being managed. SNMP defines a set of variables that the host must keep and specifies that all operations on the gateway are side effects of getting, putting, or setting the data variables. Because different network-management services are used for different types of devices or for different network-management protocols, each service has its own set of objects. The entire set of objects that any service or protocol uses is referred to as its *management information base* (MIB).

The Windows NT SNMP service includes MIB II (based on RFC 1213) and LAN Manager MIB II plus MIBs for DHCP and WINS servers, as described in Appendix A, "MIB Object Types for Windows NT." The SNMP service allows SNMP-based managers to perform standard SNMP commands, such as reading the counters in the standard MIBs included with the service. Windows NT SNMP has an extensible architecture, so it can be used to create custom functionality on a Windows NT computer, such as starting and stopping specific services or shutting down the system.

The SNMP service works with any computer running Windows NT and the TCP/IP protocol. With the SNMP service, a Windows NT computer can report its current status to an SNMP management system on a TCP/IP network. The service sends status information to a host in the following two cases:

- When a management system requests such information
- When a significant event occurs on the Windows NT computer

The SNMP service can handle requests from one or more hosts, and it can also report network-management information to one or more hosts, in discrete blocks of data called *traps*.

The SNMP service uses the unique host names and IP addresses of devices to recognize the host(s) to which it reports information and from which it receives requests.

When a network manager requests information about a device on the network, SNMP management software can be used to determine object values that represent network status. MIB objects represent various types of information about the device. For example, the management station might request an object called **SvStatOpen**, which would be the total number of files open on the Windows NT computer.

The SNMP service for Windows NT supports multiple MIBs through an agent Application Programming Interface (API) extension interface. At SNMP service startup time, the SNMP service loads all of the extension-agent dynamic link libraries (DLLs) that are defined in the Windows NT Registry. Two extension-agent DLLs come with Windows NT; others might be developed and added by users.

C H A P T E R   1 3

Installing and Configuring DHCP Servers

A Dynamic Host Configuration Protocol (DHCP) server is a Windows NT Server computer running Microsoft TCP/IP and the DHCP-compatible server software. DHCP is defined in Requests for Comments (RFCs) 1533, 1534, and 1541.

This chapter describes how to install and manage servers to support DHCP in Windows NT and also presents strategies for implementing DHCP. The following topics are included in this chapter:

- Overview of the DHCP client-server model
- Installing DHCP servers and using DHCP Manager
- Defining DHCP scopes
- Configuring DHCP options
- Administering DHCP clients
- Managing the DHCP database files
- Troubleshooting DHCP
- Advanced configuration parameters for DHCP
- Guidelines for setting local policies
- Planning a strategy for DHCP

Important If you want to use a DHCP server to support subnetworks that span multiple routers, you might need a firmware upgrade for your routers. Your routers must support RFCs 1532, 1533, and 1541.

To find out about DHCP-relay agent support, contact your router vendor. For more information, refer to RFC1541.TXT available via anonymous FTP from ftp.internic.net:/rfc.

Overview of DHCP Clients and Servers

Configuring DHCP servers for a network provides these benefits:

- The administrator can centrally define global and subnet TCP/IP parameters for the entire internetwork and define parameters for reserved clients.
- Client computers do not require manual TCP/IP configuration. When a client computer moves between subnets, it is reconfigured for TCP/IP automatically at system startup time.

DHCP uses a client-server model. The network administrator establishes one or more DHCP servers that maintain TCP/IP configuration information to be provided to clients that make requests.

The DHCP server database includes the following items:

- Valid configuration parameters for all clients on the internetwork.
- Valid IP addresses maintained in a pool for assignment to clients, plus reserved addresses for manual assignment.
- Duration of leases and other configuration parameters offered by the server. The lease defines the length of time for which the assigned IP address can be used.

A Windows NT computer becomes a DHCP client if the Enable Automatic DHCP Configuration option is checked in the Windows NT TCP/IP Installation Options dialog box. When a DHCP client computer is started, it communicates with a DHCP server to receive the required TCP/IP configuration information. This configuration information includes at least an IP address and submask plus the lease associated with the configuration.

Note DHCP client software is part of the Microsoft TCP/IP-32 for Windows for Workgroups software and the Microsoft Network Client 2.0 software that are included on the Windows NT Server compact disc. For information about installing this software, see the *Windows NT Server Installation Guide*.

For an overview of how DHCP works, see "Dynamic Host Configuration Protocol" in Chapter 12, "Networking Concepts for TCP/IP."

Note DHCP can be monitored using SNMP. For a list of DHCP MIB object types, see Appendix A, "MIB Object Types for Windows NT."

Installing DHCP Servers

You install a DHCP server as part of the process of installing Microsoft TCP/IP. These instructions assume you have already installed the Windows NT Server operating system on the computer.

Caution Before installing a new DHCP server, check for other DHCP servers on the network to avoid interfering with them.

You must be a member of the Administrators group for the computer you are installing or administering as a DHCP server.

▶ **To install a DHCP server**

1. Double-click the Network icon in Control Panel to display the Network Settings dialog box, and then choose the Add Software button to display the Add Network Software dialog box.

2. In the Network Software box, select TCP/IP Protocol And Related Components, and then choose the Continue button.

3. In the Windows NT TCP/IP Installation Options dialog box, select the appropriate options to be installed, including at least DHCP Server Service. Also select the SNMP Service option if you want to use Performance Monitor or SNMP to monitor DHCP.

4. Choose the OK button. When Windows NT Setup prompts you for the full path to the Windows NT Server distribution files, provide the appropriate location, and then choose the Continue button.

   All necessary files are copied to your hard disk.

   After you finish configuring TCP/IP and the Network Settings dialog box is displayed, choose the OK button.

5. Complete all the required procedures for manually configuring TCP/IP as described in "Configuring TCP/IP" in Chapter 11, "Installing and Configuring Microsoft TCP/IP and SNMP."

   If this DHCP server is multihomed (has multiple network adapters), you must use the Advanced Microsoft TCP/IP Configuration dialog box to specify IP addresses and other information for each network adapter.

   Also, if any adapter on the DHCP server is connected to a subnet that you do not want this server to support, then you must disable the bindings to that subnet for the particular adapter. To do this, double-click the Network icon in Control Panel, choose the Bindings button in the Network Settings dialog box, and then disable the related binding.

Note You cannot use DHCP to automatically configure a new DHCP server, because a computer cannot be a DHCP client and server simultaneously.

All the appropriate TCP/IP and DHCP software is ready for use after you reboot the computer.

The DHCP Client service is a Windows NT service running on a Windows NT computer. The supporting DHCP client software is automatically installed for computers running Windows NT Server or Windows NT Workstation when you install the basic operating system software.

The Microsoft DHCP Server service starts automatically during system startup if you have installed this service. You will probably want to pause the service while you are configuring scopes for the first time.

▶ **To pause the DHCP Server service at any Windows NT computer**

1. Double-click the Services icon in Control Panel.

   –Or–

   In Server Manager, choose Services from the Computer menu.

2. In the Services dialog box, select the Microsoft DHCP Server service.

3. Choose the Pause button, and then choose the Close button.

You can also start, stop, pause, and continue the DHCP service at the command prompt using the following commands: **net start dhcpserver**, **net stop dhcpserver**, **net pause dhcpserver**, and **net continue dhcpserver**.

Using DHCP Manager

The DHCP Manager icon is added to the Network Administration Tools group in Program Manager when you set up a Windows NT Server computer to be a DHCP server. You must use DHCP Manager to perform the following basic tasks:

- Create one or more DHCP scopes to begin providing DHCP services
- Define properties for the scope, including the lease duration and IP address ranges to be distributed to potential DHCP clients in the scope
- Define default values for options such as the default gateway, DNS server, or WINS server to be assigned together with an IP address, or add any custom options

The procedures for completing these tasks are described in the following sections.

▶   **To start DHCP Manager**

- From Program Manager, double-click the DHCP Manager icon in the Network Administration group.

  –Or–

  At the command prompt, type the **start dhcpadmn** command, and then press ENTER.

DHCP Manager window shows the local computer the first time you start DHCP Manager. Subsequently, the window shows a list of the DHCP servers to which DHCP Manager has connected, plus their scopes. The status bar reports the current DHCP Manager activities.

⌐ Select a server or scope name
   to expand or contract the list of servers.

⌐ This list shows the DHCP options for the
   selected scope, and the icon shows
   whether it is a global or scope option.

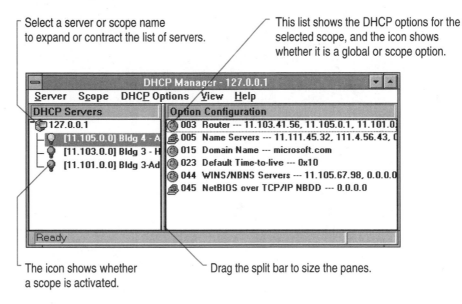

└ The icon shows whether
   a scope is activated.

└ Drag the split bar to size the panes.

Important When you are working with DHCP Manager, all computer names are DNS host names only. The full path specification might be used, such as **accounting.trey.com**, or a name might be specified relative to the local domain. In the previous example, other computers in the **trey.com** DNS domain can refer simply to **accounting**. The DNS host name is not necessarily the same as the NetBIOS computer name used in Windows-based networking.

▶ **To connect to a DHCP server**

1. From the Server menu, choose the Add command to display the Add DHCP Server To Known Server List dialog box.

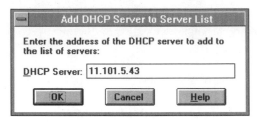

2. In the DHCP Server box, type the DNS short name or IP address for the DHCP server in which you want to connect, and then choose the OK button.

   For example, type an address such as **11.1.26.30** or type a DNS name, such as **corp01.trey.com**, in this box.

▶ **To disconnect from a selected DHCP server**

• From the Server menu, choose Remove.

   −Or−

   Press DEL.

Defining DHCP Scopes

A DHCP scope is an administrative grouping of computers running the DHCP Client service. You create a scope for each subnet on the network to define parameters for that subnet.

Each scope has the following properties:

▪ A unique subnet mask used to determine the subnet related to a given IP address

▪ A scope name assigned by the administrator when the scope is created

▪ Lease duration values to be assigned to DHCP clients with dynamic addresses

Each subnet can have only one scope with a single continuous range of IP addresses; those addresses must be valid for the subnet. To implement several address ranges in a subnet, create a continuous range that encompasses them all, and then exclude the addresses between the intended ranges. The range can be expanded later if you need more addresses.

Creating Scopes

You must use DHCP Manager to create, manage, or remove scopes.

▶ **To create a new DHCP scope**

1. In the DHCP Servers list in the DHCP Manager window, select the server for which you want to create a scope.

2. From the Scope menu, choose Create.

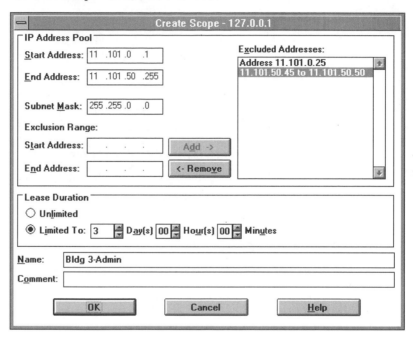

3. To define the available range of IP addresses for this scope, type the beginning and ending IP addresses for the range in the Start Address and End Address boxes.

   The IP address range includes the Start and End values. This range should not include addresses of existing statically configured machines. Either these static addresses should be outside the range for the scope or they should be immediately excluded from the range. Because the DHCP server itself is statically configured, be sure that its IP address is outside of, or excluded from, the range of the scope.

   Note   You must supply this information before this scope can be activated.

   ---

4. In the Subnet Mask box, DHCP Manager proposes a subnet mask, based on the IP address of the Start and End addresses. Accept the proposed value, unless you know that a different value is required.

5. To define excluded addresses within the IP address pool range, use the Exclusion Range controls, as follows:

- Type the first IP address that is part of the excluded range in the Start Address box, and then type the last number in the End Address box. Then choose the Add button. Continue to define any other excluded ranges in the same way.

- To exclude a single IP address, type the number in the Start Address box. Leave the End Address box empty, and then choose the Add button.

- To remove an IP address or range from the excluded range, select it in the Excluded Addresses box, and then choose the Remove button.

The excluded ranges should include all IP addresses that you assigned manually to other DHCP servers, non-DHCP clients, diskless workstations, or RAS and PPP clients.

6. To specify the lease duration for IP addresses in this scope, select Limited To. Then type values defining the number of days, hours, and seconds for the length of the address lease.

If you do not want IP address leases in this scope to expire, select the Unlimited option. As noted in "Guidelines for Lease Options" later in this chapter, infinite leases should be used with great caution.

7. In the Name box, type a scope name.

The scope name is any name you want to use to describe this subnet. The name can include any combination of letters, numbers, and hyphens. Blank spaces and underscore characters are also allowed.

Note You cannot use Unicode characters.

8. Optionally, in the Comment box, type any string to describe this scope, and then choose the OK button.

Note When you finish creating a scope, a message prompts you that the scope has not been activated, and then allows you to choose Yes to activate the scope immediately. However, you should not activate a new scope until you have defined the DHCP options to be configured for this scope.

Now you can continue with the procedures described in "Configuring DHCP Option Types" and "Administering DHCP Clients" later in this chapter. After you have configured the options for this scope, you must activate it so that DHCP client computers on the related subnet can begin using DHCP for dynamic TCP/IP configuration.

▶ **To activate a DHCP scope**

- From the Scope menu, choose the Activate command to make this scope active.

  The menu command name changes to Deactivate when the selected scope is currently active.

Changing Scope Properties

The subnet identifiers and address pool make up the properties of scopes. You can change the properties of an existing scope.

You cannot exclude a range of addresses that includes an active lease. You must first delete the active lease, as described in "Managing Client Leases" later in this chapter, and then retry the exclusion.

▶ **To change the properties of a DHCP scope**

1. In the DHCP Servers list in the DHCP Manager window, select the scope for which you want to change properties, and then choose Properties from the Scope menu.

   –Or–

   In the DHCP Servers list, double-click the scope you want to change.

2. In the Scope Properties dialog box, change any values for the IP address pool, lease duration, or name and comment as described earlier in "Creating Scopes" or in online Help. You can extend the address range of the scope, but you cannot reduce it. You can, however, exclude any unwanted addresses from the range.

3. Choose the OK button.

Removing a Scope

When a subnet is no longer in use, or any other time you want to remove an existing scope, you can remove it using DHCP Manager. If any IP address in the scope is still leased or in use, you must first deactivate the scope until all client leases expire or all client lease extension requests are denied.

When a scope is deactivated, it does not acknowledge lease or renewal requests, so existing clients lose their leases at renewal time and reconfigure with another available DHCP server. To assure that all clients migrate smoothly to a new scope, you should deactivate the old scope for at least half of the lease time, or until all clients have been moved off the scope manually. To move a client manually, from the Command Prompt of the client computer use the **ipconfig/renew** command, and then restart the computer if necessary.

▶ **To remove a scope**

1. In the DHCP Servers list in the DHCP Manager window, select the scope you want to remove.

2. From the Scope menu, choose Deactivate. (This command name changes to Activate when the scope is not active.)

   The scope must remain deactivated until you are sure the scope is not in use.

3. From the Scope menu, choose Delete.

   The Delete command is not available for an active scope.

Configuring DHCP Options

The configuration parameters that a DHCP server assigns to a client are defined as *DHCP options* using DHCP Manager. Most of the options that you will want to specify are predefined, based on standard parameters defined in RFC 1541.

When you configure a DHCP scope, you can assign DHCP options to govern all configuration parameters. You can also define, edit, or delete DHCP options. These tasks are described in the following sections.

Assigning DHCP Configuration Options

Besides the IP addressing information, other DHCP configuration options to be passed to DHCP clients must be configured for each scope. Options can be defined globally for all scopes on the current server, specifically for a selected scope, or for individual DHCP clients with reserved addresses.

- Active global options always apply unless overridden by scope options or DHCP client settings.

- Active options for a scope apply to all computers in that scope, unless overridden for an individual DHCP client.

The Microsoft DHCP network packet allocates 312 bytes for DHCP options. That is more than enough space for most option configurations. With some DHCP servers and clients, you can allocate unused space in the DHCP packet to additional options. This feature, called *option overlay,* is not supported by Microsoft DHCP Server. If you attempt to use more than 312 bytes, some options settings will be lost. In that case, you should delete any unused or low-priority options.

If you are using a third-party DHCP server, be aware that Microsoft DHCP clients do not support option overlays, either. If your option set is larger than 312 bytes, be sure that the settings used by Microsoft DHCP clients are included at the beginning of the option list. Settings beyond the first 312 bytes are not read by Microsoft DHCP clients.

The built-in options are described in "Predefined DHCP Client Configuration Options" later in this chapter.

Note Lease duration and subnet mask are defined for the scope in the Create Scope dialog box. You cannot configure them directly as options.

▶ **To assign DHCP configuration options**

1. In the DHCP Servers list in the DHCP Manager window, select the scope you want to configure.

2. From the DHCP Options menu, choose the Global or Scope command, depending on whether you want to define option settings for all scopes on the currently selected server or the scope currently selected in the DHCP Manager window.

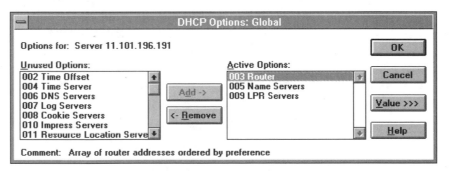

3. In the Unused Options list in the DHCP Options dialog box, select the name of the DHCP option that you want to apply, and then choose the Add button to move the name to the Active Options list.

   This list shows both predefined options and any custom options that you added.

   For example, if you want to specify DNS servers for computers, select the option named DNS Servers in the Unused Options list and choose the Add button.

   If you want to remove an active DHCP option, select its name in the Active Options box, and then choose the Remove button.

4. To define the value for an active option, select its name in the Active Options box, and then choose the Values button. Choose the Edit button, and then edit the information in the Current Value box, depending on the data type for the option, as follows:

   - For an IP address, type the assigned address for the selected option

   - For a number, type an appropriate decimal or hexadecimal value for the option

   - For a string, type an appropriate ASCII string containing letters and numbers for the option

   For example, to specify the DNS name servers to be used by DHCP clients, select DNS Servers in the Active Options list. Then choose the Edit button and type a list of IP addresses for DNS servers. The list should be in the order of preference.

   For details about the Edit Array and Edit Address dialog boxes, see the online Help.

5. When you have completed all your changes, choose the OK button.

Tip If you are using DHCP to configure WINS clients, be sure to set options #44 WINS Servers and #46 Node Type. These options will allow DHCP-configured computers to find and use the WINS server automatically.

Creating New DHCP Options

You can add custom parameters to be included with DHCP client configuration information. You can also change values or other elements of the predefined DHCP options. The option you add appears in the list of available DHCP options in the DHCP Options dialog boxes for defining options globally, per scope, and per individual reserved DHCP client.

▶ **To add new DHCP options**

1. From the DHCP Options menu, choose Defaults.

2. In the Option Class list in the DHCP Options: Default Values dialog box, select the class for which you want to add new DHCP options, and then choose the New button.

   The option class can include the DHCP standard options or any custom options that you add.

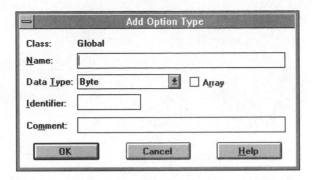

3. In the Name box of the Add Option Type dialog box, type a new option name.

4. From the Data Type list, select the data type for this option as described in the following list. If this data type represents an array, select the Array box.

Data type	Meaning
Binary	Value expressed as an array of bytes
Byte	An 8-bit, unsigned integer
Encapsulated	An array of unsigned bytes
IP address	An IP address of the form w.x.y.z
Long	A 32-bit, signed integer
Long integer	A 32-bit, unsigned integer
String	An ASCII text string
Word	A 16-bit, unsigned integer

If you select the wrong data type, an error message appears or the value is truncated or converted to the required type.

5. In the Identifier box, type a unique code number to be associated with this DHCP option. This must be a number between 0 and 255.

6. In the Comment box, type a description of the DHCP option, and then choose the OK button.

7. In the DHCP Options: Default Values dialog box, select the option, choose the Edit button, and then type the value to be configured by default for this DHCP option.

8. Choose the OK button.

You can delete custom DHCP options, but you cannot delete any predefined DHCP options.

▶ **To delete a custom DHCP option**

1. From the DHCP Options menu, choose Defaults.

2. In the DHCP Options: Default Values dialog box, select the related class in the Option Class list.

3. In the Option Name list, select the option you want to delete, and then choose the Delete button.

Changing DHCP Option Default Values

You can change the default values for the predefined and custom DHCP options for configuring clients. For example, you could change the default values for these built-in options:

- 3 = Router, to specify the IP addresses for the routers on the subnet

- 6 = DNS Servers, to specify the IP addresses of the DNS name servers used at your site

- 15 = Domain Name, to specify the DNS domain names to be used for host name resolution

Options that take an array of IP addresses have a default value of 0.0.0.0. You should reset the default value of any such options you intend to use or be sure to set a different value when you assign the option either globally or for a selected scope, as described in "Assigning DHCP Configuration Options" earlier in this chapter.

▶ **To change a DHCP option value**

1. From the DHCP Options menu, choose Defaults.

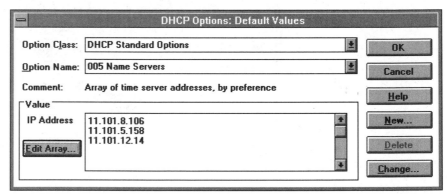

2. In the Option Class list in the DHCP Options: Default Values dialog box, select the option class for which you want to change values.

3. If you want to change the default value for an option, select the option you want to change in the Option Name list, choose the Edit button, and then type a new value in the Value box.

   Choosing the Edit button displays a special dialog box for editing strings, arrays of IP address, or binary values. For information about using the special editing dialog boxes, see the online Help for DHCP Manager.

4. If you want to change basic elements of a custom option, select it in the Option Name list, and then choose the Change button.

   You can change the name, data type, identifier, and comment for a DHCP option, following the procedures described earlier in "Creating New DHCP Options."

5. When you complete all the changes you want to make, choose the OK button.

Defining Options for Reservations

You can assign DHCP options and specify custom values for DHCP clients that use reserved IP addresses.

For information about how to reserve IP configuration information for DHCP clients, see "Managing Client Reservations" later in this chapter.

▶ **To change DHCP options for reservations**

1. From the Scope menu, choose Active Leases.

2. In the IP Address list of the Active Leases dialog box, select the reserved address whose options you want to change, and then choose the Options button.

   The Options button is only available for reserved addresses; it is not available for DHCP clients with dynamic addresses.

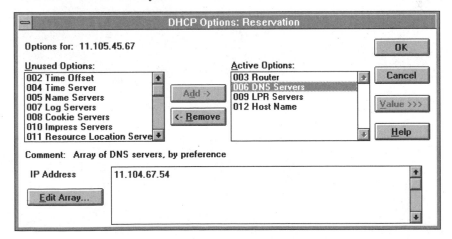

3. In the DHCP Options: Reservation dialog box, select an option name in the Unused Options list, and then choose the Add button to move the name to the Active Options list.

If you want to remove a DHCP option that has been assigned to the scope, select its name in the Active Options box, and then choose the Remove button.

4. To change a value for an option selected in the Active Options list, choose the Value button, choose the Edit button, and then enter a new value in the Current Value box.

Predefined DHCP Client Configuration Options

The tables in this section describe the predefined options available for configuration of DHCP clients. These options are defined in RFC 1533.

You can use Microsoft DHCP Server to set any of the options described in this section. Microsoft DHCP clients however, support only the options whose code and option name are listed in bold type. If you have third-party DHCP clients, you can set any option listed that is supported by the third-party client software.

Table 13.1   Basic Options

Code	Option name	Meaning
0	Pad	Causes subsequent fields to align on word boundaries.
255	End	Indicates end of options in the DHCP packet.
1	**Subnet mask**	Specifies the subnet mask of the client subnet. This option is defined in the Create Scope or Scope Properties dialog box. It cannot be set directly in an Option dialog box.
2	Time offset	Specifies the Universal Coordinated Time (UCT) offset in seconds.
3	**Router**	Specifies a list of IP addresses for routers on the client's subnet.[1]
4	Time server	Specifies a list of IP addresses for time servers available to the client.[1]
5	Name servers	Specifies a list of IP addresses for name servers available to the client.[1]
6	**DNS servers**	Specifies a list of IP addresses for DNS name servers available to the client.[1] Multihomed computers can have only one list per computer, not one per adapter card.

Table 13.1   Basic Options *(continued)*

Code	Option name	Meaning
7	Log servers	Specifies a list of IP addresses for MIT_LCS User Datagram Protocol (UDP) log servers available to the client.[1]
8	Cookie servers	Specifies a list of IP addresses for RFC 865 cookie servers available to the client.[1]
9	LPR servers	Specifies a list of IP addresses for RFC 1179 line-printer servers available to the client.[1]
10	Impress servers	Specifies a list of IP addresses for Imagen Impress servers available to the client.[1]
11	Resource location servers	Specifies a list of RFC 887 Resource Location servers available to the client.[1]
12	Host name	Specifies the host name of up to 63 characters for the client. The name must start with a letter, end with a letter or digit, and have as interior characters only letters, numbers, and hyphens. The name can be qualified with the local DNS domain name.
13	Boot file size	Specifies the size of the default boot image file for the client, in 512-octet blocks.
14	Merit dump file	Specifies the ASCII path name of a file where the client's core image is dumped if a crash occurs.
15	**Domain name**	Specifies the DNS domain name the client should use for DNS host name resolution.
16	Swap server	Specifies the IP address of the client's swap server.
17	Root path	Specifies the ASCII path name for the client's root disk.
18	Extensions path	Specifies a file retrievable via TFTP containing information interpreted the same as the vendor-extension field in the BOOTP response, except the file length is unconstrained and references to Tag 18 in the file are ignored.

[1] List is specified in order of preference.

The following table lists IP layer parameters on a per-host basis.

Table 13.2   IP Layer Parameters per Host

Code	Option name	Meaning
19	IP layer forwarding	Enables or disables forwarding of IP packet for this client. 1 enables forwarding; 0 disables it.
20	Nonlocal source routing	Enables or disables forwarding of datagrams with non-local source routes. 1 enables forwarding; 0 disables it.
21	Policy filter masks	Specifies policy filters that consist of a list of pairs of IP addresses and masks specifying destination/mask pairs for filtering nonlocal source routes. Any source routed datagram whose next-hop address does not match a filter will be discarded by the client.
22	Max DG reassembly size	Specifies the maximum size datagram that the client can reassemble. The minimum value is 576.
23	Default time-to-live	Specifies the default time-to-live (TTL) that the client uses on outgoing datagrams. The value for the octet is a number between 1 and 255.
24	Path MTU aging timeout	Specifies the timeout in seconds for aging Path Maximum Transmission Unit (MTU) values (discovered by the mechanism defined in RFC 1191).
25	Path MTU plateau table	Specifies a table of MTU sizes to use when performing Path MTU Discovered as defined in RFC 1191. The table is sorted by size from smallest to largest. The minimum MTU value is 68.

The following table lists IP parameters on a per-interface basis. These options affect the operation of the IP layer on a per-interface basis. A client can issue multiple requests, one per interface, to configure interfaces with their specific parameters.

Table 13.3   IP Parameters per Interface

Code	Option name	Meaning
26	MTU option	Specifies the MTU discovery size for this interface. The minimum MTU value is 68.
27	All subnets are local	Specifies whether the client assumes that all subnets of the client's internetwork use the same MTU as the local subnet where the client is connected. 1 indicates that all subnets share the same MTU; 0 indicates that the client should assume some subnets might have smaller MTUs.
28	Broadcast address	Specifies the broadcast address used on the client's subnet.
29	Perform mask discovery	Specifies whether the client should use Internet Control Message Protocol (ICMP) for subnet mask discovery. 1 indicates the client should perform mask discovery; 0 indicates the client should not.
30	Mask supplier	Specifies whether the client should respond to subnet mask requests using ICMP. 1 indicates the client should respond; 0 indicates the client should not respond.
31	Perform router discovery	Specifies whether the client should solicit routers using the router discovery method in RFC 1256. 1 indicates that the client should perform router discovery; 0 indicates that the client should not use it.
32	Router solicitation address	Specifies the IP address to which the client submits router solicitation requests.
33	Static route	Specifies a list of IP address pairs that indicate the static routes the client should install in its routing cache. Any multiple routes to the same destination are listed in descending order or priority. The routes are destination/router address pairs. (The default route of 0.0.0.0 is an illegal destination for a static route.)

The following table lists link layer parameters per interface. These options affect the operation of the data link layer on a per-interface basis.

Table 13.4   Link Layer Parameters per Interface

Code	Option name	Meaning
34	Trailer encapsulation	Specifies whether the client should negotiate use of trailers (RFC 983) when using the ARP protocol. 1 indicates the client should attempt to use trailer; 0 indicates the client should not use trailers.
35	ARP cache timeout	Specifies the timeout in seconds for ARP cache entries.
36	Ethernet encapsulation	Specifies whether the client should use Ethernet v. 2 (RFC 894) or IEEE 802.3 (RFC 1042) encapsulation if the interface is Ethernet. 1 indicates that the client should use RFC 1042 encapsulation; 0 indicates the client should use RFC 894 encapsulation.

The following table shows TCP parameters. These options affect the operation of the TCP layer on a per-interface basis.

Table 13.5   TCP Parameters

Code	Option name	Meaning
37	Default time-to-live	Specifies the default TTL the client should use when sending TCP segments. The minimum value of the octet is 1.
38	Keepalive interval	Specifies the interval in seconds the client TCP should wait before sending a keepalive message on a TCP connection. A value of 0 indicates that the client should not send keepalive messages on connections unless specifically requested by an application.
39	Keepalive garbage	Specifies whether the client should send TCP keepalive messages with an octet of garbage data for compatibility with older implementations. 1 indicates that a garbage octet should be sent; 0 indicates that it should not be sent.

The following table shows application layer parameters. These miscellaneous options are used to configure applications and services.

Table 13.6   Application Layer Parameters

Code	Option name	Meaning
40	NIS domain name	Specifies the name of the Network Information Service (NIS) domain as an ASCII string.
41	NIS servers	Specifies a list of IP addresses for NIS servers available to the client.[1]
42	NTP servers	Specifies a list of IP addresses for Network Time Protocol (NTP) servers available to the client.[1]

[1] List is specified in order of preference.

The following options are for vendor-specific information.

Table 13.7   Vendor-Specific Information

Code	Option name	Meaning
43	Vendor specific info	Binary information used by clients and servers to exchange vendor-specific information. Servers not equipped to interpret the information ignore it. Clients that don't receive the information attempt to operate without it.

Table 13.8   NetBIOS Over TCP/IP

Code	Option name	Meaning
44	**WINS/NBNS servers**	Specifies a list of IP addresses for NetBIOS name servers (NBNS).[1]
45	NetBIOS over TCP/IP NBDD	Specifies a list of IP addresses for NetBIOS datagram distribution servers (NBDD).[1]
46	**WINS/NBT node type**	Allows configurable NetBIOS over TCP/IP clients to be configured as described in RFC 1001/1002, where 1=b-node, 2=p-node, 4=m-node, and 8=h-node. On multihomed computers, the node type is assigned to the entire computer, not to individual adapter cards.

Table 13.8   NetBIOS Over TCP/IP (*continued*)

Code	Option name	Meaning
47	NetBIOS scope ID	Specifies as a string that is the NetBIOS over TCP/IP Scope ID for the client, as specified in RFC 1001/1002. On multihomed computers, the scope ID is assigned to the entire computer, not to individual adapter cards.
48	X Window system font	Specifies a list of IP addresses for X Window font servers available to the client.[1]
49	X Window system display	Specifies a list of IP addresses for X Window System Display Manager servers available to the client.[1]

[1] List is specified in order of preference.

Table 13.9   DHCP Extensions

Code	Option name	Meaning
51	Lease time	Specifies the time in seconds from address assignment until the client's lease on the address expires. Lease time is specified in the Create Scope or Scope Properties dialog box. It cannot be set directly in a DHCP Options dialog box.
58	Renewal (T1) time value	Specifies the time in seconds from address assignment until the client enters the renewing state. Renewal time is a function of the lease time option, which is specified in the Create Scope or Scope Properties dialog box. It cannot be set directly in a DHCP Options dialog box.
59	Rebinding (T2) time value	Specifies the time in seconds from address assignment until the client enters the rebinding state. Rebinding time is a function of the lease time option, which is specified in the Create Scope or Scope Properties dialog box. It cannot be set directly in a DHCP Options dialog box.

Administering DHCP Clients

After you have established the scope and defined the range of available and excluded IP addresses, DHCP-enabled clients can begin using the service for automatic TCP/IP configuration.

You can use DHCP Manager to manage individual client leases, including creating and managing reservations for clients.

Tip   You can use the **ipconfig** utility to troubleshoot the IP configuration on computers that use DHCP, as described in Appendix A, "TCP/IP Utilities Reference." You can also use **ipconfig** on TCP/IP-32 clients on Windows for Workgroups 3.11 computers and on computers running Microsoft Network Client version 2.0 for MS-DOS.

Managing Client Leases

The lease for the IP address assigned by a DHCP server has an expiration date, which the client must renew if it is going to continue to use that address. You can view the lease duration and other information for specific DHCP clients, and then you can add options and change settings for reserved DHCP clients.

Information about active leases in the currently selected scope is shown in the Active Leases dialog box. In addition to information on individual leases and reservations, the Active Leases dialog box also shows the total number of addresses in the scope, the number and percentage of addresses that are currently unavailable because they are active or excluded, and the number and percentage of addresses that are currently available.

Because the count of active leases and excluded addresses is an aggregate, it cannot tell you want you want to know about only the active leases. The Active/Excluded count when a scope is deactivated reflects only excluded addresses. To determine the number of active leases and reservations, compare the Active/Excluded count before and after the scope is activated.

Leases are retained in the DHCP server database approximately one day after expiration. This grace period protects a client's lease in case of client and server are in different time zones, the two computers' clocks are not synchronized, or the client computer was off the network when the lease expired. These expired leases are included in the aggregate Active/Excluded count, as well as in the list of active clients in the Active Leases dialog box. They are distinguished by a dimmed icon.

▶ **To view client lease information**

1. In the DHCP Servers list in the DHCP Manager window, select the scope for which you want to view or change client information.

2. From the Scope menu, choose Active Leases.

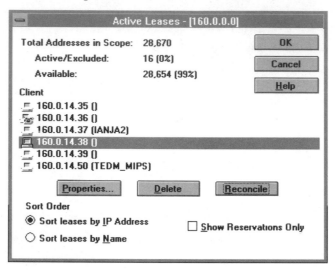

3. In the Active Leases dialog box, select the computer whose lease you want to view in the IP Address list, and then choose the Properties button.

   If you want to view only clients that use reserved IP addresses, check the Show Reservations Only box.

4. In the Client Properties dialog box, you can view the unique identifier and other client information, including the lease expiration date.

Note   You can only edit the name, unique ID, and comment, or choose the Options button in the Client Properties dialog box for clients with reserved IP addresses.

For information about the Options button in this dialog box, see "Defining Options for Reservations" earlier in this chapter.

You can delete the lease of any DHCP client in the scope. The main reason for doing so is to remove a lease that conflicts with an IP address exclusion or a client reservation that you want to add. Deleting a lease has the same effect as if the client's lease expired—the next time that client computer starts, it must enter the initialization state and obtain new TCP/IP configuration information from a DHCP server. There is nothing, however, to prevent the client from obtaining a new lease for the same IP address; you must make the address unavailable before the client requests another lease.

Important   Delete only entries for clients that are no longer using the assigned DHCP lease or that are to be moved immediately to a new address. Deleting an active client could result in duplicate IP addresses on the network, because deleted addresses will be assigned to new active clients.

After you delete a client's lease and then set a reservation or exclusion, you should always type the **ipconfig /release** command at the command prompt for a DHCP client computer to force the client to free its IP address.

▶   **To delete a client's lease**

1. In the IP Client list of the Active Leases dialog box, select the client lease you want to cancel, and then choose the Delete button.

2. Make a reservation with the IP address or exclude it from the range.

3. Force the client with the existing lease to give it up.

   From the Command Prompt on the client computer, use the **ipconfig/release** command.

5. If you want, give this client a new IP address.

   From the Command Prompt on the client computer, use the **ipconfig/renew** command.

Managing Client Reservations

You can reserve a specific IP address for a client. Typically, you need to reserve addresses in the following cases:

- For domain controllers if the network also uses LMHOSTS files that define IP addresses for domain controllers
- For clients that use IP addresses assigned using another method for TCP/IP configuration
- For assignment by RAS servers to non-DHCP clients
- For DNS servers

If multiple DHCP servers are distributing addresses in the same scope, the client reservations on each DHCP server should be identical. Otherwise, the DHCP reserved client receives different IP addresses, depending on the responding server.

Important The IP address and static name specified in WINS take precedence over the IP address assigned by the DHCP server. For such clients, create client reservations with the IP address that is defined in the WINS database.

▶ **To add a reservation for a client**

1. From the Scope menu, choose Add Reservations.

2. In the Add Reserved Clients dialog box, type information to identify the first reserved client:

   - IP Address specifies an address from the reserved address pool. You can specify any reserved, unused IP address. DHCP Manager checks and warns you if a duplicate or nonreserved address is entered.

- Unique Identifier usually specifies the media access control (MAC) address for the client computer's network adapter card. You can determine this address by typing the **net config wksta** command at the command prompt on the client computer.

- Client Name specifies the computer name for this client. This is used for identification purposes only and does not affect the actual computer name for the client. This is not available for MS-DOS–based clients; in this case, only the Unique Identifier appears.

- Client Comment is any optional text that you enter to describe this client.

3. Choose the Add button to add the reservation to the DHCP database.

   You can continue to add reservations without closing this dialog box.

4. When you have added all reservations, choose the Close button.

After the IP address is reserved in DHCP Manager, the client computer must be restarted to be configured with the new IP address.

If you want to change a reserved IP address for a client, you have to remove the old reserved address, and then add a new reservation. You can change any other information about a reserved client while keeping the reserved IP address.

Reserving an address does not automatically force a client who is currently using the address to move elsewhere. If you are reserving a new address for a client or an address that is different from the client's current one, you should verify that the address has not already been leased by the DHCP server. If the address is already in use, the client that is using it must release the address by issuing a release request. To make this happen, at the Command Prompt of the client computer, use the **ipconfig /release** command. Clients using MS-DOS, and possibly clients using third-party operating systems, will have to restart their computers for the change to take effect. Because the client's current address is now reserved, the client is moved to a different address.

Reserving an address also does not force the client for whom the reservation is made to move to the reserved address. In this case, too, the client must issue a renewal request. At the Command Prompt of the client computer, use the **ipconfig /renew** command, and then restart the computer if necessary. The DHCP server will note that the client has a reserved address, and will move the client.

▶ **To change the reserved IP address**

1. Make sure the reserved client is not using the old IP address by shutting down the client computer immediately after issuing the **ip config/release** command on that client computer.

2. In the Active Leases dialog box, select the reserved IP address in the Client list, and then choose the Delete button and the OK button.

3. From the Scope menu, choose Add Reservations, and then enter information for a new reservation as described earlier in this section.

▶ **To change basic information for a reserved client**

1. From the Scope menu, choose Active Leases.

2. In the Client list of the Active Leases dialog box, select the address of the reserved client that you want to change, and then choose the Properties button.

3. In the Client Properties dialog box, change the unique identifier, client name, or comment, and then choose the OK button.

Note   You can only change values in the Client Properties dialog box for reserved clients.

You can also view and change the options types that define configuration parameters for selected reserved clients by choosing the Options button in the Client Properties dialog box. Changing options for a reserved client follows the same procedure as use to originally define options, as described in "Defining Options for Reservations" earlier in this chapter.

Managing the DHCP Database Files

The following files are stored in the *systemroot*\SYSTEM32\DHCP directory that is created when you set up a DHCP server:

- DHCP.MDB is the DHCP database file.
- DHCP.TMP is a temporary file that DHCP creates for temporary database information.

- JET.LOG and the JET*.LOG files contain logs of all transactions done with the database. These files are used by DHCP to recover data if necessary.

- SYSTEM.MDB is used by DHCP for holding information about the structure of its database.

Caution The DHCP.TMP, DHCP.MDB, JET.LOG, and SYSTEM.MDB files should not be removed or tampered with.

The DHCP database and related Registry entries are backed up automatically at a specific interval (15 minutes by default), based on the value of Registry parameters (as described later in this chapter).

After DHCP has been running for a while, the database might need to be compacted to improve performance. You should compact the DHCP database whenever it approaches 10 MB.

▶ **To compact the DHCP database**

1. At the DHCP server, stop the Dynamic Host Configuration Protocol using the Control Panel Services option.

   –Or–

   At the command prompt, type the **net stop dhcpserver** command.

2. Run the JETPACK.EXE program (which is found in the *\systemroot*\SYSTEM32 directory) from File Manager or Program Manager.

3. Restart the Dynamic Host Configuration Protocol on the DHCP server.

Caution Do not compact the SYSTEM.MDB database.

Troubleshooting DHCP

The following error conditions can appear to indicate potential problems with the DHCP server:

- The administrator can't connect for a DHCP server using DHCP Manager. The message that appears might be "The RPC server is unavailable."

- DHCP clients cannot renew the leases for their IP addresses. The message that appears on the client computer is "The DHCP client could not renew the IP address lease."

- The DHCP Client service or Microsoft DHCP Server service might be down and cannot be restarted.

The first task is to make sure the DHCP services are running.

▶ **To ensure the DHCP services are running**

1. Use the Services option in Control Panel to verify that the DHCP services are running.

   In the Services dialog box for the client computer, Started should appear in the Status column for the DHCP Client service. For the DHCP server itself, the Started should appear in the Status column for the Microsoft DHCP Server service.

2. If a necessary service is not started on either computer, start the service.

In rare circumstances, the DHCP server cannot boot or a STOP error might occur. If the DHCP server is down, complete the following procedure to restart it.

▶ **To restart a DHCP server that is down**

1. Turn off the power to the server, and then wait about one minute.

2. Turn on the power, start Windows NT Server, and then log on under an account with Administrator rights.

3. At the command prompt, type the **net start dhcpserver** command, and then press ENTER.

Note Use Event Viewer to find the possible source of problems with DHCP services.

Restoring the DHCP Database

If you ascertain that the DHCP services are running on both the client and server computers but the error conditions described earlier persist, then the DHCP database is not available or has become corrupted. If a DHCP server fails for any reason, you can restore the database from the automatic backup files.

▶ **To restore a DHCP database**

- Restart the DHCP server using the procedure described earlier in this chapter.

  If the DHCP database has become corrupted, it is automatically restored from the DHCP backup directory specified in the Registry, as described later in this chapter.

▶ **To force the restoration of a DHCP database**

- Set the value of **RestoreFlag** in the Registry to 1, and then restart the computer.

  For information about this parameter, see "Registry Parameters for DHCP Servers" later in this chapter.

▶ **To manually restore a DHCP database**

- If the two restore methods described earlier in this chapter do not work, manually copy all DHCP database files from the backup directory to the \DHCP working directory. Then restart the Microsoft DHCP Server service.

  If the backup database is also corrupted and you have an additional backup stored elsewhere, copy the most recent usable backup to the \DHCP working directory, and then restart the DHCP Server service.

Once you have restored the DHCP database using any of these methods, you need to reconcile the database to add entries for any leased addresses that are not in the restored database.

▶ **To reconcile the DHCP database**

1. From the Scope menu, choose the Active Leases command.

2. In the Active Leases dialog box, choose the Reconcile button.

Backing up the DHCP Database onto Another Computer

The DHCP database is backed up at regular intervals, whenever the DHCP service is stopped, and whenever Windows NT is shut down. When the DHCP service restarts, if it detects a corrupt database it restores the database from the backup copy stored in the \DHCP\BACKUP\JET directory. There is no guarantee, however, that database corruption will be detected during backup; it is a good idea to periodically back up the database to another computer.

▶ **To back up a DHCP database to another computer**

* Use the Replicator service to copy the contents of the DHCP backup directory to the new computer.

If the DHCP server fails to restart because of a database problem, save the existing database to a different location, and then try restoring the database with the copy you saved to another computer. Recent new leases are noted in the Registry but not in the DHCP database; these addresses might be permanently lost from the address range.

Creating a New DHCP Database

If the database has been corrupted and you do not have a workable backup copy, you have to delete the database, and then create a new one.

▶ **To create a new database**

1. Move the file *systemroot*\SYSTEM32\DHCP.MDB to another location.
2. Delete all files in the *systemroot*\SYSTEM32\DHCP directory.
3. Delete all files in the *systemroot*\SYSTEM32\DHCP\BACKUP\JET directory.
4. Copy the file SYSTEM.MDB from the Windows NT Server CD-ROM or floppy disks to the *systemroot*\SYSTEM32\DHCP directory.
5. Restart the DHCP server.

When you check DHCP Manager, the scope still exists because the Registry holds the information on the address range of the scope, including a bitmap of the addresses in use. You need to reconcile the DHCP database to add database entries for the existing leases in the address bitmask. As clients renew, they are matched with these leases, and eventually the database is once again complete.

▶ **To reconcile the DHCP database**

1. From the Scope menu, choose the Active Leases command.

2. In the Active Leases dialog box, choose the Reconcile button.

Although it is not required, you can force clients to renew their leases in order to update the DHCP database as quickly as possible. From the Command Prompt of the client computer, type the **ipconfig/renew** command.

Advanced Configuration Parameters for DHCP

This section presents configuration parameters that affect the behavior of DHCP servers and clients, and that can be modified only through Registry Editor. For the changes to take effect after you modify any of these value entries, you must restart the Microsoft DHCP Server service for server parameters or the DHCP Client service for client parameters.

Caution   You can impair or disable Windows NT if you make incorrect changes in the Registry while using Registry Editor. Whenever possible, use DHCP Manager to make configuration changes, rather than using Registry Editor. If you make errors while changing values with Registry Editor, you will not be warned, because Registry Editor does not recognize semantic errors.

▶ **To make changes to the DHCP server or client configuration using Registry Editor**

1. Start the Registry Editor by running the REGEDT32.EXE program from File Manager or Program Manager.

    –Or–

    At the command prompt, type the **start regedt32** command, and then press ENTER.

    When the Registry Editor window appears, you can press F1 to get Help on how to make changes in Registry Editor.

2. In Registry Editor, select the window titled HKEY_LOCAL_MACHINE on Local Machine, and then click the icons for the SYSTEM subtree until you reach the subkey for the specific parameter, as described in the following sections.

The following sections describe the value entries for parameters for DHCP servers and clients that can be set only by adding an entry or changing their values in Registry Editor.

Registry Parameters for DHCP Servers

When you change any of these parameters except **RestoreFlag**, you must restart the computer for the changes to take effect. For the **RestoreFlag** parameter, you must restart the Microsoft DHCP Server service.

The Registry parameters for DHCP servers are specified under the following key:

`..SYSTEM\current\currentcontrolset\services\DHCPServer\Parameters`

APIProtocolSupport

Data type = REG_DWORD
Range = 0x1, 0x2, 0x4, 0x5, 0x7
Default = 0x1

Specifies the supported protocols for the DHCP server. You can change this value to ensure that different computers running different protocols can access the DHCP server. The values for this parameter can be the following:

0x1   For RPC over TCPIP protocols
0x2   For RPC over named pipes protocols
0x4   For RPC over local procedure call (LPC) protocols
0x5   For RPC over TCPIP and RPC over LPC
0x7   For RPC over all three protocols (TCP/IP, named pipes, and LPC)

BackupDatabasePath

Data type = REG_EXPAND_SZ
Range = *filename*
Default = %SystemRoot%\system32\dhcp\backup

Specifies the location of the backup database file where the database is backed up periodically. The best location for the backup file is on another hard drive, so that the database can be recovered in case of a system drive crash. Do not specify a network drive, because DHCP Manager cannot access a network drive for database backup and recovery.

BackupInterval

Data type = REG_DWORD
Range = no limit
Default = 15 minutes

Specifies the interval for backing up the database.

DatabaseCleanupInterval

Data type = REG_DWORD
Range = No limit
Default = 0x15180 (864,000 minutes — 24 hours)

Specifies the interval for cleaning up expired client records from the DHCP database, freeing up those IP addresses for reuse.

DatabaseLoggingFlag

Data type = REG_DWORD
Range = 0 or 1
Default = 1 (true—that is, database logging is enabled)

Specifies whether to record the database changes in the JET.LOG file. This log file is used after a system crash to recover changes that have not been made to the database file defined by **DatabaseName**. Database logging affects system performance, so **DatabaseLogging** can be turned off if you believe the system is highly stable and if logging is adversely affecting system performance.

DatabaseName

Data type = REG_SZ
Range = *filename*
Default = dhcp.mdb

Specifies the name of the database file to be used for the DHCP client information database.

DatabasePath

Data type = REG_EXPAND_SZ
Range = *pathname*
Default = %SystemRoot%\System32\dhcp

Specifies the location of the database files that have been created and opened.

RestoreFlag

Data type = REG_DWORD
Range = 0 or 1
Default = 0 (false—that is, do not restore)

Specifies whether to restore the database from the backup directory. This flag is reset automatically after the successful restoration of the database.

Registry Parameters for DHCP Clients

The Registry parameters for DHCP clients are specified under the following key:

`..SYSTEM\current\currentcontrolset\services\DHCP\Parameter\<option#>`

The *Option#* keys are a list of DHCP options that the client can request from the DHCP server. For each of the default options, the following values are defineC:

RegLocation

Data type = REG_SZ
Default = Depends on the Registry location for the specific option

Specifies the location in the Registry where the option value is written when it is obtained from the DHCP server. The "?" character expands to the adapter name for which this option value is obtained.

KeyType

Data type = REG_DWORD
Default = 0x7

Specifies the type of Registry key for the option.

Guidelines for Setting Local Policies

This section provides some suggestions for setting lease options, dividing the free address pool among DHCP servers, and avoiding DNS naming problems.

Guidelines for Managing DHCP Addressing Policy

Allocation of IP addresses for distribution by DHCP servers can be done dynamically or manually. These methods use the same DHCP client-server protocol, but the network administrator manages them differently at the DHCP server.

Dynamic Allocation of IP Addresses

Dynamic allocation enables a client to be assigned an IP address from the free address pool. The lease for the address has a lease duration (expiration date), before which the client must renew the lease to continue using that address. Depending on the local lease policies defined by the administrator, dynamically allocated addresses can be returned to the free address pool if the client computer is not being used, if it is moved to another subnet, or if its lease expires. Any IP addresses that are returned to the free address pool can be reused by the DHCP server when allocating an IP address to a new client. Usually, the local policy ensures that the same IP address is assigned to a client each time that system starts and that addresses returned to the pool are reassigned.

After the renewal time of the lease time has passed, the DHCP client enters the *renewing* state (as described in Chapter 12, "Networking Concepts for TCP/IP"). The client sends a request message to the DHCP server that provided its configuration information. If the request for a lease extension fits the local lease policy, the DHCP server sends an acknowledgment that contains the new lease and configuration parameters. The client then updates its configuration values and returns to the bound state.

When the DHCP client is in the renewing state, it must release its address immediately in the rare event that the DHCP server sends a negative acknowledgment. The DHCP server sends this message to inform a client that it has incorrect configuration information, forcing it to release its current address and acquire new information.

If the DHCP client cannot successfully renew its lease, the client enters a *rebinding* state. At this stage, the client sends a request message to all DHCP servers in its range, attempting to renew its lease. Any server that can extend the lease sends an acknowledgment containing the extended lease and updated configuration information. If the lease expires or if a DHCP server responds with a negative acknowledgment, the client must release its current configuration, and then return to the initializing state. (This happens automatically, for example, for a computer that is moved from one subnet to another.)

If the DHCP client uses more than one network adapter to connect to multiple networks, this protocol is followed for each adapter that the user wants to configure for TCP/IP. Windows NT allows multihomed systems to selectively configure any combination of the system's interfaces. You can use the **ipconfig** utility to view the local IP configuration for a client computer.

When a DHCP-enabled computer is restarted, it sends a message to the DHCP server with its current configuration information. The DHCP server either confirms this configuration or sends a negative reply so that the client must begin the initializing stage again. System startup might, therefore, result in a new IP address for a client computer, but neither the user nor the network administrator has to take any action in the configuration process.

Before loading TCP/IP with an address acquired from the DHCP server, DHCP clients check for an IP address conflict by sending an Address Resolution Protocol (ARP) request containing the address. If a conflict is found, TCP/IP does not start, and then the user receives an error message. The conflicting address should be removed from the list of active leases or it should be excluded until the conflict is identified and resolved.

Guidelines for Lease Options

To define appropriate values for lease duration, you should consider the frequency of the following events for your network:

- Changes to DHCP options and default values
- Network interface failures
- Computer removals for any purpose
- Subnet changes by users because of office moves, laptop computers docked at different workstations, and so on

All of these types of events cause IP addresses to be released by the client or cause the leases to expire at the DHCP server. Consequently, the IP addresses is returned to the free address pool to be reused.

If many changes occur on your internetwork, you should assign short lease times, such as two weeks. This way, the addresses assigned to systems that leave the subnet can be reassigned quickly to new DHCP client computers requesting TCP/IP configuration information.

Another important factor is the ratio between connected computers and available IP addresses. For example, the demand for reusing addresses is low in a network where 40 systems share a class C address (with 254 available addresses). A long lease time, such as two months, would be appropriate in such a situation. However, if 230 computers share the same address pool, demand for available addresses is much greater, so a lease time of a few days or weeks is more appropriate.

Notice, however, that short lease durations require that the DHCP server be available when the client seeks to renew the lease. Backup servers are especially important when short lease durations are specified.

Although infinite leases are allowed, they should be used with great caution. Even in a relatively stable environment, there is a certain amount of turnover among clients. At a minimum, portable computers might be added and removed, desktop computers might be moved from one office to another, and network adapter cards might be replaced. If a client with an infinite lease is removed from the network, the DHCP server is not notified, and then the IP address cannot be reused. A better option is a very long lease duration, such as six months. A long lease duration ensures that addresses are ultimately recovered.

Guidelines for Partitioning the Address Pool

You will probably decide to install more than one DHCP server, so the failure of any individual server will not prevent DHCP clients from starting. However, DHCP does not provide a way for DHCP servers to cooperate in ensuring that assigned addresses are unique. Therefore, you must divide the available address pool among the DHCP servers to prevent duplicate address assignment.

A typical scenario is a local DHCP server that maintains TCP/IP configuration information for two subnets. For each DHCP server, the network administrator allocates 70 percent of the IP address pool for local clients and 30 percent for clients from the remote subnet, and then configures a relay agent to deliver requests between the subnets.

This scenario allows the local DHCP server to respond to requests from local DHCP clients most of the time. The remote DHCP server will assign addresses to clients on the other subnet only when the local server is not available or is out of addresses. This same method of partitioning among subnets can be used in a multiple subnet scenario to ensure the availability of a responding server when a DHCP client requests configuration information.

Guidelines for Avoiding DNS Naming Conflicts

DNS can be used to provide names for network resources, as described in Chapter 12, "Networking Concepts for TCP/IP." However, DNS configuration is static. With DHCP, a host can easily have a different IP address if its lease expires or for other reasons, but there is no standard for updating DNS servers dynamically when IP address information changes. Therefore, DNS naming conflicts can occur if you are using DHCP for dynamic allocation of IP addresses.

This problem primarily affects systems that extend internetworking services to local network users. For example, a server acting as an anonymous FTP server or as an electronic mail gateway might require users to contact it using DNS names. In such cases, such clients should have reserved leases with an unlimited duration.

For workstations in environments that do not require the computers to register in the DNS name space, DHCP dynamic allocation can be used without problems.

Using DHCP with BOOTP

BOOTP is the Bootstrap Protocol used to configure systems across internetworks. DHCP is an extension of BOOTP. Although Microsoft DHCP Server does not support BOOTP, it has no problem interoperating with an existing BOOTP installation. The DHCP server simply ignores BOOTP packets that it receives.

You can continue to manage BOOTP clients with your existing BOOTP server as you manage other clients on the same subnet using DHCP. If you want your BOOTP clients to migrate to DHCP, you can take as much time as you need to do so.

You must make sure, however, that the BOOTP server and the DHCP server do not manage leases for the same IP addresses. The best way to ensure that there is no overlap in managed addresses is to define the scope of the DHCP server as the entire address range that is managed by both the DHCP server and the BOOTP server, and then exclude the address range that is managed by the BOOTP server. As BOOTP clients are dropped or upgraded to DHCP, the exclusion range can be adjusted accordingly.

For information on defining address and exclusion ranges, see "Defining DHCP Scopes" earlier in this chapter.

Planning a Strategy for DHCP

This section describes how to develop strategies for placing DHCP servers on small-scale and large-scale installations. Most network administrators implementing DHCP will also be planning a strategy for implementing WINS servers. The planning tasks described here also apply for WINS servers. In fact, the administrator will probably want to plan DHCP and WINS implementation in tandem. The following procedure describes the general planning tasks for planning DHCP and WINS implementation.

▶ **To plan for DHCP and WINS implementation**

1. Compile a list of requirements including the following types of requirements:

   - Client support (numbers and kinds of systems to be supported)

   - Interoperability with existing systems (including your requirements for mission-critical accounting, personnel, and similar information systems)

   - Hardware support and related software compatibility (including routers, switches, and servers)

   - Network monitoring software (including SNMP requirements and other tools)

2. Isolate the areas of the network where processes must continue uninterrupted, and then target these areas for the last stages of implementation.

3. Review the geographic and physical structure of the network to determine the best plan for defining logical subnets as segments of the internetwork.

4. Define the components in the new system that require testing, and then develop a phase plan for testing and adding components.

   For example, the plan could define units of the organization to be phased into using DHCP and the order for types of computers to be phased in (including Windows NT servers and workstations, Microsoft RAS servers and clients, Windows for Workgroups computers, and MS-DOS clients).

5. Create a pilot project for testing.

   Be sure that the pilot project addresses all the requirements identified in step 1.

6. Create a second test phase, including tuning the DHCP (and WINS) server-client configuration for efficiency.

   This task can include determining strategies for backup servers and for partitioning the address pool at each server to be provided to local versus remote clients.

7. Document all architecture and administration issues for network administrators.

8. Implement a final phase for bringing all organizational units into using DHCP.

While planning, remember that the actual placement of the servers in the physical network need not be a major planning issue. DHCP servers (and WINS servers) do not participate in the Windows NT Server domain model; domain membership is not, therefore, an issue in planning for server placement. Because most routers can forward DHCP configuration requests, DHCP servers are not required on every subnet in the internetwork. Also, because these servers can be administered remotely from any Windows NT Server computer that is DHCP- or WINS-enabled, location is not a major issue in planning for server placement.

Planning a Small-scale Strategy for DHCP Servers

For a small LAN that does not include routers and subnetting, the server needs for the network can probably be provided with a single DHCP server.

In this case, planning includes determining the following types of information:

- The hardware and storage requirements for the DHCP server
- Which computers can immediately become DHCP clients for dynamic addressing and which computers should keep their static addresses
- The DHCP option types and their values to be predefined for the DHCP clients

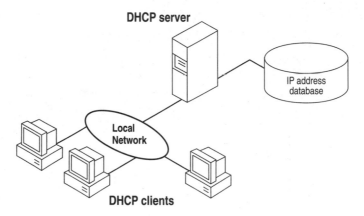

Figure 13.1   A Single Local Network Using Automatic TCP/IP Configuration with DHCP

Planning a Large-scale Strategy for DHCP Servers

The network administrator can use relay agents implementing RFC 1541 (usually IP routers) so that DHCP servers located on one node of the internetwork can respond to TCP/IP configuration requests from remote nodes. The relay agent forwards requests from local DHCP clients to the DHCP server and subsequently relays responses back to the clients.

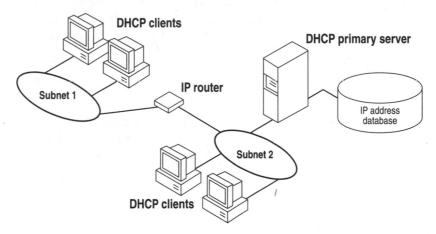

Figure 13.2   An Internetwork Using Automatic TCP/IP Configuration with DHCP

The additional planning issues for a large enterprise network includes:

- Compatibility of hardware and software routers with DHCP, as described at the beginning of this chapter.

- Planning the physical subnetting of the network and relative placement of DHCP servers. This includes planning for placement of DHCP (and WINS servers) among subnets in a way that reduces b-node broadcasts across routers.

- Specifying the DHCP option types and their values to be predefined per scope for the DHCP clients. This might include planning for scopes based on the needs of particular groups of users. For example, for a marketing group that uses portable computers docked at different stations, or for a unit that frequently moves computers to different locations, shorter lease durations can be defined for the related scopes. This way, frequently changed IP addresses can be freed for reuse.

As one example, the segmenting of the WAN into logical subnets could match the physical structure of the internetwork. Then one IP subnet can serve as the backbone, and off this backbone each physical subnet would maintain a separate IP subnet address.

In this case, for each subnet a single computer running Windows NT Server could be configured as both the DHCP and WINS server. Each server would administer a defined number of IP addresses with a specific subnet mask, and would also be defined as the default gateway. Because the server is also acting as the WINS server, it can respond to name resolution requests from all systems on its subnet.

These DHCP and WINS servers can in turn be backup servers for each other. The administrator can partition the address pool for each server to provide addresses to remote clients.

There is no limit to the maximum number of clients that can be served by a single DHCP server. However, your network can have practical constraints based on the IP address class and server configuration issues such as disk capacity and CPU speed.

C H A P T E R   1 4

Installing and Configuring WINS Servers

A WINS server is a Windows NT Server computer running the Microsoft TCP/IP protocol and the Windows Internet Name Service (WINS) server software. WINS servers maintain a database that maps computer names to IP addresses, allowing users to easily communicate with other computers while gaining all of the benefits of using TCP/IP.

This chapter describes how to install WINS servers and how to use WINS Manager to manage these servers. The following topics are included in this chapter:

- WINS benefits
- Installing and administering WINS servers
- Configuring WINS servers and replication partners
- Managing static mappings
- Setting preferences for WINS Manager
- Managing the WINS database
- Troubleshooting WINS
- Advanced configuration parameters for WINS
- Planning a strategy for WINS servers

For an overview of how WINS works, see "Windows Internet Name Service and Broadcast Name Resolution" in Chapter 12, "Networking Concepts for TCP/IP."

Note WINS can also be configured and monitored using SNMP. All configuration parameters can be set using SNMP, including configuration parameters that can otherwise only be set by editing the Registry. For a list of WINS MIB object types, see Appendix A, "MIB Object Types for Windows NT."

You can also use Performance Monitor to track WINS server performance, as described in Chapter 17, "Using Performance Monitor with TCP/IP Services."

Benefits of Using WINS

WINS servers offer the following benefits for your internetwork:

- Dynamic database maintenance to support computer name registration and name resolution. Although WINS provides dynamic name services, it offers a NetBIOS namespace, making it much more flexible than the Domain Name System (DNS) for name resolution.

- Centralized management of the computer name database and the database replication policies, alleviating the need for managing LMHOSTS files.

- Dramatic reduction of IP broadcast traffic in Microsoft internetworks, while allowing client computers to easily locate remote systems across local or wide area networks.

- The ability for clients on a Windows NT Server network (including Windows NT, Windows for Workgroups, and LAN Manager 2.*x*) to browse domains on the far side of a router without a local domain controller being present on the other side of the router.

- A scalable design, making it a good choice for name resolution for medium to very large internetworks.

Note WINS client software is part of the Microsoft TCP/IP-32 for Windows for Workgroups and the Microsoft Network Client 2.0 software that is included on the Windows NT Server compact disc. For information about installing these clients, see the *Windows NT Server Installation Guide*.

Installing WINS Servers

You install a WINS server as part of the process of installing Microsoft TCP/IP in Windows NT Server. The following instructions assume you have already installed the Windows NT Server operating system on the computer.

You must be logged on as a member of the Administrators group to install a WINS server.

▶ **To install a WINS server**

1. Double-click the Network option in Control Panel to display the Network Settings dialog box.

2. Choose the Add Software button to display the Add Network Software dialog box.

3. In the Network Software box, select TCP/IP Protocol And Related Components, and then choose the Continue button to display the Windows NT TCP/IP Installation Options dialog box.

4. Check the appropriate options to install, including at least one of the following options:

   - WINS Server Service

   - SNMP Service (for configuring and monitoring WINS using SNMP or Performance Monitor)

5. Choose the OK button.

   Windows NT Setup prompts you for the full path to the Windows NT Server distribution files.

6. Type the full path to the Windows NT Server distribution files, and then choose the Continue button.

   All necessary files are copied to your hard disk.

7. Complete all the required procedures for manually configuring TCP/IP as described in Chapter 11, "Installing and Configuring TCP/IP and SNMP."

   The Network Settings dialog box is displayed again after you finish configuring TCP/IP.

8. Choose the Close button, and then reboot the computer.

   The TCP/IP and WINS server software is now ready for use.

The Windows Internet Name Service is a Windows NT service running on a Windows NT computer. The supporting WINS client software is automatically installed for Windows NT Server and for Windows NT computers when the basic operating system is installed.

▶ **To start, stop, pause, or continue the WINS service on any Windows NT computer**

1. In Control Panel, double-click the Services option.

   –Or–

   In Server Manager, choose Services from the Computer menu.

2. In the Services dialog box, select the Windows Internet Name Service, and then choose the Start, Stop, Pause, or Continue button. Then, choose the Close button.

You can start, stop, pause, or continue the WINS service at the command prompt using the commands **net start wins**, **net stop wins**, **net pause wins**, or **net continue wins**.

Administering WINS Servers

When you install a WINS server, an icon for WINS Manager is added to the Network Administration group in Program Manager. You can use this tool to view and change parameters for any WINS server on the internetwork. To administer a WINS server remotely, you can run WINS Manager on a Windows NT Server computer that is not a WINS server.

You can also administer a WINS server remotely using SNMP. When you do so, if some WINS queries from SNMP work and others time out, you should increase the timeout on the SNMP tool you are using.

You must be logged on as a member of the Administrators group for a WINS server to configure that server.

▶ **To start WINS Manager**

1. Double-click the WINS Manager icon in Program Manager.

   –Or–

   At the command prompt, type the **start winsadmn** command, and then press ENTER.

   You can include a WINS server name or IP address with the command, for example, **start winsadmn 11.103.41.12** or **start winsadmn myserver**.

2. If the Windows Internet Name Service is running on the local computer, that WINS server is opened automatically for administration. If the Windows Internet Name Service is not running when you start WINS, the Add WINS Server dialog box appears, as described in the following procedure.

Settings in the Preferences dialog box determine whether the
IP address or computer name appears first in the list.

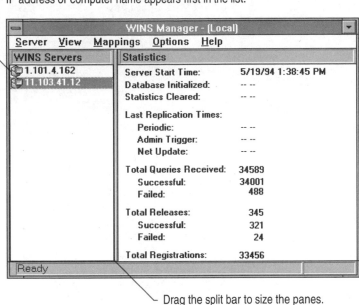

Drag the split bar to size the panes.

Note If you specify an IP address when connecting to a WINS server, the
connection is made using the TCP/IP protocol. If you specify a computer name, the
connection is made over NetBIOS. The list that appears in the WINS Server
window shows the IP address first if you connected using TCP/IP, or the computer
name first, if the connection was made over NetBIOS.

▶ **To connect to a WINS server for administration**

- In the WINS Manager window, select a server in the WINS Servers list.

  This list contains all WINS servers that you previously connected to or that have
  been reported by partners of this WINS server.

▶ **To connect to a server to which you have not previously been connected**

1. Choose the Add WINS Server command from the Server menu to display the Add WINS Server dialog box.

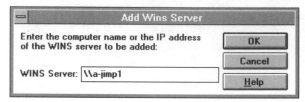

2. In the WINS Server box, type the IP address or computer name of the WINS server you want to work with, and then choose the OK button.

Note   You do not have to include double backslashes (\\)before the name. WINS Manager adds these for you.

The title bar in the WINS Manager window shows the IP address or computer name for the currently selected server, depending on whether you used the address or name to connect to the server. WINS Manager also shows some basic statistics for the selected server, as described in the following table. Additional statistics can be displayed by choosing the Detailed Information command from the Server menu.

Table 14.1   Statistics in WINS Manager

Statistic	Description
Database Initialized	The last time static mappings were imported into the WINS database.
Statistics Cleared	The time when statistics for the WINS server were last cleared with the Clear Statistics command from the View menu.
Last Replication Times	The times at which the WINS database was last replicated.
Periodic	The last time the WINS database was replicated based on the replication interval specified in the Preferences dialog box.
Admin Trigger	The last time the WINS database was replicated because the administrator chose the Replicate Now button in the Replication Partners dialog box.

Table 14.1   Statistics in WINS Manager (*continued*)

Statistic	Description
Net Update	The last time the WINS database was replicated as a result of a network request, which is a push notification message that requests propagation.
Total Queries Received	The number of *name query request* messages received by this WINS server. Successful indicates how many names were successfully matched in the database, and Failed indicates how many names this WINS server could not resolve.
Total Releases	The number of messages received that indicate a NetBIOS application has shut itself down. Successful indicates how many names were successfully released, and Failed indicates how many names this WINS server could not release.
Total Registrations	The number of messages received that indicate name registrations for clients.

▸ **To refresh the statistical display in WINS Manager**

- From the View menu, choose the Refresh Statistics command (or press F5).

  –Or–

  From the View menu, choose the Clear Statistics command to reset all statistical counters.

  –Or–

  Use automatic screen refreshing, based on the interval you specify in the Preferences dialog box, as described in "Setting Preferences for WINS Manager" later in this chapter.

▶ **To see information about the current WINS server**

1. From the Server menu, choose the Detailed Information command.

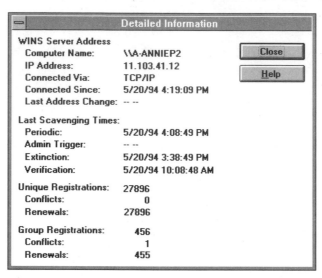

The Detailed Information dialog box shows information about the selected WINS server, as described in the table below.

2. To close the Detail Information dialog box, choose the Close button.

Table 14.2   Detailed Information Statistics for WINS Manager

Statistic	Meaning
Last Address Change	Indicates the time at which the last WINS database change was replicated.
Last Scavenging Times	Indicates the last times that the database was cleaned for specific types of entries. (For information about database scavenging, see "Managing the WINS Database" later in this chapter.
Periodic	Indicates when the database was cleaned based on the renewal interval specified in the WINS Server Configuration dialog box.
Admin Trigger	Indicates when the database was last cleaned because the administrator chose the Initiate Scavenging command.
Extinction	Indicates when the database was last cleaned based on the Extinction interval specified in the WINS Server Configuration dialog box.

Table 14.2   Detailed Information Statistics for WINS Manager (*continued*)

Statistic	Meaning
Verification	Indicates when the database was last cleaned based on the Verify interval specified in the WINS Server Configuration dialog box.
Unique Registrations	Indicates the number of *name registration requests* that have been accepted by this WINS server.
Unique Conflicts	The number of conflicts encountered during registration of unique names owned by this WINS server.
Unique Renewals	The number of renewals received for unique names.
Group Registrations	The number of registration requests for groups that have been accepted by this WINS server. For information about groups, see "Managing Special Names" later in this chapter.
Group Conflicts	The number of conflicts encountered during registration of group names.
Group Renewals	The number of renewals received for group names.

For descriptions of the related intervals, see "Configuring WINS Servers" later in this chapter.

Configuring WINS Servers and Replication Partners

You will want to configure multiple WINS servers to increase the availability and balance the load among servers. Each WINS server must be configured with at least one other WINS server as its replication partner.

Configuring a WINS server includes specifying information about when database entries are replicated between partners. A *pull partner* is a WINS server that pulls in replicas of database entries from its partner by requesting and then accepting replicas. A *push partner* is a WINS server that sends update notification messages to its partner when its WINS database has changed. When its partner responds to the notification with a replication request, the push partner sends a copy of its current WINS database to the partner. For the databases on the primary and backup WINS servers to remain consistent, they must be both push and pull partners with each other. It is always a good idea for replication partners to be both push and pull partners of each other.

For information about configuring preferences, see "Setting Preferences for WINS Manager" later in this chapter.

Configuring WINS Servers

For each WINS server, you must configure threshold intervals for triggering database replication, based on a specific time, a time period, or a certain number of new records. If you designate a specific time for replication, this occurs one time only. If a time period is specified, replication is repeated at that interval.

▶ **To configure a WINS server**

1. From the Server menu, choose the Configuration command.

   This command is available only if you are logged on as a member of the Administrators group for the WINS server you want to configure.

2. To view all the options in this dialog box, choose the Advanced button.

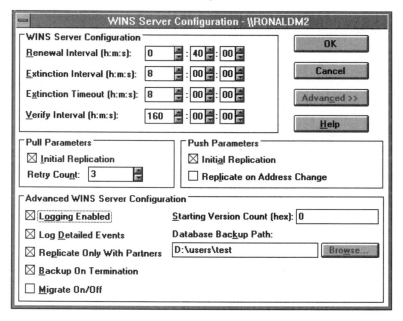

3. For the configuration options in the WINS Server Configuration dialog box, specify time intervals as described in the following list.

Configuration option	Description
Renewal Interval	Specifies how often a client reregisters its name. The default is five hours.
Extinction Interval	Specifies the interval between when an entry is marked as *released* and when it is marked as *extinct*. The default is dependent on the renewal interval and, if the WINS server has replication partners, on the maximum replication time interval. maximum allowable value is four days.
Extinction Timeout	Specifies the interval between when an entry is marked *extinct* and when the entry is finally scavenged from the database. The default is dependent on the renewal interval and, if the WINS server has replication partners, on the maximum replication time interval. minimum allowable value is one day.
Verify Interval	Specifies the interval after which the WINS server must verify that old names it does not own are still active. The default is dependent on the extinction interval. . The maximum allowable value is 24 days.

The replication interval for this WINS server's pull partner is defined in the Preferences dialog box, as described in "Setting Preferences for WINS Manager" later in this chapter. The extinction interval, extinction timeout, and verify interval are derived from the renewal interval and the replication interval specified. The WINS server adjusts the values specified by the administrator to keep the inconsistency between a WINS server and its partners as small as possible.

4. If you want this WINS server to pull replicas of new WINS database entries from its partners when the system is initialized or when a replication-related parameter changes, select the Initial Replication in the Pull Parameters checkbox, and then type a value for Retry Count.

The retry count is the number of times the server should attempt to connect (in case of failure) with a partner for pulling replicas. Retries are attempted at the replication interval specified in the Preferences dialog box. If all retries are unsuccessful, WINS waits for a period before starting replication again. For information about setting the start time and replication interval for pull and push partners, see "Setting Preferences for WINS Manager" later in this chapter.

5. To inform partners of the database status when the system is initialized, select the Initial Replication checkbox in the Push Parameters group. To inform partners of the database status when an address changes in a mapping record, select the Replicate On Address Change checkbox.

6. Set any Advanced WINS Server Configuration options, as described in the following table.

Table 14.3   Advanced WINS Server Configuration Options

Configuration option	Description
Logging Enabled	Specifies whether logging of database changes to JET.LOG should be turned on.
Log Detailed Events	Specifies whether logging events is verbose. (This requires considerable system resources and should be turned off if you are tuning for performance.)
Replicate Only With Partners	Specifies that replication will be done only with WINS pull or push partners. If this option is not checked, an administrator can ask a WINS server to pull or push from or to a non-listed WINS server partner. By default, this option is checked.
Backup On Termination	Specifies that the database will be backed up automatically when WINS Manager is stopped, except when the system is being shut down.
Migrate On/Off	Specifies that static unique and multihomed records in the database are treated as dynamic when they conflict with a new registration or replica. This means that if they are no longer valid, they will be overwritten by the new registration or replica. Check this option if you are upgrading non-Windows NT systems to Windows NT. By default, this option is not checked.
Starting Version Count	Specifies the highest version ID number for the database. Usually, you will not need to change this value unless the database becomes corrupted and needs to start fresh. In such a case, set this value to a number higher than appears as the version number counter for this WINS server on all the remote partners that earlier replicated the local WINS server's records. WINS may adjust the value you specify to a higher one to ensure that database records are quickly replicated to other WINS servers. The maximum allowable value is $2^{31} - 1$. This value can be seen in the View Database dialog box in WINS Manager.
Database Backup Path	Specifies the directory where the WINS database backups will be stored. If you specify a backup path, WINS automatically performs a full backup of its database to this directory every 24 hours. WINS uses this directory to perform an automatic restoration of the database in the event that the database is found to be corrupted when WINS is started. Do not specify a network directory.

7. When you have completed all changes in the WINS Server Configuration dialog box, choose the OK button.

Configuring Replication Partners

WINS servers communicate among themselves to fully replicate their databases, ensuring that a name registered with one WINS server is eventually replicated to all other WINS servers within the internetwork. All mapping changes converge within the *replication period* for the entire WINS system, which is the maximum time for propagating changes to all WINS servers. All released names are propagated to all WINS servers after they become extinct, based on the interval specified in WINS Manager.

Replication is carried out among replication partners, rather than each server replicating to all other servers. In the following illustration, Server1 has only Server2 as a partner, but Server2 has three partners. So, for example, Server1 gets all replicated information from Server2, but Server2 gets information from Server1, Server3, and Server4.

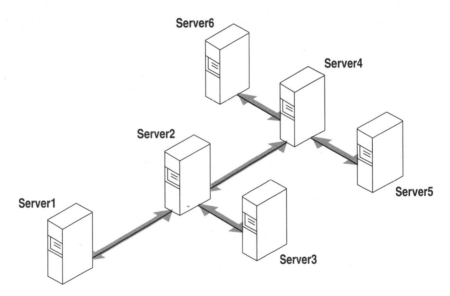

Figure 14.1   Replication Configuration Example for WINS Servers

Ultimately, all replications are pulled from the other WINS servers on an internetwork, but triggers are sent by WINS servers to indicate when a replication should be pulled. To achieve replication, each WINS server is a push partner or pull partner with at least one other WINS server. A pull partner is a WINS server that pulls in database replicas from its push partner by requesting and then accepting replicas of new database entries in order to synchronize its own database. A push partner is a WINS server that sends notification of changes and then sends replicas to its pull partner upon receiving a request. When the server's pull partner replicates the information, it pulls replicas by asking for all records with a higher version number than the last record stored from the last replication with the server or another partner.

Choosing whether to configure another WINS server as a push partner or pull partner depends on several considerations, including the specific configuration of servers at your site, whether the partner is across a wide area network (WAN), and how important it is to propagate the changes.

- If Server2, for example, needs to perform pull replications with ServerB, make sure it is a push partner of Server3.
- If Server2 needs to push replications to Server3, it should be a pull partner of WINS ServerB.

Replication is triggered when a WINS server polls another server to get a replica. This can begin at system startup and can then repeat at the time interval specified for periodic replication. Replication is also triggered when a WINS server reaches a threshold set by the administrator, which is an *update count* for registrations and changes. In this case, the server notifies its pull partners that it has reached this threshold, and the other servers may then decide to pull replicas. Additionally, the administrator can cause a replication immediately or at a specified time. Replication at a specified time is a one-time only event. If the time specified has already passed, replication does not occur.

▶ **To add a replication partner for a WINS server**

1. From the Server menu, choose the Replication Partners command to display the Replication Partners dialog box.

    This command is available only if you are logged on as a member of the Administrators group for the local server.

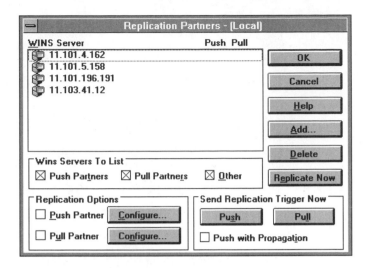

2. Choose the Add button to display the Add WINS Server dialog box.

3. Type the name or IP address of the WINS server that you want to add to the list, and then choose the OK button.

   If WINS Manager can find this server, it adds it to the WINS Server list in the Replication Partners dialog box.

4. From the WINS Server list in the Replication Partners dialog box, select the server you want to configure, and then complete the actions described in "Configuring Replication Partner Properties" later in this chapter.

5. If you want to limit which WINS servers are displayed in the Replication Partners dialog box, check or clear the options as follows:

   - Check Push Partners to display push partners for the current WINS server.

   - Check Pull Partners to display pull partners for the current WINS server.

   - Check Other to display the WINS servers that are neither push partners nor pull partners for the current WINS server.

6. To specify replication triggers for the partners you add, follow the procedures described in "Triggering Replication Between Partners" later in this chapter.

7. When you finish adding replication partners, choose the OK button.

▸ **To delete replication partners**

1. From the Server menu, choose the Replication Partners command to display the Replication Partners dialog box.

2. Select one or more servers in the WINS Server list, and then choose the Delete button, or press DEL.

   WINS Manager asks you to confirm the deletion if you checked the related confirmation option in the Preference dialog box, as described in "Setting Preferences for WINS Manager" later in this chapter.

Configuring Replication Partner Properties

When you designate replication partners, you need to specify parameters for when replication will begin.

▸ **To configure replication partners for a WINS server**

1. In the WINS Server list of the Replication Partners dialog box, select the server you want to configure.

2. Check either Push Partner or Pull Partner or both to indicate the replication partnership you want, and then choose the related Configure button.

3. Complete the entries in the appropriate Properties dialog box, as described in the following procedures.

▸ **To define pull partner properties**

1. In the Start Time box of the Pull Partner Properties dialog box, type a time to indicate when replication should begin.

   You can use any separator for hours, minutes, and seconds. You can type AM or PM, for example, only if these designators are part of your time setting, as defined using the International option in Control Panel.

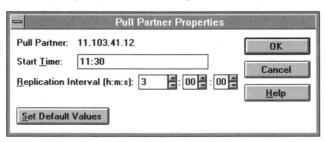

2. In the Replication Interval box, type a time in hours, minutes, and seconds to indicate how often replications will occur, or use the spin buttons to set the time you want.

   If you want to return to the values specified in the Preferences dialog box, choose the Set Default Values button.

3. Choose the OK button to return to the Replication Partners dialog box.

▶ **To define push partner properties**

1. In the Update Count box of the Push Partner Properties dialog box, type a number for how many additions and updates made to records in the database will result in changes that need replication.

   Replications that have been pulled in from partners do not count as insertions or updates in this context.

   The minimum value for Update Count is 5.

   If you want to return to the value specified in the Preferences dialog box, choose the Set Default Values button.

2. Choose the OK button to return to the Replication Partners dialog box.

Triggering Replication Between Partners

You can also replicate the database between the partners immediately, rather than waiting for the start time or replication interval specified in the Preference dialog box, as described in "Setting Preferences for WINS Manager" later in this chapter.

You probably want to begin replication immediately after you make a series of changes, such as entering a range of static address mappings.

▶ **To send a replication trigger**

- Complete one of the following tasks using the Replication Partners dialog box.

  ▪ Select the WINS servers to which you want to send a replication trigger, and then choose the Push or Pull button, depending on whether you want to send the trigger to push partners or pull partners.

  –Or–

  ▪ If you want the selected WINS server to propagate the trigger to all its pull partners, select the Push With Propagation checkbox.

  If the Push With Propagation checkbox is not selected, the selected WINS server does not propagate the trigger to its other partners.

  If the Push With Propagation checkbox is selected, the selected WINS server sends a propagate push trigger to its pull partners after it has pulled in the latest information from the source WINS server. If it does not need to pull in any replicas because it has the same or more up-to-date replicas than the source WINS server, it does not propagate the trigger to its pull partners.

▶ **To start replication immediately**

- In the Replication Partners dialog box, choose the Replicate Now button.

Managing Static Mappings

Static mappings are permanent lists of computer name-to-IP address mappings that cannot be challenged or removed, except when the administrator removes the specific mapping. You use the Static Mappings command in WINS Manager to add, edit, import, or delete static mappings for clients on the network that are not WINS enabled.

Important If DHCP is also used on the network, a reserved (or static) IP address will override any WINS server settings. Static mappings should not be assigned to WINS-enabled computers.

▶ **To view static mappings**

1. From the Mappings menu, choose the Static Mappings command to display the Static Mappings dialog box.

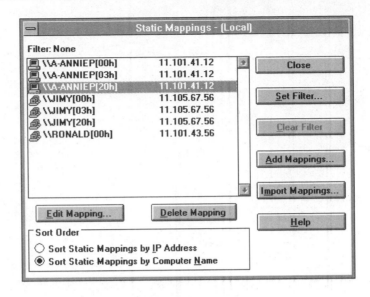

Caution All changes made to the WINS database using the Static Mappings dialog box take effect immediately. For this reason, you cannot cancel changes made to the WINS database while working in the Static Mappings dialog box. You must manually delete any entries that are added in error or manually add back any entries that you mistakenly delete.

2. In the Sort Order group box, indicate whether you want to sort static mappings by IP address or computer name.

   This selection determines the order in which entries appear in the list of static mappings.

3. Complete any of the following tasks:

   - To edit or add a mapping, follow the procedures described in "Adding Static Mappings" and "Editing Static Mappings" later in this chapter.

   - To remove existing static mappings, select the mappings you want to delete from the list, and then choose the Delete Mapping button.

   - To limit the range of mappings displayed in the list of static mappings, choose the Set Filter button, and then follow the procedure in "Filtering the Range of Mappings" later in this chapter.

   - To turn off filtering, choose the Clear Filter button.

4. When you have finished viewing or changing the static mappings, choose the Close button.

Adding Static Mappings

You can add static mappings to the WINS database for specific IP addresses using two methods:

- Type static mappings in a dialog box
- Import files that contain static mappings

▶ **To add static mappings to the WINS database by typing entries**

1. In the Static Mappings dialog box, choose the Add Mappings button to display the Add Static Mappings dialog box.

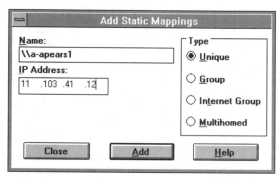

2. In the Name box, type the computer name of the system for which you are adding a static mapping.

   You do not need to type two backslashes (\\) when entering the computer name, because WINS Manager adds these for you.

3. In the IP Address box, type the address for the computer.

   If Internet Group or Multihomed is selected in the Type group box, the dialog box shows additional controls for adding multiple addresses. Use the down-arrow button to move the address you type into the list of addresses for the group. Use the up-arrow button to change the order of a selected address in the list.

4. Select an option in the Type group box to indicate whether this entry is a unique name or a kind of group with a special name, as described in the following table.

Type option	Description
Unique	Unique name in the database, with one address per name.
Group	Normal group, where addresses of individual members are not stored. The client broadcasts name packets to normal groups.

Type option	Description
Internet group	Groups with NetBIOS names that have 0x1C as the 16th byte. An internet group stores up to 25 addresses for members. The maximum number of addresses is 25. For registrations after the 25th address, WINS overwrites a replica address or, if none is present, it overwrites the oldest registration.
Multihomed	Unique name that can have more than one address (multihomed computers). The maximum number of addresses is 25. For registrations after the 25th address, WINS overwrites a replica address or, if none is present, it overwrites the oldest registration.

Important For internet group names defined in this dialog box (that is, added statically), make sure that the primary domain controller (PDC) for that domain is defined in the group if the PDC is running Windows NT Advanced Server version 3.1.

For more information, see "Managing Special Names" later in this chapter.

5. Choose the Add button.

   The mapping is immediately added to the database for that entry, and then the checkboxes are cleared so that you can add another entry.

6. Repeat this process for each static mapping you want to add to the database, and then choose the Close button.

Important Because each static mapping is added to the database when you choose the Add button, you cannot cancel work in this dialog box. If you make a mistake in entering a name or address for a mapping, you must return to the Static Mappings dialog box and delete the mapping there.

You can also import entries for static mappings for unique and special group names from any file that has the same format as the LMHOSTS file (as described in Chapter 15, "Setting Up LMHOSTS"). Scope names and keywords other than #DOM are ignored. However, normal group and multihomed names can be added only by typing entries in the Add Static Mappings dialog box.

▶ **To import a file containing static mapping entries**

1. In the Static Mappings dialog box, choose the Import Mappings button to display the Select Static Mapping File dialog box.

2. Specify a filename for a static mappings file by typing its name in the box.

   –Or–

   Select one or more filenames in the list, and then choose the OK button to import the file.

The specified file is read, and then a static mapping is created for each computer name and address. If the #DOM keyword is included for any record, an internet group is created (if it is not already present), and the address is added to that group.

Editing Static Mappings

You can change the IP addresses in static mappings owned by the WINS server you are currently administering.

▶ **To edit a static mapping entry**

1. In the Static Mappings dialog box, select the mapping you want to change, and then choose the Edit Mapping button, or double-click the mapping entry in the list.

   The Edit Static Mapping dialog box is displayed.

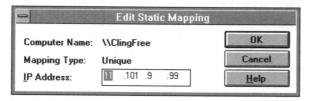

Note You can view, but not edit, the Computer Name and Mapping Type option for the mapping in the Edit Static Mappings dialog box.

2. In the IP Address box, type a new address for the computer, and then choose the OK button.

   The change is made in the WINS database immediately.

Note If you want to change the computer name or group type related to a specific IP address, you must delete the entry and redefine it using the Add Static Mappings dialog box.

Filtering the Range of Mappings

You might want to limit the range of IP addresses or computer names displayed in the Static Mappings or Show Database dialog boxes.

You can specify a portion of the computer name or IP address or both when filtering the list of mappings.

▶ **To filter mappings by address or name**

1. In the dialog box for Static Mappings or Show Database, choose the Set Filter button to display the Set Filter dialog box.

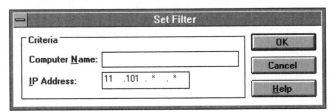

2. In the Computer Name or IP Address boxes, type portions of the computer name, IP address, or both.

   You can use the asterisk (*) wildcard for portions of the name or address or both. For example, you could type **\\acct*** to filter all computers with names that begin with **acct**. However, for the address, a wildcard can be used only for a complete octet. That is, you can type **11.101.*.***, but you cannot enter **11.1*.1.1** in these boxes.

3. Choose the OK button.

   The selected range is displayed in the Static Mappings or Show Database dialog box. The filtered range remains until you clear the filter.

   If no mappings are found to match the range you specified, an information message is displayed and the list of mappings will be empty.

If a filter is in effect for the range of mappings, the Clear Filter button is available for restoring the entire list.

▶ **To clear the filtered range of mappings**

- In the Static Mappings or Show Database dialog box, choose the Clear Filter button.

  The list now shows all mappings found in the database.

Managing Special Names

WINS recognizes special names for groups, multihomed devices, and internet groups. This section describes these special names and presents some background details to help you understand how WINS manages these groups.

Normal Group Names

A group name does not have an address associated with it. It can be valid on any subnet and can be registered with more than one WINS server. A group's timestamp shows the last time for any change received for the group. If the WINS server receives a query for the group name, it returns FFFFFFFF (the limited broadcast address). The client then broadcasts on the subnet. The group name is renewed when any member of the group renews the group name.

Multihomed Names

A multihomed name is a single, unique name storing multiple addresses. A multihomed device is a computer with multiple network cards and/or multiple IP addresses bound to NetBIOS over TCP/IP. A multihomed device with multiple IP addresses can register one or more addresses by sending one address at a time in a special name registration packet. A multihomed name in a WINS database can have one or more addresses. The timestamp for the record reflects any changes made for any members of the name.

Each multihomed group name can contain a maximum of 25 IP addresses.

When you configure TCP/IP manually on a Windows NT computer, you use the Advanced Microsoft TCP/IP dialog box to specify the IP address and other information for each adapter on a multihomed computer.

If WINS is running on a multihomed computer, the IP address of the WINS service is that of the first adapter to which Netbt is bound. When you configure clients' WINS addresses, you must specify this address, and not another one, such as that of an adapter that might be on the same subnet as the client. In some cases, the client needs to determine when WINS sends a message, and all WINS messages originate from the first adapter to which Netbt is bound.

A multihomed computer that runs on more than one network should not be used as a WINS server. Because a multihomed computer running WINS server always registers its names locally and a computer can run only one instance of WINS, the computer cannot register its name with two networks. Additionally, MS-DOS–based clients always use the first IP address supplied by the WINS server. When a client attempts a connection, the WINS server could give it the IP address for the other network as the first address. In that case, the client's connection attempt would fail.

A multihomed WINS client on more than one network can be configured to register with a different WINS server for each adapter card. The computers on each network would use the WINS server on their network to resolve names.

Internet Group Names

The internet group name is read as configuration data. When dynamic name registrations for internet groups are received, the actual address (rather than the subnet broadcast address) is stored in the group with a timestamp and the owner ID, which indicates the WINS server registering that address.

The internet group name (which has a 16th byte ending in 0x1C reserved for domain names, as described in the following section) can contain a maximum of 25 IP addresses for primary and backup domain controllers in a domain. Dynamically registered names are added if the list is not static and has fewer than 25 members. If the list has 25 members, WINS removes a replica member (that is, a member registered by another WINS server) and then adds the new member. If all members are owned by this WINS server, the oldest member is replaced by the new one.

WINS gives precedence over remote members to members in an internet group name that registered with it. This preference means that the group name always contains the geographically closest Windows NT Server computers. To establish the preference of members of internet groups registered with other WINS servers under the \Partners\Pull key in the Registry, a precedence is assigned for each WINS partner as a value of the MemberPrec Registry parameter. Preference should be given to WINS servers near the WINS server you are configuring. For more information about the value of this parameter, see its entry in "Advanced Configuration Parameters for WINS" later in this chapter.

The internet group name is handled specially by WINS, which returns the 24 closest Windows NT Server computers in the domain, plus the domain controller. The name ending in 1C is also used to discover a Windows NT Server computer in a domain when a computer running Windows NT Workstation or Windows NT Server needs a server for pass-through authentication.

If your network still has domain controllers running Windows NT Advanced Server version 3.1 to be included in the internet group name, you must add these to the group manually using WINS Manager. When you manually add such a computer to the internet group name, the list becomes static and no longer accepts dynamic updates from WINS-enabled computers.

For information about related issues in LMHOSTS for #DOM entries, see "Designating Domain Controllers Using #DOM" in Chapter 15, "Setting Up LMHOSTS."

How WINS Handles Special Names

Special names are indicated by a 16th byte appended to the computer name or
domain name. The following table shows some special names that can be defined
for static entries in the Add Static Mappings dialog box.

Table 14.4   Special Names for Static Mappings

Name ending	Usage	How WINS handles queries
0x1E	A normal group. Browsers broadcast to this name and listen on it to elect a master browser. The broadcast is done on the local subnet and should not cross routers.	WINS always returns the limited broadcast address (FFFFFFFF).
0x1D	Clients resolve this name to access the master browser for server lists. There is one master browser on a subnet.	WINS always returns a negative response. If the node is h-node or m-node, the client broadcasts a name query to resolve the name. For registrations, WINS returns a positive response even though the names are not put into the database.
0x1C	The internet group name, which contains a list of the specific addresses of systems that have registered the name. The domain controller registers this name.	WINS treats this as an internet group, where each member of the group must renew its name individually or be released. The internet group is limited to 25 names. (Note, however, that there is no limit for #DOM entries in LMHOSTS.)
		WINS returns a positive response for a dynamic registration of a static 1C name, but the address is not added to the list. When a static 1C name is replicated that clashes with a dynamic 1C name on another WINS server, a union of the members is added, and the record is marked as static. If the record is static, members of the group do not have to renew their IP addresses.

The following example illustrates a sample NetBIOS name table for a Windows NT Server domain controller, such as the list that appears if you type **nbtstat -n** at the command prompt. This example shows the 16th byte for special names, plus the type (unique or group).

```
                  NetBIOS Local Name Table

Name                      Type     Status
-------------------------------------------------------------
<0C29870B>                Unique   Registered
ANNIEP5          <20>     UNIQUE   Registered
ANNIEP5          <00>     UNIQUE   Registered
ANNIEPDOM        <00>     GROUP    Registered
ANNIEPDOM        <1C>     GROUP    Registered
ANNIEPDOM        <1B>     UNIQUE   Registered
ANNIEP5          <03>     UNIQUE   Registered
ANNIEP5          <1E>     GROUP    Registered
ANNIEP5          <1D>     UNIQUE   Registered
.._MSBROWSE_.    <01>     GROUP    Registered
```

As shown in this example, several special names are identified for both the computer and the domain. These special names include the following:

- 0x0 (shown as <00> in the example), the redirector name, which is used with **net view**.
- 0x3, the Messenger service name for sending messages.
- 0x20, the LAN Manager server name.
- _MSBROWSE_, the name master browsers broadcast to on the local subnet to announce their domains to other master browsers. WINS handles this name by returning the broadcast address FFFFFFFF.
- 0x1B, the domain master browser name, which clients and browsers use to contact the domain master browser. A domain master browser gets the names of all domain master browsers. When WINS is queried for the domain master browser name, it handles the query like any other name query and returns its address.

  WINS assumes that the computer that registers a domain name with the 1B character is the primary domain controller (PDC). This name is registered by the browser running on the PDC. This ensures that the PDC is in the internet group name list that is returned when a 1C name is queried, for which WINS always returns the address of the 1B name along with the members of a 1C name.

  If the PDC is not a Windows NT Server 3.5 computer, you should statically initialize WINS with the 0x1B name of the PDC. The address should be the IP address of the primary domain controller. Using 0x1B in this situation is not required, but clients will find the PDC much more quickly and with less network traffic.

Setting Preferences for WINS Manager

You can configure several options for administration of WINS servers. The commands for controlling preferences are on the Options menu.

▶ **To display the status bar for help on commands**

• From the Options menu, choose the Status Bar command.

When this command is active, its name is checked on the menu, and the status bar at the bottom of the WINS Manager window displays descriptions of commands as they are highlighted in the menu bar.

▶ **To set preferences for WINS Manager**

1. From the Options menu, choose the Preferences command to display the Preferences dialog box.

Tip To see all the available preferences, choose the Partners button.

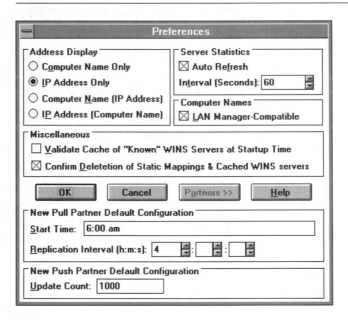

2. Specify settings for the options in which you want to change, and then choose the OK button.

The following list describes the various preferences in which you can set using this dialog box:

Address Display group box

Select an option to indicate how you want address information to be displayed throughout WINS Manager—as computer name, IP address, or an ordered combination of both.

> **Note** Remember that the kind of address display affects how a connection is made to the WINS server — for IP addresses, the connection is made via TCP/IP; for computer names, the connection is made via named pipes.

Server Statistics group box

If you want the statistics in the WINS Manager window to be refreshed automatically, select the Auto Refresh checkbox, and then enter a number in the Interval box to specify the number of seconds between refresh actions. WINS Manager also refreshes the statistical display automatically each time an action is initiated while you are working in WINS Manager.

Computer Names

Select the LAN Manager-Compatible checkbox if you want computer names to adhere to the LAN Manager naming convention.

LAN Manager computer names are limited to 15 characters, as opposed to 16-character NetBIOS names used by some other sources, such as Lotus Notes®. In LAN Manager names, the 16th byte is used to indicate whether the device is a server, workstation, messenger, and so on. When this option is selected, WINS adds and imports static mappings with 0, 0x03, and 0x20 as the 16th byte.

All Windows-based networking, including Windows NT, follows the LAN Manager convention. This checkbox should, therefore, be selected unless your network accepts NetBIOS name from other sources.

Miscellaneous group box

If you want the system to query the list of servers each time the system starts to find out if each server is available, select the Validate Cache Of Known WINS Servers At Startup Time checkbox. If you want a warning message to appear each time you delete a static mapping or the cached name of a WINS server, select the Confirm Deletion Of Static Mappings And Cached WINS Servers checkbox.

New Pull Partner Default Configuration group box

In the Start Time box, type a time to specify the default for replication start time for new pull partners, and then specify values in the Replication Interval box to indicate how often data replicas will be exchanged between the partners.

The Replication Interval should be the same as, or less than, the lowest refresh time interval that is set on any of the replicating WINS servers. The minimum value for the Replication Interval is 40 minutes.

New Push Partner Default Configuration
In the Update Count box, type a number to specify a default for how many registrations and changes can occur locally before a replication trigger is sent by this server when it is a push partner. The minimum value is 20.

Managing the WINS Database

The following files are stored in the *\systemroot*\SYSTEM32\WINS directory that is created when you set up a WINS server:

- JET.LOG is a log of all transactions done with the database. This file is used by WINS to recover data if necessary.
- SYSTEM.MDB is used by WINS for holding information about the structure of its database.
- WINS.MDB is the WINS database file.
- WINSTMP.MDB is a temporary file that WINS creates. This file may remain in the \WINS directory after a crash.

You should back up these files when you back up other files on the WINS server.

Caution The JET.LOG, SYSTEM.MDB, WINS.MDB, and WINSTMP.MDB files should not be removed or tampered with in any manner.

Like any database, the WINS database of address mappings needs to be periodically cleaned and backed up. WINS Manager provides the tools you need for maintaining the database. This section describes how to scavenge (clean), view, and back up the database. For information on restoring and moving the WINS database, see "Troubleshooting WINS" later in this chapter.

Scavenging the Database

The local WINS database should periodically be cleared of released entries and old entries that were registered at another WINS server but did not get removed from this WINS database for some reason. This process, called scavenging, is done automatically over intervals defined by the relationship between the Renewal and Extinct intervals defined in the Configuration dialog box. You can also clean the database manually.

For example, if you want to verify old replicas immediately instead of waiting the time interval specified for verification, you can manually scavenge the database.

▶ **To scavenge the WINS database**

- From the Mappings menu, choose the Initiate Scavenging command.

  The database is cleaned, with the results as shown in the following table.

State before scavenging	State after scavenging
Owned active names for which the Renewal interval has expired	Marked *released*
Owned released name for which the Extinct interval has expired	Marked *extinct*
Owned extinct names for which the Extinct timeout has expired	Deleted
Replicas of extinct names for which the Extinct timeout has expired	Deleted
Replicas of active names for which the Verify interval has expired	Revalidated
Replicas of extinct or deleted names	Deleted

For information about the intervals and timeouts that govern database scavenging, see "Configuring WINS Servers" earlier in this chapter.

After WINS has been running for a while, the database might need to be compacted to improve WINS performance. You should compact the WINS database whenever it approaches 30 MB.

▶ **To compact the WINS database**

1. At the WINS server, stop the Windows Internet Name Service using the Control Panel Services option or by typing **net stop wins** at the command prompt.

2. Run the JETPACK.EXE program (which is found in the *systemroot*\SYSTEM32 directory).

3. Restart the Windows Internet Name Service on the WINS server.

Caution Do not compact the SYSTEM.MDB database.

Viewing the WINS Database

You can view the actual active and static mappings stored in the WINS database, based on the WINS server that owns the entries.

▶ **To view the WINS database**

1. From the Mappings menu, choose the Show Database command to display the Show Database dialog box.

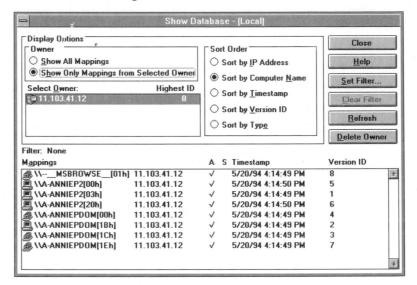

2. To view the mappings in the database for a specific WINS server, select Show Only Mappings From Specific Owner, and then from the Select Owner list, select the WINS server whose database you want to view.

    By default, the Show Database dialog box shows all mappings for the WINS database on the currently selected WINS server.

3. Select a Sort Order option to sort by IP address, computer name, timestamp for the mapping, version ID, or type. (For information about types, see "Adding Static Mappings" earlier in this chapter.)

4. If you want to view only a range of mappings, choose the Set Filter button, and then follow the procedures described in "Filtering the Range of Mappings" earlier in this chapter.

Tip To turn off filtering, choose the Clear Filter button.

---

5. Use the scroll bars in the Mappings box to view entries in the database. Then choose the Close button when you are finished viewing.

As shown in the Mappings list, each registration record in the WINS database includes these elements:

Item	Description
📇	Unique
📇	Group, internet group, or multihomed
Computer name	The NetBIOS computer name
IP address	The assigned Internet Protocol address
A or S	Indicates whether the mapping is active (dynamic) or static
Timestamp	Indicates when the record is set to expire.
Version ID	A unique hexadecimal number assigned by the WINS server during name registration, which is used by the server's pull partner during replication to find new records

You can also use the Show Database dialog box to remove all references to a specific WINS server in the database, including all database entries owned by the WINS server.

▶ **To delete a specific WINS server's entries in the database**

- In the Show Database dialog box, select a WINS server in the Select Owner list, and then choose the Delete Owner button.

Backing Up the Database

WINS Manager provides backup tools so that you can back up the WINS database. After you specify a backup directory for the database, WINS performs complete database backups every 24 hours, using the specified directory.

▶ **To back up a WINS database**

1. From the Mappings menu, choose the Backup Database command to display the Select Backup Directory dialog box.

2. Specify the location for saving the backup files.

   Windows NT proposes a subdirectory of the \WINS directory. You can accept this proposed directory. The most secure location is to back up the database on another hard disk. Do not back up to a network drive, because WINS Manager cannot restore from a network source.

3. If you want to back up only the newest version numbers in the database (that is, changes that have occurred since the last backup), select the Perform Incremental Backup checkbox.

   Note You must have performed a complete backup before this option can be used successfully.

   ---

4. Choose the OK button.

You should also periodically back up the Registry entries for the WINS server.

▶ **To back up the WINS Registry entries**

1. Run the REGEDT32.EXE program from File Manager or Program Manager to start the Registry Editor.

2. In Registry Editor, select the HKEY_LOCAL_MACHINE window, and then select the following key:

   ```
   ..SYSTEM\CurrentControlSet\Services\WINS
   ```

3. From the Registry menu, choose the Save Key command to display the Save Key dialog box.

4. Specify the path where you store backup versions of the WINS database files.

For information about restoring the WINS database, see the following section, "Troubleshooting WINS."

Troubleshooting WINS

This section describes some basic troubleshooting steps for common problems and also describes how to restore or rebuild the WINS database.

Basic WINS Troubleshooting

The following error conditions can indicate potential problems with the WINS server:

- The administrator can't connect to a WINS server using WINS Manager. The message that appears might be, "The RPC server is unavailable."

- The WINS Client service or Windows Internet Name Service might be down and cannot be restarted.

The first troubleshooting task is to make sure the appropriate services are running.

▶ **To ensure the WINS services are running**

1. Use the Services option in Control Panel to verify that the WINS services are running.

   In the Services dialog box for the client computer, Started should appear in the Status column for the WINS Client service. For the WINS server itself, Started should appear in the Status column for the Windows Internet Name Service.

2. If a necessary service is not started on either computer, start the service.

The following describes solutions to common WINS problems.

▶ **To locate the source of "duplicate name" error messages**

- Check the WINS database for the name. If there is a static record, remove it from the database of the primary WINS server.

    –Or–

    Set the value of MigrateOn in the Registry to 1, so the static records in the database can be updated by dynamic registrations (after WINS successfully challenges the old address).

▶ **To locate the source of "network path not found" error messages on a WINS client**

- Check the WINS database for the name. If the name is not present in the database, check whether the computer uses b-node name resolution. If so, add a static mapping for it in the WINS database.

    If the computer is configured as a p-node, m-node, or h-node and if its IP address is different from the one in the WINS database, then it may be that its address changed recently and the new address has not yet replicated to the local WINS server. To get the latest records, ask the WINS server that registered the address to perform a push replication with propagation to the local WINS server.

▶ **To discover why a WINS server cannot pull or push replications to another WINS server**

1. Confirm that the router is working.

2. Ensure that each server is correctly configured as either a pull or push partner.

    - If ServerA needs to perform pull replications with ServerB, make sure it is a push partner of ServerB.

    - If ServerA needs to push replications to ServerB, it should be a pull partner of WINS ServerB.

    To determine the configuration of a replication partner, check the values under the \Pull and \Push keys in the Registry, as described in "Advanced Configuration Parameters for WINS" later in this chapter.

▶ **To determine why WINS backup is failing consistently**

- Make sure the path for the WINS backup directory is on a local disk on the WINS server.

    WINS cannot back up its database files to a remote drive.

Restoring or Moving the WINS Database

This section describes how to restore, rebuild, or move the WINS database.

Restoring a WINS Database

If you have determined that the Windows Internet Name Service is running on the WINS server, but you cannot connect to the server using WINS Manager, then the WINS database is not available or has becomes corrupted. If a WINS server fails for any reason, you can restore the database from a backup copy.

You can use the menu commands to restore the WINS database or restore it manually.

▶ **To restore a WINS database using menu commands**

1. From the Mappings menu, choose the Restore Database command to display the Select Directory to Restore From dialog box.

2. Select the location where the backup files are stored, and then choose the OK button.

▶ **To restore a WINS database manually**

1. In the *systemroot*\SYSTEM32\WINS directory, delete the JET.LOG, JET*.LOG, WINS.TMP, and SYSTEM.MDB files.

2. From the Windows NT Server installation source, copy SYSTEM.MDB to the *systemroot*\SYSTEM32\WINS directory on the WINS server.

   The installation source can be the Windows NT Server compact disc, the installation floppy disks, or a network directory that contains the master files for Windows NT Server.

3. Copy an uncorrupted backup version of WINS.MDB to the *systemroot*\SYSTEM32\WINS directory.

4. Restart the Windows Internet Name Service on the WINS server.

Restarting and Rebuilding a Down WINS Server

In rare circumstances, the WINS server may not boot or a STOP error might occur. If the WINS server is down, use the following procedure to restart it.

▶ **To restart a WINS server that is down**

1. Turn off the power to the server and wait one minute.

2. Turn on the power, start Windows NT Server, and then logon under an account with Administrator rights.

3. At the command prompt, type the **net start wins** command, and then press ENTER.

If the hardware for the WINS server is malfunctioning or other problems prevent you from running Windows NT, you will have to rebuild the WINS database on another computer.

▶ **To rebuild a WINS server**

1. If you can start the original WINS server using MS-DOS, use MS-DOS to make backup copies of the files in the *systemroot*\SYSTEM32\WINS directory. If you cannot start the computer with MS-DOS, you will have to use the last backup version of the WINS database files.

2. Install Windows NT Server and Microsoft TCP/IP to create a new WINS server using the same hard drive location and *systemroot* directory. That is, if the original server stored the WINS files on C:\WINNT35\SYSTEM32\WINS, then the new WINS server should use this same path to the WINS files.

3. Make sure the WINS services on the new server are stopped, and then use Registry Editor to restore the WINS keys from backup files.

4. Copy the WINS backup files to the *systemroot*\SYSTEM32\WINS directory.

5. Restart the new, rebuilt WINS server.

Moving the WINS Database

You may find a situation where you need to move a WINS database to another computer. To do this, use the following procedure.

▶ **To move a WINS database**

1. Stop the Windows Internet Name Service on the current computer.

2. Copy the \SYSTEM32\WINS directory to the new computer that has been configured as a WINS server.

   Make sure the new directory is under exactly the same drive letter and path as on the old computer.

   If you must copy the files to a different directory, copy WINS.MDB, but not SYSTEM.MDB. Use the version of SYSTEM.MDB created for that new computer.

3. Start the Windows Internet Name Service on the new computer. WINS will automatically use the .MDB and .LOG files copied from the old computer.

Advanced Configuration Parameters for WINS

This section presents configuration parameters that affect the behavior of WINS and that can be modified only through Registry Editor. For some parameters, WINS can detect Registry changes immediately. For other parameters, you must restart the Windows Internet Name Service for the changes to take effect.

Caution   You can impair or disable Windows NT if you make incorrect changes in the Registry while using Registry Editor. All but a few of the configuration parameters that can be set by editing the Registry can also be set using WINS Manager or SNMP. Whenever possible, use WINS Manager or SNMP to make configuration changes, rather than using Registry Editor. If you make errors while changing values with Registry Editor, you will not be warned, because Registry Editor does not recognize semantic errors.

▶   **To make changes to WINS configuration using Registry Editor**

1. Start the Registry Editor by running the REGEDT32.EXE file from File Manager or Program Manager.

   –Or–

   At the command prompt, type the **start regedt32** command, and then press ENTER.

   When the Registry Editor window appears, you can press F1 to get Help on how to make changes in Registry Editor.

2. In Registry Editor, click the window titled HKEY_LOCAL_MACHINE On Local Machine, and then click the icons for the SYSTEM subtree until you reach the appropriate subkey, as described later in this section.

The following describes the value entries for WINS parameters that can only be set by adding an entry or changing values in Registry Editor.

Registry Parameters for WINS Servers

The Registry parameters for WINS servers are specified under the following key:

```
..\SYSTEM\CurrentControlSet\Services\Wins\Parameters
```

This subkey lists all the nonreplication-related parameters needed to configure a WINS server. It also contains a \Datafiles subkey, which lists all the files that should be read by WINS to initialize or reinitialize its local database.

DbFileNm

Data type = REG_SZ or REG_EXPAND_SZ
Range = *path name*
Default = %SystemRoot%\system32\wins\wins.mdb

Specifies the full path name for the WINS database file.

DoStaticDataInit

Data type = REG_DWORD
Range = 0 or 1
Default = 0 (false—that is, the WINS server does not initialize its database)

If this parameter is set to a non-zero value, the WINS server will initialize its database with records listed in one or more files listed under the \Datafiles subkey. The initialization is done at process invocation and whenever a change is made to one or more values of the \Parameters or \Datafiles keys (unless the change is to change the value of **DoStaticDataInit** to 0).

InitTimePause

Data type = REG_DWORD
Range = 0 or 1
Default = 0 (no initial pause)

If set to 1, WINS starts in the paused state—that is, WINS does not accept any name registrations, releases, or queries—until it has replicated with its partners, or failed in the attempt, at least once. If **InitTimePause** is set to 1, the \WINS\Partners\Pull**InitTimeReplication** parameter should be either set to 1 or removed from the Registry.

LogFilePath

Data type = REG_SZ or REG_EXPAND_SZ
Default = %SystemRoot%\system32\wins

This parameter specifies the directory location of the log files created by WINS. These files are used for recovery in case of a soft failure of WINS.

McastIntvl

Data type = REG_DWORD
Default = 2400 (seconds)

This parameter specifies the time interval at which the WINS server sends a multicast to announce its presence to other WINS servers. The value is expressed in seconds. The minimum allowable value is 2400 seconds (40 minutes).

McastTtl

Data type = REG_DWORD
Range = 1 to 32
Default = 6

This parameter specifies the number of times a WINS multicast announcement can cross a router to another network.

NoOfWrkThds

Data type = REG_DWORD
Range = 1 to 40
Default = Number of processors on the computer

This parameter specifies the number of worker threads. It can be changed without restarting the WINS computer.

PriorityClassHigh

Data type = REG_DWORD
Range = 0 or 1
Default = 0 (false—that is, the priority class is normal)

If the parameter is set to a non-zero value, WINS runs in high priority class. This setting is useful to ensure that other processes, such as electronic mail or other applications, do not preempt WINS.

UseSelfFndPnrs

Data type = REG_DWORD
Range = 0 or 1
Default = 0

If the parameter is set to 1 and network routers support multicasting, WINS Server automatically finds other WINS servers on the network and configures them as push and pull partners. If the parameter is set to 1 and network routers do not support multicasting, WINS finds other WINS servers only on its subnet.

By default, partnership data created in this way is maintained automatically. When a WINS server is discovered through multicast, it is automatically removed as a replication partner when it shuts down gracefully. If the Registry information about this partnership is changed manually using WINS Manager, WINS Server no longer maintains the partnership information when there is a change.

The following parameters in this subkey can be set using the options available in the WINS Server Configuration dialog box:

LogDetailedEvents
LogFilePath
LoggingOn
RefreshInterval
TombstoneInterval (extinction interval)
TombstoneTimeout (extinction timeout)
VerifyInterval

Also, the \Wins\Parameters\Datafiles key lists one or more files that the WINS server should read to initialize or reinitialize its local database with static records. If the full path of the file is not listed, the directory of execution for the WINS server is assumed to contain the data file. The parameters can have any names (for example, DF1 or DF2). Their data types must be REG_SZ or REG_EXPAND_SZ.

Important The \Wins\Performance key contains values used for WINS performance counters that can be viewed in Performance Monitor. These values should be maintained by the system, so do not change these values.

Registry Parameters for Replication Partners

Properties of WINS replication partners are specified under the \Wins\Partners key.

PersonaNonGrata

Data type = REG_MULTI_SZ
Default = None

This parameter specifies the Internet Protocol (IP) addresses of WINS servers whose records are not to be inserted into the local database during replication. If there are incorrect records in the databases of one or more WINS servers on your network, you can prevent those records from being replicated to your WINS Server database by specifying the IP addresses of the WINS servers that own them under the **PersonaNonGrata** parameter.

The \Wins\Partners key has two subkeys, \Pull and \Push, under which are subkeys for the IP addresses of all push and pull partners, respectively, of the WINS server.

Parameters for Push Partners

A push partner, listed under the \Partners\Pull key, is one from which a WINS server pulls replicas and from which it can expect update notification messages. The following parameter appears under the IP address for a specific push partner. This parameter can be set only by changing the value in Registry Editor:

MemberPrec

> Data type = REG_DWORD
> Range = 0 or 1
> Default = 0

> Specifies the order of precedence of addresses in an internet group, those for which the sixteenth byte is 0x1C. Addresses in the 0x1C names pulled from a WINS partner are given the precedence assigned to the WINS server. 0 indicates low precedence, and 1 indicates high precedence. Locally registered names always have high precedence. Set this value to 1 if this WINS server is serving a geographic location that is nearby.

The following parameters appear under this subkey and can be set in the WINS Server Configuration dialog box:

```
..\SYSTEM\CurrentControlSet\Services\Wins\Partners\Pull
```

InitTimeReplication
CommRetryCount

The following parameters appear under this subkey and can be set using the Preferences dialog box:

```
..\SYSTEM\CurrentControlSet\Services\Wins\Partners\Pull\<Ip Address>
```

SpTime (Start Time for pull partner default configuration)
TimeInterval (Replication Interval)

For **SpTime**, WINS replicates at the set time if it is in the future for that day. After that, it replicates every number of seconds specified by **TimeInterval**. If **SpTime** is in the past for that day, WINS replicates every number of seconds specified by **TimeInterval**, starting from the current time (if **InitTimeReplication** is set to 1).

Parameters for Pull Partners

A pull partner of a WINS server, listed under the \Partners\Push key, is one from which it can expect pull requests to pull replicas and to which it sends update notification messages.

OnlyDynRecs

> Data type = REG_DWORD
> Range = 0 or 1
> Default = 0

If set to 1, only dynamically registered records are replicated to a pull partner. If set to 0, the default, all records, both dynamic and static, are replicated.

The following parameters appear under this subkey and can be set using the options available in the WINS Server Configuration dialog box:

`..\SYSTEM\CurrentControlSet\Services\Wins\Partners\Push`

InitTimeReplication
RplOnAddressChg

The following parameter appears under this subkey and can be set using the options available in the Preferences dialog box:

`..\SYSTEM\CurrentControlSet\Services\Wins\Partners\Push\<Ip Address>`

UpdateCount

Planning a Strategy for WINS Servers

The planning issues for implementing WINS servers are similar to those for implementing DHCP servers, as described in Chapter 13, "Installing and Configuring DHCP Servers." Most network administrators will be installing both kinds of servers, so the planning and implementation tasks will be undertaken jointly for DHCP and WINS servers.

This section provides some additional planning issues for WINS servers.

Planning for Server Performance

A WINS server can typically service 1500 name registrations per minute and about 760 queries per minute. There is no built-in limit to the number of records that a WINS server can replicate or store.

Based on these numbers, and planning for large-scale power outage where many computers will come on line simultaneously, the conservative recommendation is that you plan to include one WINS server and a backup server for every 10,000 computers on the network.

Two factors can particularly enhance WINS server performance. WINS performance increases almost 25 percent on a computer with two processors. Also, using NTFS as the file system also improves performance.

After you establish WINS servers in the internetwork, you can adjust the Renewal interval. Setting this interval to reduce the numbers of registrations can help tune server response time. (The Renewal interval is specified in the WINS Server Configuration dialog box.)

Planning Replication Partners and Proxies

In one possible configuration, one WINS server can be designated as the central server, and all other WINS servers can be configured as both push partner and pull partner of this central server. Such a configuration ensures that the WINS database on each server contains addresses for every node on the WAN.

Another option is to set up a chain of WINS servers, where each server is both the push partner and pull partner with a nearby WINS server. In such a configuration, the two servers at the ends of the chain would also be push and pull partners with each other. Other replication partner configurations can be established for your site's needs.

Only a limited number of WINS proxies should be designated on each domain, so that a limited number of computers are using resources to respond to broadcast name requests.

Planning Replication Frequency Between Hubs

A major tuning issue for WINS servers is replication frequency. You want replication to occur frequently enough that any server being down will not interfere with the reliability of name query responses. However, for longer wide area network (WAN) lengths, you do not want replication to interfere with network throughput.

For multiple network hubs interconnected by WAN links, replication frequency can be configured to be low compared to the replication frequency of multiple WINS servers at a single hub. For long WAN links, infrequent replication ensures that the links are available to carry client traffic without WINS affecting throughput.

For example, the WAN servers at a central site might be configured to replicate every 15 minutes. Replication between WAN hubs of a greater distance might be scheduled for every 30 minutes. Replication between servers on different continents might replicate twice a day.

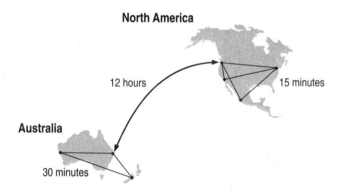

Figure 14.2   Example of an Enterprise-Wide Configuration for WINS Replication

C H A P T E R   1 5

Setting Up LMHOSTS

The LMHOSTS file is commonly used on Microsoft networks to locate remote computers for network file, print, and remote procedure services and for domain services such as logons, browsing, replication, and so on.

Use the LMHOSTS file for smaller networks or to find hosts on remote networks that are not part of the WINS database (since name query requests are not broadcast beyond the local subnet). If WINS servers are in place on an internetwork, users do not have to rely on broadcast queries for name resolution, since WINS is the preferred method for name resolution. With WINS servers in place, therefore, the LMHOSTS file might not be necessary.

This chapter presents the following topics:

- Editing the LMHOSTS file
- Using LMHOSTS with dynamic name resolution

Editing the LMHOSTS File

The LMHOSTS file used by Windows NT contains mappings of IP addresses to Windows NT computer names (which are NetBIOS names). This file is compatible with Microsoft LAN Manager 2.*x* TCP/IP LMHOSTS files.

You can use Notepad or any other text editor to edit the sample LMHOSTS file that is automatically installed in the *systemroot*\\SYSTEM32\\DRIVERS\\ETC directory.

This section provides some basic rules and guidelines for LMHOSTS.

Rules for LMHOSTS

Use the following rules for entries in LMHOSTS:

- Each entry should be placed on a separate line.
- The IP address should begin in the first column, followed by the corresponding computer name.
- The address and the computer name should be separated by at least one space or tab.
- NetBIOS names can contain uppercase and lowercase characters and special characters. If a name is placed between double quotation marks, it is used exactly as entered. For example, "AccountingPDC" is a mixed-case name, and "HumanRscSr   \\0x03" generates a name with a special character.

Note With Microsoft networks, a NetBIOS computer name displayed within straight quotation marks that is less than 16 characters long is padded with spaces. If you do not want this behavior, make sure the quoted string is 16 characters long.

- The pound sign (#) character is usually used to mark the start of a comment. However, it can also designate special keywords, as described in this section.

The keywords listed in the following table can be used in LMHOSTS under Windows NT. (LAN Manager 2.*x*, which also uses LMHOSTS for NetBIOS over TCP/IP name resolution, treats these keywords as comments.)

Table 15.1   LMHOSTS Keywords

Keyword	Description
#PRE	Added after an entry to cause that entry to be preloaded into the name cache. By default, entries are not preloaded into the name cache but are parsed only after WINS and name query broadcasts fail to resolve a name. The #PRE keyword must be appended for entries that also appear in #INCLUDE statements; otherwise, the entry in #INCLUDE is ignored.
#DOM:*<domain>*	Added after an entry to associate that entry with the domain specified by *<domain>*. This keyword affects how the Browser and Logon services behave in routed TCP/IP environments. To preload a #DOM entry, you must also add the #PRE keyword to the line.
#INCLUDE *<filename>*	Forces the system to seek the specified *<filename>* and parse it as if it were local. Specifying a Uniform Naming Convention (UNC) *<filename>* allows you to use a centralized LMHOSTS file on a server. If the server is located outside of the local broadcast area, you must add a mapping for the server before its entry in the #INCLUDE section and also append the #PRE keyword to ensure that it preloaded.
#BEGIN_ALTERNATE	Used to group multiple #INCLUDE statements. Any single successful #INCLUDE causes the group to succeed.
#END_ALTERNATE	Used to mark the end of an #INCLUDE statement grouping.
\0x*nn*	Support for nonprinting characters in NetBIOS names. Enclose the NetBIOS name in double quotation marks and use \0x*nn* notation to specify a hexadecimal value for the character. This allows custom applications that use special names to function properly in routed topologies. However, LAN Manager TCP/IP does not recognize the hexadecimal format, so you surrender backward compatibility if you use this feature. Note that the hexadecimal notation applies only to one character in the name. The name should be padded with blanks so the special character is last in the string (character 16).

The following example shows how all of these keywords are used:

```
102.54.94.98    localsrv    #PRE
102.54.94.97    trey        #PRE    #DOM:networking    #net group's PDC
102.54.94.102   "appname         \0x14"               #special app server
102.54.94.123   popular     #PRE                      #source server

#BEGIN_ALTERNATE
#INCLUDE \\localsrv\public\lmhosts    #adds LMHOSTS from this server
#INCLUDE \\trey\public\lmhosts        #adds LMHOSTS from this server
#END_ALTERNATE
```

In the above example:

- The servers named **localsrv** and **trey** are specified so they can be used later in an #INCLUDE statement in a centrally maintained LMHOSTS file.

- The server named **"appname   \0x14"** contains a special character after the 15 characters in its name (including the blanks), so its name is enclosed in double quotation marks.

- The server named **popular** is preloaded, based on the #PRE keyword.

Guidelines for LMHOSTS

When you use a host table file, be sure to keep it up to date and organized. Use the following guidelines:

- Update the LMHOSTS file whenever a computer is changed or removed from the network.

- Because LMHOSTS files are searched one line at a time from the beginning, list remote computers in priority order, with the ones used most often at the top of the file, followed by remote systems listed in #INCLUDE statements. Finally, the #PRE keyword entries should be left for the end of the file, because these are preloaded into the cache at system startup time and are not accessed later. This increases the speed of searches for the entries used most often. Because each line is processed individually, any comment lines that you add increase the parsing time.

- Use #PRE statements to preload popular entries and servers listed in #INCLUDE statements into the local computer's name cache.

Using LMHOSTS with Dynamic Name Resolution

On networks that do not use WINS, the broadcast name resolution method used by Windows NT computers provides a simple, dynamic mechanism for locating resources by name on a TCP/IP network.

Because broadcast name resolution relies on IP-level broadcasts to locate resources, unwanted effects can occur in routed IP topologies. In particular, resources located on remote subnets do not receive name query requests, because routers do not pass IP-level broadcasts. For this reason, Windows NT allows you to manually provide computer name and IP address mappings for remote resources via LMHOSTS.

This section describes how the LMHOSTS file can be used to enhance Windows NT in routed environments. This section includes the following topics:

- Specifying remote servers in LMHOSTS
- Designating primary domain controllers using the #DOM keyword
- Using centralized LMHOSTS files

Specifying Remote Servers in LMHOSTS

Computer names can be resolved outside the local broadcast area if computer name and IP address mappings are specified in the LMHOSTS file. For example, suppose the computer named ClientA wants to connect to the computer named ServerB, which is outside of its IP broadcast area. Both Windows NT computers are configured with Microsoft TCP/IP.

Under a strict b-node broadcast protocol, as defined in RFCs 1001 and 1002, ClientA's name query request for ServerB would fail (by timing out), because ServerB is located on a remote subnet and does not respond to ClientA's broadcast requests. So an alternate method is provided for name resolution. Windows NT maintains a limited cache of computer name and IP address mappings, which is initialized at system startup. When a workstation needs to resolve a name, the cache is examined first and, if there is no match in the cache, Windows NT uses b-node broadcast name resolution. If this fails, the LMHOSTS file is used. If this last method fails, the name is unresolved, and an error message appears.

This strategy allows the LMHOSTS file to contain a large number of mappings without requiring a large chunk of static memory to maintain an infrequently used cache. At system startup, the name cache is preloaded only with entries from LMHOSTS tagged with the #PRE keyword. For example, the LMHOSTS file could contain the following information:

```
102.54.94.91     accounting                #accounting server
102.54.94.94     payroll                   #payroll server
102.54.94.97     stockquote      #PRE      #stock quote server
102.54.94.102    printqueue                #print server in Bldg 10
```

In this example, the server named **stockquote** is preloaded into the name cache, because it is tagged with the #PRE keyword. Entries in the LMHOSTS file can represent Windows NT Workstation computers, Windows NT Server computers, LAN Manager servers, or Windows for Workgroups 3.11 computers running Microsoft TCP/IP. There is no need to distinguish between different platforms in LMHOSTS.

Note The Windows NT tag #PRE allows backward compatibility with LAN Manager 2.x LMHOSTS files and offers added flexibility in Windows NT. Under LAN Manager, the pound sign (#) character identifies a comment, so all characters thereafter are ignored. But #PRE is a valid tag for Windows NT.

In the above example, the servers named **accounting**, **payroll**, and **printqueue** would be resolved only after the cache entries failed to match and after broadcast queries failed to locate them. After nonpreloaded entries are resolved, their mappings are cached for a period of time for reuse.

Windows NT limits the preload name cache to 100 entries by default. This limit only affects entries marked with the #PRE keyword. If you specify more than 100 entries, only the first 100 #PRE entries are preloaded. Any additional #PRE entries are ignored at startup but are resolved when the system parses the LMHOSTS file after dynamic resolution fails.

Finally, you can reprime the name cache by using the **nbtstat -R** command to purge and reload the name cache, reread the LMHOSTS file, and then insert entries tagged with the #PRE keyword. Use the **nbtstat** command to remove or correct preloaded entries that might have been mistyped or any names cached by successful broadcast resolution.

Designating Domain Controllers Using #DOM

The most common use of LMHOSTS is for locating remote servers for file and print services. But for Windows NT, LMHOSTS can also be used to find domain controllers running TCP/IP in routed environments. Windows NT primary domain controllers (PDCs) and backup domain controllers (BDCs) maintain the user account security database and manage other network-related services. Because large Windows NT domains can span multiple IP subnets, it is possible that routers could separate the domain controllers from one another or separate other computers in the domain from domain controllers.

The #DOM keyword can be used in LMHOSTS files to distinguish a Windows NT domain controller from a Windows NT Workstation computer, a LAN Manager server, or a Windows for Workgroups computer. To use the #DOM tag, follow the name and IP address mapping in LMHOSTS with the #DOM keyword, a colon, and the domain in which the domain controller participates. For example:

```
102.54.94.97    treydc  #DOM:treycorp    #The treycorp PDC
```

Using the #DOM keyword to designate domain controllers adds entries to a special *internet group name cache* that is used to limit internetwork distribution of requests intended for the local domain controller. When domain controller activity such as a logon request occurs, the request is sent on the special internet group name. In the local IP-broadcast area, the request is sent only once and picked up by any local domain controllers. However, if you use the #DOM keyword to specify domain controllers in the LMHOSTS file, Microsoft TCP/IP uses datagrams to also forward the request to domain controllers located on remote subnets.

Examples of such domain controller activities include domain controller pulses (used for account database synchronization), logon authentication, password changes, master browser list synchronization, and other domain management activities.

For domains that span subnets, LMHOSTS files can be used to map important members of the domain using the #DOM keyword. The following list contains guidelines for doing this task.

- For each local LMHOSTS file on a Windows NT computer that is a member in a domain, there should be #DOM entries for all domain controllers in the domain that are located on remote subnets. This ensures that logon authentication, password changes, browsing, and so on all work properly for the local domain. These are the minimum entries necessary to allow a Windows NT system to participate in a Windows networking internetwork.

- For local LMHOSTS files on all servers that can be backup domain controllers, there should be mappings for the primary domain controller's name and IP address, plus mappings for all other backup domain controllers. This ensures that promoting a backup to primary domain controller status does not affect the ability to offer all services to members of the domain.

- If trust relationships exist between domains, all domain controllers for all trusted domains should also be listed in the local LMHOSTS file.

- For domains that you want to browse from your local domain, the local LMHOSTS files should contain at least the name and IP address mapping for the primary domain controller in the remote domain. Again, backup domain controllers should also be included so that promotion to primary domain controller does not impair the ability to browse remote domains.

For small to medium sized networks with fewer than 20 domains, a single common LMHOSTS file usually satisfies all workstations and servers on the internetwork. To achieve this, systems should use the Windows NT replicator service to maintain synchronized local copies of the global LMHOSTS file or use centralized LMHOSTS files, as described in the following section.

Names that appear with the #DOM keyword in LMHOSTS are placed in a special domain name list in NetBIOS over TCP/IP. When a datagram is sent to this domain using the DOMAIN<1C> name, the name is resolved first via WINS or broadcast. The datagram is then sent to all the addresses contained in the list from LMHOSTS, and there is also a broadcast on the local subnet.

Important To browse across domains, for Windows NT Advanced Server 3.1 and Windows NT 3.1, each computer must have an entry in its LMHOSTS file for the primary domain controller in each domain. This remains true for Windows NT version 3.5 clients, unless the Windows NT Server computer is also version 3.5 and, optionally, offers WINS name registration.

However, you cannot add an LMHOSTS entry for a Window NT Server that is a DHCP client, because the IP address changes dynamically. To avoid problems, any domain controllers whose names are entered in LMHOSTS files should have their IP addresses reserved as static addresses in the DHCP database rather than running as DHCP clients.

Also, all Windows NT Advanced Server 3.1 computers in a domain and its trusted domains should be upgraded to version 3.5, so that browsing across domains is possible without LMHOSTS.

Using Centralized LMHOSTS Files

With Microsoft TCP/IP, you can include other LMHOSTS files from local and remote computers. The primary LMHOSTS file is always located in the *systemroot*\SYSTEM32\DRIVERS\ETC directory on the local computers. Most networks will also have an LMHOSTS file maintained by the network administrator, so administrators should maintain one or more global LMHOSTS files that users can rely on. This is done using #INCLUDE statements rather than copying the global file locally. Then use the replicator service to distribute multiple copies of the global file(s) to multiple servers for reliable access.

Note If network clients access a computer's LMHOSTS file, that computer's Registry parameter **NullSessionShares** must include the share where the LMHOSTS file is located. The **NullSessionShares** parameter is in the Registry key HKEY_LOCAL_MACHINE\System\CurrentControlSet\Services\LanManServer\Parameters. For detailed information on Registry parameters, see Chapter 14, "Registry Value Entries," in the *Windows NT Resource Guide*.

To provide a redundant list of servers maintaining copies of the same LMHOSTS file, use the #BEGIN_ALTERNATE and #END_ALTERNATE keywords. This is known as a *block inclusion*, which allows multiple servers to be searched for a valid copy of a specific file. The following example shows the use of the #INCLUDE and #_ALTERNATE keywords to include a local LMHOSTS file (in the C:\PRIVATE directory):

```
102.54.94.97    treydc     #PRE  #DOM:treycorp    #primary DC
102.54.94.99    treybdc    #PRE  #DOM:treycorp    #backup DC in domain
102.54.94.98    localsvr   #PRE  #DOM:treycorp

#INCLUDE    c:\private\lmhosts              #include a local lmhosts

#BEGIN_ALTERNATE
#INCLUDE    \\treydc\public\lmhosts     #source for global file
#INCLUDE    \\treybdc\public\lmhosts    #backup source
#INCLUDE    \\localsvr\public\lmhosts   #backup source
#END_ALTERNATE
```

Important This feature should never be used to include a remote file from a redirected drive, because the LMHOSTS file is shared between local users who have different profiles and different logon scripts, and even on single-user systems, redirected drive mappings can change between logon sessions.

In the above example, the servers **treydc** and **treybdc** are located on remote subnets from the computer that owns the file. The local user has decided to include a list of preferred servers in a local LMHOSTS file located in the C:\PRIVATE directory. During name resolution, the Windows NT system first includes this private file, then gets the global LMHOSTS file from one of three locations: **treydc**, **treybdc**, or **localsvr**. All names of servers in the #INCLUDE statements must have their addresses preloaded using the #PRE keyword; otherwise, the #INCLUDE statement is ignored.

The block inclusion is satisfied if one of the three sources for the global LMHOSTS is available and none of the other servers are used. If no server is available, or for some reason the LMHOSTS file or path is incorrect, an event is added to the event log to indicate that the block inclusion failed.

C H A P T E R   1 6

Using the Microsoft FTP Server Service

When a Windows NT Server computer is running the FTP Server service, other computers using the FTP utility can connect to the server and transfer files. The FTP Server service supports all Windows NT **ftp** client commands. Non-Microsoft versions of FTP clients might contain commands that are not supported. The FTP Server service is implemented as a multithreaded Win32 service that complies with the requirements defined in Requests for Comments (RFCs) 959 and 1123.

The FTP Server service is integrated with the Windows NT security model. Users connecting to the FTP Server service are authenticated based on their Windows NT user accounts and receive access based on their user profiles. For this reason, it is recommended that the FTP Server service be installed on an NTFS partition so that the files and directories made available via FTP can be secured.

Caution The FTP Server protocol relies on the ability to pass user passwords over the network without data encryption. A user with physical access to the network could examine user passwords during the FTP validation process.

The following topics are included in this chapter:

- Installing the FTP Server service
- Configuring the FTP Server service
- Administering the FTP Server service
- Advanced configuration parameters for FTP Server service

For information about using performance counters to monitor FTP Server traffic, see Chapter 17, "Using Performance Monitor with TCP/IP Services."

Installing the FTP Server Service

It is assumed that you have installed any necessary devices and device drivers before trying to install the FTP Server service.

You must be logged on as a member of the Administrators group for the local computer to install and configure the FTP Server service.

▶ **To install the FTP Server service**

1. Double-click the Network option in Control Panel to display the Network Settings dialog box.

2. Choose the Add Software button to display the Add Network Software dialog box.

3. In the Network Software box, select TCP/IP Protocol And Related Components, and then choose the Continue button to display the Windows NT TCP/IP Installation Options dialog box.

4. Select the FTP Server Service option, and then choose the Continue button.

5. When prompted to confirm whether you are familiar with FTP security, choose the Yes button to continue with the FTP Server service installation.

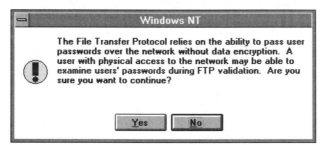

6. When prompted for the full path to the Windows NT distribution files, provide the appropriate location, and then choose the Continue button.

After the necessary files are copied to your computer, the FTP Service dialog box appears so that you can continue with the configuration procedure as described in the next section. The FTP Server service must be configured in order to operate.

Note For disk partitions that do not use the Windows NT file system (NTFS), you can apply simple read/write security by using the FTP Server tool in the Control Panel as described in the following section.

Configuring the FTP Server Service

After the FTP Server service software is installed on your computer, you must configure it to operate. When you configure the FTP Server service, your settings result in one of the following situations:

- No anonymous FTP connection allowed. In this case, each user must provide a valid Windows NT username and password. To configure the FTP Server service for this, make sure the Allow Anonymous Connection box is cleared in the FTP Service dialog box.

- Allow both anonymous and Windows NT users to connect. In this case, a user can choose to use either an anonymous connection or a Windows NT username and password. To configure the FTP Server service for this, make sure only the Allow Anonymous Connection box is selected in the FTP Service dialog box.

- Allow only anonymous FTP connections. In this case, a user cannot connect using a Windows NT username and password. To configure the FTP Server service for this, make sure both the Allow Anonymous Connections and the Allow Anonymous Connections Only boxes are selected in the FTP Service dialog box.

If anonymous connections are allowed, you must supply the Windows NT username and password to be used for anonymous FTP. When an anonymous FTP transfer takes place, Windows NT checks the username assigned in this dialog box to determine whether access is allowed to the files.

▶ **To configure or reconfigure the FTP Server service**

1. The FTP Service dialog box appears automatically after the FTP Server service software is installed on your computer.

   –Or–

   If you are reconfiguring the FTP Server service, double-click the Network option in Control Panel to display the Network Settings dialog box. In the Installed Network Software box, select FTP Server, and then choose the Configure button to display the FTP Service dialog box.

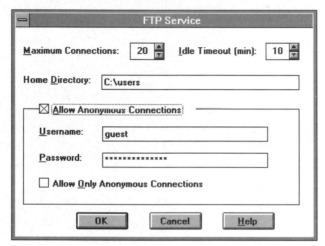

The FTP Service dialog box displays the following options:

Item	Description
Maximum Connections	Specifies the maximum number of FTP users who can connect to the system simultaneously. The default value is 20; the maximum is 50. A value of 0 means no maximum, that is, an unlimited number of simultaneous users.
	When the specified number of concurrent users are logged onto the FTP server, any subsequent attempts to connect will receive messages defined by the administrator. For information about defining custom messages, see "Advanced Configuration Parameters for FTP Server Service" later in this chapter.
Idle Timeout	Specifies how many minutes an inactive user can remain connected to the FTP Server service. The default value is 10 minutes; the maximum is 60 minutes. If the value is 0, users are never automatically disconnected.

Item	Description
Home Directory	Specifies the initial directory for users.
Allow Anonymous Connections	Enables users to connect to the FTP Server using the user name **anonymous** (or **ftp**, which is a synonym for **anonymous**). A password is not necessary, but the user is prompted to supply a mail address as the password. By default, anonymous connections are not allowed. Notice that you cannot use a Windows NT user account with the name **anonymous** with the FTP Server. The **anonymous** user name is reserved in the FTP Server for the anonymous logon function. Users logging on with the username **anonymous** receive permissions based on the FTP Server configuration for anonymous logons.
Username	Specifies which local user account to use for FTP Server users who log on under **anonymous**. Access permissions for the anonymous FTP user are the same as the specified local user account. The default is the standard Guest system account. If you change this, you must also change the password.
Password	Specifies the password for the user account specified in the Username box.
Allow Only Anonymous Connections	Allows only the user name **anonymous** to be accepted. This option is useful if you do not want users to log on using their own user names and passwords because FTP passwords are unencrypted. However, all users will have the same access privilege, defined by the anonymous account. By default, this option is not enabled.

2. Default values are provided for Maximum Connections, Idle Timeout, and Home Directory. Accept the default values, or change values for each field as necessary.

3. Choose the OK button to close the FTP Service dialog box and return to the Network Settings dialog box.

4. To complete initial FTP Server service installation and configuration, choose the OK button.

   A message reminds you that you must restart the computer so that the changes you made can take effect.

Note When you first install the FTP Server service, you must also complete the security configuration as described in the following procedure for users to access volumes on your computer.

► **To configure FTP Server security**

1. After the FTP Server has been installed and you have restarted Control Panel, double-click the FTP Server option in Control Panel.

   Windows NT Server users can also use the FTP menu in Server Manager.

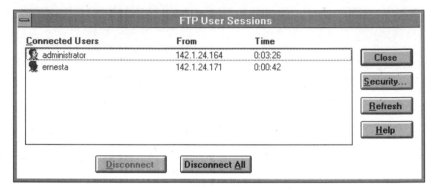

2. In the FTP User Sessions dialog box, choose the Security button to display the FTP Server Security dialog box.

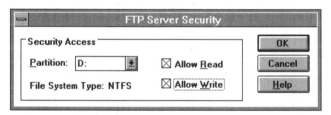

3. In the Partition box, select the drive letter on which you want to set security, and then select the Allow Read or Allow Write check box, or both check boxes, depending on the security you want for the selected partition.

   Repeat this step for each partition.

   Setting these permissions affects all files across the entire partition on file allocation table (FAT) and high-performance file system (HPFS) partitions. On NTFS partitions, this feature can be used to remove read or write access (or both) on the entire partition.

   Any restrictions set in this dialog box are enforced in addition to any security that might be part of the file system. That is, an administrator can use this dialog box to remove permissions on specific volumes but cannot use it to grant permissions beyond those maintained by the file system. For example, if a partition is marked as read-only, no one can write to the partition via FTP regardless of any permissions set in this dialog box.

4. Choose the OK button when you are finished setting security access on partitions.

The changes take effect immediately. The FTP Server service is now ready to operate.

Administering the FTP Server Service

FTP Server

After initial installation is complete, the FTP Server service is automatically started in the background each time the computer is started. Remote computers can initiate an FTP session while the FTP Server service is running on your Windows NT computer. Both computers must be running the TCP/IP protocol.

You must be logged on as a member of the Administrators group to administer the FTP Server.

Remote users can connect to the FTP Server using their account on the FTP Server, an account on the FTP Server's domain or trusted domains (Windows NT Server only), or using the **anonymous** account if the FTP Server service is configured to allow anonymous logons.

When making any configuration changes to the FTP Server (with the exception of security configuration), you must restart the FTP Server by either restarting the computer or manually stopping and restarting the server, using the **net** command or Services option in Control Panel.

▶ **To start or stop the FTP Server service**

- Double-click the Services option in Control Panel.

  –Or–

  At the command prompt, type the command **net stop ftpsvc** followed by the **net start ftpsvc** command.

Restarting the service in this way disconnects any users presently connected to the FTP Server without warning—so use the FTP Server option in Control Panel to determine if any users are connected. Pausing the FTP Server (by using the Services option in Control Panel or the **net pause** command) prevents any more users from connecting to the FTP Server but does not disconnect the currently logged on users. This feature is useful when the administrator wants to restart the server without disconnecting the current users. After the users disconnect on their own, the administrator can safely shut down the server without worrying that users might lose work. When attempting to connect to a Windows NT FTP Server that has been paused, clients receive the message "421 - Service not available, closing control connection."

Using FTP Commands at the Command Prompt

When you install the FTP service, a set of **ftp** commands are automatically installed that you can use at the command prompt. For a summary list of these commands, see the **ftp** entry in Appendix A, "TCP/IP Utilities Reference."

▶ **To get help on ftp commands**

1. In Program Manager, double-click the Windows NT Help icon in the Main window.

2. In the Windows NT Help window, choose the Command Reference Help button.

3. Choose the **ftp commands** name in the Commands window.

4. Choose an **ftp** command name in the Command Reference window to see a description of the command, plus its syntax and parameter definitions.

Managing Users

Use the FTP Server option in Control Panel to manage users connected to the FTP Server and to set security for each volume on the FTP Server. For convenience on Windows NT Server computers, the same dialog box can be reached from Server Manager by choosing the FTP menu command.

In the FTP User Sessions dialog box, the Connected Users box displays the names of connected users, their system's IP addresses, and how long they have been connected. For users who logged on using the **anonymous** user name, the display shows the passwords used when they logged on as their user names. If the user name contained a mail host name (for example, ernesta@trey-research.com) only the username (ernesta) appears. Anonymous users also have a question mark (?) over their user icons. Users who have been authenticated by Windows NT security have no question mark.

The FTP Server enables you to disconnect one or all users with the disconnect buttons. Users are not warned if you disconnect them.

The FTP Server displays users' names as they connect but does not update the display when users disconnect or when their connect time elapses. The Refresh button enables you to update the display to show only users who are currently connected.

Choosing the Security button displays the FTP Service Security dialog box, where you can set Read and Write permissions for each partition on the FTP Server, as described earlier in this chapter. You must set the permissions for each partition you want FTP users to have access to. If you do not set partition parameters, no users will be able to access files. If the partition uses a secure file system, such as NTFS, file system restrictions are also in effect.

In addition to FTP Server partition security, if a user logs on using a Windows NT account, access permissions for that account are in effect.

Controlling the FTP Server and User Access

A network administrator can control several of the FTP Server configuration variables. One such variable, Maximum Connections, can be set by using the Network option in Control Panel to define a value between 0 and 50. Any value from 1 to 50 restricts concurrent FTP sessions to the value specified. A value of 0 allows unlimited connections to be established to the FTP Server until the system exhausts the available memory.

You can specify a custom message to be displayed when the maximum number of concurrent connections is reached. To do this, enter a new value for **MaxClientsMessage** in the Registry, as described in "Advanced Configuration Parameters for FTP Server Service" later in this chapter.

Annotating Directories

You can add directory descriptions to inform FTP users of the contents of a particular directory on the server by creating a file called ~FTPSVC~.CKM in the directory that you want to annotate. You usually want to make this a hidden file so directory listings do not display this file. To do this, use File Manager or type the command **attrib +h ~ftpsvc~.ckm** at the command prompt.

Directory annotation can be toggled by FTP users on a user-by-user basis with a built-in, site-specific command called **ckm**. On most FTP client implementations (including the Windows NT FTP client), users type a command at the command prompt similar to **quote site ckm** to get this effect.

You can set the default behavior for directory annotation by setting a value for **AnnotateDirectories** in the Registry, as described in "Advanced Configuration Parameters for FTP Server Service" later in this chapter.

Changing Directory Listing Format

Some FTP client software makes assumptions based on the formatting of directory list information. The Windows NT FTP Server provides some flexibility for client software that requires directory listing similar to UNIX systems. Users can use the command **dirstyle** to toggle directory listing format between MS-DOS–style (the default) and UNIX-style listings. On most FTP client implementations (including the Windows NT FTP client), users type a command at the command prompt similar to **quote site dirstyle** to get this effect.

You can set the default style for directory listing format by setting a value for **MsDosDirOutput** in the Registry, as described in "Advanced Configuration Parameters for FTP Server Service" later in this chapter.

Customizing Greeting and Exit Messages

You can create customized greeting and exit messages by setting values for **GreetingMessage** and **ExitMessage** in the Registry, as described in "Advanced Configuration Parameters for FTP Server Service" later in this chapter. By default, these value entries are not in the Registry, so you must add them to customize the message text.

Greeting and exit messages are sent to users when they connect or disconnect from the FTP Server. When you create custom messages, you can add multiline messages of your choice.

Logging FTP Connections

You can log incoming FTP connections in the System event log by setting values for **LogAnonymous** and **LogNonAnonymous** in the Registry, as described in "Advanced Configuration Parameters for FTP Server Service" later in this chapter. By default, these value entries are not in the Registry, so you must add them to log incoming connections.

You can specify whether event log entries are made for both anonymous and nonanonymous users connecting to the FTP Server. You can view such entries in the System event log by using Event Viewer.

Advanced Configuration Parameters for FTP Server Service

This section presents configuration parameters that affect the behavior of the FTP Server service and that can be modified only through Registry Editor. After you modify any of these value entries, you must restart the FTP Server service for the changes to take effect.

Caution You can impair or disable Windows NT if you make incorrect changes in the Registry while using Registry Editor. Whenever possible, use administrative tools such as Control Panel to make configuration changes, rather than using Registry Editor. If you make errors while changing values with Registry Editor, you will not be warned, because Registry Editor does not recognize semantic errors.

▶ **To make changes to the FTP Server service configuration using Registry Editor**

1. Run the REGEDT32.EXE program from File Manager or Program Manager.

   –Or–

   At the command prompt, type the **start regedt32** command, and then press ENTER.

   When the Registry Editor window appears, you can press F1 to get Help on how to make changes in Registry Editor.

2. In Registry Editor, select HKEY_LOCAL_MACHINE On Local Machine, and then click the icons for the SYSTEM subtree until you reach this subkey:

   `..\SYSTEM\CurrentControlSet\Services\ftpsvc\Parameters`

   All of the parameters described here are located under this Registry subkey.

   You must restart the FTP Server service for the changes to take effect.

The following list describes the value entries for FTP Server service parameters that can only be set by adding an entry or changing their values in Registry Editor. These value entries do not appear by default in the Registry, so you must add an entry if you want to change its default value.

AnnotateDirectories

Data type = REG_DWORD
Range = 0 or 1
Default = 0 (false—that is, directory annotation is off)

This value entry defines the default behavior of directory annotation for newly connected users. Directory descriptions are used to inform FTP users of the contents of a directory on the server. The directory description is saved in a file named ~FTPSVC~.CKM, which is usually a hidden file. When this value is 1, directory annotation is on.

ExitMessage

Data type = REG_SZ
Range = String
Default = "Goodbye."

This value entry defines a signoff message that will be sent to FTP clients upon receipt of a **quit** command.

GreetingMessage

Data type = REG_MULTI_SZ
Range = String
Default = None (no special greeting message)

This value entry defines the message to be sent to new clients after their accounts have been validated. In accordance with Internet behavior, if the client logs on as anonymous and specifies an identity that starts with a minus sign (–), this greeting message is not sent.

LogAnonymous

Data type = REG_DWORD
Range = 0 or 1
Default = 0 (false—that is, do not log successful anonymous logons)

This value entry enables or disables logging of anonymous logons in the System event log.

LogNonAnonymous

Data type = REG_DWORD
Range = 0 or 1
Default = 0 (false—that is, do not log successful nonanonymous logons)

This value entry enables or disables logging of nonanonymous logons in the System event log.

LogFileAccess

Data type = REG_DWORD
Range = 0-2
Default = 0 (do not log file accesses to FTPSVC.LOG)

This value entry specifies the logging behavior of FTP Server file access. Allowable values are:

0 Do not log file accesses (default)

1 Log file accesses to FTPSVC.LOG in the service's current directory, typically *systemroot*\SYSTEM32.

2 Log file accesses to FT*yymmdd*.LOG, where *yy* is the current year, *mm* is the current month, and *dd* is the current day. The log file is located in the service's current directory, typically *systemroot*\SYSTEM32. New log files are opened daily, as necessary.

For each file opened by the FTP Server, the service log will contain a single line entry in the following format:

IPAddress username action path date_time

- *ip_address* is the client computer's IP address

- *username* is the user's name (or *password* for anonymous logons)

- *action* is either "opened," "created," or "appended"

- *path* is the fully qualified path of the file acted upon

- *date_time* is the date and time the action took place

Entries are also written to the log whenever the FTP Server starts or stops. For example:

```
************** FTP SERVER SERVICE STARTING Fri Apr 29 10:28:49 1994
11.101.199.173 daveo opened c:\tmp\tst.bat Fri Apr 29 10:29:42 1994
11.101.199.173 daveo created c:\tmp\new.txt Fri Apr 29 10:30:25 1994
11.101.199.173 daveo appended c:\tmp\new.txt Fri Apr 29 10:33:04 1994
************** FTP SERVER SERVICE STOPPING Fri Apr 29 10:33:08 1994
```

LogFileDirectory

Data type = REG_SZ
Default = *systemroot*\SYSTEM32

This value entry specifies the target directory for the log file or files. The target directory does not have to reside on the system partition.

LowercaseFiles

Data type = REG_DWORD
Range = 0 or 1
Default = 0 (do not map filenames to lowercase)

If this value entry is nonzero, all filenames returned by the **list** and **nlst** commands are mapped to lowercase for noncase-preserving file systems. This mapping only occurs when a directory listing is requested on a noncase-preserving file system. If this value is 0, case in all filenames is unaltered. Currently, FAT is the only noncase-preserving file system supported under Windows NT, so this flag has no effect when retrieving listings on HPFS or NTFS partitions.

MaxClientsMessage

Data type = REG_SZ
Range = String
Default = "Maximum clients reached, service unavailable."

This value entry specifies the message to be sent to an FTP client if the maximum number of clients has been reached or exceeded. This message indicates that the server is refusing additional clients because it is currently servicing the maximum number of connections (as specified in the FTP Service dialog box or the **MaxConnections** value in the Registry).

MsdosDirOutput

Data type = REG_DWORD
Range = 0 or 1
Default = 1 (true—that is, directory listings will look like MS-DOS)

This value entry specifies the default behavior for whether the output of the **list** command looks like the output of the MS-DOS **dir** command or the output of the UNIX **ls** command. This value also controls the direction of slashes in paths sent by the **pwd** command.

When this value is 1, directory listings look like MS-DOS listings, and the path will contain backward slashes (\\). If this value is 0, listings look like UNIX listings, and the path contains forward slashes (/).

The following Registry parameters can be set using the options available when configuring the FTP Server service in the Network Settings dialog box:

AllowAnonymous
AnonymousOnly
AnonymousUsername
ConnectionTimeout
HomeDirectory
MaxConnections

The following Registry parameters can be set using the options available when you select the FTP Server icon in Control Panel and then choose the Security button:

ReadAccessMask
WriteAccessMask

The ranges of values that can be entered for these parameters in Registry Editor are the same as those described in the related dialog boxes earlier in this chapter. You should use only the FTP Server service dialog boxes to set these values.

C H A P T E R   1 7

Using Performance Monitor with TCP/IP Services

This chapter describes the performance counters that can be charted in Performance Monitor so you can track performance of the IP protocols, FTP Server service traffic, and WINS servers.

The performance counters are described in the following topics in this chapter:

- Using Performance Monitor with TCP/IP
- Monitoring TCP/IP performance
- Monitoring FTP Server service traffic
- Monitoring WINS server performance

Important To use the TCP/IP performance counters in Performance Monitor, you must install the SNMP service, as described in Chapter 11, "Installing and Configuring Microsoft TCP/IP and SNMP."

Using Performance Monitor with TCP/IP

After elements of Microsoft TCP/IP are installed, you can use Performance Monitor to track performance.

▶ **To use Performance Monitor with TCP/IP**

1. In the Administrative Tools group in Program Manager, double-click Performance Monitor.

2. From the Edit menu, choose Add To Chart.

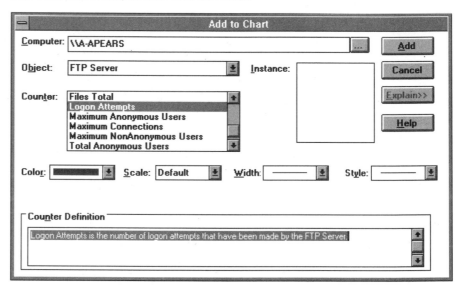

3. In the Computer list in the Add To Chart dialog box, select the computer you want to monitor.

4. In the Object list, select the TCP/IP-related process you want to monitor: FTP Server, ICMP, IP, Network Interface, TCP, UDP, or WINS Server.

5. In the Counter list, select the counters you want to monitor for each process, and then choose the Add button.

   For information about each counter, choose the Explain button, or see the definition tables later in this chapter.

6. When you have selected all the counters you want for a particular chart, choose the Done button.

For more information about using Performance Monitor, see Chapter 19, "Performance Monitor," in the *Windows NT Server System Guide*.

Monitoring TCP/IP Performance

Each of the different elements that make up the TCP/IP protocol suite can be monitored separately in Performance Monitor if SNMP services are installed on the computer.

▶ **To view counters specific to TCP/IP processes**

- In the Add To Chart dialog box in Performance Monitor, select ICMP, IP, Network Interface, TCP, or UDP in the Object list.

The counters for each of these object types are described in the following sections.

ICMP Performance Counters

The ICMP Object Type includes those counters that describe the rates that Internet Control Message Protocol (ICMP) messages are received and sent by a certain entity using the ICMP protocol. It also describes various error counts for the ICMP protocol.

Table 17.1   Internet Control Message Protocol (ICMP) Performance Counters

ICMP performance counter	Meaning
Messages Outbound Errors	The number of ICMP messages that this entity did not send because of problems discovered within ICMP, such as lack of buffers. This value should not include errors discovered outside the ICMP layer, such as the inability of IP to route the resultant datagram. In some implementations, there might be no types of error that contribute to this counter's value.
Messages Received Errors	The number of ICMP messages that the entity received, but determined as having errors (bad ICMP checksums, bad length, and so on).
Messages Received/Second	The rate at which ICMP messages are received by the entity. The rate includes those messages received in error.
Messages Sent/Second	The rate at which ICMP messages are attempted to be sent by the entity. The rate includes those messages sent in error.
Messages/Second	The total rate at which ICMP messages are received and sent by the entity. The rate includes those messages received or sent in error.
Received Address Mask	The number of ICMP Address Mask Request messages received.

Table 17.1   Internet Control Message Protocol (ICMP) Performance Counters
(continued)

ICMP performance counter	Meaning
Received Address Mask Reply	The number of ICMP Address Mask Reply messages received.
Received Destination Unreachable	The number of ICMP Destination Unreachable messages received.
Received Echo Reply/Second	The rate of ICMP Echo Reply messages received.
Received Echo/Second	The rate of ICMP Echo messages received.
Received Parameter Problem	The number of ICMP Parameter Problem messages received.
Received Redirect/Second	The rate of ICMP Redirect messages received.
Received Source Quench	The number of ICMP Source Quench messages received.
Received Time Exceeded	The number of ICMP Time Exceeded messages received.
Received Timestamp Reply/Second	The rate of ICMP Timestamp Reply messages received.
Received Timestamp/Second	The rate of ICMP Timestamp (request) messages received.
Sent Address Mask	The number of ICMP Address Mask Request messages sent.
Sent Address Mask Reply	The number of ICMP Address Mask Reply messages sent.
Sent Destination Unreachable	The number of ICMP Destination Unreachable messages sent.
Sent Echo Reply/Second	The rate of ICMP Echo Reply messages sent.
Sent Echo/Second	The rate of ICMP Echo messages sent.
Sent Parameter Problem	The number of ICMP Parameter Problem messages sent.
Sent Redirect/Second	The rate of ICMP Redirect messages sent.
Sent Source Quench	The number of ICMP Source Quench messages sent.
Sent Time Exceeded	The number of ICMP Time Exceeded messages sent.
Sent Timestamp Reply/Second	The rate of ICMP Timestamp Reply messages sent.
Sent Timestamp/Second	The rate of ICMP Timestamp (request) messages sent.

IP Performance Counters

The IP Object Type includes those counters that describe the rates that Internet Protocol (IP) datagrams are received and sent by a certain computer using the IP protocol. It also describes various error counts for the IP protocol.

Table 17.2   IP Performance Counters

IP performance counter	Meaning
Datagrams Forwarded/Second	The rate of input datagrams for which this entity was not their final IP destination that resulted in an attempt to find a route to forward them to that final destination. In entities that do not act as IP Gateways, this rate includes only those packets that were Source-Routed via this entity, when the Source-Route option processing was successful.
Datagrams Outbound Discarded	The number of output IP datagrams for which no problems were encountered to prevent their transmission to their destination, but which were discarded (for example, for lack of buffer space.) This counter would include datagrams counted in Datagrams Forwarded if any such packets met this (discretionary) discard criterion.
Datagrams Outbound No Route	The number of IP datagrams discarded because no route could be found to transmit them to their destination. This counter includes any packets counted in Datagrams Forwarded that meet this "no route" criterion.
Datagrams Received Address Errors	The number of input datagrams discarded because the IP address in their IP header's destination field was not a valid address to be received at this entity. This count includes invalid addresses (for example, 0.0.0.0) and addresses of unsupported Classes (for example, Class E). For entities that are not IP gateways and therefore do not forward datagrams, this counter includes datagrams discarded because the destination address was not a local address.
Datagrams Received Delivered/Second	The rate at which input datagrams are successfully delivered to IP user protocols (including ICMP).
Datagrams Received Discarded	The number of input IP datagrams for which no problems were encountered to prevent their continued processing, but which were discarded (for example, for lack of buffer space). This counter does not include any datagrams discarded while awaiting reassembly.
Datagrams Received Header Errors	The number of input datagrams discarded because of errors in their IP headers, including bad checksums, version number mismatch, other format errors, time-to-live exceeded, errors discovered in processing their IP options, and so on.

Table 17.2   IP Performance Counters *(continued)*

IP performance counter	Meaning
Datagrams Received Unknown Protocol	The number of locally addressed datagrams received successfully but discarded because of an unknown or unsupported protocol.
Datagrams Received/Second	The rate at which IP datagrams are received from the interfaces, including those in error.
Datagrams Sent/Second	The rate at which IP datagrams are supplied to IP for transmission by local IP user protocols (including ICMP). This counter does not include any datagrams counted in Datagrams Forwarded.
Datagrams/Second	The rate at which IP datagrams are received from or sent to the interfaces, including those in error. Any forwarded datagrams are not included in this rate.
Fragment Re-assembly Failures	The number of failures detected by the IP reassembly algorithm (for whatever reason: timed out, errors, and so on). This is not necessarily a count of discarded IP fragments, because some algorithms (notably RFC 815) can lose track of the number of fragments by combining them as they are received.
Fragmentation Failures	The number of IP datagrams that have been discarded because they needed to be fragmented at this entity but could not be, for example, because their "Don't Fragment" flag was set.
Fragmented Datagrams/Second	The rate at which datagrams are successfully fragmented at this entity.
Fragments Created/Second	The rate at which IP datagram fragments have been generated as a result of fragmentation at this entity.
Fragments Re-assembled/Second	The rate at which IP fragments are successfully reassembled.
Fragments Received/Second	The rate at which IP fragments that need to be reassembled at this entity are received.

Network Interface Performance Counters for TCP/IP

The Network Interface Object Type includes those counters that describe the rates at which bytes and packets are received and sent over a network TCP/IP connection. It also describes various error counts for the same connection.

Table 17.3   Network Interface Counters

Network Interface counter	Meaning
Bytes Received/Second	The rate at which bytes are received on the interface, including framing characters.
Bytes Sent/Second	The rate at which bytes are sent on the interface, including framing characters.
Bytes Total/Second	The rate at which bytes are sent and received on the interface, including framing characters.
Current Bandwidth	An estimate of the interface's current bandwidth in bits per second (bps). For interfaces that do not vary in bandwidth or for those where no accurate estimation can be made, this value is the nominal bandwidth.
Output Queue Length	The length of the output packet queue (in packets.) If this is longer than 2, delays are being experienced and the bottleneck should be found and eliminated if possible. Since the requests are queued by NDIS in this implementation, this will always be 0.
Packets Outbound Discarded	The number of outbound packets that were chosen to be discarded even though no errors had been detected to prevent their being transmitted. One possible reason for discarding such a packet could be to free up buffer space.
Packets Outbound Errors	The number of outbound packets that could not be transmitted because of errors.
Packets Received Discarded	The number of inbound packets that were chosen to be discarded even though no errors had been detected to prevent their being deliverable to a higher-layer protocol. One possible reason for discarding such a packet could be to free up buffer space.

Table 17.3   Network Interface Counters *(continued)*

Network Interface counter	Meaning
Packets Received Errors	The number of inbound packets that contained errors preventing them from being deliverable to a higher-layer protocol.
Packets Received Non-Unicast/Second	The rate at which non-unicast (that is, subnet broadcast or subnet multicast) packets are delivered to a higher-layer protocol.
Packets Received Unicast/Second	The rate at which (subnet) unicast packets are delivered to a higher-layer protocol.
Packets Received Unknown	The number of packets received via the interface that were discarded because of an unknown or unsupported protocol.
Packets Received/Second	The rate at which packets are received on the network interface.
Packets Sent Non-Unicast/Second	The rate at which packets are requested to be transmitted to non-unicast (that is, subnet broadcast or subnet multicast) addresses by higher-level protocols. The rate includes the packets that were discarded or not sent.
Packets Sent Unicast/Second	The rate at which packets are requested to be transmitted to subnet-unicast addresses by higher-level protocols. The rate includes the packets that were discarded or not sent.
Packets Sent/Second	The rate at which packets are sent on the network interface.
Packets/Second	The rate at which packets are sent and received on the network interface.

TCP Performance Counters

The TCP Object Type includes those counters that describe the rates that Transmission Control Protocol (TCP) segments are received and sent by a certain entity using the TCP protocol. In addition, it describes the number of TCP connections that are in each of the possible TCP connection states.

Table 17.4   TCP Performance Counters

TCP performance counter	Meaning
Connection Failures	The number of times TCP connections have made a direct transition to the CLOSED state from the SYN-SENT state or the SYN-RCVD state, plus the number of times TCP connections have made a direct transition to the LISTEN state from the SYN-RCVD state.
Connections Active	The number of times TCP connections have made a direct transition to the SYN-SENT state from the CLOSED state.
Connections Established	The number of TCP connections for which the current state is either ESTABLISHED or CLOSE-WAIT.
Connections Passive	The number of times TCP connections have made a direct transition to the SYN-RCVD state from the LISTEN state.
Connections Reset	The number of times TCP connections have made a direct transition to the CLOSED state from either the ESTABLISHED state or the CLOSE-WAIT state.
Segments Received/Second	The rate at which segments are received, including those received in error. This count includes segments received on currently established connections.
Segments Retransmitted/Second	The rate at which segments are retransmitted, that is, segments transmitted containing one or more previously transmitted bytes.
Segments Sent/Second	The rate at which segments are sent, including those on current connections, but excluding those containing only retransmitted bytes.
Segments/Second	The rate at which TCP segments are sent or received using the TCP protocol.

UDP Performance Counters

The UDP Object Type includes those counters that describe the rates that User Datagram Protocol (UDP) datagrams are received and sent by a certain entity using the UDP protocol. It also describes various error counts for the UDP protocol.

Table 17.5   UDP Performance Counters

UDP performance counter	Meaning
Datagrams No Port/Second	The rate of received UDP datagrams for which there was no application at the destination port.
Datagrams Received Errors	The number of received UDP datagrams that could not be delivered for reasons other than the lack of an application at the destination port.
Datagrams Received/Second	The rate at which UDP datagrams are delivered to UDP users.
Datagrams Sent/Second	The rate at which UDP datagrams are sent from the entity.
Datagrams/Second	The rate at which UDP datagrams are sent or received by the entity.

Monitoring FTP Server Traffic

When you install the FTP Server services, the necessary software is also installed so that you can monitor and graph various FTP Server statistics using Performance Monitor. Using Performance Monitor to view activity on remote Windows NT systems makes FTP Server administration more convenient when you are administering multiple Windows NT FTP Servers.

▶ **To view counters specific to the FTP Server service**

- In the Performance Monitor window, select FTP Server in the Object list.

The FTP Server performance counters are cleared each time you start and stop the FTP Server service.

Table 17.6   FTP Performance Counters

FTP performance counter	Meaning
Bytes Received/Second	The rate at which data bytes are received by the FTP Server.
Bytes Sent/Second	The rate at which data bytes are sent by the FTP Server.
Bytes Total/Second	The sum of Bytes Sent/Second and Bytes Received/Second. This is the total rate of bytes transferred by the FTP Server.
Connection Attempts	The number of connection attempts that have been made to the FTP Server.
Current Anonymous Users	The number of anonymous users currently connected to the FTP Server.
Current Connections	The current number of connections to the FTP Server.
Current NonAnonymous Users	The number of nonanonymous users currently connected to the FTP Server.
Files Received	The total number of files received by the FTP Server.
Files Sent	The total number of files sent by the FTP Server.
Files Total	The sum of Files Sent and Files Received. This is the total number of files transferred by the FTP Server.
Logon Attempts	The number of logon attempts that have been made to the FTP Server.
Maximum Anonymous Users	The maximum number of anonymous users simultaneously connected to the FTP Server.
Maximum Connections	The maximum number of simultaneous connections to the FTP Server.
Maximum NonAnonymous Users	The maximum number of nonanonymous users simultaneously connected to the FTP Server.
Total Anonymous Users	The total number of anonymous users that have ever connected to the FTP Server.
Total NonAnonymous Users	The total number of nonanonymous users that have ever connected to the FTP Server.

Monitoring WINS Server Performance

When you install a WINS server and SNMP services, counters are automatically installed so that you can use Performance Monitor to view WINS Server service performance.

▶ **To view counters specific to the WINS Server service**

- In the Performance Monitor window, select WINS Server in the Object list.

Table 17.7   WINS Performance Counters

WINS performance counter	Meaning
Failed Queries/Second	The total number of failed queries per second.
Failed Releases/Second	The total number of failed releases per second.
Group Conflicts/Second	The rate at which group registrations received by the WINS server resulted in conflicts with records in the database.
Group Registrations/Second	The rate at which group registrations are received by the WINS server.
Group Renewals/Second	The rate at which group renewals are received by the WINS server.
Queries/Second	The total number of queries per second, which is the rate at which queries are received by the WINS server.
Releases/Second	The total number of releases per second, which is the rate at which releases are received by the WINS server.
Successful Queries/Second	The total number of successful queries per second.
Successful Releases/Second	The total number of successful releases per second.
Total Number of Conflicts/Second	The sum of the Unique and Group conflicts per second, which is the total rate at which conflicts were seen by the WINS server.
Total Number of Registrations/Second	The sum of the Unique and Group registrations per second. This is the total rate at which registrations are received by the WINS server.
Total Number of Renewals/Second	The sum of the Unique and Group registrations per second, which is the total rate at which renewals are received by the WINS server.
Unique Conflicts/Second	The rate at which unique registrations and renewals received by the WINS server resulted in conflicts with records in the database.
Unique Registrations/Second	The rate at which unique registrations are received by the WINS server.
Unique Renewals/Second	The rate at which unique renewals are received by the WINS server.

C H A P T E R   1 8

Internetwork Printing with TCP/IP

Users on any Microsoft networking computer can print to direct-connect TCP/IP printers or to printers that are physically attached to UNIX computers if at least one Windows NT computer has Microsoft TCP/IP printing installed.

Microsoft TCP/IP printing conforms with Request for Comment (RFC) 1179.

This chapter describes how to create a TCP/IP printer when TCP/IP is installed on a Windows NT computer and how to print to a Windows NT print server from a UNIX computer.

The topics in this chapter include:

- Overview of TCP/IP printing
- Setting up Windows NT for TCP/IP printing
- Creating a printer for TCP/IP printing
- Printing to Windows NT from UNIX clients

For complete information about working with printers, see Chapter 6, "Print Manager," in the *Windows NT System Guide*.

Overview of TCP/IP Printing

In a Windows NT internetwork with multiple kinds of computers and operating systems, users can take advantage of Microsoft TCP/IP to easily print to computers that are connected through a UNIX computer or that are connected directly to the network (via a built-in network adapter card or through a serial/parallel ethernet print server).

Such an internetwork might include computers running Windows NT Workstation and Windows NT Server, plus computers with only Microsoft Windows for Workgroups 3.11 or MS-DOS with LAN Manager networking software.

To take advantage of the printing capabilities of Microsoft TCP/IP, only the single Windows NT computer that defines a TCP/IP printer needs to have TCP/IP installed. All the other client computers can print to the TCP/IP printers over any protocol they share with the Windows NT TCP/IP print server. That is, the computer acting as the Windows NT TCP/IP print server must be configured with all protocols used by any clients that will be printing to the TCP/IP printer.

Any Windows NT computer with TCP/IP printing installed can print directly to these kinds of printers and can function as a gateway for other network users.

In the following sample configuration of a Microsoft network, all computers can connect to printers named **\\nt\p1** and **\\nt\p2** on the network. The Windows NT computer with Microsoft TCP/IP installed created these TCP/IP printers, which consist of a direct-connect printer and a printer connected to a UNIX computer. The Windows NT computer with TCP/IP is named **nt** in this example, and the printers are named **p1** and **p2**, respectively.

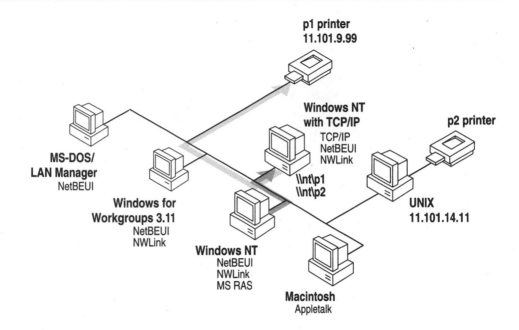

Figure 18.1   Printing to TCP/IP or UNIX Printers Using Microsoft TCP/IP

Setting Up Windows NT for TCP/IP Printing

Any Windows NT computer can be used to create a TCP/IP printer if Microsoft TCP/IP is installed with TCP/IP printing support.

▶ **To configure a Windows NT computer for TCP/IP printing**

1. Double-click the Network option in Control Panel to display the Network Settings dialog box, and then choose the Add Software button to display the Add Network Software dialog box.

2. Select TCP/IP Protocol And Related Components in the Network Software box, and then choose the Continue button.

3. In the Windows NT TCP/IP Installation Options dialog box, check the TCP/IP Network Printing Support option.

   If Microsoft TCP/IP is not already installed on this computer, select the other options you want, as described in Chapter 11, "Installing and Configuring Microsoft TCP/IP and SNMP."

4. Choose the OK button. Windows NT Setup displays a message prompting for the full path to the Windows NT distribution files. Provide the appropriate location, and then choose the Continue button.

   All necessary files are copied to your hard disk.

   Note If the Enable Automatic DHCP Configuration option is not selected in the Windows NT TCP/IP Installation Options dialog box, you must complete all the required procedures for manually configuring TCP/IP as described in Chapter 11, "Installing and Configuring Microsoft TCP/IP and SNMP."

   After you finish configuring TCP/IP, the Network Settings dialog box is displayed again.

5. Choose the Close button, and then restart your computer for the changes to take effect.

You can now create a TCP/IP printer on this Windows NT computer.

Creating a Printer for TCP/IP Printing

You can use Print Manager to create a TCP/IP printer in the same way that you create any printer to be used on a Windows NT network. You need the following information to create a TCP/IP printer:

- The IP identifier of the host where the printer is connected.

   This can be the DNS name or the IP address. A direct-connect printer has its own IP identifier. For a printer connected to a UNIX computer, this is the computer's IP identifier.

- The printer name as it is identified on the host.

   This is the name defined on the UNIX computer or the name defined by the manufacturer for the direct-connect printer.

The computer where you create the TCP/IP printer must have TCP/IP installed and configured with the TCP/IP Network Printing Support option, as described in Chapter 11, "Installing and Configuring Microsoft TCP/IP and SNMP."

▸ **To create a TCP/IP printer**

1. From the Printer menu in Print Manager, choose Create Printer to display the Create Printer dialog box.

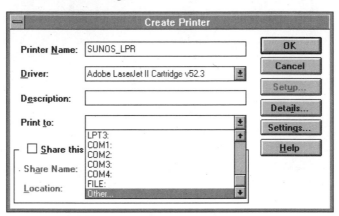

2. In the Printer Name box, type a name of up to 32 characters.

   This name appears in the title bar of the printer window, and Windows NT users see this name when connecting to this printer if it is shared.

   This name can be the same as the printer name as it is identified on the printer's UNIX host, but it does not have to be.

   For a direct-connect printer, see the hardware documentation to find the name by which the network printer identifies the print queue.

3. In the Driver list, select the appropriate driver.

   In addition, you can type text in the Description box to inform network users about the printer.

4. In the Print To box, select Other to display the Print Destinations dialog box.

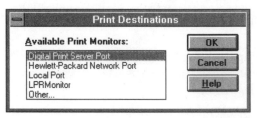

5. In the Available Print Destinations list, select LPR Print Monitor, and then choose OK to display the Add LPR Compatible Printer dialog box.

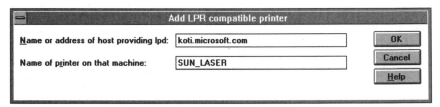

6. In the Name Or Address Of Host Providing LPD box, type the DNS name or IP address of the host for the printer you are adding.

The name can be the DNS name or IP address of the direct-connect TCP/IP printer or of the UNIX computer to which the printer is connected. The DNS name can be the name specified for the host in the HOSTS file.

LPR stands for Line Printing utility; and LPD stands for Line Printing Daemon, which is how these elements are known on UNIX.

Note   Windows NT 3.5 supports TCP/IP printing only for UNIX computers running the LPD service. It does not support UNIX computers running LPSCHED. If your UNIX computer is running LPSCHED and you want it to support Windows NT TCP/IP printing, you need to install a publicly available LPD program.

---

7. In the Name Of Printer On That Machine box, type the name of the printer as it is identified by the host, which is either the direct-connect printer itself or the UNIX computer.

    For example, you might have a UNIX computer running the print server component (**lpd**) with which the TCP/IP printer you are creating will interact. If **lpd** recognizes a printer attached to the UNIX computer by the name Crisp, the name you should type in this box is **Crisp**.

    For a direct-connect printer, this is whatever name was used to create the printer while running **lpd**.

8. When the Create Printer dialog box reappears, select the Share This Printer On The Network option if this definition is being created on a Windows NT computer that will serve as a print server for other users to access this printer.

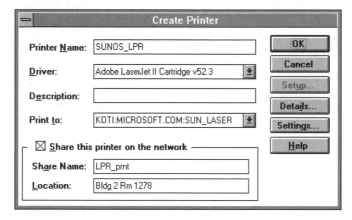

9. By default, in the Share Name box, Printer Manager creates a shared resource name that is compatible with MS-DOS–based computers. You can edit this name, which users will see when browsing to find this printer on the network.

10. Optionally, in the Location box, you can type information about where this printer is located.

    Users can see this location information when they connect to the printer.

11. Complete any other configuration information in the Create Printer dialog box, as described in Chapter 6 of the *Windows NT System Guide*, and then choose the OK button.

In Print Manager, the printer name you specified in the Create Printer dialog box appears in the title bar of the printer's window. For client computers configured with Microsoft Network Client version 2.0 for MS-DOS, users see only the shared name, not the printer name. Users who connect to this TCP/IP printer can select it and then print to it from applications like any other printer. Users and administrators can use Print Manager to secure and audit the use of the printer and change its properties.

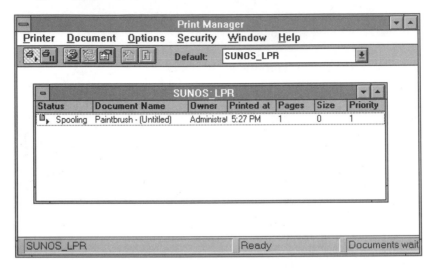

Tip You can use the **lpr** connectivity utility at the command prompt to print a file to a host running an LPD server. You can also use the **lpq** diagnostic utility to obtain the status of a print queue on a host running the LPD server. For information, see the entries for **lpr** and **lpq** in Appendix A, "TCP/IP Utilities Reference."

Printing to Windows NT from UNIX Clients

The Lpdsvc service is the server side of TCP/IP printing for UNIX clients. If any UNIX clients on the network want to print to a printer connected to a Windows NT computer, this service needs to be running on the Windows NT computer so it can accept requests from the UNIX clients. The Lpdsvc service supports any print format, including plain-text. It does not perform any additional processing.

The Lpdsvc service cannot send print jobs to network shares on a Microsoft OS/2 LAN Manager server.

▶ **To start or stop the Lpdsvc service**

- At the command prompt, type the **net start lpdsvc** or **net stop lpdsvc** command, and then press ENTER.

  –Or–

  Double-click the Services option in Control Panel, select Lpdsvc, and then choose the Start button.

On the UNIX computer, you can use the **lpr** utility to send jobs to Windows NT print queues. For details on the UNIX **lpr** utility, see your UNIX documentation.

The Lpdsvc service is independent of the Lprmon service. The Lprmon service runs automatically to allow a Windows NT computer (and all clients who can access this computer) to print to a printer connected to a UNIX system, as described in the previous section.

For the Lpdsvc service to support print jobs sent to a Windows NT shared printer specified by its universal naming convention (UNC) name, such as \\MYSERVER\MYPRINTER, the shared printer must be designated in the Registry as a null share. You must change the setting of the **NullSessionShares** parameter under the Registry key HKEY_LOCAL_MACHINE\SYSTEM\CurrentControlSet\Services\LanmanServer\Parameters. For detailed information about this parameter, see Chapter 14, "Registry Value Entries," in the *Windows NT Resource Guide*.

Note When you use the **lpr** utility to submit a print job, check Print Manager to be sure the target printer does not have the Job Prints While Spooling option set in the Printer Details dialog box. When this option is not set, the **lpr** utility processes the print job much more efficiently.

CHAPTER 19

Troubleshooting TCP/IP

The following diagnostic utilities included with Microsoft TCP/IP can be used to find solutions to TCP/IP networking problems.

Table 19.1   TCP/IP Diagnostic Utilities

Utility	Usage
arp	View the ARP (address resolution protocol) table on the local computer to detect invalid entries.
hostname	Print the name of the current host.
ipconfig	Display current TCP/IP network configuration values, and update or release TCP/IP network configuration values.
nbtstat	Check the state of current NetBIOS over TCP/IP connections, update the LMHOSTS cache, and determine the registered name and scope ID.
netstat	Display protocol statistics and the state of current TCP/IP connections.
ping	Verify whether TCP/IP is configured correctly and that a remote TCP/IP system is available.
tracert	Check the route to a remote system.

For complete details about the utilities included with Windows NT, see Appendix A, "TCP/IP Utilities Reference." See also the online Command Reference.

These other Windows NT tools can be used for TCP/IP troubleshooting:

- Microsoft SNMP service, to supply statistical information to SNMP management systems, as described in Chapter 11, "Installing Microsoft TCP/IP and SNMP."
- Event Viewer, to track errors and events, as described in the Event Viewer chapter in the *System Guide*.
- Performance Monitor, to analyze TCP/IP, FTP, and WINS server performance, as described in Chapter 17, "Using Performance Monitor with TCP/IP Services." (Microsoft SNMP must be installed if you want to monitor TCP/IP.)
- Registry Editor, to browse and edit Registry parameters, as described in README.WRI in your *\systemroot* directory.

Troubleshooting IP Configuration

If you have trouble installing Microsoft TCP/IP on your computer, follow the suggestions in the error messages. You can also use the **ping** utility to isolate network hardware problems and incompatible configurations, allowing you to verify a physical connection to a remote computer.

Use the **ping** utility to test both the host name and the IP address of the host. For the syntax and description of the **ping** command, see Appendix A, "TCP/IP Utilities Reference."

▷ **To test TCP/IP using the ping utility**

1. If the computer was configured using DHCP, use **ipconfig** to learn the IP address.

2. Use **ping** to check the loopback address by typing **ping 127.0.0.1** and pressing ENTER at the command prompt. The computer should respond immediately.

   If **ping** is not found or the command fails, check the event log with Event Viewer and look for problems reported by Setup or the TCP/IP service.

3. To determine whether you configured IP properly, use **ping** with the IP address of your computer, your default gateway, and a remote host.

If you cannot use **ping** successfully at any point, check the following:

- The computer was restarted after TCP/IP was installed and configured
- The local computer's IP address is valid and appears correctly in the TCP/IP Configuration dialog box
- The IP address of the default gateway and remote host are correct
- IP routing is enabled and the link between routers is operational

If you can use **ping** to connect to other Windows NT computers on a different subnet but cannot connect through File Manager or with **net use** *server**share*, check the following:

- The computer is WINS-enabled (if the network includes WINS servers).
- The WINS server addresses are correct, and the WINS servers are functioning.
- The correct computer name was used.
- The target host uses NetBIOS. If not, you must use FTP or Telnet to make a connection; in this case, the target host must be configured with the FTP server daemon or Telnet server daemon, and you must have correct permissions on the target host.
- The scope ID on the target host is the same as the local computer.
- A router exists between your system and the target system.
- LMHOSTS contains correct entries, so that the computer name can be resolved. For more information, see "Troubleshooting Name Resolution Problems" later in this chapter.
- The computer is not configured to use WINS.

Troubleshooting Name Resolution Problems

If the IP address responds but the host name does not when you use **ping**, you have a name resolution problem. In this case, use the following lists of common problems in name resolution to find solutions.

Name Resolution Problems in HOSTS

These problems can occur because of errors related to the HOSTS file:

- The HOSTS file or DNS do not contain the particular host name.
- The host name in the HOSTS file or in the command is misspelled or uses different capitalization. (Host names are case-sensitive.)
- An invalid IP address is entered for the host name in the HOSTS file.
- The HOSTS file contains multiple entries for the same host on separate lines.
- A mapping for a computer name-to-IP address was mistakenly added to the HOSTS file (rather than LMHOSTS).

Name Resolution Problems in LMHOSTS

These problems can occur because of errors related to the LMHOSTS file:

- The LMHOSTS file does not contain an entry for the remote server.
- The computer name in LMHOSTS is misspelled. (Notice that LMHOSTS names are converted to uppercase.)
- The IP address for a computer name in LMHOSTS is not valid.

Troubleshooting Other Connection Problems

In addition to **ping**, the other diagnostic utilities such as **netstat** and **nbtstat** can be used to find and resolve connection problems. Although this is not a complete list, these examples show how you might use these utilities to track down problems on the network.

▶ **To determine the cause of Error 53 when connecting to a server**

1. If the computer is on the local subnet, confirm that the name is spelled correctly and that the target computer is running TCP/IP as well. If the computer is not on the local subnet, be sure that its name and IP address mapping are available in the LMHOSTS file or the WINS database.

   Error 53 is returned if name resolution fails for a particular computer name.

2. If all TCP/IP elements appear to be installed properly, use **ping** with the remote computer to be sure that its TCP/IP software is working.

▶ **To determine the cause of long connect times after adding to LMHOSTS**

- Because this behavior can occur with a large LMHOSTS file with an entry at the end of the file, mark the entry in LMHOSTS as a preloaded entry by following the mapping with the #PRE tag. Then use the **nbtstat -R** command to update the local name cache immediately.

  −Or−

  Place the mapping higher in the LMHOSTS file.

  As discussed in Chapter 15, "Setting Up LMHOSTS," the LMHOSTS file is parsed sequentially to locate entries without the #PRE keyword. Therefore, you should place frequently used entries near the top of the file and place the #PRE entries near the bottom.

▶ **To determine the cause of connection problems when specifying a server name**

- Use the **nbtstat -n** command to determine what name the server registered on the network.

  The output of this command lists several names that the computer has registered. A name resembling the computer's computer name should be present. If not, try one of the other unique names displayed by **nbtstat**.

  The **nbtstat** utility can also be used to display the cached entries for remote computers from either #PRE entries in LMHOSTS or recently resolved names. If the name the remote computers are using for the server is the same, and the other computers are on a remote subnet, be sure that they have the computer's mapping in their LMHOSTS files.

▶ **To determine why only IP addresses work for connections to foreign systems but not host names**

1. Make sure that the appropriate HOSTS file and DNS setup have been configured for the computer by checking the host name resolution configuration using the Network icon in Control Panel and then choosing the DNS button in the TCP/IP Configuration dialog box.

2. If you are using a HOSTS file, make sure that the name of the remote computer is spelled the same and capitalized the same in the file and by the application using it.

3. If you are using DNS, be sure that the IP addresses of the DNS servers are correct and in the proper order. Use **ping** with the remote computer by typing both the host name and IP address to determine whether the host name is being resolved properly.

▶ **To determine why a TCP/IP connection to a remote computer is not working properly**

- Use the **netstat -a** command to show the status of all activity on TCP and UDP ports on the local computer.

  The state of a good TCP connection is usually established with 0 bytes in the send and receive queues. If data is blocked in either queue or if the state is irregular, there is probably a problem with the connection. If not, you are probably experiencing network or application delay.

Troubleshooting Other Problems

This section presents some possible TCP/IP symptoms with recommendations for using the diagnostic utilities to determine the source of the problems.

Troubleshooting the FTP Server Service

▶ **To determine whether the FTP Server service is installed correctly**

- Use **ftp** on the local computer by typing the IP loopback address from the command line; for example, type **ftp 127.0.0.1** and press ENTER.

  The interaction with the server locally is identical to the interaction expected for other Windows NT (and most UNIX) clients. You can also use this utility to determine whether the directories, permissions, and so on are configured properly for the FTP Server service.

Troubleshooting Telnet

▶ **To determine why the banner displayed with Telnet identifies a different computer, even when specifying the correct IP address**

1. Make sure the DNS name and hosts table are up to date.

2. Make sure that two computers on the same network are not mistakenly configured with the same IP address.

   The ethernet and IP address mapping is done by the ARP (address resolution protocol) module, which believes the first response it receives. Therefore, the impostor computer's reply sometimes comes back before the intended computer's reply.

   These problems are difficult to isolate and track down. Use the **arp -g** command to display the mappings in the ARP cache. If you know the ethernet address for the intended remote computer, you can easily determine whether the two match. If not, use **arp -d** to delete the entry, then use **ping** with the same address (forcing an ARP), and check the ethernet address in the cache again by using **arp -g**.

   Chances are that if both computers are on the same network, you will eventually get a different response. If not, you might have to filter the traffic from the impostor host to determine the owner or location of the system.

Troubleshooting Gateways

▶ **To determine the cause of the message, "Your default gateway does not belong to one of the configured interfaces..." during Setup**

- Find out whether the default gateway is located on the same logical network as the computer's network adapter by comparing the network ID portion of the default gateway's IP address with the network ID(s) of any of the computer's network adapters.

  For example, a computer with a single network adapter configured with an IP address of 102.54.0.1 and a subnet mask of 255.255.0.0 would require that the default gateway be of the form 102.54.*a.b* because the network ID portion of the IP interface is 102.54.

Troubleshooting TCP/IP Database Files

The following UNIX-style database files are stored in the *systemroot*\SYSTEM32\DRIVERS\ETC when you install Microsoft TCP/IP:

Table 19.2   UNIX-style Database Files

Filename	Use
HOSTS	Provides hostname-to-IP address resolution for Windows Sockets applications
LMHOSTS	Provides NetBIOS name-to-IP address resolution for Windows-based networking
NETWORKS	Provides network name-to-network ID resolution for TCP/IP management
PROTOCOLS	Provides protocol name-to-protocol ID resolution for Windows Sockets applications
SERVICES	Provides service name-to-port ID resolution for Windows Sockets applications

To troubleshoot any of these files on a local computer:

- Make sure the format of entries in each file matches the format defined in the sample file originally installed with Microsoft TCP/IP.
- Check for spelling or capitalization errors.
- Check for invalid IP addresses and identifiers.

PART IV

Windows NT and the Internet

C H A P T E R   2 0

Using Windows NT on the Internet

Although the Internet has been a vast, complex system that is difficult to join, Windows NT simplifies connecting to the Internet. You can create a file transfer protocol (FTP) server, ready to join the Internet, during initial installation of Windows NT. With minimal hardware and knowledge you can use Windows NT to publish information for world consumption.

This chapter explains typical scenarios for connecting a Windows NT computer or network to the Internet and describes logistical details about setting up Windows NT on the Internet. For information about specific Internet server services or client applications, and their protocols, see Chapter 21, "Setting Up Internet Servers and Clients on Windows NT Computers."

This chapter contains the following topics:

- Using Windows NT to Connect to the Internet
- Configuring TCP/IP and RAS for Internet Gateway
- Planning Internet Service for Your LAN
- Establishing the Infrastructure

Using Windows NT to Connect to the Internet

Windows NT provides the necessary foundation required to supply you with access to the Internet and to create your own space and presence on the Internet. The primary Windows NT tools you will use are the TCP/IP protocol, utilities, and services. You can also use the Remote Access Service (RAS). To compliment the base technologies, you might also want to use utilities in the Windows NT Resource Kit, public domain programs available on the Internet, or commercial products that might include more features and technical support.

You also need a connection to the Internet. Depending on your needs, the connection might be a 14.4 bps (bits per second) modem and dial-in Point-to-Point Protocol (PPP) account, or a dedicated high-volume line supplied by an Internet service provider (for an Internet server or providing Internet gateway to a LAN).

This section explains the many types of Internet service you can provide with Windows NT, starting with the simplest types of connections first. See the table below for more cross references.

For more information about	See
Configuring Windows NT components	"Configuring TCP/IP and RAS for Internet Gateway."
Connections to the Internet	"Link Types," and "Internet Service and Providers."
Installing the Internet tools provided in this resource kit	Chapter 21, "Setting Up Internet Servers and Clients on Windows NT Computers."

Single-Computer Connections

The simplest connection to the Internet is as a client, using Internet tools to search for information. For this type of connection, you need: TCP/IP, RAS, a modem, a PPP or serial line internet protocol (SLIP) dial-in account, and Internet tools, such as FTP, Telnet, or Mosaic applications.

This configuration allows outbound traffic to the Internet only, as illustrated in the following figure.

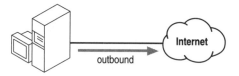

Figure 20.1   Windows NT Internet Client

Using the preceding configuration, you can install Internet server services, such as a World-Wide-Web (WWW) or FTP server and create two-way communication with the Internet as illustrated in the following figure. To participate as an Internet server, you'll need additional Internet-specific settings (such as a domain name) as described in the section, "Establishing the Infrastructure," later in this chapter.

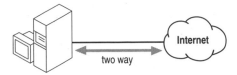

Figure 20.2   Windows NT Internet Server and Client

Note   Security becomes an important issue when you are connected to the Internet. This section describes only basic Internet service configurations. Many options exist to protect your computer or LAN from external Internet clients that are not mentioned in this section. For more information on security, see "Planning Internet Service for your LAN" later in this chapter.

Connecting a LAN to the Internet

If you have a small business you might want your LAN clients to access the Internet. By installing Windows NT with a network adapter card connected to your LAN, and another network card for your Internet connection, you can create two-way communication with the Internet by configuring Windows NT as a simple router.

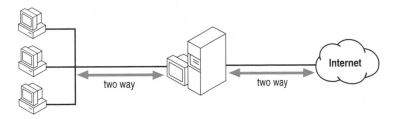

Figure 20.3   Small LAN Client Access to the Internet Using Windows NT

Windows NT is suited as a TCP/IP router only in small, single subnet networks because Windows NT does not process the RIP requests that automatically maintain a TCP/IP router table. If you have a larger network, with more that one subnet, you probably need the performance of a dedicated router (and likely have routers in your network already).

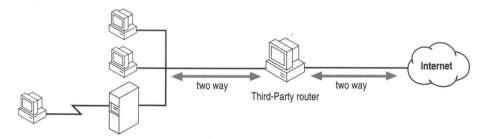

Figure 20.4   Large LAN Client Access to the Internet Using Third-party Router

Connecting Computers to the Internet with RAS

Windows NT Server's Remote Access Service (RAS) can also be used to provide remote clients with Internet gateway. This requires additional communication equipment that allows multiple remote clients to dial into the RAS computer. This type of configuration allows communication to the Internet as illustrated in the following figure.

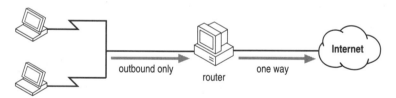

Figure 20.5   Remote Client Internet Gateway

On small LANs, you can also use RAS and a PPP connection in place of a router. This allows you to connect both LAN clients and RAS clients to the Internet.

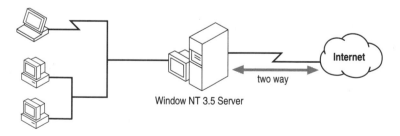

Figure 20.6   Small LAN and Remote Client Internet Gateway

Combining Windows NT Internet Functions

Because Windows NT is flexible, you can combine as many of the types of Internet connections just described to suit your needs. For example, you could create an Internet server that is also configured for remote client Internet gateway. Thus, you would have a computer serving information to external Internet users, and that same computer can be used by mobile workers to access the Internet.

Configuring TCP/IP and RAS for Internet Gateway

You must install the TCP/IP network protocol to use the Internet.

You must install and configure RAS unless you purchase leased-line services from your Internet service provider to create Internet servers or provide Internet gateway. If you create an Internet server, have a high volume of traffic, or multiple subnets, you will most likely use a leased line and a dedicated router. If you are using Windows NT as an Internet client only, a modem and dial-in PPP or SLIP line is all that is needed.

You install TCP/IP and RAS using the Network option in Control Panel or during installation of Windows NT. See your Windows NT *Installation Guide* for detailed installation information or see the following table:

For more information about	See
TCP/IP installation and configuration	Windows NT Server *TCP/IP* manual, or online Help (TCPIP.HLP).
RAS installation and configuration	Windows NT Server *Remote Access Service* manual or online Help (RASPHONE.HLP).
Using RAS on the Internet	Chapter 22, "Remote Access Service and the Internet" and online Help (RASPHONE.HLP).

Configuring TCP/IP

For a Windows NT installation that will use the Internet, you can install the components listed in the following table with TCP/IP:

Table 20.1   Components for a Windows NT Server Installation

Option	Usage	Internet use or implications
TCP/IP internetworking	Includes the TCP/IP protocol, NetBIOS over TCP/IP, Windows Sockets interface 1.1, and the TCP/IP diagnostic utilities.	Required.
Connectivity utilities	Installs the TCP/IP utilities. Select this option to install the connectivity utilities **finger**, **ftp** (client), **lpr**, **rcp**, **rexec**, **rsh**, **telnet**, and **tftp**, and the diagnostic utilities **arp**, **hostname**, **ipconfig**, **lpq**, **nbtstat**, **netstat**, **ping**, **route**, and **tracert**.	Permits you to access remote computers and troubleshoot your Internet connections.
SNMP Service	Installs the SNMP service. Select this option to allow this computer to be administered remotely using management tools, such as SUN Net Manager or HP Open View. This option also allows you to monitor statistics for TCP/IP services using Performance Monitor.	Supported.
TCP/IP network printing support	Allows this computer to print directly over the network using TCP/IP. Select this option if you want to print to UNIX print queues or TCP/IP printers that are connected directly to the network, or if you want UNIX computers on the network to print to Windows NT print servers.	Supported.
FTP Server Service	Allows files on this computer to be shared over the network with any remote computers that support the file transfer protocol (FTP) and TCP/IP. Select this option if you want to use TCP/IP to share files with other computers.	Fully Internet compatible. Any FTP client can use a Windows NT FTP server to download files. The FTP server on Windows NT Workstation permits only 10 simultaneous connections. Windows NT also includes the FTP command at the command prompt.

Table 20.1   Components for a Windows NT Server Installation *(continued)*

Option	Usage	Internet use or implications
Simple TCP/IP Services	Provides the TCP/IP services Chargen, Daytime, Discard, Echo, and Quote. Select this option to allow this computer to respond to requests from other systems that support these protocols.	Fully Internet compatible.
Enable Automatic DHCP Configuration	Turns on automatic configuration of TCP/IP parameters for this computer. Select this option if there is a DHCP server on your internetwork to support dynamic host configuration.	If you are connecting a large number of computers to the Internet, a DHCP server can simplify network administration of IP addresses.

Configuring RAS

Windows NT 3.5 RAS can be configured to accomplish the following three uses on the Internet:

- As a dial-in client to the Internet
- As an Internet service provider for remote access clients
- As a simple router to the Internet for LAN computers

See Chapter 22, "Remote Access Service and the Internet," and RAS online Help (RASPHONE.HLP) for information about installing and configuring RAS for each of the uses described in the preceding list.

Planning Internet Service for Your LAN

This section helps you understand the network and security implications of different Windows NT Internet service scenarios.

Network Protocols and LANs

As the name implies, the Internet is a group of interconnected networks. When you create an Internet server, you are adding another network to the network of networks. The network you add to the Internet can be one computer, a small workgroup, or your entire corporation's local area network.

The protocol used on a network configures the packets of data sent over the network cable.

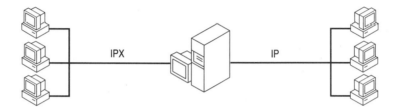

Figure 20.7   Windows NT Computer Connected to Two Networks

The Internet is primarily a TCP/IP network. That means your computer must use the TCP/IP network protocol (it is actually a suite of protocols) to participate. Internet Protocol (IP) is one of the protocols in the suite of protocols. You can install TCP/IP during or after installation of Windows NT.

If your computer uses TCP/IP on both your LAN and the Internet, and you configure Windows NT as a TCP/IP as a router, your computer acts as a gateway to the Internet, passing packets of information in both directions—to the Internet from the LAN, and from the Internet into your LAN.

Using Network Topology to Provide Security

Although you might want the users on your corporate network to use the Internet, and users from the Internet to access certain information, you probably do not want Internet users to have full access to your corporate network.

You can use physical isolation, protocol isolation, third-party routers, and Windows NT router security in your network to provide security, although the topology you choose affects the service you provide to LAN users.

The following figure illustrates the different network topology scenarios you can implement and how each scenario influences security and service for LAN users.

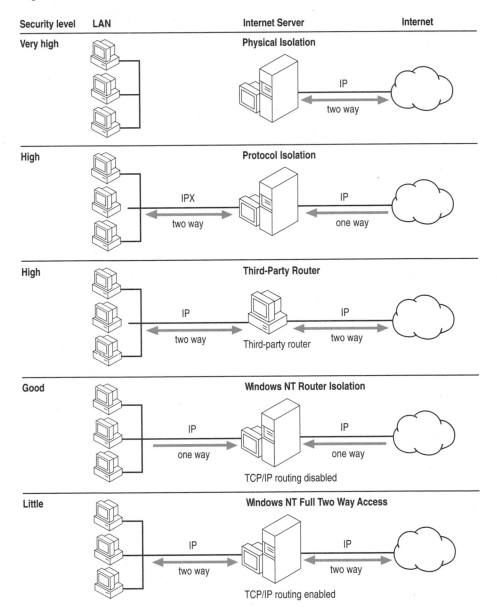

Figure 20.8   Network Topology Affects Security Levels

Physical Isolation

A computer physically isolated from your LAN is the safest and easiest to plan and configure. Only the Internet server can see and be seen by the Internet. Even the most clever hacker cannot browse your corporate network without physical access. Of course, the Internet server is still open to attack.

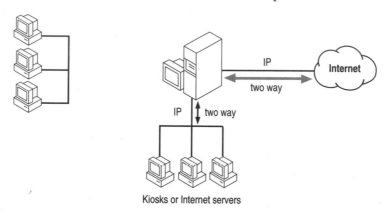

Figure 20.9 **Physical Isolation Security Model**

A limitation to this configuration is that you cannot share files between the corporate network and the Internet. You have to use floppy disks to share information between the two systems.

You can expand this scenario to create a small LAN connected to the Internet server. The type of configuration you choose depends on the size of your organization and on how much Internet gateway you want to give your users.

For example, if you have a single computer connected to the Internet, it serves as an Internet server that provides information to share with Internet users, and (optionally) as an Internet client that allows the users in your organization access to the Internet. For this computer to serve as an Internet client, however, it must be physically accessible to employees because it is not on the corporate net.

To give users in your organization easier access to the Internet, you can set up a small, separate network consisting of the Internet server, additional Internet servers, and individual workstations, or *kiosks*. The kiosks can be located in conference rooms, hallways, libraries, or in special offices scattered throughout the company. Individuals who need to make heavy use of the Internet can have kiosks in their offices. The kiosks can be used to retrieve information from your Internet server, to place new information on the server, and to gather information from the Internet at large. This type of scenario, however, might require additional cable installation.

Protocol Isolation

If you want both Internet and LAN computers to see the Internet server, you can use protocol isolation security. In this model the Internet server has two network adapters. The network adapter connected to the Internet is bound to TCP/IP. The network adapter connected to the LAN runs IPX or any other network protocol except TCP/IP.

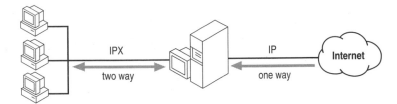

Figure 20.10   Protocol Isolation Security Model

The key to this model is that the Internet requires use of the IP protocol. If a different protocol, such as IPX, connects your Internet server to the corporate network, then the corporate network cannot be accessed by Internet users because they aren't using the correct protocol. Likewise, corporate network users cannot directly access the Internet because they are not using TCP/IP.

The protocol isolation security model is useful for users who spend most of their time making information available to Internet users and who want to copy files directly from the corporate network to the Internet server. Or, some users might need to frequently download information that is left in a "drop box" by Internet users, and then integrate that material with information from corporate electronic mail and other resources on the corporate network.

The resources on this server are accessible from either direction, but data cannot be passed through. In this way, there is a virtual barrier to passing packets through the server. Such barriers are often referred to as *firewalls*.

The advantage of the protocol isolation security model is that your users can share information with Internet users from their workstations on the corporate net, without exposing the corporate net to unauthorized use. One disadvantage of using this type of model is that your users cannot directly access the Internet. The users cannot search for or retrieve Internet resources, other than those resources on the Internet server you have set up. Users also cannot exchange mail with other Internet users unless you have provided the necessary Internet mail server services on the server. Another disadvantage is that, theoretically, an Internet hacker could penetrate this security model, but it is very challenging since the server does no protocol conversion.

Replicating the Internet Server on Your Network

A variation on the protocol isolation security model is to replicate the data on the Internet server onto another computer on the internal LAN using the Windows NT Replication service.

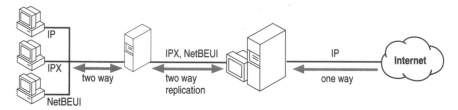

Figure 20.11   Using the Windows NT Replication Service for Security

For example, if you are using the Internet server as a drop-box for customer questions and suggestions, Internet users leave information on the Internet server, and then the Windows NT Replication service replicates the contents of the Internet server to the LAN computer. Conversely, if your LAN users need to post information to the public, users on your corporate net copy the information to be shared to the LAN intermediary computer, and then that information is replicated to your Internet server.

A replication scenario also allows more control over what is brought into the LAN and permitted out of the LAN. Files can be checked for viruses or other problems. This is a scenario used in Microsoft's corporate network.

Third-party Router Security on TCP/IP-based LANs

If you are using TCP/IP on a large corporate network with high volume or multiple subnets, you will probably use a third-party router and a leased-line connection to the Internet. Some third-party routers can create a firewall by filtering packets.

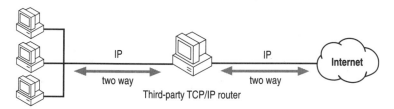

Figure 20.12   Third-party TCP/IP Router Security

Windows NT Router Security on TCP/IP-based LANs

If you are using TCP/IP on your corporate network, you can create a firewall in the Internet server by disabling TCP/IP routing.

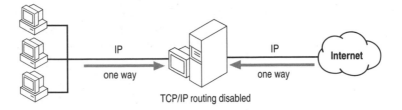

Figure 20.13   Disabled TCP/IP Router Security

This feature controls whether data is passed through the Internet server to and from the corporate network; that is, it controls whether the computer acts as a gateway.

The router feature works both ways. Either traffic can pass both ways or traffic cannot pass through the server at all. This type of security model has all the advantages and disadvantages of the protocol isolation model.

A major concern with this model is that the separation between the Internet and your corporate network depends on a single checkbox in the TCP/IP configuration dialog box (or on the associated Registry entries). Assuming an intruder somehow entered your Windows NT gateway, the intruder need only change one Registry value to expose your internal TCP/IP network.

If you use this type of security model, you also need to be especially careful to control physical and administrative access to the computer used as an Internet server. An individual familiar with Windows NT configuration tools and administrative privilege can find and change the router checkbox in a matter of moments.

Full Internet Gateway

Some organizations need to provide unrestricted Internet gateway to their users. For example, you might have researchers in your organization who need to scan the Internet directly as a major part of their work, and then combine information gleaned from the Internet with information that is on the corporate network. Rather than have each of these users connect to the Internet through a modem, you can have one computer running Windows NT that serves as a simple gateway to the Internet.

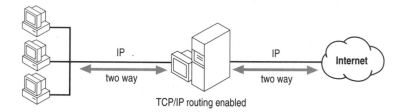

Figure 20.14   A Windows NT Computer Serving as a Gateway to the Internet

The computer that serves as a gateway must have a physical connection to the Internet, must be running the TCP/IP protocol, and the Router feature must be enabled.

See the Windows NT *Installation Guide, TCP/IP* manual, or TCP/IP online Help (TCPIP.HLP) for information on configuring TCP/IP routing.

The router feature works both ways. Either traffic can pass both ways or traffic cannot traverse the server at all. If you enable the router feature, you need to protect sensitive data by other means, such as file protections and access control as described later in this chapter.

Make sure that the users who have direct Internet gateway are aware of the security issues. In fact, you might want to periodically remind them of these issues.

You'll probably want to use the computer that serves as the gateway to the Internet configured for some Internet server services as well. It is an ideal place for shared directories where Internet users and users of the corporate network can deposit and retrieve files, and for indexes of those files.

Note   Windows NT is suited as a TCP/IP router only in small, single subnet networks because Windows NT does not process RIP requests that automatically maintain a TCP/IP router's table. If you have a larger network with more that one subnet, you probably need the performance of a dedicated router (and likely have routers in your network already).

Additional Security Methods

You can use methods other than network topology to secure your network. Third-party routers use packet filtering to prevent unwanted access. File system security can prevent access to portions of a disk (or partition). User account security should be configured to control access of the Guest account and others. Log on authentication in FTP and Telnet can prevent unauthorized users from accessing your servers. You can also audit access to you Internet servers using Event Log.

Using Firewalls and Other Inbound Security

Commercial products exist that can create firewalls between the Internet and your LAN. Most of these products are based on filtering packets. Many third-party routers used to connect your LAN to the Internet can be configured to filter packets based on the source or destination IP address. You are able to specify the IP addresses that are allowed into your LAN. Consult dedicated router vendors for more information about the packet filtering products available.

Using File System Security

If you create an FTP server, you can and should use NTFS security settings to control specific access to files and directories and to configure the behavior of files and directories. This security method requires the disk or disk partition to be formatted as NTFS. It is a good idea keep the files available through FTP on.a disk or disk partition separate from your operating system, application, or personal files.

You use File Manager to set permissions on NTFS partitions. See the Windows NT *System Guide* for more information about setting file permissions with File Manager.

A basic use of file system security is creating read-only directories so Internet users will not change files. However, NTFS security is flexible and can be used for creative problem solving.

One example of using file system security to control the behavior of directories is creating a drop box for your Internet customers to leave files in. By setting the permissions on the drop box directory to write only, Internet users can place files in the drop box directory, but cannot see or copy any of the files left there by other customers. Only internal users with appropriate permissions can access the files.

File system security can also be used with other Internet server services for additional security, although the inherent nature of most other Internet server services provide more security than an FTP server.

Windows NT User Account Security

A primary security measure that should be observed at all times is guarding the Administrator account and administrative privilege on computers connected to the Internet. Only employees with appropriate security clearances should be given the passwords for these accounts.

External Internet users access your LAN under the Guest account. You should ensure that the permissions for the Guest account on your Internet gateway is configured to provide adequate security.

If your Internet users are using any Microsoft networking client, you can use Windows NT user accounts to validate these users and define the user's permissions. These uses can still access the system without a Windows NT user account using Guest or an anonymous FTP log on.

Also note that users of two computers on the Internet with Microsoft Windows-based networking software (such as Windows NT, Windows for Workgroups, LAN Manager, or MS-DOS clients) can issue **net use** commands, or use File Manager or Print Manager to connect to resource on the distant computer—even if that computer is on another continent. A hacker using Windows-based software could issue a **net view** command and then see a list of your corporate servers. Windows-based networking client security is controlled through Windows NT user account permissions and NTFS file permissions, just as it is on the local LAN.

FTP and Telnet Logon Security

The FTP and Telnet server services use the Windows NT user account database to authenticate users logging on.

Important FTP and Telnet logons use clear-text for username and passwords. This is a potential security weakness.

FTP always uses user-level security, meaning you must log on to use an FTP server. You can configure the FTP server service to allow only users with valid Windows NT accounts to log on. An FTP server can also be configured to permit anonymous log on. Anonymous log on requires the user to type **anonymous** as their username and their Internet email address as their password. Anonymous users access files under the Guest account. You can also allow only anonymous log to a Windows NT FTP server. Anonymous-only log on is useful because real passwords are not used, thus, a valid password cannot be revealed to network snoops.

Auditing Access with the Event Log

The event log can be used to track access to all of the Internet server services. The FTP server service and Telnet server service can be configured to record logons in the event log. Other Internet server services can create entries each time a file is downloaded.

Establishing the Infrastructure

Once you have planned your Internet service, you are faced with the logistics of implementing your plan. This section explains Internet link types, service providers, and formal requirements and procedures for participating in the Internet.

Link Types

A connection to the Internet is measured in the amount of data transferred per second. The link types described in the following table are typical types of service. The Internet services and providers in your area might differ slightly.

The following table lists the common connection types. Only true Internet connections are described. Some services (not listed) only provide Internet mail service or Internet news service.

Table 20.2   Common Internet Service Connection Types

Connection type	Bits per second (bps)	Approximate cost
PPP dial-in	modem speed	$20-30 mo.
SLIP dial-in	modem speed	$20-30 mo.
Dedicated PPP/SLIP	modem speed	$200-300 mo.
56K	56 thousand bps	$150-300 mo.
PPP ISDN	128 thousand bps	$70-100 mo plus equipment
T1	1.5 million bps	$1,500-2,000 mo.
T3	45 million bps	$65,000-80,000 mo.

If you just want to browse the servers on the Internet using a hypertext browser, you probably want to get a PPP dial-in account. These accounts can transfer data up to the speed of your modem and usually are metered or have time use restrictions. Costs range from about $20 to $40 per month.

To establish a light traffic FTP or World-Wide Web (WWW) server, you could probably use a dedicated PPP account. These accounts can transfer data up to the speed of your modem and are available 24 hours a day. Costs range from $20 to $300 per month. Speeds faster than modem speeds are possible using integrated services digital network (ISDN) lines.

A server with medium traffic might want a larger pipe to the Internet and have a T1 or some fraction of a T1 line installed.

Internet Service and Providers

The services available on the Internet varies widely. The basic services used by Internet clients are:

- Internet gateway (default gateway)
- TCP/IP addresses and subnet mask
- DNS name resolution
- Simple network mail protocol (SMTP) services
- Network news transfer protocol (NNTP) news groups

You can find Internet service providers listed in your local phone book (usually under computer network services). Internet service providers also frequently advertise in local newspapers. The Windows NT RAS online Help (RASPHONE.HLP) also lists many PPP and SLIP service providers in locations around the world.

IP Addresses and Domain Names

Each computer on the Internet must have an IP address. If you use a PPP dial-up connection the Internet, to use Internet tools, it does not matter if you are assigned a random IP address by the PPP server for the duration of your call.

If you want to start a WWW server you will want a permanent IP address. If you want to connect a network to the Internet, you must have as many IP addresses as you have computers on the network.

For an Internet server or servers to become reachable by a friendly name, such as **microsoft.com**, rather than an IP address of 12 numerals, you must use a domain name. Most Internet service providers can register a domain name for your Internet service and provide IP addresses. Both are required to be seen and used by others on the Internet.

If you must apply for your own domain name or IP addresses, you should have a good understanding of the Domain Name System (DNS) and TCP/IP networking.

C H A P T E R   2 1

Setting Up Internet Servers and Clients on Windows NT Computers

This chapter briefly describes Internet services and how Internet server applications interact with client applications. Many client services are generally available for use with Windows and Windows NT computers. In addition, several server services are included in this resource kit. This chapter provides information to help you decide whether to provide specific Internet services, and how to set up an Internet server with the services you choose to provide. This chapter discusses two types of tools:

- *Information publishing tools*, which you can use to share your company's information
- *Locator and retrieval tools*, which are used to locate addresses and resources across the Internet

The following Internet information publishing tools are described in this chapter.

Table 21.1   Internet Information Publishing Tools

Service	Use to
File Transfer Protocol (FTP) server service	Transfer files from one computer to another.
Gopher server service	Search files and directories distributed across thousands of gopher servers.
World Wide Web (WWW) server service	Provide access to multi-media information via the Hyper Text Transfer Protocol (HTTP).
Wide Area Information Server (WAIS) service	Permit users to query full-content indexes of distributed databases and retrieve requested data.
WAIS Toolkit	Build and query indexes of words used in a set of files.

The following Internet locator and retrieval tools are described in this chapter.

Table 21.2   Internet Locator and Retrieval Tools

Service	Use to
Domain Name System (DNS)	Let the user specify user friendly computer names, which are then mapped to numeric IP addresses. DNS servers query other DNS servers to resolve portions of the address that they cannot map, until the entire IP address has been built.
Windows Internet Name Service (WINS)	Map the computer names of computers running Windows or Windows NT to IP addresses.

The Internet provides a vast collection of information with many tools that are used to publish and access the information. Consult the Internet or your local library or bookstore for comprehensive discussions of the tools available for using the Internet.

The Internet has been evolving since the early 1970's. Early servers on the Internet conformed to original Internet protocols, such as the file transfer protocol (FTP) or virtual terminal protocol (VTP, now called Telnet). These protocols let you copy files and/or issue commands or start programs through a character-based interface or a graphical user interface (such as Windows or XWindows).

Recently, Internet technology has grown beyond the simple file transfers on character-based FTP or Telnet clients. Newer protocols and clients on the Internet now have graphical interfaces and present information and services to Internet users using hypertext documents. Gopher servers and World Wide Web (WWW) servers now provide formatted text, sounds, and animation to Internet users. You must use the proper browser (such as Cello or Mosaic, or a Gopher client) to use these Internet services. Fortunately, these browsers often support the older standards, such as FTP, so you can use the newer browsers to access multiple services and data types.

Windows NT on the Internet

Now you can use Windows NT to connect to the Internet without having to remember arcane commands. You can even set up an Internet server on a Windows NT computer, taking advantage of Windows NT's scalability, easy interface, and ease of configuration. All you need is Windows NT, the Internet server services that are included in this resource kit, and a connection to the Internet.

Software for many client and server Internet services is also available in the public domain (free) software. In the case of client software especially, more powerful and better-supported commercial programs have been written based on the public domain tools, and are available through the usual software outlets and also through the Internet itself.

The EMWAC Documents

The European Microsoft Windows NT Academic Centre (EMWAC) has prepared software and documentation for several Internet server services. Copies of the documentation is included in this resource kit, in the same directories as the programs they describe. The documents are available in Word for Windows format (*.DOC) and Write format (*.WRI). A version in PostScript (*.PS), ready for copying to a PostScript printer, is also included.

Publishing Tools

This section describes the following information publishing tools, which can be used on Windows NT computers to share information with Internet users: File Transfer Protocol (FTP), Gopher, World-Wide Web (WWW), Wide Area Information Server (WAIS), the WAIS toolkit, and the Telnet Server.

FTP Server Service

File Transfer Protocol (FTP) is used only to transfer files from one computer to another. However, FTP isn't just for the Internet. You can also set up an FTP server on your local network to help users within your corporation find the information they need. Several versions of FTP clients are available, including both character-based and graphical-interface varieties. Software programs, such as Mosaic, can also provide a friendly client interface to the FTP server service.

▶ **To create an FTP server and install the FTP server service**

1. Install Windows NT Server on your computer.

2. Enable the TCP/IP protocol on the Windows NT computer.

3. Acquire a connection to the Internet.

4. Install and enable the FTP server service.

   The FTP server service is included with Windows NT and is documented in the *TCP/IP* book of your Windows NT Server documentation set. You can also review the information in the online Help file, TCPIP.HLP.

Note Before you install the FTP server service, read the following section, "Operating and Security Issues," for some tips on security and efficiency issues.

The hardware resources you require depend on the activity your FTP server handles and the kind of link you have to the Internet. For example, a Pentium-based computer with 48 MB of RAM can easily support 100 simultaneous FTP connections, if the link to the Internet can handle it.

Operating and Security Issues

For basic information on operating the FTP server service, see the *TCP/IP* book of your Windows NT Server documentation set, or the online Help file, TCPIP.HLP. This section provides some additional tips on operating a Windows NT FTP server on the Internet.

Since FTP requires users to explicitly log on to the computer where the files they are accessing are kept, it is best to keep all the material you want to share via FTP on one computer.

You can specify the directory that FTP clients will be in when they connect to your FTP server. The files you want to share can be organized into subdirectories of this directory, or, if there are relatively few files, you can just keep them all in the FTP directory itself.

You can also use Windows NT security to create one or more subdirectories to act as drop-boxes. Use the Security menu in File Manager to grant only Add privileges for the drop box directories to the public accounts (for example, Guest) that Internet users use to access your FTP server. Internet users can write to these directories, but cannot read or copy from them.

FTP passwords travel as clear text on the Internet. For this reason, many FTP server programs support anonymous (unsecured) FTP. If your users will be accessing a secure Windows NT computer acting as a FTP server from computers running any Microsoft networking software, and you want to use passwords, use the Windows NT Server service, which does encrypt passwords. The Internet user then connects to the Internet through any provider, and uses File Manager or the **net use** command to connect to your Internet server. The server prompts for a password and the client software encrypts and sends the password typed in by the user. With this method, you can grant different permissions to different usernames. However, users who are not using Windows NT client software cannot send the encrypted passwords. You might want to have them log on as anonymous.

FTP does not prevent users from changing directories from the initial FTP directory in which they were given access to parents of that directory. For example, if you specify **d:\welcome** as the initial FTP directory, the FTP users who connect to your FTP server can change to the root directory on **d:**, and to any of its subdirectories, if the permissions you have set on those directories let them do so. To protect the data you don't want to share with the public, either use NTFS and set protections on the root directory and other subdirectories for the logical drive you are using for the FTP directory, or (more simply) create a separate partition for FTP use. This is not an issue when you are using Gopher or World Wide Web (WWW) because these tools do not let users move up from the directory they initially connect to.

Gopher Server Service

The Gopher service offers access to files and directories on Gopher servers throughout the Internet. With Gopher, users get an easier interface, links to other Gopher servers and resources, and access to *aliases* (descriptive names) for files and directories on Gopher servers. The information is presented in a hierarchical structure. Depending on the client software being used and the selections available on the Gopher server, the user might be able to choose how information is viewed (for example, as a text file, as a Word for Windows document, or in a particular language).

The Gopher client presents the individual user with directory lists. If the user chooses a subdirectory from the displayed list, the listing for that subdirectory is displayed. If the user chooses a file, it is downloaded. Each directory and file can be on a different Gopher server.

You can also configure your Gopher server to search local WAIS databases. Information on how to do this, along with information on installing and configuring the Gopher Server service, is available in the EMWAC document, *Gopher Server Manual*. WAIS is discussed later in this chapter.

Gopher isn't just an Internet tool. Many organizations use Gopher on their local area network, or on the corporate internet, to help users within the organization find the information they need quickly and efficiently.

Installing the Gopher Server Service

The EMWAC document, *Gopher Server Manual* (included in this resource kit) gives you complete information on installing and configuring the Gopher server service. It is in the same directory with the files for the Gopher server program; these files are named GOPHERS.*.

The files you need to install the Gopher Server service are included with this resource kit.

Operating the Gopher Server Service

The Gopher Server service is started and stopped like any other Windows NT service, through the Services option in Control Panel. The EMWAC document, *Gopher Server Manual*, gives specific information about controlling and monitoring this service.

When you first install the service, and periodically thereafter, it is a good idea to use Performance Monitor to make sure users of the service are not putting too great a load on the computer. You can divide the load among several different computers if necessary. However, one computer can usually distribute a tremendous amount of information via the Gopher Server service.

Organizing Information for Users

Gopher servers are set up so that information can be readily accessed, even by users who don't know the name of the specific file or directory where the information they seek is kept. To meet these goals, it is important to use descriptive directory names, filenames, and aliases. Descriptive directory names and filenames are an obvious step, and help users of FTP as well as users of Gopher. For example, your Gopher directory could have a subdirectory named \RESEARCH, which has a subdirectory for each type of project (\RESEARCH\DEMOGRPH for demographics, \RESEARCH\USABILTY for usability studies, and so forth.). Each of these subdirectories would have two subdirectories: \RESULTS and \RAWDATA. Anyone searching your Gopher server could locate the information they want by following the directory tree.

Aliases (also called friendly names) let you present Gopher users with descriptive names for files and directories. This is especially helpful to Internet users working from computers that do not support long filenames. When a Gopher user searches for information you have provided on your Gopher server, the Gopher client searches for filenames in the server's directory and subdirectories, and also searches for aliases you might have created for the files and directories. For example, for the directory \RESEARCH\DEMOGRPH\RESULTS you could create the alias "Demographic Research at XYZ University: Results." The user sees the alias instead of the directory name. The result is less ambiguous, and the presentation is more polished. Aliases are discussed in the EMWAC document, *Gopher Server Manual*.

World-Wide Web Server

World-Wide Web (WWW) is a network within the Internet consisting of servers that provide information in hypertext format and clients that relay input from the user to the server and display information on the servers in the format specified by the user. While the FTP server and Gopher server present information in a hierarchical directory structure, WWW information is presented in *pages*. A page can be an index or a document. Pages have hypertext entries, like those in Windows Help files, that are linked to other WWW pages; a link can refer to a page on any of the thousands of WWW servers. A link can also connect to other kinds of Internet resources. Users access information, or navigate through the Internet, by selecting highlighted words in the documents, including indexes, that are shared on WWW servers.

The commands used by the WWW are defined in the *HyperText Transfer Protocol* (HTTP). Mosaic is a commonly used client software application for use on the WWW. Often the terms "World-Wide Web," "HTTP," and "Mosaic" are used interchangeably. For example, the filename for the WWW server in this resource kit is HTTPS.EXE for HTTP Server.

To specify the location of a resource, HTTP uses Uniform Resource Locators (URLs), which follow a naming convention that uniquely identifies the location of a computer, directory, or file on the Internet. The URL also specifies the Internet protocol (Gopher, HTTP, etc.) needed to retrieve the resource. If you know the URL of a resource, you can locate it directly, or you can link to it in a document you make available to WWW users.

The advantage of using WWW is that it makes it easy for Internet users to find and retrieve the information you have made available to them. However, publishing information via WWW involves more than just sharing files, since WWW uses hypertext. You must format your files to conform to the *HyperText Markup Language* (HTML), which is the standard format of the WWW. HTML authoring tools are available to make this job easier and are described later in this chapter.

The HTTP Server service currently does not do logon authentication, while the FTP Server service does. This means that the WWW server can handle a greater load because it isn't doing verification for each user. It also means that the information you share through WWW is available to everyone using the Internet.

Installing the HTTP Server Service

For your Windows NT computer to act as a server on the World-Wide Web, you must install the Windows NT HTTP Server service, which is included with this resource kit.

The EMWAC document, *HTTP Server Manual*, is included in this resource kit and gives you complete information on installing and configuring the HTTP Server service. It is in the same directory with the files for the HTTP Server program (HTTPS.*).

Operating the HTTP Server Service

The HTTP Server service is started, stopped, and paused through the Services option in Control Panel, like any other Windows NT service. Errors are logged to an Event Log and can be viewed with the Event Viewer. In addition, you can log all HTTP requests that the server receives by marking the Log HTTP Transactions checkbox in the HTTP Server Configuration dialog.

You can also have the HTTP Server search WAIS databases and return the results to the World-Wide Web user in the form of an HTML document. For more information on this feature, see the EMWAC document, *HTTP Server Manual*. This document also tells you how to create scripts and forms for use by World-Wide Web users.

Authoring HTML Pages

A page in the WWW is an ASCII text file that contains formatting commands that conform to the HyperText Markup Language (HTML). HTML files are transferred in plain ASCII over the Internet, and then the client software interprets the embedded formatting commands and displays the file, using fonts and colors as specified by the client user.

The formatting commands appear as markers in the text file. For example, to make text appear bold, you would surround it with the markers <B> to begin bolding and </B> to end bolding, like this: <B>**Bold text**</B>. Heading styles, fill-in forms, pictures, and hypertext all have their own markers, and are used to supply links to bookmark markers elsewhere in the same document or to other documents on the Web. The user does not normally see the markers, just their effects. Some WWW browsers let you to see the document source, with codes, which lets you see for yourself how a document is formatted.

There are many HTML authoring tools available on the Internet, freeware and shareware. Some of these are text-based, with menu items that let you add markup codes to highlighted text. Some are add-ons to Microsoft Word or Microsoft Word for Windows that let you author documents in Word using a provided template, producing an HTML file instead of a Word file. There are also many conversion utilities, for example one to convert .RTF (Rich Text Format) files to HTML files. Some examples of these programs, and the locations where they might be found, are shown in the following table.

Note Names on the Internet are case-sensitive; if a letter is capitalized in the directory name you should capitalize it when specifying the directory.

Table 21.3   HTML Authoring Tools Available on the Internet

Application	Site	Directory	File name
HotMetaL	ftp.ncsa.uiuc.edu	Web\html\hotmetal\Windows	hotmetal.exe
HTML Writer	diable.upc.es	pub\software\www\html	htmlwrit.zip
HTML Assistant[1]	ftp.cs.dal.ca	htmlasst	htmlasst.zip
HTMLed	pringle.mta.ca	pub\HTMLed	htmed11.zip
HTML Hyperedit	info.curtin.edu.au	pub\internet\windows\hyperedit	htmledit.zip
ANT-HTML[2] (Word 6.0 templ.)	ftp.einet.net	einet\pc	ant_html.zip
CU-HTML (Word template)	ftp.cuhk.hk	pub\www\windows\util	cu_html.zip
GT-HTML (Word template	ftp.ncsa.uiuc.edu	Web\html\hotmetal\Windows	gt_html.zip
TagWiz	ftp.cica.indiana.edu	pub\pc\win3\winword	html.zip

[1] HTML Assistant is freeware for non-commercial purposes.

[2] ANT-HTML is shareware

For instructions on using HTML, access the following file through the Internet:
`http://www.ncsa.uiuc.edu/General/Internet/WWW/HTMLPrimer.html`

The file is itself an HTML document, as well as a primer on using HTML.

Troubleshooting HTML Documents

The links in HTML documents point to a specific marker, or to the URL for a specific directory or file. It sometimes happens that, after an HTML document has been posted, a file or directory that it points to is removed, or the name is changed. When this happens, the link ceases to work. A user who finds a failed link is likely to contact the author directly to find out where the resource is, and to report the failure of the link.

Of course, you should always test the links in your HTML documents before making them available. A simple typographical error can cause a link to fail.

If you are trying to track down a lost link (one that used to work but now fails), and you know the owner of the page you were linking to, you can contact the owner and ask for the new URL for the page. If you do not know the author, you might be able to find the page by browsing directories near the last known source. (A file might have been moved from a subdirectory to a parent directory, for example, or new subdirectories might have been created to better organize a growing collection of files.) If you cannot find the page, you need to edit the HTML file to remove the link. Check the text of the document to make sure that it does not lead the reader to expect a link at that point.

Once you make resources available on the WWW, people can start linking to them in their own HTML pages. This means that moving or renaming a resource after it has been shared can cause links to fail in other pages throughout the web, and bring you an avalanche of mail and phone calls asking for the new URL. Plan carefully when naming and organizing the resources you want to share.

WAIS Server

The Wide Area Information Server (WAIS) lets users query full-content indexes of distributed databases and retrieve requested data. Working with tools in the WAIS Toolkit, which is also included in this resource kit, WAIS responds to client connections and queries, returning information on the files shared in the WAIS data directory. In addition, you can log transactions involving the WAIS Server service.

For more information, see the "WAIS Toolkit" section later in this chapter. The WAIS Toolkit is used to build and maintain the WAIS database (index) for the WAIS Server. See also the sections "Gopher Server" and "World Wide Web Server." Both of these services use WAIS databases.

Overview and Requirements

WAIS servers can be accessed from a variety of WAIS client software programs. When a user queries a WAIS database, a list is returned of the files containing the words specified in the query. When an item is chosen from that list, WAIS server returns that item for display on the user's screen.

While WAIS is used primarily to provide Internet users with access to the information you want to share, you can also use it on your local area network, or on the corporate internet, to help users within the organization find the information they need quickly and efficiently.

To run the WAIS Server service, you'll need a computer with Windows NT 3.5 installed, at least 16 MB of RAM, and a network connection. When you install the WAIS Server (WAISS) you also need to install the WAISINDEX.EXE and WAISSERV.EXE files. These files are part of the WAIS Toolkit.

Installing a WAIS Server

The EMWAC document, *WAIS Server Manual* (included in this resource kit) gives you complete information on installing and configuring the WAIS server service. It is in the same directory with the files for the WAIS Server program (WAISS.*).

Operating the WAIS Server Service

The WAIS Server service is controlled like any other Windows NT service, through the Services option in Control Panel. The EMWAC document, *WAIS Server Manual*, gives specific information about controlling and monitoring this service.

When you first install the service, and periodically thereafter, it is a good idea to use Performance Monitor to make sure users of the service are not putting too great a load on the computer. You can divide the load among several different computers if necessary.

You'll need to maintain an index of the information available on your WAIS server, so that users can find the information you have provided. For this, use the programs described in "WAIS Toolkit" later in this chapter.

WAIS Toolkit

The WAIS Toolkit is a companion to the WAIS Server service, Gopher Server service, and HTTP Server service. The toolkit includes the following files:

Table 21.4   WAIS Toolkit Files

File	Description
WAISINDEX.EXE or WAISINDX.EXE	Creates an index of all the words used in a set of files.
WAISLOOK.EXE	Constructs a list of files containing user-specified words, ranked according to how often the specified words occur, from the index created by the WAISINDEX.EXE program.
WAISSERV.EXE	Functions as an intermediary between the WAIS Server and the WAISLOOK tool.

To install the WAIS Toolkit software, your computer must meet the following requirements:

- The computer must have an Intel, Digital Alpha, or MIPS processor.
- At least 16 MB of RAM must be installed on the computer.
- The Windows NT operating system must be installed on the computer.

Installing the WAIS Toolkit

The WAIS Toolkit software is generally installed at the same time as the WAIS, Gopher, or HTTP Server services. The EMWAC document, *WAIS Toolkit*, (included in this resource kit) gives you complete information on installing the WAIS Toolkit. It is in the same directory with the files for the WAIS Server program (WAISS.EXE) and toolkit files listed in the section immediately preceding this one. The EMWAC document is in WAISTOOL.DOC (the Word for Windows file) and WAISTOOL.PS (the PostScript file ready for printing).

Using the WAIS Toolkit

The EMWAC document, *WAIS Toolkit*, contains information on using the tools. Read the section "Using the Tools" in that document for a thorough discussion of the command syntax for the tools and for information on making the WAIS index more usable by the use of synonym files. There are many parameters and options to these commands. You will probably want to test the tools on your files and make adjustment to your commands before making your WAIS server public.

If files are constantly being added to your WAIS server, you will probably want to set up a batch file to create a new index on a regular basis. If new information appears all at once and at irregular intervals, you might prefer to create a new index explicitly at those times.

Locator Tools

Several locator tools are used to locate computers, directories, and files that are on the Internet. Locator tools that are included in this resource kit for use with Windows NT are displayed in the following list.

- Domain Name System (DNS), which lets the user specify user friendly computer names. DNS maps friendly computer names to numeric IP addresses. DNS servers query other DNS servers to resolve portions of the address that they cannot map, until the entire IP address has been built.
- Windows Internet Name Service (WINS), which maps the computer names of computers running Windows or Windows NT to IP addresses.

DNS Server

The Domain Name System is a protocol and system used throughout the Internet. Its best-known function is mapping IP addresses to user-friendly names. A major advantage of this service is that the name of a computer can remain the same, even if the address changes. For example, suppose the FTP site provided by Microsoft had the IP address **11.101.54.134**. Most people would reach this computer by specifying **ftp.microsoft.com**. Besides being easier to remember, the name is more reliable. The numeric address could change for any of a number of reasons, but the name can always be used.

The IP address that matches this name is found by DNS servers on the Internet, using the following procedure. When the address name is specified, it is sent to the DNS server specified in the TCP/IP configuration of the computer sending the message. This can be a server on the local area network that is running the DNS Server service, or it can be one that your Internet service provider makes available. It is generally one that is physically nearby. If that DNS server cannot resolve the address, it passes it to the DNS server it deems most likely to be able to resolve the address. If that server can resolve the address it does so; otherwise, it responds with a referral to another server more likely to have the answer. This process is repeated as needed, resolving the address from the most general to the most specific, until the correct address is returned. This address is then used for communication with the target computer for the remainder of the session. The client software for DNS (called the *resolver*) is built into the TCP/IP software that ships with Windows NT.

In the extreme case, the queries must work down from the servers governing the root addresses to those on the individual sub-domains. However, DNS servers keep a record of recently requested addresses that lets them start further down the chain in most instances, or even to return the specific address immediately.

The Domain Name System is a complex topic, and this document does not attempt to explain it fully. An excellent book on the subject is *DNS and BIND* by Paul Albitz and Cricket Liu, published by O'Reilly and Associates. This book is a great introduction to the Domain Name System. Another good source of information is *Connecting to the Internet*, also published by O'Reilly and Associates.

Determining Whether You Should Maintain a DNS Server

In many cases, you do not need to maintain a DNS server. If you have a small network, or a single network rather than an internetwork, you will probably find it simpler and more effective to have the DNS client software query a nearby DNS server such as the one maintained by your Internet service provider. Most providers will maintain your domain information for a fee.

You will want to provide your own DNS server if you have your own domain on the Internet or if you want to access DNS from your LAN, rather than going through your Internet provider.

If you do maintain a DNS server, you will probably want to assign the task to at least two computers: a primary and a secondary name server. Data should be replicated from the primary name server to the secondary name server. This lets the Internet-wide DNS locate computers on your network even if one of the name servers is down. How often you schedule replication will depend on how often names change in your domain. Replicate often enough that changes are known to both servers. Excessive replication can tie up your network and servers unnecessarily.

Preparing and Installing the DNS Server Service

To use the DNS Server service, you must first create (or modify) the configuration files used by the service. Then install the service as you would any other service, through Services in Control Panel.

Configuration

You must have a set of configuration files in place for the DNS service to start. These files are:

- A file named BOOT in the %systemroot%\system32\drivers\etc directory.
- Database files specified by the BOOT file.

You can use files from a UNIX BIND installation at your site, or you can use the included files, which contain comments to help explain their format. The included files are:

- BOOT
- CACHE
- ARPA-127.REV
- ARPA-257.REV
- PLACE.DOM

These files are used as follows:

BOOT

This file controls the startup behavior of the DNS server. The syntax of Windows NT DNS boot files is mostly compatible with that of BIND boot files. (Some out-of-date commands are not supported.) Commands must begin at the beginning of a line. No spaces can precede commands. Recognized commands and their syntax are as follows:

directory *pathname*

Causes the server to read database files from the directory given by *pathname* instead of from the %systemroot%\system32\drivers\etc directory. This should be the first command in the file.

cache *filename*

Specifies a file used to help the DNS service contact name servers for the root domain. This command and the file it refers to must be present. A cache file suitable for use on the Internet is provided. To get an up-to-date root name server cache file, connect via anonymous FTP to ftp.rs.internic.net and download the file /domain/named.root.

primary *domain filename*

Specifies a domain for which this name server is authoritative and a database file which contains the name information for that domain.

secondary *domain hostlist* [*filename*]

Specifies a domain for which this name server is authoritative, and a list of host's IP addresses from which to attempt downloading the zone information, rather than reading it from a file. The optional filename instructs the DNS service to maintain a backup copy of the downloaded information, in the specified file.

CACHE

This file contains host information that is needed to achieve usable DNS connectivity. For users on the Internet, the provided file generally should suffice. However, if there is a firewall (hardware or software that inhibits Internet traffic in one or both directions) between you and the Internet, you might be unable to reach Internet name servers. In this case, contact your Internet provider for a valid CACHE file.

ARPA-127.REV

A database file for the 127.in-addr.arpa. domain. This domain is used for reverse-lookups of IP numbers in the 127 network, such as localhost. This file should be usable as provided.

ARPA-257.REV

A fictitious database file for reverse lookups in the fictitious 257 network. This file must be edited and renamed before use on a production DNS server.

PLACE.DOM

A fictitious database file for looking up host names in the PLACE.DOM domain. This file must be edited and renamed before use on a production DNS server. The corresponding entry in the BOOT file must also be changed.

To use these files, you must change the database information to match your company's information. Note that information in ARPA-257.REV and PLACE.DOM is fictitious.

Setting up WINS Name Resolution

The Windows NT DNS Server service can use the WINS service to resolve the names of computers running Windows or Windows NT. For example, you might want to use a UNIX computer to connect to a computer that has a WINS name and a changing IP address (for example, an address acquired through the DHCP service). In this case, configure the UNIX computer's resolver to use the Windows NT computer running the DNS service, and make sure that the computer running the DNS service has a properly configured WINS Server service. Then, decide which domain the WINS names will belong in. For example, you might decide that the domain **nt.place.dom** is the name space in which all WINS computers will be named. You would then expect queries for **testcomputer.nt.place.dom** to be handled via WINS lookup, looking for the **TestComputer** computer.

Note Windows NT servers that run DNS and also provide WINS lookup must not be configured to use DNS for Windows name resolution. This setting is reached by choosing Network from the Control Panel, and going to the advanced configuration settings for the TCP/IP protocol. The checkbox "Use DNS for Windows Name Resolution" should be cleared.

▶ **To provide WINS names through the DNS service**

1. Open the PLACE.DOM file with any text editor.

2. Find or create the "Start of Authority" (SOA) record for the domain in which you want to use WINS names.

   The SOA record points to the computer that is the best source of information on computer names in the domain. The record can span more than one line if enclosed in parenthesis so that the program reads it as a single line.

3. Create a new line under this line, consisting of the string **$WINS**.

   Note that this must be on a line by itself and start in column 1.

4. Save the file.

For an example, see the PLACE.DOM file.

Note Do not put the **$WINS** line in reverse-lookup (IN-ADDR.ARPA.) domains.

Installing the Domain Name Server Service

Before beginning to install the Domain Name Server service, be sure to read all the directions carefully.

▶ **To install the Domain Name Server Service**

1. Install the TCP/IP protocol software on your computer if you have not done so already.

2. Run the INSTALL batch file from the directory that contains the DNS service files.

   This batch file will complete the following tasks:

   - Copy the DNS Server service executable file to your system directory.
   - Configure the registry entries that control the DNS Server service.

3. Edit the files as described under "Configuration" earlier in this chapter, and make sure that the boot file and the database files are in the proper directories.

4. Open the Control Panel, and choose Services.

5. From the Services dialog, select DNS.

6. Choose Startup.

7. Choose Automatic Startup

8. Choose OK.

Registering with the Parent Domain

Once you have your DNS server or servers configured and installed, you need to register with the DNS server that is above you in the hierarchical naming structure of DNS. The parent system needs the name and addresses of your name servers, and will probably want other information such as the date that the domain will be available and the names and addresses of contact people.

If you are registering with a parent below the second level, check with the administrator of that system to find out what information you need to supply and how to submit it.

Operating the DNS Service

Once the DNS service is installed, there is very little work involved in maintaining it. As with all services, you will want to use Performance Monitor and the Event Log to make sure that everything is going well and that the computer resources available to the service are sufficient.

When you add addresses (for a computer or for a new sub-domain) to the Internet domain you are administering, you need to consider a few issues. The first consideration is the name you choose for the new address, which should be easy to remember, hard to misspell, and indicative of what the address represents.

Also, you will need to enter the new address in the reverse mapping file (which generally has a file type of .REV).

The remaining consideration is the "time to live" (TTL) value. When any DNS server receives an address, it retains the address for possible re-use, until the TTL for that address has expired. After that it must go to the next higher level of DNS server that it knows of, to get the address again. The TTL for each address is assigned by the administrator for that address. If your network is growing rapidly, you'll want to assign small TTLs so that information in the DNS system remains current. If your network is relatively stable, assign a larger TTL to reduce traffic and improve performance for those seeking addresses on your network.

The default TTL for your DNS server is specified in the SOA record in the BOOT file. If you want to specify a different TTL for a specific address, specify it in the record in the database file. The TTL appears before the word "in" toward the beginning of the line. This is the same convention as is used in BIND.

See the readme that accompanies the DNS Server files in this resource kit for troubleshooting suggestions.

WINS Service

The Windows Internetwork Name Service (WINS) is used to resolve names on an internet of computers running any combination of Windows NT and other Windows family operating systems. WINS can be used in conjunction with DNS to resolve names on your Windows internet for Internet users.

See Chapter 14, "Installing and Configuring WINS Servers" in this manual for information on the WINS service.

Other Internet Tools

New tools appear on the Internet all the time. You might want to install some of these on the Internet server you set up. This section discusses where to look for tools and how to install them.

Windows NT TCP/IP provides FTP client and server services, and the TELNET client service, when you install the TCP/IP protocol. FTP is a character-based utility used to connect client computers to FTP servers, and to list and transfer files that are on the FTP servers. The TELNET client service is a graphical application that lets you log in to remote computers and issue commands as if you were at the computer's keyboard. See NTCMDS.HLP for a complete list of the other TCP/IP character-based network tools available with Windows NT. Many variations of FTP, TELNET, and other programs based on earlier Internet standards are also available on the Internet or commercially.

Finding Other Internet Tools

Public-domain tools are found by browsing the Internet. You will need to obtain one or more Internet browsers to access the hypertext documents available on WWW servers. Many of these browsers have been developed at universities, research institutions, or educational institutions and are in the public domain, meaning they are freely distributed. Two popular FTP sites for obtaining public-domain Internet browsers (and other Windows Sockets applications) are **sunsite.unc.edu** and **ftp.cica.indiana.edu**. Mosaic is a popular Internet browser with a version that takes advantage of Windows NT's 32-bit technology. Most public domain software designed for Windows 3.1 or Windows for Workgroups will work on Windows NT. Mosaic is available at **ftp.ncsa.uiuc.edu**.

Installing Other Internet Tools

Once you have a connection to an Internet service provider, you can use the **ftp** program provided with Windows NT TCP/IP to connect to an FTP server and download files, including Internet tools. The same tool can exist for different operating systems or processors. Ensure you obtain the correct version of the tool.

The files might have been compressed using a shareware program such as **pkzip**. If so, use the appropriate program to uncompress the files on your local hard drive. The shareware compression tools are often available on local bulletin boards or FTP servers in an uncompressed format.

After you have uncompressed the files for a particular program, you should read any available readme files or other documentation for specific information about installing and configuring the program and comply with those instructions. Most public domain software designed for Windows 3.1 or Windows for Workgroups will work on Windows NT without modification.

After you've copied the program files, you might want to add an icon for that program to a Program Manager group, to make it easier to find and start the program.

You should now be able to start the Internet tool from the Windows NT desktop.

Integrating Multiple Internet Services on One Windows NT Computer

You don't need to set up a different server for every Internet service you want to provide. One Windows NT server can provide several different services. You can set up a separate directory (or even a separate partition) for each service, which makes it easier to keep track of the files for the different services. Or, you can keep files for several different services in one directory. The only real restrictions are the resources of the computer: bandwidth, disk size, memory, and so forth.

CHAPTER 22

Remote Access Service and the Internet

This chapter focuses on Internet support in RAS. It also describes how Windows NT Server 3.5 can be deployed as an Internet gateway server and as a router to the Internet for a small network.

For a more general overview of RAS, see Chapter 9, "Using Remote Access Service," in this manual and Chapter 1, "Understanding Remote Access Service," in the Windows NT *Remote Access Service* manual. You can also refer to the Remote Access online Help file (RASPHONE.HLP).

RAS: A Ramp to the Internet

Perhaps the most exciting development in networking during the 1990's has been the explosive growth in Internet use. The latest figures indicate that over 20 million people have access to this world-wide network. The Internet's diverse services appeal to a broad spectrum of business people, academics, government users, and others. The Internet is the best model in existence today for the information superhighway of tomorrow.

Traditionally, connecting to the Internet has been a difficult process that is daunting for a beginner. Early tools, such as FTP and Telnet, featured character-based commands suited for the technical elite who knew how to connect and maneuver through the intertwined network with 32-bit IP addresses. Today's tools, such as Gopher and World Wide Web (WWW), provide front-end viewers that allow users to scan through and search for information without much knowledge of where information resides and without having to logon to the source computer.

With Windows NT and RAS, Microsoft provides an operating system that fully supports the Internet. There are several different scenarios for connecting to the Internet using Windows NT and RAS:

- Using Windows NT and RAS, a user can make an IP over Point-to-Point Protocol (PPP) connection to any Internet host. Speeds of 2400 bits per second (bps) up to 128 Kbps are supported. Once the RAS connection is established, the user can choose from a variety of tools, from the traditional, non-graphical to those that fully exploit the Windows interface.

- A corporation can establish a RAS server with direct connections (through a router) to the Internet. The server can be isolated from the rest of the corporate network to provide for security. Users can dial one number for access to the Internet, and then dial one number for access to the corporate LAN.

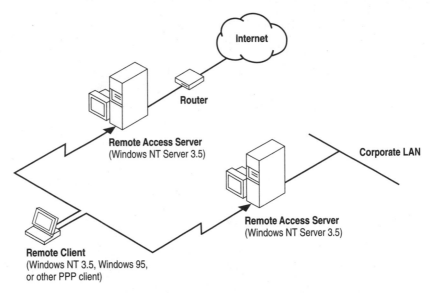

Figure 22.1   Microsoft's RAS Server with Direct Connections to the Internet

- An Internet service provider can set up an information service network where they provide a shared Internet connection, plus value-added services, such as mail and fax gateways, custom databases, software distribution, and other custom applications. RAS is an excellent solution for this scenario because it offers up to 256 connections at very high speeds, with a variety of protocols and client software supported.

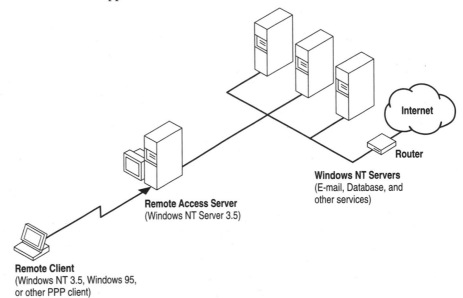

Figure 22.2   Acquiring a Shared Internet Connection and Value-Added Services

- Using Windows NT, RAS and a PPP connection, a small network can be added to the Internet, allowing a small company or workgroup to create multiple servers on the Internet and also provide Internet gateway for the computers on the small network or workgroup.

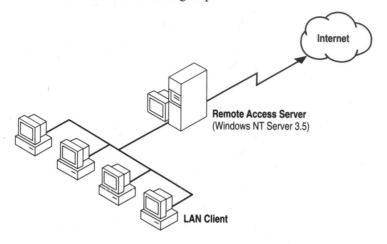

Figure 22.3   Using Windows NT Simple Internet Router Using PPP

Windows NT as an Internet Gateway Server

Before final release of Windows NT 3.5, Microsoft conducted a limited pilot test of Windows NT 3.5 as an Internet gateway server. For security reasons, the Internet gateway server was installed on an isolated network, which was in turn connected to the Internet via Cisco routers. The RAS server and the Cisco routers were not connected to the corporate network.

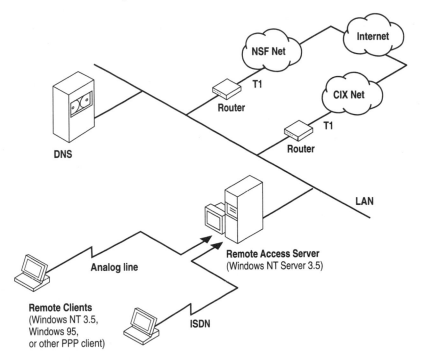

Figure 22.4   Windows NT as an Internet Gateway Server

The Internet gateway server for the pilot test had the following configuration:

- MIPS R4000, a RISC-based microprocessor
- 32 MB of RAM
- Digi International PC/2e serial adapter
- Digi International PCIMAC4 ISDN adapter
- One 16550 internal serial port
- Two Hayes Accura 14400 modems
- One Microcom Deskporte fast modem
- Four ISDN lines from GTE
- Three analog lines

Connecting Windows NT to the Internet

With Windows NT and Windows95 workstations, connecting to the Internet is easy. The connection process is as follows:

1. The remote user dials a phone number.

2. PPP negotiation occurs.

   First user authentication takes place, and then PPP protocol configuration occurs.

   If the remote workstation is running Windows NT 3.5 or Windows95, PPP negotiation automatically assigns an IP address, subnet mask, default gateway address, Domain Name System (DNS), and Windows Internet Name Service (WINS) address.

   For more details on IP address, DNS, and default gateway, see the following sections in this chapter. For more information about PPP protocols and authentication, see Chapter 9, "Using Remote Access Service."

   Note Non-Microsoft PPP client software may not negotiate all the necessary IP configuration information. In this case, users need to manually configure their TCP/IP protocol with the appropriate information.

   ---

3. The remote workstation is then connected to the Internet.

   The remote workstation is now a node on the network. The remote user can now run any Windows Sockets-compliant application to browse for information, exchange electronic mail, or download files from the Internet.

It's that simple. If the remote workstation is running Windows NT 3.5 or Windows95, PPP negotiation automatically assigns an IP address, subnet mask, default gateway address, Domain Name System (DNS) address, and Windows Internet Name Service (WINS). With Windows NT and Windows95 workstations, dialing into the Internet is very easy.

Installing an Internet Gateway Server

Before describing how to install RAS as an Internet Gateway server, it is useful to explain a few TCP/IP networking terms, and how they relate to RAS.

IP Address

An IP address is used to identify a node on a network (workstation, server, printer, etc.) and to specify routing information on an internetwork. Each node on the internetwork must be assigned a unique IP address. In Windows NT, the IP address can be configured statically or configured dynamically from a Dynamic Host Configuration Protocol (DHCP) server.

The remote access server can automatically assign IP addresses to remote workstations when they connect. The addresses is generated from a static pool that has been reserved for use by the RAS server, or via dynamic allocation from a DHCP server.

Where needed, the RAS server can be configured to allow remote clients to specify their own IP addresses. This is useful for the case where remote workstations each want to be guaranteed a specific IP address when they are connected to the network.

Dynamic Host Configuration Protocol

Dynamic host configuration protocol (DHCP) is an industry-standard protocol for automatic assignment of IP configuration to workstations. DHCP uses a client-server model for address allocation. The network administrator establishes one or more DHCP servers that maintain TCP/IP configuration to be provided to clients. LAN workstations request leases on TCP/IP configuration from the DHCP server, thus eliminating the need for administrators to manually configure each workstation.

A remote access server can act as a DHCP client, thereby attaining TCP/IP configuration information on behalf of remote workstations. The RAS server leases a pool of IP configuration information from the DHCP server(s). When remote workstations dial in to the network, the RAS server allocates IP configuration information out of this pool to each workstation.

Domain Name System

Domain Name System (DNS) is sometimes referred to as the BIND service in BSD UNIX. The Domain Name System presents friendly names to users and resolves friendly computer names to IP addresses.

Workstations on the internetwork are typically configured to use one or two DNS servers directly. If a DNS server is unable to identify the IP address of a name requested by the workstation, it sends back information about other DNS servers that might be able to resolve the address. The workstation then queries the new set of DNS servers.

DNS makes it easy for users to access information from servers on the Internet. For example, it is easier to remember ftp.microsoft.com than to remember the IP address for that server.

To use the Domain Name System, workstations must be configured to know at least one DNS server's IP address. DNS server addresses are typically assigned to LAN workstations in one of two ways:

- Statically configured on the workstation
- Dynamically assigned by a DHCP server

In the specific case of Remote Access, DNS server addresses are assigned to remote workstations in one of three ways:

- Statically assigned on the workstation.
- Statically assigned on the remote access server, which in turn assigns that address to remote workstations.
- Dynamically assigned to the remote access server via DHCP. The RAS server in turn assigns that address to remote workstations.

For Windows NT or Windows95 workstations dialing into a Windows NT server, the remote access server always assigns the DNS address. The address is either statically assigned on the remote access server or dynamically assigned to the remote access server via DHCP. For non-Microsoft remote access solutions, remote users might need to statically assign their DNS server.

Default Gateway

The default gateway is the intermediate network node on the local network that has knowledge of the network IDs of other networks in the internetwork. When a workstation sends data, the default gateway can forward the packets to other gateways until the data is eventually delivered to its final destination. Gateways are usually dedicated computers called *routers*.

TCP/IP workstations can each be configured only for one default gateway. This poses an interesting situation for remote workstations that are also connected to a LAN. For example, a workstation at a branch office dials into the corporate network, while it is still connected to the branch office network. This type of a workstation is referred to as a *multihomed* workstation.

When a multihomed remote Windows NT 3.5 workstation attempts to access a particular IP address, the destination server is located using the following process:

- If the destination IP address indicates that it is on the same IP subnet as the workstation's LAN adapter, then data is sent via the LAN adapter.

- If the destination IP address indicates that it is not on the same subnet as the workstation's LAN adapter, then data is sent to the default gateway assigned by the RAS server. The default gateway then locates the destination route on behalf of the remote workstation.

If a default gateway IP address was previously configured for the LAN adapter, it is ignored by default. If required, the remote workstation can be configured so that the default gateway on the LAN adapter is used instead of the default gateway on the remote link.

Before Installing RAS

Before installing RAS, you need to perform the following tasks in order for the computer to become an Internet gateway.

▶ **To prepare a computer to become an Internet gateway**

1. Select an Internet service provider.

   For a complete list of Internet service providers, refer to Estrada, Susan Connecting to the Internet, O'Reilly and Associates.

2. Assign a dedicated pool of IP addresses for remote clients.

   –Or–

   If you prefer to use a DHCP server, install a DHCP server on your network. For details, see Chapter 13, "Installing and Configuring DHCP Servers."

3. Configure a Domain Name System (DNS) system either locally on your LAN or contact the Internet service provider for the IP address of their DNS computer.

4. Install optional communication hardware in the Internet server.

   Your server can be configured with Serial, ISDN, and X.25 adapters.

5. Install Windows NT Server 3.5 on your computer.

   For details, see the Windows NT Server *Installation Guide*.

Installing the Microsoft TCP/IP Protocol

This section describes how to install Microsoft TCP/IP on a Windows NT computer, and then how to manually configuring or reconfigure the TCP/IP protocol.

▸ **To install Microsoft TCP/IP on a Windows NT computer**

1. Double-click the Network icon in the Control Panel window to display the Network Settings dialog box.

2. In the Network Software and Adapter Cards box, choose the Add Software button to display the Add Network Software dialog box.

3. From the Network Software list box, select the TCP/IP and Related Components option, and then choose the Continue button.

   The Windows NT TCP/IP Installation Options dialog box is displayed.

4. From the Components group box, select the desired options, and then choose the Continue button. TCP/IP will be installed on your computer.

After the Microsoft TCP/IP protocol software is installed on your computer, you must provide valid addressing, subnet mask, default gateway, and DNS information as described in the following procedure.

▸ **To manually configure or reconfigure the TCP/IP protocol**

1. Complete one of the following tasks depending on whether you want to manually configure or reconfigure the TCP/IP protocol.

   ▪ The TCP/IP Configuration dialog box appears automatically when you choose the OK button in the Network Settings dialog box after completing all options in the Microsoft TCP/IP Installation Options dialog box.

   ▪ If you are reconfiguring the TCP/IP protocol, double-click the Network icon in the Control Panel window to display the Network Settings dialog box. In the Installed Network Software list box, select TCP/IP Protocol, and then choose the Configure button to display the TCP/IP Configuration dialog box.

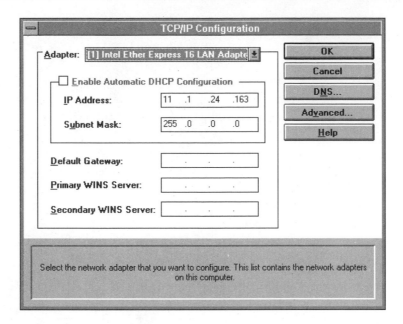

2. In the Adapter box, select the network adapter for which you want to set IP addresses.

3. Type values in the IP Address and Subnet Mask boxes. These parameters must be configured for each adapter with correct values.

   The Subnet Mask will be passed to remote dial-in clients upon connection.

4. For each network adapter, type the correct IP address value in the Default Gateway box.

   The Default Gateway location will pass to remote dial-in clients.

5. If you want DNS host name resolution, choose the DNS button, and continue with the DNS configuration procedure.

Configuring TCP/IP to use DNS

If you currently have an Internet connection, most likely there is DNS server located at your facility. If you are installing a new Internet connection and do not plan on having a DNS server of your own, contact your service provider for the IP address of their DNS server.

▶ **To configure the TCP/IP protocol using DNS**

1. Use the Network option in Control Panel to configure TCP/IP. In the Microsoft TCP/IP Configuration dialog box, choose the DNS button.

2. The DNS Configuration dialog box Host Name box will default to your Internet gateway's computer name. You can optionally type a different host name to identify the local computer by name. Host names are stored on the DNS server in a table that maps to IP addresses for use by DNS.

3. Optionally, type a name in the TCP Domain Name box. This is usually an organization name followed by a period and an extension that indicates the type of organization, such as microsoft.com.

4. In the Domain Name System (DNS) Server Search Order box, type the IP Address of the DNS server that will provide name resolution, and then choose the Add button. The IP address is displayed in the right column.

5. When you are done setting DNS options, choose the OK button.

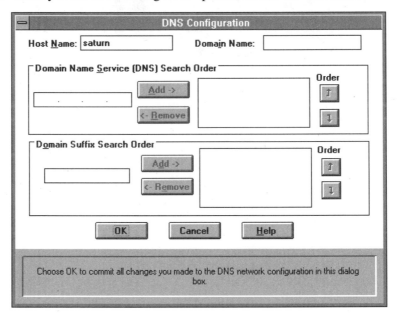

You can add up to three addresses for DNS servers. The servers running DNS will be queried in the listed order. To change the order of the IP addresses, select an IP address to move, and then use the up and down arrow buttons. To remove an IP address, select it, and choose the Remove button.

Installing a Simple Internet Router Using PPP

Windows NT version 3.5 RAS was not designed to route packets from a local area network over a WAN link. However, by correctly configuring both the RAS computer acting as a router and the other computers on your small LAN, you can use the computer running Windows NT RAS as a simple router to the Internet.

The following items are the primary requirements to use Windows NT RAS as router between your LAN and the Internet.

- A Windows NT computer with a high speed modem and a network adapter card.
- A PPP connection to the Internet.

Note The Internet service provider you connect to cannot be a Windows NT 3.5 computer.

- A valid class "C" network or a subnet, different from the subnet of the Internet service provider.
- The proper registry and Default Gateway configurations on the computer acting as a router and the LAN clients. The configurations are described later in this section.

To be identified using names rather than IP addresses, you also need a domain name. Your Internet service provider might help you obtain a domain name.

When you establish your PPP account, you must also ensure your Internet service provider provides you with a valid class C network (255 nodes) or a valid IP subnet (and subnet mask) that contains sufficient IP addresses for every computer on your LAN.

Once you have a PPP connection, IP addresses for your subnet (and correct subnet mask), and (optionally) a domain name, you can then configure the RAS and LAN computers for Internet gateway as described below.

▶ **To configure a small LAN for routing to the Internet over a dedicated PPP account**

1. Using the Registry path shown below, add the value **DisableOtherSrcPackets** to the Registry of the RAS computer that will route packets from the LAN to the Internet.

```
\HKEY_LOCAL_MACHINE\System\CurrentControlSet\Services
   \RasArp\Parameters
```

DisableOtherSrcPackets   **REG_DWORD**

By default, the header of each packet sent by the RAS computer over the PPP link uses the IP address of the RAS computer as the source. Since the packets that come from LAN clients are not originating from the RAS computer, you must set **DisableOtherSrcPacket** to 1 so the header sent over the PPP link retains the IP address of the LAN clients.

Range: 0-1
Default: 0 (not in registry)

2. If the subnet you have is in the same network class as your service provider, which is very likely in this scenario, you must also add the value **PriorityBasedOnSubNetwork** to the Registry of the RAS computer that routes packets from the LAN to the Internet.

```
\HKEY_LOCAL_MACHINE\System\CurrentControlSet\Services\RasMan\PPP\IPCP
```

PriorityBasedOnSubNetwork   **REG_DWORD**

A computer can connect to the LAN using a network card and a RAS connection. If the RAS connection and the LAN network adapter card are assigned addresses with the same network number and the Use Default Gateway On Remote Network check box is selected, then all packets are sent over the RAS connection, though the two addresses are in different subnetworks within the same network.

Set this parameter to 1 to send packets over the network card. For example, if the network adapter card has IP address 10.1.1.1 (subnet mask 255.255.0.0) and the RAS connection is assigned the address 10.2.1.1, RAS sends all 10.x.x.x packets using the RAS connection. If the parameter is set, RAS sends 10.2.x.x packets using the RAS connection and 10.1.x.x packets using the network adapter card.

Range: 0-1
Default: 0 (not in registry)

3. Configure the default gateway of all the computers on the LAN using the Network option in Control Panel.

The default gateway is set when you configure the TCP/IP protocol.

Use the IP address of the network card adapter in the RAS computer as the default gateway for all computers on the LAN except the computer acting as a router to the Internet. The default gateway for the computer acting as the router to the Internet should be left blank. Consult the following figure to determine the correct assignment pattern of IP addresses, subnet masks, and default gateways.

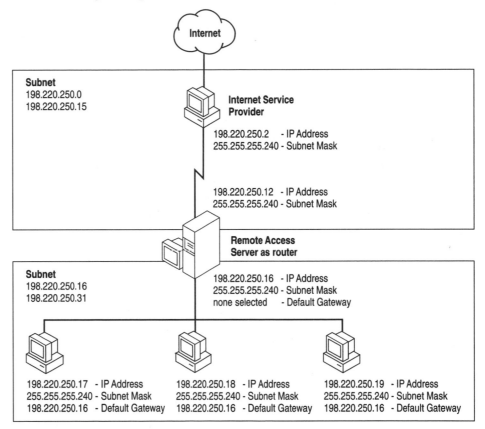

Figure 22.5   Sample Configuration using RAS as a Simple Internet Router

APPENDIX A

TCP/IP Utilities Reference

This appendix is a reference for using Microsoft TCP/IP utilities, which provide diagnostic and connectivity utilities for network and connectivity administration. These client utilities are provided for file transfer, terminal emulation, and network diagnostics. Besides the connectivity support built into Windows NT, some third-party vendors are developing advanced connectivity utilities such as X Window servers, Network File System (NFS) implementations, and so on.

Diagnostic commands help you detect TCP/IP networking problems. *Connectivity commands* enable users to interact with and use resources on non-Microsoft hosts such as UNIX workstations. The following commands are includec:

- Diagnostic commands: **arp**, **hostname**, **ipconfig**, **lpq**, **nbtstat**, **netstat**, **ping**, **route**, and **tracert**
- Connectivity commands: **finger**, **ftp**, **lpr**, **rcp**, **rexec**, **rsh**, **telnet**, and **tftp**

Important The **ftp**, **ftpsvc**, **rexec**, and **telnet** utilities all rely on password authentication by the remote computer. Passwords are not encrypted before being sent over the network. This enables another user equipped with a network analyzer on the same network to steal a user's remote account password. For this reason, it is strongly recommended that users of these utilities choose different passwords for their Windows NT workgroup, workstation, or domain from the passwords used on systems they are connecting to that are not Microsoft systems. All passwords used by Windows networking services are encrypted.

▸ **To get help on TCP/IP utilities**

- Complete one of the following tasks:

  ▪ At the command prompt, type the command name followed by **-?**. For example, type **nbtstat -?** to get help on this command.

  –Or–

  ▪ Choose the Search button in the Command Reference window, and then type a command name in the box or select a command name from the list.

  –Or–

  ▪ Invoke Windows NT Help from Program Manager using the following procedure:

  a. In the Program Manager Main group, double-click the Windows NT Help icon.

  b. In the Windows NT Help window, click the Command Reference Help button.

  c. In the Commands window, click a command name.

Note Switches used in the syntax for TCP/IP commands are case-sensitive. For example, for **nbtstat**, the switch **-R** has a different effect from the **-r** switch.

---

arp

This diagnostic command displays and modifies the IP-to-Ethernet or Token Ring physical address translation tables used by the Address Resolution Protocol (ARP).

Syntax
arp -a [*inet_addr*] [**-N** [*if_addr*]]
arp -d *inet_addr* [*if_addr*]
arp -s *inet_addr ether_addr* [*if_addr*]

Parameters
-a
Displays current ARP entries by querying TCP/IP. If *inet_addr* is specified, only the IP and physical addresses for the specified computer are displayed.

-d
Deletes the entry specified by *inet_addr*.

-s

> Adds an entry in the ARP cache to associate the IP address *inet_addr* with the physical address *ether_addr*. The physical address is given as 6 hexadecimal bytes separated by hyphens. The IP address is specified using dotted decimal notation. The entry is permanent, that is, it will not be automatically removed from the cache after the timeout expires.

-N [*if_addr*]

> Displays the ARP entries for the network interface specified by *if_addr*.

ether_addr

> Specifies a physical address.

if_addr

> Specifies, if present, the IP address of the interface whose address translation table should be modified. If not present, the first applicable interface will be used.

inet_addr

> Specifies an IP address in dotted decimal notation.

finger

This connectivity command displays information about a user on a specified system running the Finger service. Output varies based on the remote system.

Syntax   **finger** [**-l**] [*user*]@*host* [...]

Parameters   **-l**

> Displays information in long list format; not supported on all remote systems.

user

> Specifies the user you want information about. Omit the *user* parameter to display information about all users on the specified host.

@*host*

> Specifies the host name or the IP address of the remote system whose users you want information about.

ftp

This connectivity command transfers files to and from a computer running an FTP service. **Ftp** can be used interactively or by processing ASCII text files.

Syntax

ftp [-**v**] [-**n**] [-**i**] [-**d**] [-**g**] [*host*] [-**s:** *filename*]

Parameters

-**v**

Suppresses display of remote server responses.

-**n**

Suppresses autologon upon initial connection.

-**i**

Turns off interactive prompting during multiple file transfers.

-**d**

Enables debugging, displaying all **ftp** commands passed between the client and server.

-**g**

Disables filename globbing, which permits the use of wildcard characters in local file and path names. (See the **glob** command in the online Command Reference.)

host

Specifies the host name or IP address of the remote host to connect to.

-**s:** *filename*

Specifies a text file containing **ftp** commands; the commands automatically run after **ftp** starts. Use this switch instead of redirection (>).

The following table shows the **ftp** commands available when the FTP service is installed on a Windows NT computer. For details about syntax for individual **ftp** commands, choose the **ftp commands** topic in the Commands list in Command Reference.

Table A.1   FTP Commands in Windows NT

Command	Purpose
!	Runs the specified command on the local computer.
?	Displays descriptions for **ftp** commands. **?** is identical to **help**.
append	Appends a local file to a file on the remote computer using the current file type setting.
ascii	Sets the file transfer type to ASCII, which is the default.
bell	Toggles a bell to ring after each file transfer command is completed. By default, the bell is off.

Table A.1   FTP Commands in Windows NT *(continued)*

Command	Purpose
binary	Sets the file transfer type to binary.
bye	Ends the FTP session with the remote computer and exits **ftp**.
cd	Changes the working directory on the remote computer.
close	Ends the FTP session with the remote server and returns to the command interpreter.
debug	Toggles debugging. When debugging is on, each command sent to the remote computer is printed, preceded by the string --->. By default, debugging is off.
delete	Deletes files on remote computers.
dir	Displays a list of a remote directory's files and subdirectories.
disconnect	Disconnects from the remote computer, retaining the **ftp** prompt.
get	Copies a remote file to the local computer using the current file transfer type.
glob	Toggles filename globbing. Globbing permits use of wildcard characters in local file or path names. By default, globbing is on.
hash	Toggles hash-sign (#) printing for each data block transferred. The size of a data block is 2048 bytes. By default, hash-sign printing is off.
help	Displays descriptions for **ftp** commands.
lcd	Changes the working directory on the local computer. By default, the current directory on the local computer is used.
literal	Sends arguments, verbatim, to the remote FTP server. A single FTP reply code is expected in return.
ls	Displays an abbreviated list of a remote directory's files and subdirectories.
mdelete	Deletes files on remote computers.
mdir	Displays a list of a remote directory's files and subdirectories. **Mdir** enables you to specify multiple files.
mget	Copies remote files to the local computer using the current file transfer type.
mkdir	Creates a remote directory.
mls	Displays an abbreviated list of a remote directory's files and subdirectories.
mput	Copies local files to the remote computer using the current file transfer type.
open	Connects to the specified FTP server.

Table A.1   FTP Commands in Windows NT *(continued)*

Command	Purpose
prompt	Toggles prompting. **Ftp** prompts during multiple file transfers to enable you to selectively retrieve or store files; **mget** and **mput** transfer all files if prompting is turned off. By default, prompting is on.
put	Copies a local file to the remote computer using the current file transfer type.
pwd	Displays the current directory on the remote computer.
quit	Ends the FTP session with the remote computer and exits **ftp**.
quote	Sends arguments, verbatim, to the remote FTP server. A single FTP reply code is expected in return. **Quote** is identical to **literal**.
recv	Copies a remote file to the local computer using the current file transfer type. **Recv** is identical to **get**.
remotehelp	Displays help for remote commands.
rename	Renames remote files.
rmdir	Deletes a remote directory.
send	Copies a local file to the remote computer using the current file transfer type. **Send** is identical to **put**.
status	Displays the current status of FTP connections and toggles.
trace	Toggles packet tracing; **trace** displays the route of each packet when running an **ftp** command.
type	Sets or displays the file transfer type.
user	Specifies a user to the remote computer.
verbose	Toggles verbose mode. If on, all **ftp** responses are displayed; when a file transfer completes, statistics regarding the efficiency of the transfer are also displayed. By default, verbose is on.

hostname

This diagnostic command prints the name of the current host.

Syntax   **hostname**

ipconfig

This diagnostic command displays all current TCP/IP network configuration values. This command is of particular use on systems running DHCP, enabling users to determine which TCP/IP configuration values have been configured by DHCP. With no parameters, **ipconfig** displays all of the current TCP/IP configuration values, including IP address, subnet mask, and WINS and DNS configuration.

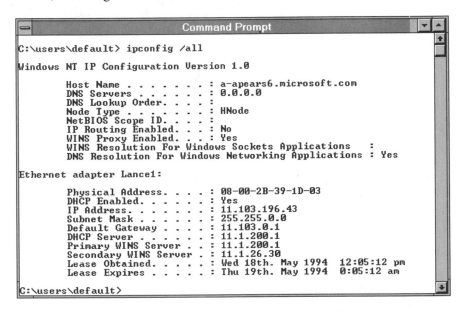

```
─                          Command Prompt                          ▼ ▲

C:\users\default> ipconfig /all

Windows NT IP Configuration Version 1.0

        Host Name . . . . . . . : a-apears6.microsoft.com
        DNS Servers . . . . . . : 0.0.0.0
        DNS Lookup Order. . . . :
        Node Type . . . . . . . : HNode
        NetBIOS Scope ID. . . . :
        IP Routing Enabled. . . : No
        WINS Proxy Enabled. . . : Yes
        WINS Resolution For Windows Sockets Applications   :
        DNS Resolution For Windows Networking Applications : Yes

Ethernet adapter Lance1:

        Physical Address. . . . : 08-00-2B-39-1D-03
        DHCP Enabled. . . . . . : Yes
        IP Address. . . . . . . : 11.103.196.43
        Subnet Mask . . . . . . : 255.255.0.0
        Default Gateway . . . . : 11.103.0.1
        DHCP Server . . . . . . : 11.1.200.1
        Primary WINS Server . . : 11.1.200.1
        Secondary WINS Server . : 11.1.26.30
        Lease Obtained. . . . . : Wed 18th. May 1994  12:05:12 pm
        Lease Expires . . . . . : Thu 19th. May 1994   0:05:12 am

C:\users\default>
```

Syntax

ipconfig [**/all** | **/renew** [*adapter*] | **/release** [*adapter*]]

Parameters

all

Produces a full display. Without this switch, **ipconfig** displays only the IP address, subnet mask, and default gateway values for each network card.

renew [*adapter*]

Renews DHCP configuration parameters. This option is available only on systems running the DHCP Client service. To specify an adapter name, type the adapter name that appears when you use **ipconfig** without parameters. For example, in the illustration above, the adapter name is Lance1.

release [*adapter*]

Releases the current DHCP configuration. This option disables TCP/IP on the local system and is available only on DHCP clients. To specify an adapter name, type the adapter name that appears when you use **ipconfig** without parameters.

lpq

This diagnostic utility is used to obtain status of a print queue on a host running the LPD server.

Syntax   **lpq** -**S**_Server_ -**P**_Printer_ [-**l**]

Parameters   -**S**_Server_
Specifies the name of the host that has the printer attached to it.

-**P**_Printer_
Specifies the name of the printer for the desired queue.

-**l**
Specifies that a detailed status should be given.

lpr

This connectivity utility is used to print a file to a host running an LPD server.

Syntax   **lpr** -**S**_Server_ -**P**_Printer_ [-**o**_Options_] [-**C**_Class_] [-**J**_Jobname_] _filename_

Parameters   -**o**_Options_
Specifies options that the **lpr** utility passes to the Lpdsvc service. Options available are specified in RFC 1179.

-**S**_Server_
Specifies the name of the host that has the printer attached to it.

-**P**_Printer_
Specifies the name of the printer for the desired queue.

-**C**_Class_
Specifies the content of the banner page for the class.

-**J**_Jobname_
Specifies the name of this job.

filename
The name of the file to be printed.

Notes   To print a nontext file, such as a PostScript file, from a Windows NT computer to a printer controlled by a UNIX computer, use the **lpr** utility with the **-ol** switch. The **l** option specifies that the print file should be passed as is to the printer, with no processing by the Lpdsvc service.

To print a nontext file from a UNIX computer to a printer controlled by a Windows NT computer, use the **lpr** utility on the UNIX computer with the **-l** switch. For details on the UNIX **lpr** utility, see your UNIX documentation.

nbtstat

This diagnostic command displays protocol statistics and current TCP/IP connections using NetBIOS over TCP/IP.

Syntax   **nbtstat** [**-a** *remotename*] [**-A** *IPaddress*] [**-c**] [**-n**] [**-R**] [**-r**] [**-S**] [**-s**] [*interval*]

Parameters   **-a** *remotename*
    Lists the remote computer's name table using the computer's name.

-A *IPaddress*
    Lists the remote computer's name table using the computer's IP address.

-c
    Lists the contents of the NetBIOS name cache, giving the IP address of each name.

-n
    Lists local NetBIOS names.

-R
    Reloads the LMHOSTS file after purging all names from the NetBIOS name cache.

-r
    Lists name resolution statistics for Windows networking. On a Windows NT computer configured to use WINS, this option returns the number of names resolved and registered via broadcast or via WINS.

-S
    Displays both workstation and server sessions, listing the remote hosts by IP address only.

-s

Displays both workstation and server sessions. It attempts to convert the remote host IP address to a name using the HOSTS file.

interval

Redisplays selected statistics, pausing *interval* seconds between each display. Press CTRL+C to stop redisplaying statistics. If this parameter is omitted, **nbtstat** prints the current configuration information once.

Notes

The column headings generated by the **nbtstat** utility have the following meanings.

In

Number of bytes received.

Out

Number of bytes sent.

In/Out

Whether the connection is from the computer (outbound) or from another system to the local computer (inbound).

Life

The remaining time that a name table cache entry will live before it is purged.

Local Name

The local NetBIOS name associated with the connection.

Remote Host

The name or IP address associated with the remote host.

Type

This refers to the type of name. A name can either be a unique name or a group name.

<03>

Each NetBIOS name is 16 characters long. The last byte often has special significance, because the same name can be present several times on a computer. This notation is simply the last byte converted to hexadecimal. For example, <20> is a space in ASCII.

State

The state of NetBIOS connections. The possible states are shown in the following list:

State	Meaning
Connected	The session has been established
Associated	A connection endpoint has been created and associated with an IP address
Listening	This endpoint is available for an inbound connection
Idle	This endpoint has been opened but cannot receive connections

State	Meaning
Connecting	The session is in the connecting phase where the name-to-IP address mapping of the destination is being resolved
Accepting	An inbound session is currently being accepted and will be connected shortly
Reconnecting	A session is trying to reconnect if it failed to connect on the first attempt
Outbound	A session is in the connecting phase where the TCP connection is currently being created
Inbound	An inbound session is in the connecting phase
Disconnecting	A session is in the process of disconnecting
Disconnected	The local computer has issued a disconnect, and it is waiting for confirmation from the remote system

netstat

This diagnostic command displays protocol statistics and current TCP/IP network connections.

Syntax

netstat [**-a**] [**-e**][**n**][**s**] [**-p** *protocol*] [**-r**] [*interval*]

Parameters

-a
Displays all connections and listening ports; server connections are usually not shown.

-e
Displays Ethernet statistics. This can be combined with the **-s** option.

-n
Displays addresses and port numbers in numerical form (rather than attempting name lookups).

-p *protocol*
Shows connections for the protocol specified by *protocol*; *protocol* can be **tcp** or **udp**. If used with the **-s** option to display per-protocol statistics, *protocol* can be **tcp**, **udp**, or **ip**.

-r
Displays the contents of the routing table.

-s

Displays per-protocol statistics. By default, statistics are shown for TCP, UDP and IP; the **-p** option can be used to specify a subset of the default.

interval

Redisplays selected statistics, pausing *interval* seconds between each display. Press CTRL+C to stop redisplaying statistics. If this parameter is omitted, **netstat** prints the current configuration information once.

Notes

The **netstat** utility provides statistics on the following network components.

Statistic	Purpose
Foreign Address	The IP address and port number of the remote computer to which the socket is connected. The name corresponding to the IP address is shown instead of the number if the HOSTS file contains an entry for the IP address. In cases where the port is not yet established, the port number is shown as an asterisk (*).
Local Address	The IP address of the local computer, as well as the port number the connection is using. The name corresponding to the IP address is shown instead of the number if the HOSTS file contains an entry for the IP address. In cases where the port is not yet established, the port number is shown as an asterisk (*).
Proto	The name of the protocol used by the connection.
(state)	Indicates the state of TCP connections only. The possible states are:

CLOSED   FIN_WAIT_1   SYN_RECEIVED

CLOSE_WAIT   FIN_WAIT_2   SYN_SEND

ESTABLISHED   LISTEN   TIMED_WAIT

LAST_ACK

ping

This diagnostic command verifies connections to one or more remote hosts.

Syntax

ping [**-t**] [**-a**] [**-n** *count*] [**-l** *length*] [**-f**] [**-i** *ttl*] [**-v** *tos*] [**-r** *count*] [**-s** *count*] [[**-j** *host-list*] | [**-k** *host-list*]] [**-w** *timeout*] *destination-list*

Parameters

-t

Pings the specified host until interrupted.

-a

Resolve addresses to hostnames.

-n *count*

Sends the number of ECHO packets specified by *count*. The default is 4.

-l *length*

Sends ECHO packets containing the amount of data specified by *length*. The default is 64 bytes; the maximum is 8192.

-f

Sends a Do Not Fragment flag in the packet. The packet will not be fragmented by gateways on the route.

-i *ttl*

Sets the Time To Live field to the value specified by *ttl*.

-v *tos*

Sets the Type Of Service field to the value specified by *tos*.

-r *count*

Records the route of the outgoing packet and the returning packet in the Record Route field. A minimum of 1 to a maximum of 9 hosts must be specified by *count*.

-s *count*

Specifies the timestamp for the number of hops specified by *count*.

-j *host-list*

Routes packets via the list of hosts specified by *host-list*. Consecutive hosts can be separated by intermediate gateways (loose source routed). The maximum number allowed by IP is 9.

-k *host-list*

Routes packets via the list of hosts specified by *host-list*. Consecutive hosts cannot be separated by intermediate gateways (strict source routed). The maximum number allowed by IP is 9.

-w *timeout*

Specifies a timeout interval in milliseconds.

destination-list

Specifies the remote hosts to ping.

Note

The **ping** command verifies connections to remote host or hosts by sending ICMP echo packets to the host and listening for echo reply packets. **Ping** waits for up to 1 second for each packet sent and prints the number of packets transmitted and received. Each received packet is validated against the transmitted message. By default, four echo packets containing 64 bytes of data (a periodic uppercase sequence of alphabetic characters) are transmitted.

You can use the **ping** utility to test both the host name and the IP address of the host. If the IP address is verified but the host name is not, you might have a name resolution problem. In this case, be sure that the host name you are querying is in either the local HOSTS file or in the DNS database.

The following shows sample output for **ping**:

```
C:\>ping ds.internic.net

Pinging ds.internic.net [192.20.239.132] with 32 bytes of data:

Reply from 192.20.239.132: bytes=32 time=101ms TTL=243
Reply from 192.20.239.132: bytes=32 time=100ms TTL=243
Reply from 192.20.239.132: bytes=32 time=120ms TTL=243
Reply from 192.20.239.132: bytes=32 time=120ms TTL=243
```

rcp

This connectivity command copies files between a Window NT computer and a system running **rshd**, the remote shell server. The **rcp** command can also be used for third-party transfer to copy files between two computers running **rshd** when the command is issued from a Windows NT computer. The **rshd** server is available on UNIX computers, but not on Windows NT, so the Windows NT computer can only participate as the system from which the commands are issued.

Syntax

rcp [-a | -b] [-h] [-r] *source1 source2 ... sourceN destination*

Parameters

-a

Specifies ASCII transfer mode. This mode converts the carriage return/linefeed characters to carriage returns on outgoing files, and linefeed characters to carriage return/linefeeds for incoming files. This is the default transfer mode.

-b

Specifies binary image transfer mode. No carriage return/linefeed conversion is performed.

-h

Transfers source files marked with the hidden attribute on the Windows NT computer. Without this option, specifying a hidden file on the **rcp** command line has the same effect as if the file did not exist.

-r

Recursively copies the contents of all subdirectories of the source to the destination. Both the *source* and *destination* must be directories.

source and *destination*

Must be of the form [*host*[.*user*]:]*filename*. If the [*host*[.*user*]:] portion is omitted, the host is assumed to be the local computer. If the *user* portion is omitted, the currently logged on Windows NT username is used. If a fully qualified host name is used, which contains the period (.) separators, then the [.*user*] must be included. Otherwise, the last part of the hostname is interpreted as the username. If multiple source files are specified, the *destination* must be a directory.

If the filename does not begin with a forward slash (/) for UNIX or a backward slash (\) for Windows NT systems, it is assumed to be relative to the current working directory. On Windows NT, this is the directory from which the command is issued. On the remote system, it is the logon directory for the remote user. A period (.) means the current directory. Use the escape characters (\, ", or ') in remote paths to use wildcard characters on the remote host.

Notes

Remote Privileges

The **rcp** command does not prompt for passwords; the current or specified user name must exist on the remote host and enable remote command execution via **rcp**.

The .rhosts file specifies which remote system or users can assess a local account using **rsh** or **rcp**. This file (or a HOSTS equivalent) is required on the remote system for access to a remote system using these commands. **Rsh** and **rcp** both transmit the local username to the remote system. The remote system uses this name plus the IP address (usually resolved to a host name) or the requesting system to determine whether access is granted. There is no provision for specifying a password to access an account using these commands.

If the user is logged on to a Windows NT Server domain, the domain controller must be available to resolve the currently logged on name, because the logged on name is not cached on the local computer. Because the username is required as part of the **rsh** protocol, the command fails if the username cannot be obtained.

The .rhosts File

The .rhosts file is a text file where each line is an entry. An entry consists of the local host name, the local user name, and any comments about the entry. Each entry is separated by a tab or space, and comments begin with a hash mark (#), for example:

```
computer5   marie   #This computer is in room 31A
```

The .rhosts file must be in the user's home directory on the remote computer. For more information about a remote computer's specific implementation of the .rhosts file, see the remote system's documentation.

Additionally, have your host name added to the remote system's /ETC/HOSTS file. This enables the remote system to authenticate remote requests for your computer using the Microsoft TCP/IP utilities.

Specifying Hosts

Use the *host.user* variables to use a user name other than the current user name. If *host.user* is specified with *source*, the .rhosts file on the remote host must contain an entry for *user*. For example,

```
rcp rhino.johnb:file1  buffalo.admin:file2
```

The .rhosts file on BUFFALO should have an entry for Johnb on RHINO.

If a host name is supplied as a full domain name containing dots, a user name must be appended to the host name, as previously described. This prevents the last element of the domain name from being interpreted as a user name. For example,

```
rcp domain-name1.user:johnm  domain-name2.user:billr
```

Remote Processing

Remote processing is performed by a command run from the user's logon shell on most UNIX systems. The user's .profile or .cshrc is executed before parsing filenames, and exported shell variables can be used (using the escape character or quotation marks) in remote filenames.

Copying Files

If you attempt to copy a number of files to a file rather than a directory, only the last file is copied. Also, the **rcp** command cannot copy a file onto itself.

Examples

These examples show syntax for some common uses of **rcp**.

To copy a local file to the logon directory of a remote computer:

```
rcp filename remotecomputer:
```

To copy a local file to an existing directory and a new filename on a remote computer:

```
rcp filename remotecomputer:/directory/newfilename
```

To copy multiple local files to a subdirectory of a remote logon directory:

```
rcp file1 file2 file3 remotecomputer:subdirectory/filesdirectory
```

To copy from a remote source to the current directory of the local computer:

```
rcp remotecomputer:filename .
```

To copy from multiple files from multiple remote sources to a remote destination with different usernames:

```
rcp remote1.user1:file1 remote2.user2:file2
   remotedest.destuser:directory
```

To copy from a remote system using an IP address to a local computer (where the username is mandatory because a period is used in the remote system name):

```
rcp 11.101.12.1.user:filename filename
```

rexec

This connectivity command runs commands on remote hosts running the **rexecd** service. **Rexec** authenticates the user name on the remote host by using a password, before executing the specified command.

Syntax

rexec *host* [**-l** *username*] [**-n**] *command*

Parameters

host
    Specifies the remote host on which to run *command*.

-l *username*
    Specifies the user name on the remote host.

-n
    Redirects the input of **rexec** to NUL.

command
    Specifies the command to run.

Notes

Rexec prompts the user for a password and authenticates the password on the remote host. If the authentication succeeds, the command is executed.

Rexec copies standard input to the remote command, standard output to its standard output, and standard error to its standard error. Interrupt, quit, and terminate signals are propagated to the remote command. **Rexec** normally terminates when the remote command does.

Use quotation marks around redirection symbols to redirect onto the remote host. If quotation marks are not used, redirection occurs on the local computer. For example, the following command appends the remote file *remotefile* to the local file *localfile*:

```
rexec otherhost cat remotefile >> localfile
```

The following command appends the remote file *remotefile* to the remote file *otherremotefile*:

```
rexec otherhost cat remotefile ">>" otherremotefile
```

Using Interactive Commands

You cannot run most interactive commands. For example, **vi** or **emacs** cannot be run using **rexec**. Use **telnet** to run interactive commands.

route

This diagnostic command manipulates network routing tables.

Syntax   **route** [**-f**] [*command* [*destination*] [**MASK** *netmask*] [*gateway*]]

Parameters   **-f**

Clears the routing tables of all gateway entries. If this parameter is used in conjunction with one of the commands, the tables are cleared prior to running the command.

command

Specifies one of four commands.

Command	Purpose
print	Prints a route
add	Adds a route
delete	Deletes a route
change	Modifies an existing route

destination

Specifies the host to send *command*.

MASK

Specifies, if present, that the next parameter be interpreted as the *netmask* parameter.

netmask
Specifies, if present, the subnet mask value to be associated with this route entry. If not present, this parameter defaults to 255.255.255.255.

gateway
Specifies the gateway.

Notes   The **route** utility does not accept a subnet mask value of 255.255.255.255 on the command line. To specify a subnet mask with this value, you must accept the default.

On a multihomed computer on which a network is available from more than one adapter card, all network traffic is passed over the first gateway defined. If you add a second gateway to the same network, the entry is added to the route table, but it is never used.

The **route** utility uses the NETWORKS file to convert destination names to addresses. For the **route** utility to work correctly, the network numbers in the NETWORKS file must specify all four octets in dotted decimal notation. For example, a network number of 284.122.107 must be specified in the NETWORKS file as 284.122.107.0, with trailing zeroes appended.

rsh

This connectivity command runs commands on remote hosts running the RSH service. For information about the .rhosts file, see the **Rcp** command.

Syntax   **rsh** *host* [**-l** *username*] [**-n**] *command*

Parameters   *host*
Specifies the remote host on which to run *command*.

-l *username*
Specifies the user name to use on the remote host. If omitted, the logged on user name is used.

-n
Redirects the input of **rsh** to NUL.

command
Specifies the command to run.

Notes   **Rsh** copies standard input to the remote *command*, standard output of the remote *command* to its standard output, and the standard error of the remote *command* to its standard error. **Rsh** normally terminates when the remote command does.

Using Redirection Symbols

Use quotation marks around redirection symbols to redirect onto the remote host. If quotation marks are not used, redirection occurs on the local computer. For example, the following command appends the remote file *remotefile* to the local file *localfile*:

```
rsh otherhost cat remotefile >> localfile
```

The following command appends the remote file *remotefile* to the remote file *otherremotefile*:

```
rsh otherhost cat remotefile ">>" otherremotefile
```

Using Rsh on a Windows NT Server Domain

If the user is logged on to a Windows NT Server domain, the domain controller must be available to resolve the currently logged on name, because the logged on name is not cached on the local computer. Because the *username* is required as part of the **rsh** protocol, the command fails if the *username* cannot be obtained.

telnet

This connectivity command starts terminal emulation with a remote system running a Telnet service. Telnet provides DEC™ VT 100, DEC VT 52, or TTY emulation, using connection-based services of TCP.

To provide terminal emulation from a Windows NT computer, the foreign host must be configured with the TCP/IP program, the Telnet server program or daemon, and a user account for the Windows NT computer.

Note Microsoft does not provide the Telnet server daemon (**telnetd**).

Syntax   **telnet** [*host* [*port*]]

Parameters   *host*
Specifies the host name or IP address of the remote system you want to connect to, providing compatibility with applications such as Gopher and Mosaic.

port

Specifies the remote port you want to connect to, providing compatibility with applications such as Gopher and Mosaic. The default value is specified by the **telnet** entry in the SERVICES file. If no entry exists in the SERVICES file, the default connection port value is decimal 23.

Notes

The Telnet application is found in the Accessories program group after you install the TCP/IP connectivity utilities. Telnet is a Windows Sockets-based application that simplifies TCP/IP terminal emulation with Windows NT.

▶   **To use Telnet**

1. Double-click the Telnet icon in the Accessories program group.

    –Or–

    At the command prompt, type **telnet** and press ENTER.

2. From the Connect menu in the Telnet window, choose Remote System.

3. In the Connect dialog box, type the host name you want to connect to, and then choose the Connect button.

    A connection is made, and you can begin a work session.

4. To end a session, choose the Disconnect command from the Connect menu.

You can specify your preferences for items such as emulation options, the screen font, and color by choosing Preferences from the Terminal menu. You can also use commands from the Edit menu to select, copy, and paste text from the Clipboard. For information about Telnet options, see the online Help.

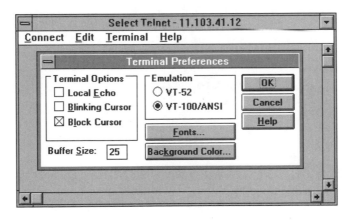

tftp

This connectivity command transfers files to and from a remote computer running the Trivial File Transfer Protocol (TFTP) service. This utility is similar to **ftp**, but it does not provide user authentication, although the files require read and write UNIX permissions.

Syntax

tftp [**-i**] *host* [**get** | **put**] *source* [*destination*]

Parameters

-i

Specifies binary image transfer mode (also called octet). In binary image mode, the file is moved literally byte by byte. Use this mode when transferring binary files.

If **-i** is omitted, the file is transferred in ASCII mode. This is the default transfer mode. This mode converts the end-of-line (EOL) characters to a carriage return for UNIX and a carriage return/linefeed for personal computers. This mode should be used when transferring text files. If a file transfer is successful, the data transfer rate is displayed.

host

Specifies the local or remote host.

get

Transfers *destination* on the remote computer to *source* on the local computer.

Since the TFTP protocol does not support user authentication, the user must be logged on, and the files must be writable on the remote computer.

put

Transfers *source* on the local computer to *destination* on the remote computer.

source

Specifies the file to transfer.

destination

Specifies where to transfer the file.

tracert

This diagnostic utility determines the route taken to a destination by sending Internet Control Message Protocol (ICMP) echo packets with varying Time-To-Live (TTL) values to the destination. Each router along the path is required to decrement the TTL on a packet by at least 1 before forwarding it, so the TTL is effectively a hop count. When the TTL on a packet reaches 0, the router is supposed to send back an ICMP Time Exceeded message to the source system. **Tracert** determines the route by sending the first echo packet with a TTL of 1 and incrementing the TTL by 1 on each subsequent transmission until the target responds or the maximum TTL is reached. The route is determined by examining the ICMP Time Exceeded messages sent back by intermediate routers. Notice that some routers silently drop packets with expired time-to-live (TTLs) and will be invisible to **tracert**.

Syntax

tracert [**-d**] [**-h** *maximum_hops*] [**-j** *host-list*] [**-w** *timeout*] *target_name*

Parameters

-d
   Specifies not to resolve addresses to hostnames.

-h *maximum_hops*
   Specifies maximum number of hops to search for target.

-j *host-list*
   Specifies loose source route along *host-list*.

-w *timeout*
   Waits the number of milliseconds specified by *timeout* for each reply.

Notes

The following shows sample output for **tracert**. The first column is the hop number, which is the Time To Live (TTL) value set in the packet. The next three columns are the round-trip times in milliseconds for three attempts to reach the destination with that TTL value. An asterisk (*) means that the attempt timed out. The fourth column is the hostname (if it was resolved) and IP address of the responding system.

```
C:\>tracert ds.internic.net

Tracing route to ds.internic.net [198.49.45.10]
over a maximum of 30 hops:

1   <10 ms  <10 ms    *      [131.107.1.100]
2    10 ms  <10 ms   10 ms seattle1-gw.nwnet.net [192.80.12.82]
3    *       10 ms   10 ms enss143-enet.nwnet.net [192.35.180.2]
4    20 ms    *      10 ms t3-3.seattle-cnss8.t3.ans.net [140.222.88.4]
5    30 ms   30 ms   20 ms t3-0.los-angeles-cnss8.t3.ans.net [140.222.8.1
6    70 ms   70 ms   80 ms t3-0.new-york-cnss24.t3.ans.net [140.222.24.1]
7    80 ms   81 ms   80 ms t3-0.denver-cnss40.t3.ans.net [140.222.40.1]
8   100 ms   91 ms   90 ms t3-1.new-york-cnss32.t3.ans.net [140.222.32.2]
9    90 ms   90 ms   91 ms mf-0.new-york-cnss36.t3.ans.net [140.222.32.196]
10  100 ms   90 ms   91 ms t1-0.enss222.t3.ans.net [140.222.222.1]
11  140 ms  191 ms  100 ms ds.internic.net [198.49.45.10]

Trace complete.
```

MIB Object Types for Windows NT

This appendix lists the objects in the LAN Manager MIB II, DHCP MIB, and WINS MIB, and provides a brief description of each.

The following MIB objects are listed in this appendix:

- LAN Manager MIB II for Windows NT objects, including Common group, Server group, Workstation group, and Domain group
- Microsoft DHCP objects
- Microsoft WINS objects

This appendix assumes that you are familiar with network management, TCP/IP, and SNMP. It also assumes that you are familiar with the concept of a *management information base* (MIB). If you are not familiar with TCP/IP or the Internet MIB 2, see *Internetworking with TCP/IP* by Douglas E. Comer (Prentice Hall, 1991) and *The Simple Book* by Marshall T. Rose (Prentice Hall, 1991).

LAN Manager MIB II for Windows NT Objects

The LAN Manager MIB II for Windows NT contains a set of objects specifically designed to support computers running Windows NT. Notice that there are fewer objects in the LAN Manager MIB II for Windows NT than the LAN Manager MIB II for OS/2 because of differences in the operating system.

All LAN Manager MIB II objects apply to computers running Windows NT Workstation and Windows NT Server.

Common Group

comVersionMaj {common 1}
The major release version number of the Windows NT software.

comVersionMin {common 2}
The minor release version number of the Windows NT software.

comType {common 3}
The type of Windows NT software this system is running.

comStatStart {common 4}
The time, in seconds, since January 1, 1970, at which time the Windows NT statistics on this node were last cleared. The **comStatStart** object applies to the following statistical objects:

comStatNumNetIOs	**svStatErrorOuts**	**wkstaStatSessStarts**
comStatFiNetIOs	**svStatPwErrors**	**wkstaStatSessFails**
comStatFcNetIOs	**svStatPermErrors**	**wkstaStatUses**
svStatOpens	**svStatSysErrors**	**wkstaStatUseFails**
svStatDevOpens	**svStatSentBytes**	**wkstaStatAutoRecs**
svStatJobsQueued	**svStatRcvdBytes**	
svStatSOpens	**svStatAvResponse**	

comStatNumNetIOs {common 5}
The number of network I/O operations submitted on this node.

comStatFiNetIOs {common 6}
The number of network I/O operations on this node that failed issue.

comStatFcNetIOs {common 7}
The number of network I/O operations on this node that failed completion.

Server Group

svDescription {server 1}
A comment describing the server.

svSvcNumber {server 2}
The number of network services installed on the server.

svSvcTable {server 3}
A list of service entries describing the network service installed on the server.

svSvcEntry {svSvcTable 1}
The names of the network services installed on the server.

svSvcName {svSvcEntry 1}
The name of a Windows NT network service.

svSvcInstalledState {svSvcEntry 2}
The installation status of a network.

svSvcOperatingState {svSvcEntry 3}
The operating status of a network service.

svSvcCanBeUninstalled {svSvcEntry 4}
Indicates whether the network service specified by this entry can be removed.

svSvcCanBePaused {svSvcEntry 5}
Indicates whether the network service specified by this entry can be paused.

svStatsOpen {server 4}
The total number of files that were opened on the server.

svStatDevOpens {server 5}
The total number of communication devices that were opened on the server.

svStatQueuedJobs {server 6}
The total number of print jobs that were spooled on the server.

svStatSOpens {server 7}
The number of sessions that were started on the server.

svStatErrorOuts {server 8]
The number of sessions disconnected because of an error on the server.

svStatPwErrors {server 9}
The number of password violations encountered on the server.

svStatPermErrors {server 10}
The number of access-permission violations encountered on the server.

svStatSysErrors {server 11}
The number of system errors encountered on the server.

svStatSentBytes {server 12}
The number of bytes sent by the server.

svStatRcvdBytes {server 13}

The number of bytes received by the server.

svStatAvResponse {server 14}

The mean number of milliseconds it took the server to process a workstation I/O request (for example, the average time an NCB sat at the server).

svSecurityMode {server 15}

The type of security running on the server.

svUsers {server 16}

The number of concurrent users the server can support.

svStatReqBufsNeeded {server 17}

The number of times the server requested allocation of additional buffers.

svStatBigBufsNeeded {server 18}

The number of times the server needed but could not allocate a big buffer while processing a client request.

svSessionNumber {server 19}

The number of sessions on the server.

svSessionTable {server 20}

A list of session entries corresponding to the current sessions that clients have with the server.

svSessionEntry {svSessionTable 1}

A session that is currently established on the server.

svSesClientName {svSessionEntry 1}

The name of the remote computer that established the session.

svSesUserName {svSessionEntry 2}

The number of connections to server resources that are active in the current session.

svSesNumConns {svSessionEntry 3}

The number of connections to server resources that are active in the current session.

svSesNumOpens {svSessionEntry 4}

The number of files, devices, and pipes that are open in the current session.

svSesTime {svSessionEntry 5}

The length of time, in seconds, since the current session began.

svSesIdleTime {svSessionEntry 6}

The length of time, in seconds, that the session has been idle.

svClientType {svSessionEntry 7}

The type of client that established the session.

svSesState {svSessionEntry 8}

The state of the current session. (Setting the state of an active session to **deleted** with **netSessionDel** deletes the client session. The session state cannot be set to **active**.)

svAutoDisconnects {server 21}

The number of sessions that the server automatically disconnected because of inactivity.

svDisConTime {server 22}

The number of seconds the server waits before disconnecting an idle session.

svAuditLogSize {server 23}

The maximum size, in kilobytes, of the server's audit log.

svUserNumber {server 24}

The number of users who have accounts on the server.

svUserTable {server 25}

A table of active user accounts on the server.

svUserEntry {svUserTable 1}

A user account on the server.

svUserName {svUserEntry 1}

The name of a user account.

svShareNumber {server 26}

The number of shared resources on the server.

svShareTable {server 27}

A table of the shared resources on the server.

svShareEntry {svShareTable 1}

A table corresponding to a single shared resource on the server.

svShareName {svShareEntry 1}

The name of a shared resource.

svSharePath {svShareEntry 2}

The local name of a shared resource.

svShareComment {svShareEntry 3}

A comment associated with a shared resource.

svPrintQNumber {server 28}

The number of printer queues on the server.

svPrintQTable {server 29}

A table of the printer queues on the server.

svPrintQEntry {svPrintQTable 1}

A table entry corresponding to a single printer queue on the server.

svPrintQName {svPrintQEntry 1}

The name of a printer queue.

svPrintQNumJobs {svPrintQEntry 2}

The number of jobs currently in a printer.

Workstation Group

wkstaStatSessStarts {workstation 1}

The number of sessions the workstation initiated.

wkstaStatSessFails {workstation 2}

The number of failed sessions the workstation had.

wkstaStatUses {workstation 3}

The number of connections the workstation initiated.

wkstaStatUseFails {workstation 4}

The number of failed connections the workstation had.

wkstaStatAutoRecs {workstation 5}

The number of sessions that were broken and then automatically reestablished.

wkstaErrorLogSize {workstation 6}

The maximum size, in kilobytes, of the workstation error log.

wkstaUseNumber {workstation 7}

This object will always return the value 0.

Domain Group

domPrimaryDomain {domain 1}

The name of the primary domain to which the computer belongs.

Microsoft DHCP Objects

Enterprises are defined in RFC 1155-SMI. Object Type is defined in RFC 1212. DisplayString is defined in RFC 1213.

DHCP MIB Parameters

ParDhcpStartTime {DhcpPar 1}
DHCP Server start time.

ParDhcpTotalNoOfDiscovers {DhcpPar 2}
Indicates the number of discovery messages received.

ParDhcpTotalNoOfRequests {DhcpPar 3}
Indicates the number of requests received.

ParDhcpTotalNoOfReleases {DhcpPar 4}
Indicates the number of releases received.

ParDhcpTotalNoOfOffers {DhcpPar 5}
Indicates the number of offers sent.

ParDhcpTotalNoOfAcks {DhcpPar 6}
Indicates the number of acknowledgments sent.

ParDhcpTotalNoOfNacks {DhcpPar 7}
Indicates the number of negative acknowledgments sent.

ParDhcpTotalNoOfDeclines {DhcpPar 8}
Indicates the number of declines received.

DHCP Scope Group

ScopeTable {DhcpScope 1}
A list of subnets maintained by the server.

sScopeTableEntry {ScopeTable 1}
The row corresponding to a subnet.

SubnetAdd {sScopeTableEntry 1}
The subnet address.

NoAddInUse {sScopeTableEntry 2}
The number of addresses in use.

NoAddFree {sScopeTableEntry 3}
The number of free addresses available.

NoPendingOffers {sScopeTableEntry 4}
The number of addresses currently in the offer state — that is, those that are used temporarily.

Microsoft WINS Objects

Enterprises are defined in RFC 1155-SMI. Object Type is defined in RFC 1212. DisplayString is defined in RFC 1213.

WINS Parameters

ParWinsStartTime {Par 1}

WINS start time.

ParLastPScvTime {Par 2}

Most recent date and time at which planned scavenging took place. Planned scavenging happens at intervals specified in the Registry. Scavenging involves changing owned nonrenewed entries to the released state. Further, released records might be changed to extinct records, extinct records might be deleted, and revalidation of old replicas can take place.

ParLastATScvTime {Par 3}

Most recent date and time at which scavenging took place as a result of administrative action.

ParLastTombScvTime {Par 4}

Most recent date and time at which extinction scavenging took place.

ParLastVerifyScvTime {Par 5}

Most recent date and time at which revalidation of old active replicas took place.

ParLastPRplTime {Par 6}

Most recent date and time at which planned replication took place. Planned replication happens at intervals specified in the Registry.

ParLastATRplTime {Par 7}

Most recent date and time at which administrator-triggered replication took place.

ParLastNTRplTime {Par 8}

Most recent date and time at which network-triggered replication took place. Network-triggered replication happens as a result of an update notification message from a remote WINS.

ParLastACTRplTime {Par 9}

Most recent date and time at which address change-triggered replication took place. Address change-triggered replication happens when the address of an owned name changes because of a new registration.

ParLastInitDbTime {Par 10}

Most recent date and time at which the local database was generated statically from one or more data files.

ParLastCounterResetTime {Par 11}

Most recent date and time at which the local counters were initialized to zero.

ParWinsTotalNoOfReg {Par 12}

Indicates the number of registrations received.

ParWinsTotalNoOfQueries {Par 13}

Indicates the number of queries received.

ParWinsTotalNoOfRel {Par 14}

Indicates the number of releases received.

ParWinsTotalNoOfSuccRel {Par 15}

Indicates the number of releases that succeeded.

ParWinsTotalNoOfFailRel {Par 16}

Indicates the number of releases that failed because the address of the requester did not match the address of the name.

ParWinsTotalNoOfSuccQueries {Par 17}

Indicates the number of queries that succeeded.

ParWinsTotalNoOfFailQueries {Par 18}

Indicates the number of queries that failed.

ParRefreshInterval {Par 19}

Indicates the Renewal interval in seconds (sometimes called the refresh interval).

ParTombstoneInterval {Par 20}

Indicates the Extinct interval in seconds.

ParTombstoneTimeout {Par 21}

Indicates the Extinct timeout in seconds.

ParVerifyInterval {Par 22}

Indicates the Verify interval in seconds.

ParVersCounterStartVal_LowWord {Par 23}

Indicates the Low Word of the version counter that WINS should start with.

ParVersCounterStartVal_HighWord {Par 24}

Indicates the High Word of the version counter that WINS should start with.

ParRplOnlyWCnfPnrs {Par 25}

Indicates whether replication is allowed with nonconfigured partners. If not set to zero, replication will be done only with partners listed in the Registry (except when an update notification comes in).

ParStaticDataInit {Par 26}

Indicates whether static data should be read in at initialization and reconfiguration time. Update of any MIB variable in the parameters group constitutes reconfiguration.

ParLogFlag {Par 27}

Indicates whether logging should be done. Logging is the default behavior.

ParLogFileName {Par 28}

Specifies the path to the log file.

ParBackupDirPath {Par 29}

Specifies the path to the backup directory.

ParDoBackupOnTerm {Par30}

Specifies whether WINS should perform a database backup upon termination. Values can be 0 (no) or 1 (yes). Setting this value to 1 has no meaning unless **ParBackupDirPath** is also set.

ParMigration (Par 31}

Specifies whether static records in the WINS database should be treated as dynamic records during conflict with new name registrations. Values can be 0 (no) or 1 (yes).

WINS Datafiles Group

DFDatafilesTable {Datafiles 1}

A list of datafiles specified under the \Datafiles key in the Registry. These files are used for static initialization of the WINS database.

dDFDatafileEntry {DFDatafilesTable 1}

Data file name record.

dFDatafileIndex {dDFDatafileEntry 1}

Used for indexing entries in the datafiles table. It has no other use.

dFDatafileName {dDFDatafileEntry 2}

Name of the datafile to use for static initialization.

WINS Pull Group

PullInitTime {Pull 1}

Indicates whether pull should be done at WINS invocation and at reconfiguration. If any pull or push group's MIB variable is set, that constitutes reconfiguration.

PullCommRetryCount {Pull 2}

Specifies the retry count in case of communication failure when doing pull replication. This is the maximum number of retries to be done at the interval specified for the partner before WINS stops for a set number of replication-time intervals before trying again.

PullPnrTable {Pull 3}

A list of partners with which pull replication needs to be done.

pPullPnrEntry {PullPnrTable 1}

The row corresponding to a partner.

PullPnrAdd {pPullPnrEntry 1}

The address of the remote WINS partner.

PullPnrSpTime {pPullPnrEntry 2}

Specifies the specific time at which pull replication should occur.

PullPnrTimeInterval {pPullPnrEntry 3}

Specifies the time interval for pull replication.

PullPnrMemberPrec {pPullPnrEntry 4}

The precedence to be given to members of the special group pulled from the WINS. The precedence of locally registered members of a special group is more than any replicas pulled in.

PullPnrNoOfSuccRpls {pPullPnrEntry 5}

The number of times replication was successful with the WINS after invocation or reset of counters.

PullPnrNoOfCommFails {pPullPnrEntry 6}

The number of times replication was unsuccessful with the WINS because of communication failure (after invocation or reset of counters).

PullPnrVersNoLowWord {pPullPnrEntry 7}

The Low Word of the highest version number found in records owned by this WINS.

PullPnrVersNoHighWord {pPullPnrEntry 8}

The High Word of the highest version number found in records owned by this WINS.

WINS Push Group

PushInitTime {Push 1}

Indicates whether a push (that is, notification message) should be done at invocation.

PushRplOnAddChg {Push 2}

Indicates whether a notification message should be sent when an address changes.

PushPnrTable {Push 3}

A list of WINS partners with which push replication is to be initiated.

pPushPnrEntry {PushPnrTable 1}

The row corresponding to the WINS partner.

PushPnrAdd {pPushPnrEntry 1}

Address of the WINS partner.

PushPnrUpdateCount {pPushPnrEntry 2}

Indicates the number of updates that should result in a push message.

WINS Cmd Group

CmdPullTrigger {Cmd 1}

This variable, when set, causes the WINS to pull replicas from the remote WINS server identified by the IP address.

CmdPushTrigger {Cmd 2}

If set, causes WINS to push a notification message to the remote WINS server identified by the IP address.

CmdDeleteWins {Cmd 3}

If set, causes all information pertaining to a WINS server (data records, context information) to be deleted from the local WINS server . Use this only when the owner-address mapping table is nearing capacity. Deleting all information pertaining to the managed WINS is not permitted.

CmdDoScavenging {Cmd 4}

If set, causes WINS to do scavenging.

CmdDoStaticInit {Cmd 5}

If set, WINS performs static initialization using the file specified as the value. If 0 is specified, WINS performs static initialization using the files specified in the Registry (filenames can be read and written to using the Datafile table).

CmdNoOfWrkThds {Cmd 6}

Reads the number of worker threads in WINS.

CmdPriorityClass {Cmd 7}

Reads the priority class of WINS to normal or high.

CmdResetCounters {Cmd 8}

Resets the counters. Value is ignored.

CmdDeleteDbRecs {Cmd 9}

If set, causes all data records pertaining to a WINS server to be deleted from the local WINS server. Only data records are deleted.

CmdDRPopulateTable {Cmd 10}

Retrieves records of a WINS server whose IP address is provided. When this variable is set, the following table is generated immediately.

CmdDRDataRecordsTable {Cmd 11}

The table that stores the data records. The records are sorted lexicographically by name. The table is cached for a certain time (to save overhead on WINS). To regenerate the table, set the **CmdDRPopulateTable** MIB variable.

CmdDRRecordEntry {CmdDRDataRecordsTable 1}

Data record owned by the WINS server whose address was specified when **CmdDRPopulateTable** was set.

CmdDRRecordName {cCmdDRRecordEntry 1}

Name in the record.

CmdDRRecordAddress {cCmdDRRecordEntry 2}

Address(es) of the record. If the record is a multihomed record or an internet group, the addresses are returned sequentially in pairs. Each pair comprises the address of the owner WINS server followed by the address of the computer or of the internet group member. The records are always returned in network byte order.

CmdDRRecordType {cCmdDRRecordEntry 3}

Type of record as unique, multihomed, normal group, or internet group.

CmdDRRecordPersistenceType {cCmdDRRecordEntry 4}

Persistence type of the record as static or dynamic.

CmdDRRecordState {cCmdDRRecordEntry 5}

State of the record as active, released, or extinct.

CmdWinsVersNoLowWord {Cmd 12}

The Low Word of the version number counter of the record.

CmdWinsVersNoHighWord {Cmd 13}

The High Word of the version number counter of the record.

APPENDIX C

Windows Sockets Applications

Vendors

AGE Logic, Inc.
9985 Pacific Heights Blvd.
San Diego, CA 92121
Phone: (619) 455-8600
Fax: (619) 597-6030
X Window software

American Computer &
 Electronics Corp.
209 Perry Parkway
Gaithersburg, MD 20877
Phone: (301) 258-9850
Fax: (301) 921-0434
Network management

Attachmate Corporation
3617 131st Avenue SE
Bellevue, WA 98006-9930
Phone: (800) 426-6283
Fax: (206) 747-9924
Terminal emulation

Beame and Whiteside
P.O. Box 8130
Dundas, Ontario L9H 5E7
CANADA
Phone: (416) 765-0822
Fax: (416) 765-0815
*Terminal emulation, file transfer,
remote process execution, e-mail,
NFS, network printing*

Digital Equipment Corporation
Attn: Lori Heron
2 Results Way
MR02-2/D10
Marlboro, MA 01752-3011
Phone: (508) 467-7855
Fax: (508) 467-1926
*eXcursion, X Window server and client
libraries*

Distinct Corporation
14395 Saratoga Ave. Suite 120
Saratoga, CA 95070
Phone: (408) 741-0781
Fax: (408) 741-0795
*Terminal emulation, file transfer,
X Window, remote process execution,
e-mail, NFS, ONC/RPC*

Esker, Inc.
1181 Chess Drive, Suite C
Foster City, CA 94404
Phone: (415) 341-9065
Fax: (415) 341-6412
*Terminal emulation, file transfer,
X Window, remote process execution,
NFS*

Executive Systems/XTree Company
4115 Broad Street Bldg. #1
San Luis Obispo, CA 93401-7993
Phone: (805) 541-0604
Fax: (805) 541-4762
Network management

Frontier Technologies Corporation
10201 North Port Washington Road
Mequon, Wisconsin 53092
Phone: (414) 241-4555
Fax: (414) 241-7084
Terminal emulation, file transfer,
remote process execution, e-mail,
NFS, NNTP, TelnetD, network
printing

Gallagher & Robertson A/S
Postboks 1824, Vika
0123 OSLO
NORWAY
Phone: (+47) 2 41 85 51
Fax: (+47) 2 42 89 22
Terminal emulation, file transfer

Genisys Comm, Inc.
314 S. Jay Street
Rome, NY 13440
Phone: (315) 339-5502
Fax: (315) 339-5528
Terminal emulation, file transfer

Gradient Technologies, Inc.
577 Main Street, Suite 4
Hudson, MA 01749
Phone: (508) 562-2882
Fax: (508) 562-3549
DCE (OSF distributed computing
environment)

Hummingbird Communications Ltd.
2900 John Street, Unit 4
Markham, Ontario L3R 5G3
CANADA
Phone: (416) 470-1203
Fax: (416) 470-1207
File transfer, remote process execution,
terminal emulation, X Window

Hypercube, Inc.
Unit 7-419 Phillip Street
Waterloo, Ontario N2L 3X2
CANADA
Phone: (519) 725-4040
Fax: (519) 725-5193
Modeling software, remote process
execution

I-Kinetics, Inc.
19 Bishop Allen Drive
Cambridge, MA 02139
Phone: (617) 661-8181
Fax: (617) 661-8625
Middleware, remote process execution

John Fluke Mfg. Co.
P.O. Box 9090
Everett, WA 98206
Phone: (206) 356-5847
Fax: (206) 356-5790
Instrument control software

JSB Computer Systems Ltd.
Cheshire House, Castle Street
Macclesfield, Cheshire
ENGLAND SK11 6AF
Phone: (+44) 625-433618
Fax: (+44) 625-433948

JSB Corporation [USA]
Suite 115, 108 Whispering Pines Drive
Scotts Valley, CA 95066
Phone: (408) 438-8300
Fax: (408) 438-8360
Terminal emulation, file transfer,
X Window, remote process execution,
virtual sockets library

Lanera Corporation
516 Valley Way
Milpitas, CA 95035
Phone: (408) 956-8344
Fax: (408) 956-8343
Terminal emulation, file transfer,
X Window, remote process execution,
NFS, SNMP

Microdyne Corp.
239 Littleton Road
Westford, MA 01886
Phone: (508) 392-9953
Fax: (508) 392-9962
File transfer

NetManage, Inc.
20823 Stevens Creek Blvd.
Cupertino, CA 95014
Phone: (408) 973-7171
Fax: (408) 257-6405
Terminal emulation, file transfer,
X Window, e-mail, NFS, TN3270,
BIND, SNMP

Network Computing Devices
9590 SW Gemini
Beaverton, OR 97005
Phone: (503) 641-2200
Fax: (503) 643-8642
X Window

Spry, Inc.
1319 Dexter Ave. N
Seattle, WA 98109
Phone: (206) 286-1412
Fax: (206) 286-1722
Terminal emulation, file transfer,
e-mail, network printing

SunSelect
2 Elizabeth Drive
Chelmsford, MA 01824-4195
Phone: (508) 442-2300
Fax: (508) 250-2300
E-mail

TurboSoft Pty Ltd.
248 Johnston Street
Annandale, NSW 2038
AUSTRALIA
Phone: (+612) 552-1266
Fax: (+612) 552-3256
Terminal emulation, file transfer,
network printing

Unipalm Ltd.
216, Science Park, Milton Road
Cambridge, Cambridgeshire
CB4 4WA ENGLAND
Phone: (+44) 223-420002
Fax: (+44) 223-426868
E-mail

VisionWare UK
57 Cardigan Lane
Leeds, ENGLAND LS4 2LE
Phone: (+44) 532-788858
Fax: (+44) 532-304676

VisionWare USA
1020 Marsh Road
Suite 220
Menlo Park, CA 94025
Phone: (415) 325-2113
Fax: (415) 325-8710
Terminal emulation, file transfer,
X Window, remote process execution

VisiSoft
430 10th Street NW, Suite S008
Atlanta, GA 30318
Phone: (404) 874-0428
Fax: (404) 874-6412
Network management

Walker Richer & Quinn, Inc.
1500 Dexter Ave. N.
Seattle, WA 98109
Phone: (206) 217-7500
Fax: (206) 217-0293
Terminal emulation, file transfer,
X Window

XSoft
3400 Hillview Ave.
Palo Alto, CA 92304
Phone: (800) 428-2995
Fax: (415) 813-7028
Document management

Internet Sources for Applications

Cello
ftp.law.cornell.edu
/pub/LII/Cello
cello.zip, lview31.zip, gswin.zip,
cellofaq.zip, wingif14.zip,
wplny09b.zip

Cookie Server
sunsite.unc.edu
/pub/micro/pc-stuff
   /ms-windows/winsock/apps
cooksock.zip

EINet Wais Client
ftp.cica.indiana.edu
/pub/pc/win3/winsock
ewais154.zip

Finger Daemon
sunsite.unc.edu
/pub/micro/pc-stuff
   /ms-windows/winsock/apps
fingerd.zip

Finger31
ftp.cica.indiana.edu
/pub/pc/win3/winsock
finger31.zip

GopherBook
ftp.cica.indiana.edu
/pub/pc/win3/winsock
gophbk11.zip

GopherS
emwac.ed.ac.uk
/pub/gophers
gsi386.zip or gsalpha.zip

HGopher
ftp.cica.indiana.edu
/pub/pc/win3/winsock
hgoph24.zip

HTTPS
emwac.ed.ac.uk
/pub/https
hsi386.zip or hsalpha.zip

Internet Help File
ftp.ccs.queensu.ca
/pub/msdos/tcpip
ipwin.zip

Micro X-Win
bart.starnet.com
/pub
xwindemo.exe or xwin287b.exe

Mosaic
ftp.ncsa.uiuc.edu
/PC/Mosaic
wmos20a1.zip

NCSA Telnet
ftp.cica.indiana.edu
/pub/pc/win3/winsock
wintelb3.zip

PCEudora
ftp.qualcomm.com
/pceudora/windows
eudora14.exe

QWS3270
ftp.ccs.queensu.ca
/pub/msdos/tcpip
qws3270.zip

SerWeb
ftp.cica.indiana.edu
/pub/pc/win3/winsock
serweb03.zip

Text Server
sunsite.unc.edu
/pub/micro/pc-stuff
   /ms-windows/winsock/apps
txtsrv.zip

TimeSync
ftphost.cac.washington.edu
/pub/winsock
tsync1_4.zip

Trumpet for Windows
ftp.utas.edu.au
/pub/trumpet/wintrump
wtwsk10a.zip

Trumpet Telnet
petros.psychol.utas.edu.au
/pc/trumpet/trmptel
trmptel.exe

Trumpet Winsock
ftp.utas.edu.au
/pc/trumpet/wintrump
winsock.zip

USGS WAIS Client
ridgisd.er.usgs.gov
/software/wais
wwais23.zip

Wais Manager
ftp.cnidr.org
/pub/NIDR.tools/wais/pc/windows
waisman3.zip

WFTPD
sunsite.unc.edu
/pub/micro/pc-stuff/ms-
windows/winsock/apps
wftpd18b.zip

Windows SMTP
sunsite.unc.edu
/pub/micro/pc-stuff
   /ms-windows/winsock/apps
wsmtpd16.zip

WinFSP
ftp.cica.indiana.edu
/pub/pc/win3/winsock
winfsp12.zip

WinIRC
dorm.rutgers.edu (ftp.utas.edu.au)
/pub/msdos/trumpet/irc

/pc/trumpet/irc/winirc-beta
winirc.exe, winirc.doc

WinLPR
sunsite.unc.edu
/pub/micro/pc-stuff
   /ms-windows/winsock/apps
winlpr10.zip

WinQVT/Net
sunsite.unc.edu
/pub/micro/pc-stuff
   /ms-windows/winsock/apps
qvtne394.zip

WinQVT/Net for NT
sunsite.unc.edu
/pub/micro/pc-stuff
   /ms-windows/winsock/apps
qvtnt394.zip

WinQVTNet
biochemistry.cwru.edu
/pub/qvtnet
qvtws396.zip

WinTalk
elf.com
/pub/wintalk
wintalk.zip

WinVN
titan.ksc.nasa.gov
/pub/win3/winvn
winvnstd90_2.zip

WS Gopher
sunsite.unc.edu
/pub/micro/pc-stuff
   /ms-windows/winsock/apps
wsg-09g.exe

WS_Finger
sunsite.unc.edu
/pub/micro/pc-stuff
  /ms-windows/winsock/apps
wsfinger.zip

WS_FTP
ftp.usma.edu
/pub/msdos
ws_ftp.zip

WS_FTPb
sunsite.unc.edu
/pub/micro/pc-stuff
  /ms-windows/winsock/apps
ws_ftpb.zip, view.zip

WSArchie
ftp.demon.co.uk
/pub/ibmpc/winsock/apps/wsarchie
wsarchie.zip

Index

X

The Information and Tools You Need...

to Roll Out and Support Word on All Platforms

If you need to get users up to speed quickly, customize your installation of Word, and have somewhere to turn for answers to commonly asked questions, the MICROSOFT WORD 6 RESOURCE KIT is your one-stop solution.

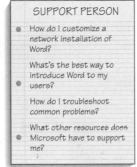

END USER

- What new features does Word 6 have?
- Can Word read my WordPerfect® files?
- What are the top tips and tricks for Word 6?
- What can I do with Word's macros?
- Can I share my files with Word users on other platforms?

SUPPORT PERSON

- How do I customize a network installation of Word?
- What's the best way to introduce Word to my users?
- How do I troubleshoot common problems?
- What other resources does Microsoft have to support me?

Whether you're moving to Word from another word processor or simply upgrading from an older version of Word, the MICROSOFT WORD 6 RESOURCE KIT has all the information and tools you need.

Microsoft® Word 6 Resource Kit
SECOND EDITION
For Windows™, Windows NT™, Macintosh®, and Power Macintosh™

ISBN 1-55615-682-0
$39.95 ($53.95 Canada)
896 pages, with three 3.5-inch disks

The MICROSOFT WORD 6 RESOURCE KIT provides all the answers to the questions you and your users might have.

- Learn how to install Word over a network and customize Word to meet your needs. A customization utility is included on an accompanying disk.

- Get help introducing Word 6 to experienced Word users and those new to Microsoft Word. The MICROSOFT WORD 6 RESOURCE KIT includes information on file conversion, keystrokes, and menus.

- Train your users. The MICROSOFT WORD 6 RESOURCE KIT disks include self-paced exercises, tips and tricks, and a sample newsletter article about Word that you can include in your own group or company newsletter.

- Support advanced Word users. Besides answers to common questions, you'll find technical information on customizing user settings, a guide to supplied macros, and information on creating custom solutions with Word 6.

Your Guide to
Applying the
Security and Audit
Capabilities of
Windows NT™ 3.5

ISBN 1-55615-814-9
304 pages
$49.95 ($67.95 Canada)

**A joint research
project by Citibank
N.A., Coopers & Lybrand,
The Institute of Internal Auditors,
and Microsoft Corporation**

The technology of interconnecting personal workstations, servers, and multiple wide-area networks, although young in comparison with more traditional information systems, is affecting every sector of society. This explosion in technology is not without risks. As organizations and individuals become increasingly reliant on networked information systems, adequate levels of security and control over these systems have become critical concerns. Mission-critical business applications placed on networks need to provide internal controls, security, and auditing capabilities.

This book is designed to help managers, network security specialists, auditors, and users understand the control, security, and audit implications of the Microsoft® Windows NT Server Operating System.